The Economies of Violence

Studies in Critical Social Sciences Book Series

Haymarket Books is proud to be working with Brill Academic Publishers (www.brill.nl) to republish the *Studies in Critical Social Sciences* book series in paperback editions. This peer-reviewed book series offers insights into our current reality by exploring the content and consequences of power relationships under capitalism, and by considering the spaces of opposition and resistance to these changes that have been defining our new age. Our full catalog of *SCSS* volumes can be viewed at https://www.haymarketbooks.org/series_collections/4-studies-in-critical-social-sciences.

Series Editor
David Fasenfest (York University, Canada)

Editorial Board
Eduardo Bonilla-Silva (Duke University)
Chris Chase-Dunn (University of California–Riverside)
William Carroll (University of Victoria)
Raewyn Connell (University of Sydney)
Kimberlé W. Crenshaw (University of California–LA and Columbia University)
Heidi Gottfried (Wayne State University)
Alfredo Saad-Filho (Queen's University, Belfast)
Chizuko Ueno (University of Tokyo)
Sylvia Walby (Lancaster University)
Raju Das (York University)

The Economies of Violence

The Forgotten Variable

Edited by
Guillaume Soto-Mayor

Haymarket Books
Chicago, IL

First published in 2024 by Brill Academic Publishers, The Netherlands
© 2024 Koninklijke Brill NV, Leiden, The Netherlands

Published in paperback in 2025 by
Haymarket Books
P.O. Box 180165
Chicago, IL 60618
773-583-7884
www.haymarketbooks.org

ISBN: 979-8-88890-550-0

Distributed to the trade in the US through Consortium Book Sales and Distribution (www.cbsd.com) and internationally through Ingram Publisher Services International (www.ingramcontent.com).

This book was published with the generous support of Lannan Foundation, Wallace Action Fund, and the Marguerite Casey Foundation.

Special discounts are available for bulk purchases by organizations and institutions. Please call 773-583-7884 or email info@haymarketbooks.org for more information.

Cover design by Jamie Kerry and Ragina Johnson.

Printed in the United States.

Library of Congress Cataloging-in-Publication data is available.

In memoriam to my beloved grandfather and eternal source of inspiration, Gaston Soto, who, after a first critical reading of this book, would have reminded me of Honoré de Balzac words: "Behind every great fortune lies a great crime"

Contents

Preface   IX
Acknowledgements   X
List of Illustrations   XI
Note on Contributors   XII

General Introduction   1
   Alain Bauer and Guillaume Soto-Mayor

1   Economics and Violence: Hidden Forces and Unaccounted Tales   19
   Clotilde Champeyrache

2   Human Trafficking and the Economy of Violence   42
   Louise Shelley

3   The Economy of Violence in Afghanistan 2001–2021   61
   David Izadifar

4   Mapping the Politics of Water and the Hidden Violence of the Legal Economy through the Small-scale Water Providers of Metro Manila   123
   Nazia Hussain

5   Illicit Urban Economies: The Toll of Local and Global Illegalities in the Making of Cities   155
   Arturo Alvarado

6   Warlords and Violent Entrepreneurs   220
   Guillaume Soto-Mayor

7   The Digital Realm: An Amplifier of the Economy of Violence   276
   Julien Dechanet

Conclusion   315
   Clotilde Champeyrache and Guillaume Soto-Mayor

Index   329

Preface

In 2019, the Security and Defense Research Team (SDRTI3C) at the Conservatoire National des Arts et Métiers (CNAM) gathered distinguished researchers from all around the world, and brought their richly diverse perspectives, to study a forgotten variable of the economies: violence. We produced at the time a report which was published by the International Journal on Criminology, which acknowledged the need for a broader framework beyond mere inventory, suggesting avenues for further research and exploration. This book is the prolonged effort of researchers from the original team and two excellent additions.

Hence, this book delves into the intricate relationship between violence and traditional economic mechanisms worldwide, exemplified through real-life instances ranging from drug dealers to multinational companies. By analyzing violence within economic and financial markets through political, sociological, and anthropological lenses, the book reveals how both illicit and licit economic agents exploit violence for personal gain.

Emphasizing violence as a pivotal economic factor, the book seeks to deepen understanding, raise awareness, and propose innovative solutions to combat its destructive consequences. It highlights the concept of "Economies of Violence," showcasing how violence permeates various economic sectors, often through sophisticated means. The book underscores the multifaceted nature of violence, encompassing both explicit and implicit forms, and its systemic role in maintaining social hierarchies.

Ultimately, the report grapples with defining violence—whether it must be measurable or tangible—and navigates the intricate web of economic, social, and moral implications inherent in its analysis. Through rigorous examination and insightful discourse, it offers a nuanced understanding of violence as a pervasive force shaping economic landscapes worldwide.

The inclusion of extensive case studies makes it a valuable resource for students, researchers, practitioners, and policymakers alike, and from all regions of the world.

Acknowledgements

I first would like to thank every author of this collective effort for their invaluable contributions, academic guidance and original vision. This research has been enlightened by the quality of their field work, the uniqueness of the data and the complementary analysis they have provided to study different aspects of a complex phenomenon such as the economies of violence.

I also pay tribute to Alice Gagliano, and to my assistant Mame Yacine Niang, for their unwavering efforts and who were instrumental in conducting the research for this book.

I would like to thank my family for their unwavering love, support, and understanding throughout this endeavor. Your belief in me has been a constant source of encouragement, and I am profoundly grateful for your patience, your inspiring determination and motivation in times where I could not see the end of the tunnel.

The transition from a sparse and vastly unexplored analytical field to a finished product and a coherent writing style matching the Brill excellency requirements presented many challenges. I am therefore truly grateful to those who contributed to this research work and to the birth of this book. I would also like to express my sincere thanks to David Fasenfest for his trust, his patience and guidance throughout this process. This book wouldn't exist without him.

Illustrations

Figures

4.1 Households with piped water source   131
4.2 Households experiencing water shortages (percentage)   134
4.3 An informal settlement   135
4.4 Coping strategies during daily water shortages   135
4.5 Storing water in an informal settlement   136
4.6 Cooperative-set prices for water supply   138
4.7 Members of a water cooperative   139
4.8 Laying down water pipelines on public land   141
4.9 Tapping legal water connections   142

Tables

4.1 Urban communities—a profile   133
5.1 Demographic, economic and social characteristics of Sao Paulo and Ciudad de Mexico   158
5.2 Government, regulatory systems and structure of public security   182
5.3 Typology of urban violences   190
5.3b Trends in illicit activities   193
5.4 Criminal actors in the Ciudad de México   205

Maps

5.1 Spatial distribution of socioeconomic conditions and violence (homicide rates) in Mexico City (2020) and Sao Paulo (2019)   179
6.1 Roadblocks in the Central African Republic   235

Note on Contributors

Arturo Alvarado
has been a visiting Professor at the Paris Institute for Advanced Study, France (2021); at the Program on Latin America Studies at Princeton University in the United States (in 2019), as well as Visiting Researcher, from the University of São Paulo (USP/NEV), Brasil. (2019). He has been the *Directeurs d'Etudes Associés* of the Fondation Maison des Sciences de l'Homme, Paris, France (2018), the *Maitre de Conférences* (Chair-Mexique), Institute de hautes etudes D'Amerique latine (IHEAL) Universite Sorbonne Nouvelle 3 (2009), and a Cogut Visiting Professor at the Watson Institute at Brown University (2006). He was a Visiting Scholar at the Woodrow Wilson International Center for Scholars (2004), a Member of spurs at the Massachusetts Institute of Technology (MIT) in the USA (2004), a Fulbright Fellow, and a Member of the International Sociological Association. From 2018–2023, he was Chair of the Research Committee RC 29 Deviance and Social Control, of the International Sociological Association, ISA. He is also a national representative at ISA Council of National Associations. He is a Founder and Director of Democracia, Derechos Humanos y Seguridad, CSO. His areas of research include: Justice, Human rights, violence, security and urban democratic governance. He has conducted several investigations on violence prevention, crime, justice, urban governance and security in Latin America. He has been a consultant for international organizations such as UN Women, Mexico; UNDP, UNDOC, and the World Bank. His recent research projects funded were by FACI-Colmex, Conacyt, México; Fapespe, Brasil; Harvard Innovation Fund & Fondo de Cooperación México-Uruguay. He won the following awards: National Research, National System of Researchers, level III, the Medal of Merit National category—Universidad Veracruzana, México in 2022, and the Juchimán Award, Universidad Juárez, Autónoma de Tabasco, México 2015. He is the author of numerous academic books and publications.

Alain Bauer
is Professor of Criminology (Chair) at the *Conservatoire National des Arts et Métiers* (CNAM) and head of the Security, Defense and Intelligence Department an member of the Security and Defense Research Team—Intelligence, Criminality, Crisis, Cyberthreats (SDRT-I3C). He is also Associate Professor at Fudan University (Shanghai) and Senior Research Fellow at the Center of Terrorism of the John Jay College of Criminal Justice in New York (USA) and at the University of Law and Political Science of Beijing. He is Director of the

Chair of Police and Criminal Sciences of the MBA "Security Management" at the EOGN (*Ecole des officiers de la Gendarmerie Nationale*), editor of the *International Journal on Criminology*, as well as President of the Higher Council for Strategic Training and Research (CSFRS) of the Republic Presidency (2009–2019). He notably held the position of President of the Orientation Council of the National Observatory of Delinquency (ONDRP) from 2003 to 2012. He is also consultant for the New York Police Department (NYPD), the sûreté du Québec (SQ) (Canada) and the Los Angeles Sheriff Department (LASD). He is a member of the OECD Task Force on Illicit Trade and the EUROPOL Expert Group on Organized Crime (SOCTA). He seats at the French Customs scientific Council. He is currently serving as a Colonel (Air) in the Citizen's Reserve. He is the Editor of the International Journal on Criminology, Member of the editorial Board of PRISM at NDU. He is the author of numerous academic and non-academic books. His latest published books are *Au commencement était la Guerre* (Fayard, 2023), *Encyclopédie du crime au cinéma* (Gründ 2023), *Tu ne tueras point* (Fayard 2024), and his latest TV series are *Au bout de l'enquête* (Season 1 and 2, 2023 and First 2024).

Clotilde Champeyrache
is Lecturer with an accreditation to direct research (HDR) at the *Conservatoire national des arts et métiers* (CNAM). She is an economist and mafia specialist. Her research focuses on the issues and developments of the illicit economy. Her current work focuses on the question of power and territory in economics, as well as on criminalities in economics. She is the author of numerous books, notably *Géopolitique des Mafias* (2022), *La Face Cachée de l'Economie* (2019) and *Quand la Mafia se Légalise* (2016).

Julien Dechanet
is a high-ranking officer, a Capitaine de Frégate (Commander), in the French Navy. He is one of the most renowned French specialists in cyber security and cyber defense. He has held commanding position in the Eléments Français du Sénégal, at NATO, at the French Cyber Command and for the French special forces, always as expert in cybersecurity.

Nazia Hussain
is an Assistant Professor at the Institute for Future Initiatives (IFI) at the University of Tokyo. Her work focuses on complex stresses in cities. In particular, she studies interactions among dynamics of informality, criminal and political violence, and politics of water in cities in developing countries. She holds a PhD in Public Policy from the Schar School of Policy and Government,

George Mason University. She was a recipient of the Japan Society for the Promotion of Science postdoctoral fellowship at the Center for Policy Research, United Nations University, and a Fulbright scholarship for an MA in International Relations from Boston University. This chapter was supported by the Japan Society for Promotion of Science KAKENHI under Grant number JP19H00577 (Grant-in-Aid for Scientific Research (A)).

David Izadifar
is a distinguished expert in counter-terrorism and crime intelligence, political and religious violence, terrorism financing, PCVE and conflict analysis, boasting a career spanning over two decades across diverse regions worldwide. His expertise covers areas such as the Great Lakes of Africa, West and Central Africa, the Middle East and North Africa, Central Asia, Southeast Asia, and the Pacific. Throughout his career, David has held numerous positions with various United Nations organizations, including UNODC, UN DPA, and IOM. Notably, he has served as a high-level research team leader during his tenure with UNODC.

Louise Shelley
is the Omer L. and Nancy Hirst Endowed Chair and a University Professor at George Mason University. She is in the Schar School of Policy and Government and directs the Terrorism, Transnational Crime and Corruption Center (TraCCC) that she founded. She is a leading expert on the relationship among terrorism, organized crime and corruption as well as human trafficking, transnational crime and terrorism with a particular focus on the former Soviet Union. She also specializes in illicit financial flows and money laundering. She was an inaugural Andrew Carnegie Fellow.

Guillaume Soto-Mayor
is currently an independent consultant and is a non-resident scholar at the Middle East Institute and senior fellow at the CRTG-Working Group and the Timbuktu Institute. He is the co-founder of Egregor, a catalyst of energies at the service of social innovators. Priorly, Guillaume Soto-Mayor was a program manager for Altai Consulting's West Africa & the Sahel office, and he is a former research engineer of the Security and Defense research team (SDRTI3C) at CNAM Paris and is now an associated expert with SDRTI3C. He has especially conducted field research and analysis on terrorism, organize crime, religious, social and political violence across Africa. He founded the

economies of violence research working group at CNAM SDRTI3C in 2019 as he thought necessary to alert public opinion and decision-makers to the origins of violence in our societies, the existence and functioning of its main protagonists, the consequences of their growing powers and the factors explaining their success.

General Introduction

Alain Bauer and Guillaume Soto-Mayor

Economies of violence are ever-present issues that determine our past, our present, and our collective future. Understanding what they are, who the core players are, and how they impact our world is therefore absolutely crucial.

The foundation of violence is not only determined by sociological, biological, or psychological factors but is shaped by the interwoven fields of politics and economy. Violence in all its facets has a significant impact on entire nations as well as the lives of countless individuals, and so does the economy. This book shows that from the corridors of power to the busy market squares, the mutually reinforcing interactions between violence and economic systems, relationships, and interactions shape the course of society.

Violence is a pervasive phenomenon in the complex individual and collective webs of social structures. It spreads through marketplaces, where economic inequities feed dissatisfaction and discontent, and it flourishes within the halls of power, where political maneuvering frequently breeds conflict and strife. Violence in the economy and politics is by no means a tale of the so-called "Global South."[1] Economic exploitation is most prevalent in politically unstable circumstances, often due to the weakness of public institutions, the absence of the rule of law, and because of the abundance of corruption. Economic disparities also fuel enmity and violence, which are further exacerbated by the instability that follows. These phenomena might be most common in the "Global South," however, they often implicate actors of the "Global North" and the economies of violence are also extremely common in European, American, Chinese, and Japanese territories.

To frame our research, we propose the following definition of the term "violence," strictly reflecting the term as understood in the previously outlined

---

1 Definition of Aude Darnal, Stimson Center: "Global south" as a synonym for developing countries—or what was once called the "third world"—but the label has a broader meaning. The *global south* is not strictly delineated by either geography or *economics*, instead taking into account shared experiences and inequalities rooted in the colonial era and sustained by global capitalism. The term remains imperfect: It is not neutral, and it should not be used to homogenize different geopolitical contexts. Beyond semantics, appreciating the global south means parting ways with a hierarchy among states and approaching Western dominance of the international system more critically". Source: Aude Darnal, "U.S. Foreign Policy Must Consider the Global South," *Foreign Policy* (blog), March 26, 2024, https://foreignpolicy.com/2023/03/06/us-global-south-diplomacy-multilateralism/.

notion of *Economies of violence*. There is no simple qualification to what violence is in that sense. The distinction between peaceful and violent methods in the pursuit of political or social objectives is often difficult to make, due to the subtle nature of violence. While physical violence is easily identifiable, more insidious forms of violence, such as economic coercion, media manipulation, and psychological repression, can be equally damaging and difficult to recognize. As a result, the boundaries between peaceful and violent methods can become blurred, as economic, political, and social actors often employ strategies that oscillate between the legitimate expression of rights and the use of oppressive tactics to achieve their goals.

However, a prevalent characteristic of violence within the framework limited to the concept of economies of violence entails the presence of intentionality and premeditation aimed at power acquisition and enrichment. Within this context, acts of violence are propelled by aspirations for profit and/or the consolidation of power dynamics that guarantee a privileged financial and economic status. Ultimately, the harm inflicted upon another individual or entity consequent to the executed action, which yields financial benefits, whether it be physical, moral, or psychological, serves as a unifying factor in categorizing said action as "violent."

0.1 The Economies of Violence: A New Lens to Study Our Economies

The concept of "economies of violence," which we use as an innovative frame to study the intricate connection between economic systems and the continuation of violent acts, is at the center of our investigation. Economies of violence entail the systemic integration of violence into the fundamental fabric of economic systems and organizations, as opposed to merely being isolated instances of conflict or criminal behavior. This integration can take many different forms, such as the use of coercive measures to keep power and control or the exploitation of weaker groups for financial benefit.

The relationships between mafias and the financial sector in the 20th and 21st centuries serve as an example of how closely actors of violence may be tied to important players within our economies, exploiting its weaknesses to bolster their power and violent enterprises. Warlords and private military firms have also used their coercive power to exploit natural resources to their benefit. Another aspect of the economics of violence is the exploitation of weaker, marginalized populations for financial gain. Human trafficking networks, for example, take advantage of people's financial hardships by forcing them to work as slaves or to be sexually exploited for financial gain.

Comparably, the practice of "land grabbing" entails the use of force or violence by strong individuals to take land from smallholders or indigenous people to harvest resources or carry out extensive development projects. These illustrations show how violence infiltrates economic structures, sustaining cycles of injustice and inequality while benefiting those in positions of authority. Essentially, economies of violence show how the institutionalization of violence within economic frameworks influences the choices and behaviors of people on an individual, group, and sometimes national level.

Interestingly, the idea of the economies of violence and the role of violence in the economy have been concealed from the public for a long time. This notion has been considerably understudied and is rarely mentioned by decision-makers. No particular academic nor non-academic work has indeed attempted to analyze this notion transversally and from a global standpoint. Interestingly, in the 90s, many democracies avoided discussing the influence of violent players in their domestic affairs, declaring themselves and the world "free from violence" or entering a "liberal peace."[2] However as Pr. Alain Bauer shows in his recent research, violence has always been and remains more present than ever in our societies.

0.2 Broadening Classical Concepts Linking Violence and the Economy

To fully comprehend economies of violence, it is necessary to explore related ideas that provide complex perspectives on its complex nature. Although the frameworks of the conflict economy, war economy, and criminal economy are important, it is imperative to expand the investigation beyond these limits. Approaches based on political and sociological theory offer insightful viewpoints on how economic systems and violence interact. These theories provide insight into the institutional structures, power relationships, and structural injustices that support violence in economies. We may create a more comprehensive knowledge of economies of violence and their effects on society by combining these larger theoretical frameworks.

The concept of conflict economics as notably developed by Paul Collier and Anke Hoeffler[3] clarifies how political unrest and military conflicts provide a

---

2 Oliver P. Richmond, "Liberal Peace and Its Critiques," in *The Palgrave Encyclopedia of Peace and Conflict Studies*, ed. Oliver P. Richmond and Gëzim Visoka (Cham: Springer International Publishing, 2022), 715–33, https://doi.org/10.1007/978-3-030-77954-2_186.
3 Paul Collier and Anke Hoeffler, "High-Value Natural Resources, Development, and Conflict: Channels of Causation," in *High-Value Natural Resources and Post-Conflict Peacebuilding* (Routledge, 2011).

range of entities, from corrupt authorities and multinational businesses to rebel organizations and militias, with economic opportunities.[4] This concept is that intricate network of economic activity that develops amid instability caused by conflict, such as the illegal trade in goods, weapons, and natural resources.[5] Ballentine and Nitzschke highlight the shift in research focus, acknowledging that many civil wars have become increasingly self-financing.[6] Other political scientists who have made substantial contributions to our knowledge of the political and social dynamics that fuel conflicts include David Laitin and James Fearon.

In a similar vein, the study of war economics explores the economic aspects of conflict and how armed conflicts impact local and international decision-making processes.[7] This idea emphasizes how economic activity is fueled during times of conflict by war profiteering, military spending, and reconstruction efforts.[8] Key authors include Mark Harrison, Richard Overy, Paul A.C. Koistinen, Michael Geyer, and Adam Tooze.[9,10] A famous example illustrating the notion of war economies, and the interlinkages between the two notions is the extension of the number of taxpayers in the United States during World War II, to finance the war.[11]

This concept is perfectly exemplified by the way private or para-public military companies such as Africa Corp, formerly known as the Wagner Group, operate. Africa Corp is involved in wars throughout Africa and its misdeeds are a prime example of how violence may become intertwined with global economic goals. Africa Corp, a for-profit military corporation with connections

---

4   Karen Ballentine and Jake Sherman, eds., *The Political Economy of Armed Conflict: Beyond Greed and Grievance* (Lynne Rienner Publishers, 2003).
5   Koen Vlassenroot and Timothy Raeymaekers, eds., *Conflict and Social Transformation in Eastern DR Congo* (Academia Press, 2004).
6   Karen Ballentine and Heiko Nitzschke, "The Political Economy of Civil War and Conflict Transformation," 2005, https://berghof-foundation.org/files/publications/dialogue3_ballentine_nitzschke.pdf.
7   Pyt S Douma, "Political Economy of Internal Conflict: A Review of Contemporary Trends and Issues," *Netherlands Institute of International Relations, Clingendael*, 2001, https://www.clingendael.org/sites/default/files/pdfs/20011000_cru_working_paper_1.pdf.
8   Paul Poast, "Economics and War," in *Understanding War and Peace* (Cambridge University Press, 2023).
9   Michael Geyer and Adam Tooze, eds., *The Cambridge History of the Second World War: Volume 3: Total War: Economy, Society and Culture*, vol. 3, The Cambridge History of the Second World War (Cambridge: Cambridge University Press, 2015), https://doi.org/10.1017/CHO9781139626859.
10 R. J. Overy, *Why the Allies Won* (w.w. Norton, 1997).
11 Lily Rothman, "How World War II Still Determines Your Tax Bill," TIME, April 14, 2016, https://time.com/4289687/1942-tax-day-history/.

to the Russian government, takes advantage of conflicts, weak public institutions, and its capacity to "sell violence" (both physical and digital), in places like the Central African Republic to advance its geopolitical clout and resource extraction goals.[12] The way that violence and economic exploitation coexist highlights the part that state-sponsored actors play in sustaining violent and unstable cycles to benefit financially.

Furthermore, the investigation of the economies of violence is also related to the study of the notion of "criminal economies" which examines the intersections between violence and crime and black markets, including those associated with organized crime, drug trafficking, and human trafficking. Key authors having established this concept include Vanda Felbab-Brown, Moisés Naím, Peter Reuter, as well as Pr. Alain Bauer and Pr. Louise Shelley, who are both contributing to this book.[13,14] This statement elucidates how criminal organizations exploit vulnerabilities in the legal and regulatory frameworks to generate profits from unlawful activities, often perpetuating detrimental cycles of exploitation and violence. The criminal activities concerned notably include drug trafficking, human trafficking, medicine trafficking, cigarette trafficking, natural resources trafficking, thefts and robberies, cybercrime, and counterfeiting.[15]

However, beyond classical situations and actors of violence such as confrontations and organized crime, economies of violence comprise a broader range of individual and collective acts driven by self-interest at the financial expense of others. This broad viewpoint highlights the various ways that violence, which takes the shape of both overt and covert forms of exploitation, is entwined with economic processes. We already mentioned the role of States as actors of the economies of violence.

Take now the example of unethical, illicit, and/or violent business practices in local and global private companies. Unethical executives may engage in bribery, fraud, and environmental abuse for the sake of maximizing profits,

---

12 Redazione Agenzia Nova, "Moscow Laundered 2,5 Billion from Illegal Gold Mining in Central African Republic, Sudan and Mali," *Agenzia Nova* (blog), December 13, 2023, https://www.agenzianova.com/en/news/Russia-laundered-%2425-billion-from-illegal-gold-mining-in-Central-African-Republic%2C-Sudan-and-Mali/.

13 Felbab-Brown, Vanda. *The Extinction Market: Wildlife Trafficking and How to Counter It.* Oxford: Oxford University Press, 2017; Naím, Moisés. *Illicit: How Smugglers, Traffickers, and Copycats are Hijacking the Global Economy.* New York: Anchor Books, 2007.

14 Moisés Naím, *Illicit: How Smugglers, Traffickers, and Copycats Are Hijacking the Global Economy* (Doubleday, 2005).

15 Louise I. Shelley, *Dark Commerce: How a New Illicit Economy Is Threatening Our Future* (Princeton University Press, 2018), https://doi.org/10.2307/j.ctv346n56.

with little regard for the welfare of workers, communities, and ecosystems. Such activities not only feed social unrest and erode trust in institutions, but they also prolong cycles of inequality and environmental damages, negatively impacting the lives of many for the financial interests of a few.

The financial activities of multinational companies shed light on how corporate interests can encourage brutality and abuse for financial gains.[16,17] The history of land expropriation by multinational companies demonstrates how economic power can be used to take advantage of natural resources and uproot communities, demonstrating the widespread impact of economies of violence on a worldwide basis.[18] Multinational corporations have indeed been associated with environmental destruction and violent land seizures in multiple regions of the world.

Hence in recent years, a discernible transformation in the role of violence within global economies emerged. It evolved beyond being a tool of one continental group over another, becoming exploitable by individuals and nations alike, with the core focus on the exploitation of natural resources. This transformation has given rise to various designations, including the term "new wars" as developed recently by Mary Kaldor.[19] However, many historical examples cited align perfectly with the characterization of "new wars." The exploitation of humans we evoked, remains indeed a contemporary phenomenon, enduring centuries beyond the abolition of slavery, establishing itself as the most enduring form of commerce.[20]

Instances of such exploitation are rife across the globe. In the Middle East, men and women originating from the African continent continue to be vulnerable, particularly young women seeking improved living conditions

---

16 Facing Finance, "Dirty Profits 11: Report on Companies and Financial Institutions Benefiting from Violations of Human Rights," 2013, https://www.facing-finance.org/wp-content/blogs.dir/16/files/2012/12/ff_dirtyprofits.pdf.

17 Victoria Schneider, "Bolloré Blacklisted over Alleged Rights Violations on Plantations in Africa and Asia," Mongabay Environmental News, September 29, 2023, https://news.mongabay.com/2023/09/bollore-blacklisted-over-alleged-rights-violations-on-plantations-in-africa-and-asia/.

18 Angelika Rettberg et al., *Different Resources, Different Conflicts?: The Subnational Political Economy of Armed Conflict and Crime in Colombia* (Universidad de los Andes, 2023).

19 Mary Kaldor, *New and Old Wars: Organised Violence in a Global Era* (John Wiley & Sons, 2013).

20 "GMG Thematic Paper on the Exploitation and Abuse of International Migrants, Particularly Those in an Irregular Situation—A Human Rights Approach (2013)," International Organization for Migration, 2013, https://www.iom.int/resources/gmg-thematic-paper-exploitation-and-abuse-international-migrants-particularly-those-irregular-situation-human-rights-approach-2013.

in countries such as Libya and the United Arab Emirates.[21] They often fall victim to countless forms of violence, including immolation, rape, assault, and forced prostitution. This exploitation of women is not confined to Europe or America, as mafias are implicated in these heinous acts. Women from Romania and Latin America, deported for mere illegal immigration, find themselves enslaved in other European or North American countries.[22]

Criminal exploitation remains prevalent in other labor markets. In the agricultural sectors in Libya, employers who want to take advantage of inexpensive labor take advantage of the economic gaps and weaknesses of immigrants.[23] Recent investigations on North Koreans being modern-day slaves in Chinese fish-processing factories shed light on the conditions of North Korean workers in the fish industries.[24] The article describes how the North Korean government orchestrates this exploitation by providing its citizens to serve the Chinese elite. The government not only supplies the workforce but also withholds wages to finance the bureau responsible for this human trafficking.

Moreover, the prevalence of cybercrime and online fraud highlights how flexible economies of violence are in the digital era. Cybercriminals take advantage of holes in digital platforms to swindle gullible people and businesses, draining their funds and eroding confidence in online transactions. The anonymity provided by the digital environment makes it easier for offenders to avoid punishment, which makes it more difficult to stop economic violence in the virtual world.

Expanding our conceptualization of the economies of violence to include individual behaviors helps us better grasp the complex ways in which violence is embedded in economic and social systems.[25] These seemingly small actions, which range from price gouging and land grabbing to wage theft and psychological workplace violence, support structural injustices and economic

---

21 Human Rights Watch, "Middle East and North Africa: End Curbs on Women's Mobility | Human Rights Watch," July 18, 2023, https://www.hrw.org/news/2023/07/18/middle-east-and-north-africa-end-curbs-womens-mobility.
22 Louise Shelley, *Human Trafficking: A Global Perspective* (Cambridge University Press, 2010).
23 International Organization for Migration (IOM), "Libya Migrant Vulnerability and Humanitarian Needs Assessment," 2019, https://dtm.iom.int/sites/g/files/tmzbdl461/files/reports/DTM_LBY_MVHNA_Report_Dec2019.pdf.
24 Ian Urbina, "North Koreans Are Used as Modern Slaves in China's Fish Processing Plants," *Le Monde.Fr*, February 29, 2024, https://www.lemonde.fr/en/international/article/2024/02/29/north-koreans-are-used-as-modern-slaves-in-china-s-fish-processing-plants_6573255_4.html.
25 Karen Ballentine and Jake Sherman, *The Political Economy of Armed Conflict: Beyond Greed and Grievance* (Lynne Rienner Publishers, 2003).

exploitations. This comprehensive viewpoint forces us to address the moral ramifications of our economic decisions. The only way we can create a more just and democratic economic system is by tackling the underlying causes of economic violence.

In the physical and digital spheres, victims of the economies of violence often endure psychological anguish, displacement, and loss of employment, among other social and economic hardships. We can learn more about the intricate dynamics behind economies of violence and the consequences they have on various individuals and communities by looking at the range of players involved and comprehending the effects of their practices.

0.3 The Economies of Violence: A Global Concern

Relying on research (which is the first objective of this collective effort), we can better dissect the complex web of political and economic systems that propel economies of violence. These occurrences function as potent reminders of the human toll that violence inflicts and the urgent requirement for reform, irrespective of their location—in the political sphere, in market economies, and in the pathways of authority.

It is critical to underscore the significance of the economies of violence, both in historical and contemporary terms, given that the repercussions of violence transcend a mere number of immediate casualties. A comprehensive understanding of the underlying causes and thorough consequences of the economies of violence is needed. It is nonetheless a difficult task for us to comprehend and deal with the complex economic effects of violence. Compounded by historical legacies, geopolitical dynamics, and socioeconomic inequality, the intricacies of the economy of violence provide enormous obstacles to effective intervention. Furthermore, attempts to lessen the long-lasting effects of violence on communities and economies are frequently thwarted by vested interests, firmly established power structures and systematic imbalances.

Understanding the depth of this violence within societies is crucial, as is identifying the primary beneficiaries involved. A comprehensive analysis is warranted to unravel why violence persists so prominently in our societies and to assess its underlying purposes. As we delve into an examination of the pervasive nature of violence in our societies, it becomes imperative to trace its origins. Is violence in economies a phenomenon more deeply rooted in human history than commonly believed? Could it be ingrained in the very fabric of our collective past?

Certain phases in the history of humanity serve as vivid reminders of the centrality of violence in the making of nations and communities, as well as its intractable links to the functioning of the economic systems of the time. Let's travel back. As America was on the verge of a disastrous civil war in 1861, all the features of economic violence took shape that nourished this deadly conflict.[26] The institution of slavery served as the cornerstone of an oppressive and exploitative socioeconomic system, contributing to the nation's economic division in addition to its ideological and geographic divisions.[27]

As the war dragged on, the violence of the fight grew more intense, emphasizing the need for a thorough comprehension of the underlying dynamics. It went beyond simple military conflicts to include social unrest and economic compulsion. The work that was taken from people who were enslaved propelled the war machine, keeping the fighting going not just on the battlefield but also in the fields and factories where industry thrived.

The complex interactions between violence, money, and social systems are highlighted by this historical incident. We can better understand the long-lasting effects of economies of violence by going deeper into history and appreciating the part played by colonialism and economic exploitation. It becomes clear that the foundations of contemporary capitalism are firmly rooted in oppressive and exploitative institutions, underscoring the need for a critical analysis of past injustices and their continuing influence on the formation of present socioeconomic environments.[28] The foundation of economic prosperity for colonial powers was the exploitation of human labor, especially through systems like slavery, which fueled cycles of violence and inequality that still affect modern nations.[29] The genesis of early large-scale international trade was indeed marked by violence.

Post the abolition of slavery, a new form of exploitation took center stage, heralding the era of European imperialism in the 19th century. This imperialism aimed to "civilize" indigenous populations worldwide while ensuring Europe's industrial development.[30] This specific case serves as just one example,

---

26   Roger Lowenstein, *Ways and Means: Lincoln and His Cabinet and the Financing of the Civil War* (Penguin Publishing Group, 2022).
27   Roger L. Ransom, *Conflict and Compromise: The Political Economy of Slavery, Emancipation and the American Civil War* (Cambridge University Press, 1989).
28   Heide Gerstenberger, "Market and Violence: The Functioning of Capitalism in History," in *Market and Violence* (Brill, 2022), https://brill.com/display/title/55937.
29   Gerstenberger.
30   Claude Serfati, "Economies de guerre et ressources naturelles : les visages de la mondialisation," *Annuaire suisse de politique de développement*, no. 25–2 (October 1, 2006): 107–26, https://doi.org/10.4000/aspd.258.

highlighting the historical role of governments in so-called illicit economies. This complexity adds nuance to the phenomenon of "economies of violence." Contrary to prevalent narratives that depict the architects of these economies as rebels or powerless individuals, many of these illicit exchanges are directed by governments to serve the powerful economic authorities of their nations.

Violence is entrenched in the core of every illicit economic activity, especially in conflict-ridden regions worldwide, particularly those endowed with abundant natural resources. October 2023 notably marked the resumption of hostilities in the East of the Democratic Republic of the Congo.[31] This conflict notably pits the M23 against the Armed Forces of the Democratic Republic of the Congo (DRC) since the 1990s.[32] At least six million people have died in this conflict and another six million have been displaced.[33] Most international powers exclusively frame this war as an ethnic conflict.[34] The United States condemned Rwanda this Saturday, February 17, 2024, and urged it to withdraw its support for the M23.[35] Nonetheless, in addition to the inter-communal dimension, the violence unfolding has also a significant economic dimension. The DRC is an immense reservoir of natural resources, including diamonds, gold, and coltan, a highly sought-after mineral in the manufacturing of

---

31 Vincent Duhem, "Dans l'est de la RDC, comment et pourquoi les hostilités ont repris—Jeune Afrique.com," JeuneAfrique.com, November 1, 2023, https://www.jeuneafrique.com/1499582/politique/dans-lest-de-la-rdc-comment-et-pourquoi-les-hostilites-ont-repris/.

32 The M23 is composed of Tutsi ethnic generals who fled Rwanda during the 1994 genocide, as these survivors found refuge in the East of the DRC. At the end of the genocide, the instigators, who are of the Hutu ethnicity, were forced to leave Rwanda to escape reprisals for their actions. When these two Rwandan-origin ethnicities found themselves once again on the same soil, intimidation and xenophobia from the Hutus toward the Tutsis quickly resurfaced. In order to defend themselves and prevent a new massacre, the Tutsis, with the support of the Rwandan government, have deployed the necessary human and military resources. The ethnic origin of this war points today all fingers at the Rwandan President, Paul Kagame. Center for Preventive Action, "Conflict in the Democratic Republic of Congo," Global Conflict Tracker, February 21, 2024, https://cfr.org/global-conflict-tracker/conflict/violence-democratic-republic-congo.

33 Shola Lawal, "A Guide to the Decades-Long Conflict in DR Congo," Al Jazeera, February 21, 2024, https://www.aljazeera.com/news/2024/2/21/a-guide-to-the-decades-long-conflict-in-dr-congo.

34 Delphin R. Ntanyoma, "DRC Violence Has Many Causes—the UN's Narrow Focus on Ethnicity Won't Help End Conflict," The Conversation, July 10, 2023, http://theconversation.com/drc-violence-has-many-causes-the-uns-narrow-focus-on-ethnicity-wont-help-end-conflict-208774.

35 Associated Press, "US Condemns Rwanda's Support of Armed M23 Rebels in Eastern Congo and Calls for Troop Withdrawal," AP News, February 18, 2024, https://apnews.com/article/congo-rwanda-m23-us-troop-withdrawal-971e0c1a162598cfcf84934c163a7a67.

technological materials. Being a region rich in resources, the DRC is a strategically important area in the global economic future. The region is, therefore, a playground for many actors, including the Congolese government, other rebel groups, Rwanda, and Uganda, as well as multinational corporations and major world powers. Hence, violence in the DRC is intrinsically linked to our modern economic systems and outlets, the law of international trade, of supply and demand.

However, another example illustrates the complexity of analysis when it comes to unraveling who the actors of violence are. The government in power in Myanmar has maintained a longstanding cultural association with global drug production. In 2023, Myanmar became the world's leading producer of opium.[36] The nation has held a firm grip on opium production since the 1980s.[37] The ethnic tensions arising from Myanmar's independence in 1948 provided fertile ground for the expansion of the drug trade in the region. Rebel groups, Burmese both also Chinese emerging in the aftermath, seized control of opium production to fund their armed campaigns. As is often observed in countries experiencing civil conflicts, the trade of primary commodities becomes a natural source of financing for rebel groups and feeds violence. The Myanmar government, whether through direct support or the enactment of legislation favorable to ongoing production and trade, has consistently played a role in the regulation of opium production.[38]

Today, we can witness how economic collapse brought on by political unrest in nations like Venezuela has resulted in widespread violence as an elite embezzles state resources and participates in international criminal activities thanks to their use of violence while people fight for limited resources and strive to meet their fundamental requirements.[39] As also demonstrated in nations like Iran, North Korea, and Syria, the establishment of authoritarian governments frequently depends on the simultaneous violent repression

36   UN News, "Myanmar Overtakes Afghanistan as World's Top Opium Producer," December 12, 2023, https://news.un.org/en/story/2023/12/1144702.
37   UNODC: Global Illicit Drug Trends 2001, "'Myanmar: How Did Myanmar Become a Major Supplier of Illicit Opium.,'" June 26, 2001, https://www.unodc.org/pdf/report_2001-06-26_1/analysis_myanmar.pdf.
38   Ruosui Zhang, "To Suspend or Not to Suspend: A Cost-Benefit Analysis of Three Chinese Mega-Projects in Myanmar," *The Pacific Review* 34, no. 6 (October 7, 2021): 946–72, https://doi.org/10.1080/09512748.2020.1776757.
39   Bram Ebus and Thomas Martinelli, "Venezuela's Gold Heist: The Symbiotic Relationship between the State, Criminal Networks and Resource Extraction," *Bulletin of Latin American Research* 41, no. 1 (2022): 105–22, https://doi.org/10.1111/blar.13246.

of dissent and the establishment of an economy of violence.[40] Under such regimes, economic exploitation and organized crime feed the vicious cycles of violence and repression. North Korea and Syria have indeed been involved in large-scale drug production, notably amphetamine-type stimulants, and international drug trafficking operations, as well as human trafficking and cybercrime.[41] North Korea also produces and ships weapons illicitly throughout the world. Despite international bans and condemnations, the revenues generated could amount to $1 billion (only from its sales to Russia).[42]

Economies of violence are not limited to conflicts in Africa. They also aren't limited to autocracies. As such, it is of the utmost importance that we identify the true beneficiaries of the economies of violence—those who stand to profit monetarily from violence. It is far too simple to place the guilt for acts of violence on the backs of criminals, warlords, and private military companies. In practice, the real offenders are also frequently concealed under the mask of respectability. By bringing these unseen beneficiaries to light, we can start to disentangle the complex network of cooperation that underpins economies of violence. These economies of violence are not the consequences of faceless forces of nature but rather a planned and purposeful act carried out by those who stand to benefit the most. As a matter of fact, the economies of violence are profoundly antagonistic to democracy.

In regions across the globe, we are witnessing an escalation of violence within the income production chain, particularly impacting economic development and creating social unrest. This is demonstrated by the central role in the economies of violence played by corrupt politicians who take advantage of their positions of power to exploit other people's suffering for financial gain. Consider the latest discoveries surrounding the Panama Papers controversy, for example. To illustrate the breadth of corruption in business and political circles, consider the Panama Papers incident, which revealed how elites and politicians throughout the world exploited offshore accounts to conceal income and avoid paying taxes. Through the use of offshore bank accounts, a network of politicians, businesspeople, and corporations that had amassed

---

40   Claudia Chiappa, "Drug That Makes Syrian Regime Millions Trafficked through Europe, Report Says," POLITICO, September 13, 2023, https://www.politico.eu/article/europe-key-transit-hub-for-captagon-trafficking-new-report-finds/.

41   U.S. Department of the Treasury, "Treasury Designates Financial Institution Involved in Facilitating North Korea's Illicit Activities," U.S. Department of the Treasury, April 19, 2011, https://home.treasury.gov/news/press-releases/tg1146.

42   Andrew Yeo, "Expect to See More North Korean Weapons Reach Nonstate Armed Actors in 2024," Brookings, February 21, 2024, https://www.brookings.edu/articles/expect-to-see-more-north-korean-weapons-reach-nonstate-armed-actors-in-2024/.

wealth through unethical means or by taking advantage of conflict zones was revealed by these leaks.[43]

Inequalities grow as money and power concentrate in the hands of a few individuals, escalating social tensions and igniting public unrest. Ongoing violence weakens people's faith in the public institutions that are in charge of maintaining justice and safety. People become disillusioned with governing structures due to inefficiencies and corruption. Because communities believe those tasked with their protection have abandoned them and rule for themselves, this mistrust breeds instability. When there are no trustworthy institutions and rule of law, insecurity grows and economic development stops as the examples of Russia and Southern Italy show.[44]

Trade disruptions, infrastructure destruction, and investment deterrence are some of the ways that violence impedes economic development and innovation. Limited resources are directed away from worthwhile projects, detached from the public good. Furthermore, an environment of violence discourages invention since actors of violence appropriate people's creative energies for their own economic gains. Progress and prosperity are hampered by this inertia, which further embeds communities in cycles of poverty and underdevelopment.

By understanding the complex relationships between violence and economy, this book will help us to better comprehend the fundamental causes of the perpetuation of social inequalities and conflict cycles, of contemporary obstacles to peace and prosperity. We seek to understand the underlying mechanisms at work and devise solutions for these intricate problems through our investigation of economies of violence.

0.4   Presentation/Book Outline

This book will dig into the economies of violence, examining its various manifestations and the part societal actors play in maintaining its pernicious hold. The profound integration of economies of violence into political and economic landscapes is a multifaceted phenomenon that reflects the maze of human affairs. The fundamental essence of violence is revealed inside this complex

---

43   David Dominguez et al., "Panama Papers' Offshoring Network Behavior," *Heliyon* 6, no. 6 (June 1, 2020): e04293, https://doi.org/10.1016/j.heliyon.2020.e04293.

44   Alberto Aziani, Serena Favarin, and Gian Maria Campedelli, "Security Governance: Mafia Control over Ordinary Crimes," *Journal of Research in Crime and Delinquency* 57, no. 4 (July 1, 2020): 444–92, https://doi.org/10.1177/0022427819893417.

web of power relationships and economic pressures; it is not an act of hostility committed inadvertently, but rather a planned force motivated by the desire for both profit and power.

Studying this highly complex and multilayered notion required a collective effort which resulted in this book. We hope that this investigation will pique readers' curiosity and encourage more in-depth discussion on the issue. We offer readers the possibility to dissect the economies of violence and to finally comprehend its tremendous effects on people, communities, and societies as a whole by presenting it as a multifaceted and ubiquitous characteristic. The incredible variety and profiles of the authors of this book match that requirement, as they come from different regions of the world, have all a first hand knowledge and have access to first hand high quality data.

We will set out to explore the complex economic mechanisms that underlie this ubiquitous phenomenon in the introductory chapter to our study of the economies of violence, *Economics and Violence: Hidden Forces and Unaccounted Tales, written* by Pr. Clotilde Champeyrache. We provide readers with a thorough introduction to the idea to highlight its complexity and its centrality in modern-day economic systems. The chapters explore how violence permeates economic systems and uncover the ways in which it shapes and reshapes social institutions.

Building on the foundations established in the introduction, we investigate the regions and the diverse actors involved in economies of violence. From conflict-ridden areas in the Global South to the thriving financial hubs of the Global North, these economies take many different forms and have a lasting impact on societies all over the world. In her chapter on *Human Trafficking and the Economy of Violence*, Professor Louise Shelley provides an analysis on the importance of labor and sexual exploitation in the United States. In the following chapters, David Izadifar presents a detailed story of the naissance, growth, and consequences of the *Economy of Violence in Afghanistan*. In her fascinating chapter, Nazia Hussain *maps the politics of water and hidden violence of the legal economy in Metro Manila* and demonstrates how local politics, economic exploitations, and the handling of natural resources can be deeply intertwined.

In the continuity of our investigation, our team highlighted the complex network of players at play in the economies of violence, individuals and groups, global companies, conflict actors, government-sponsored organizations, and criminal organizations all motivated by self-interest and power. In his chapter on the illicit urban economies, focusing on Mexico City and São Paulo Metropolitan Regions, Pr. Artur Alvarado provides a detailed understanding of how various social settings and landscapes interact with economic systems to sustain violent practices. The chapter written by Guillaume Soto-Mayor, *Warlords and Violent Entrepreneurs*, provides a greater understanding of the intricacy of economies of violence and their worldwide influence by shedding light on the interconnection of these actors, dynamics of violence, and our globalized modern economy.

We finally explore the deep effects of the economies of violence across various systems, showing that it applies also to the digital world thanks to Commander Julien Dechanet's chapter *The Digital Realm: an Amplifier of the Economy of Violence*. The effects of the economy of violence spreading to the digital spaces range from the economic exploitation of socio-political weaknesses to the weakening of democratic institutions. By drawing attention to these significant ramifications, we emphasize how urgent it is to deal with the underlying causes of economic violence and to promote all-encompassing solutions that put the welfare of people and sustainable development first.

Bibliography

Associated Press. "US Condemns Rwanda's Support of Armed M23 Rebels in Eastern Congo and Calls for Troop Withdrawal." AP News, February 18, 2024. https://apnews.com/article/congo-rwanda-m23-us-troop-withdrawal-971e0c1a162598cfcf84934c163a7a67.

Aziani, Alberto, Serena, Favarin, and Gian Maria, Campedelli. "Security Governance: Mafia Control over Ordinary Crimes." *Journal of Research in Crime and Delinquency* 57, no. 4 (July 1, 2020): 444–92. https://doi.org/10.1177/0022427819893417.

Ballentine, Karen, and Heiko, Nitzschke. "The Political Economy of Civil War and Conflict Transformation," 2005. https://berghof-foundation.org/files/publications/dialogue3_ballentine_nitzschke.pdf.

Ballentine, Karen, and Jake, Sherman, eds. *The Political Economy of Armed Conflict: Beyond Greed and Grievance*. Lynne Rienner Publishers, 2003.

Center for Preventive Action. "Conflict in the Democratic Republic of Congo." Global Conflict Tracker, February 21, 2024. https://cfr.org/global-conflict-tracker/conflict/violence-democratic-republic-congo.

Chiappa, Claudia. "Drug That Makes Syrian Regime Millions Trafficked through Europe, Report Says." POLITICO, September 13, 2023. https://www.politico.eu/article/europe-key-transit-hub-for-captagon-trafficking-new-report-finds/.

Collier, Paul, and Anke, Hoeffler. "High-Value Natural Resources, Development, and Conflict: Channels of Causation." In *High-Value Natural Resources and Post-Conflict Peacebuilding*. Routledge, 2011.

Darnal, Aude. "U.S. Foreign Policy Must Consider the Global South." *Foreign Policy* (blog), March 26, 2024. https://foreignpolicy.com/2023/03/06/us-global-south-diplomacy-multilateralism/.

Dominguez, David, Odette, Pantoja, Pablo, Pico, Miguel, Mateos, María del Mar, Alonso-Almeida, and Mario, González. "Panama Papers' Offshoring Network Behavior." *Heliyon* 6, no. 6 (June 1, 2020): e04293. https://doi.org/10.1016/j.heliyon.2020.e04293.

Douma, Pyt S. "Political Economy of Internal Conflict: A Review of Contemporary Trends and Issues." *Netherlands Institute of International Relations, Clingendael*, 2001. https://www.clingendael.org/sites/default/files/pdfs/20011000_cru_working_paper_1.pdf.

Duhem, Vincent. "Dans l'est de la RDC, comment et pourquoi les hostilités ont repris—Jeune Afrique.com." JeuneAfrique.com, November 1, 2023. https://www.jeuneafrique.com/1499582/politique/dans-lest-de-la-rdc-comment-et-pourquoi-les-hostilites-ont-repris/.

Ebus, Bram, and Thomas, Martinelli. "Venezuela's Gold Heist: The Symbiotic Relationship between the State, Criminal Networks and Resource Extraction." *Bulletin of Latin American Research* 41, no. 1 (2022): 105–22. https://doi.org/10.1111/blar.13246.

Facing Finance. "Dirty Profits II: Report on Companies and Financial Institutions Benefiting from Violations of Human Rights," 2013. https://www.facing-finance.org/wp-content/blogs.dir/16/files/2012/12/ff_dirtyprofits.pdf.

Gerstenberger, Heide. "Market and Violence: The Functioning of Capitalism in History." In *Market and Violence*. Brill, 2022. https://brill.com/display/title/55937.

Geyer, Michael, and Adam, Tooze, eds. *The Cambridge History of the Second World War: Volume 3: Total War: Economy, Society and Culture.* Vol. 3. The Cambridge History of the Second World War. Cambridge: Cambridge University Press, 2015. https://doi.org/10.1017/CHO9781139626859.

Human Rights Watch. "Middle East and North Africa: End Curbs on Women's Mobility | Human Rights Watch," July 18, 2023. https://www.hrw.org/news/2023/07/18/middle-east-and-north-africa-end-curbs-womens-mobility.

International Organization for Migration. "GMG Thematic Paper on the Exploitation and Abuse of International Migrants, Particularly Those in an Irregular Situation—A Human Rights Approach (2013)," 2013. https://www.iom.int/resources/gmg-thematic-paper-exploitation-and-abuse-international-migrants-particularly-those-irregular-situation-human-rights-approach-2013.

International Organization for Migration (IOM). "Libya Migrant Vulnerability and Humanitarian Needs Assessment," 2019. https://dtm.iom.int/sites/g/files/tmzbdl461/files/reports/DTM_LBY_MVHNA_Report_Dec2019.pdf.

Kaldor, Mary. *New and Old Wars: Organised Violence in a Global Era.* John Wiley & Sons, 2013.

Lawal, Shola. "A Guide to the Decades-Long Conflict in DR Congo." Al Jazeera, February 21, 2024. https://www.aljazeera.com/news/2024/2/21/a-guide-to-the-decades-long-conflict-in-dr-congo.

Lowenstein, Roger. *Ways and Means: Lincoln and His Cabinet and the Financing of the Civil War*. Penguin Publishing Group, 2022.

Naím, Moisés. *Illicit: How Smugglers, Traffickers, and Copycats Are Hijacking the Global Economy*. Doubleday, 2005.

Nova, Redazione Agenzia. "Moscow Laundered 2,5 Billion from Illegal Gold Mining in Central African Republic, Sudan and Mali." *Agenzia Nova* (blog), December 13, 2023. https://www.agenzianova.com/en/news/Russia-laundered-%2425-billion-from-illegal-gold-mining-in-Central-African-Republic%2C-Sudan-and-Mali/.

Ntanyoma, Delphin R. "DRC Violence Has Many Causes—the UN's Narrow Focus on Ethnicity Won't Help End Conflict." The Conversation, July 10, 2023. http://theconversation.com/drc-violence-has-many-causes-the-uns-narrow-focus-on-ethnicity-wont-help-end-conflict-208774.

Overy, R. J. *Why the Allies Won*. W.W. Norton, 1997.

Poast, Paul. "Economics and War." In *Understanding War and Peace*. Cambridge University Press, 2023.

Ransom, Roger L. *Conflict and Compromise: The Political Economy of Slavery, Emancipation and the American Civil War*. Cambridge University Press, 1989.

Rettberg, Angelika, Carlo, Nasi, Ralf, Leiteritz, and Juan Diego, Prieto. *Different Resources, Different Conflicts?: The Subnational Political Economy of Armed Conflict and Crime in Colombia*. Universidad de los Andes, 2023.

Richmond, Oliver P. "Liberal Peace and Its Critiques." In *The Palgrave Encyclopedia of Peace and Conflict Studies*, edited by Oliver P. Richmond and Gëzim Visoka, 715–33. Cham: Springer International Publishing, 2022. https://doi.org/10.1007/978-3-030-77954-2_186.

Rothman, Lily. "How World War II Still Determines Your Tax Bill." TIME, April 14, 2016. https://time.com/4289687/1942-tax-day-history/.

Schneider, Victoria. "Bolloré Blacklisted over Alleged Rights Violations on Plantations in Africa and Asia." Mongabay Environmental News, September 29, 2023. https://news.mongabay.com/2023/09/bollore-blacklisted-over-alleged-rights-violations-on-plantations-in-africa-and-asia/.

Serfati, Claude. "Economies de guerre et ressources naturelles : les visages de la mondialisation." *Annuaire suisse de politique de développement*, no. 25–2 (October 1, 2006): 107–26. https://doi.org/10.4000/aspd.258.

Shelley, Louise. *Human Trafficking: A Global Perspective*. Cambridge University Press, 2010.

Shelley, Louise I. *Dark Commerce: How a New Illicit Economy Is Threatening Our Future*. Princeton University Press, 2018. https://doi.org/10.2307/j.ctv346n56.

UN News. "Myanmar Overtakes Afghanistan as World's Top Opium Producer," December 12, 2023. https://news.un.org/en/story/2023/12/1144702.

UNODC: Global Illicit Drug Trends 2001. "'Myanmar: How Did Myanmar Become a Major Supplier of Illicit Opium.,'" June 26, 2001. https://www.unodc.org/pdf/report_2001-06-26_1/analysis_myanmar.pdf.

Urbina, Ian. "North Koreans Are Used as Modern Slaves in China's Fish Processing Plants." *Le Monde.Fr*, February 29, 2024. https://www.lemonde.fr/en/international/article/2024/02/29/north-koreans-are-used-as-modern-slaves-in-china-s-fish-processing-plants_6573255_4.html.

U.S. Department of the Treasury. "Treasury Designates Financial Institution Involved in Facilitating North Korea's Illicit Activities." U.S. Department of the Treasury, April 19, 2011. https://home.treasury.gov/news/press-releases/tg1146.

Vlassenroot, Koen, and Timothy, Raeymaekers, eds. *Conflict and Social Transformation in Eastern DR Congo*. Academia Press, 2004.

Yeo, Andrew. "Expect to See More North Korean Weapons Reach Nonstate Armed Actors in 2024." Brookings, February 21, 2024. https://www.brookings.edu/articles/expect-to-see-more-north-korean-weapons-reach-nonstate-armed-actors-in-2024/.

Zhang, Ruosui. "To Suspend or Not to Suspend: A Cost-Benefit Analysis of Three Chinese Mega-Projects in Myanmar." *The Pacific Review* 34, no. 6 (October 7, 2021): 946–72. https://doi.org/10.1080/09512748.2020.1776757.

CHAPTER 1

Economics and Violence: Hidden Forces and Unaccounted Tales

Clotilde Champeyrache

The history of the relationship between economists and violence is, on the whole, that of a long silence. Generally absent from the reflection, the term "violence" itself does not appear either as a main subject or even as a possible modality of interaction between economic agents. This is even more striking for recent works. In the best of cases, we can find references to similar notions such as blackmail.[1,2,3,4] The question arises as to the reason or reasons for such an omission. The idea here is to show that the question of violence in economics is notably overshadowed by two biases: the first is that of the idealization of the market because this idealization is based on an exaggeratedly pacified vision of the economic world; the second is based on the illusion of the dichotomy between the legal and illegal spheres, with violence being intrinsically confined to the latter.

This double blindness has recently been marginally challenged by the emergence of conflict theory. However, it seems necessary to move away from the dominant thinking in economics to lay the groundwork for a better understanding and consideration of violence in economics. In particular, it is certainly appropriate to start from the observation of the real economy, i.e. as it functions and not as it is modeled, in order to identify what violence can be in economics. It also appears that the approach can be made through notions such as that of coercion and power: violence is effectively a tool for asserting power, which can be legitimate (the State holds the "monopoly of violence" according to the established expression) or not (in which case violence falls

---

1 See, for example, the criticisms of Coase (1960) and the idea that private negotiation leads to an economically optimal solution in the case of negative externalities, notably those of Cheung (1970) and Coase's response (1988).
2 R. H. Coase, "The Problem of Social Cost," *The Journal of Law and Economics* 3 (October 1960): 1–44, https://doi.org/10.1086/466560.
3 Steven N. S. Cheung, "The Structure of a Contract and the Theory of a Non-Exclusive Resource," *The Journal of Law & Economics* 13, no. 1 (1970): 49–70.
4 Ronald H. Coase, "Blackmail," *Occasional Papers from the Law School, the University of Chicago* 24 (1988).

into the realm of the illegal). However, these notions of power and coercion are present in the thought known as "old American institutionalism" and especially in the work of John Rogers Commons. Moreover, the notion of coercion opens the door to a more subtle apprehension of what falls within the scope of violence. Violence can be visible, even quantifiable (we have statistics on the number of homicides, attacks on people and property, etc.). But violence can also be masked, sometimes even reduced to a threat that does not even need to be carried out because it is so credible (as in the case of intimidation or even blackmail). Rethinking the variety of registers of violence gives substance to the notion of violence in economics. It also allows us to move away from the legal/illegal dichotomy: intangible violence—especially that which involves conditioning strategies—is manifested in both the legal and illegal spheres. The economic functioning of criminal organizations such as mafias illustrates this fact well.

1.1 Economists: A Pacified Vision of the World

From the classical founders of political economy to the current mainstream of economics, economists have conscientiously avoided addressing the issue of violence. Following the teachings of Adam Smith and his famous "invisible hand" metaphor, economics as a discipline has mainly developed a positive and pacified view of economic relations. The mainstream literature that has developed around the representation of the market—an idealized market—has emphasized coordination mechanisms between agents that mainly allow for the convergence of individual interests, i.e. a harmonious vision of economic relations. Even the factors likely to create tensions and conflicts are finally presented as elements of pacification: this is the case in particular with the treatment of scarcity. The whole is carried by the idea that the actions undertaken by individuals are always the expression of their free choice. This type of reasoning, taken to its extreme, implicitly leads to forms of obliteration of the law in favor of the economy. The result is that economics is characterized by irenism and is in many ways incapable of grasping the question of violence, except by confining it to the illegal sphere.

1.1.1 *The Market as an Unquestionable and Uncontested Natural Order*
When classical economists, and particularly Adam Smith, studied the market in order to understand its mechanisms, they considered that the economic laws they were going to enunciate were, by nature, natural laws: they were valid at all times and in all places. Among these natural laws, one predominates: that

of supply and demand. It determines the price of goods and therefore what makes the transaction acceptable or not for each of the suppliers and the applicants, independently of any characteristic specific to each individual. It is the meeting of supply and demand in a competitive market that sets the price level, not human action. The market thus becomes a natural order and not the largely political product of human decisions. Opposing the law of the market then amounts to an "unnatural" position.[5,6,7] Presenting the law of the market as a natural law thus validates that one must submit to it and accept its fruits, even when the functioning of the market produces inequalities. These inequalities are themselves considered natural.

The mainstream economy that developed at the end of the 19th century and the mathematical modeling that accompanied it reinforced this vision. Natural inequalities even become just in the sense that they are interpreted as resulting from the just retribution of each person's actions. The idealization of the market is transformed into its model: the market in pure and perfect competition. This strictly normative model, disconnected from any empirical realism, is used to demonstrate the superiority of the market over other economic systems. This is done by identifying an equilibrium—also called natural—that is optimal in terms of resource allocation since it allows for a maximum number of transactions between free buyers and sellers. This result therefore implies maximum satisfaction for the participants in the exchanges. In this sense, it also contributes to irenism. But to achieve this result, mainstream economists use a certain number of hypotheses that can be considered as biased with respect to the problem of violence. On the one hand, the model dismisses the possibility that scarcity—although crucial—produces conflict. On the other hand, it assumes a freedom of economic agents which, because it lacks tangible content, is potentially illusory.

1.1.2 *Scarcity: From Conflict to Harmony Via the Market*

Scarcity is an essential element for economists. Some of them even make it the crucial element in the definition of the discipline. Thus, according to Lionel Robbins, economics is "the science which studies human behavior as

---

5 See in particular Dugger (1989) on the construction of the market myth or Nooteboom (2014).
6 William M. Dugger, "Instituted Process and Enabling Myth: The Two Faces of the Market," *Journal of Economic Issues*, June 1, 1989, https://www.tandfonline.com/doi/abs/10.1080/00213624.1989.11504927.
7 Bart Nooteboom, *How Markets Work and Fail, and What to Make of Them* (Edward Elgar Publishing, 2014).

a relationship between ends and scarce means which have alternative uses"[8] The central question for the economist then becomes that of the optimal allocation of scarce resources. This quest fits in well with the methodological evolution introduced by the transition from political economy to the so-called "economic science": the reasoning based on methodological individualism proposes a rational, calculating, and maximizing economic agent as the reference individual. The scarcity of available resources forces him to make choices; his rationality allows him to make rational choices. This model of the behavior of agents under constraint also contributes to the irenique vision of the economic world in mainstream thinking.

Where scarcity would normally introduce conflicts, and therefore potentially violence, between individuals competing for resources, the dominant economists will make scarcity an instrument of harmony in human relations. Once again, it is the market that is a factor in the pacification of the economy. The state of nature would see the appropriation of most of the rare resources according to the law of the strongest. The thesis of the liberal economists is that the creation of the market makes it possible to respond to the difficulties caused by scarcity. The market then becomes the main institution of modern societies. It guarantees the proper functioning of exchanges, but above all, it creates a harmony of interests that are nevertheless divergent. This presupposes that property rights are clearly defined, implemented, and enforceable in case of dispute. Scarcity thus leads to the creation of the market and the definition of property rights so that it can function: scarcity thus creates order and avoids the use of violence.

The competitive market allows the meeting and matching of private individual interests. It does so in a harmonious and non-conflictual way because the free will of each market participant is respected: no one is obliged to sell or not to sell; no one is obliged to buy or not to buy because the free entry, free exit of the market is a starting hypothesis. The economy is thus reduced to its sole market dimension. And, by hypothesis, exchanges are only finalized when they are considered mutually advantageous by rational market participants. Scarcity then no longer leads to conflicts over the appropriation of resources but to the constitution of peacemaking institutions.

---

8   Lionel Robbins, *An Essay on the Nature and Significance of Economic Science* (Ludwig von Mises Institute, 1935), p.16.

1.1.3 *The Illusion of Free and Equal Agents*

If the market is peacemaking, it is also because of the assumptions made about the agents present in the market. The dominant economics, as opposed to the classical and Marxist currents, no longer thinks in terms of social classes. Yet thinking in terms of classes opens up the possibility that these classes are in conflict because they are driven by divergent, even contradictory, interests. Thus, for the classics, the sharing of the fruits of labor-value is done between three classes (the capitalists, the working class, and the landowners): the increase in the share captured by one of the classes is done at the expense of one or both of the other classes. The classical authors do not dwell on the conflictual dimension of this sharing. Marxists, on the other hand, explore the conflictual potential through the question of class struggle and proletarian revolution.

Mainstream economics dismisses the problem by removing all reference to social classes and by resorting to methodological individualism. In this way, the problem of power (and power asymmetry) is removed from the field of economics. Yet the question of violence is an integral part of that of power: the legitimate power of the state is embodied in the monopoly of violence; violence against others is the expression of a will to establish power over that person.

The competitive market offers the guarantee of mutually agreed and unconstrained exchanges insofar as individuals are assumed to be free and equal. Freedom (to produce, to sell, to consume ... or not to carry out each of these options) rules out the possibility of one individual exercising a constraint on one or more others. Equality also plays a major role in the pacification of the representation of the economic world. It is not a question of equality in terms of initial endowments (budgetary, social, material) but of equality in the face of market mechanisms and laws. From the hypothesis of the atomicity of agents in the market, an equality of these agents follows, an equality that must be understood as the absence of power of these agents in the market. In concrete terms, no agent has the power to influence the price level in a competitive market. We say that they are "price takers" and not "price makers." The ideal world of pure and perfect competition excludes the possibility that some agents might seek to manipulate markets[9] (through corruption or cartels, for example) or that they might adopt behaviors such as deception, blackmail, threats, or any other non-peaceful method. Visible violence, or violence that is

---

9   The exercise of market power (typically cases of monopoly) is analyzed in terms of deviation from the ideal pure and perfect competition model.

invisible because it does not take the form of physical harm to people or property, is considered incompatible with the market.

These models enrich the thesis dating back to the philosophers of the Enlightenment, such as Montesquieu and Voltaire, and taken up by the classics, such as Adam Smith[10] of "sweet trade." According to this thesis, free trade—especially when extended to the international level—is a source of well-being because it is supposed to increase the wealth of all participants through mutually beneficial exchanges. It is also supposed to develop more virtuous individual behaviors such as honesty and loyalty to create the trust necessary to continue trading. Once again, the market appears to be a vehicle for peace, removing the specter of violence. In reality, Adam Smith's analysis was more nuanced than that, since he also envisaged that the wealth obtained through trade would also be used to finance wars in order to conquer new markets. Although in favor of trade and the market, Adam Smith did not assume that peace was necessarily achieved.[11][12] These nuances were gradually swept away by liberal thought, to the point that the term "war" did not appear in the keywords of a work such as Marshall's *Principles of Economics* (1920).[13]

1.1.4   The Effacement of the Law before the Economy

If market transactions make it possible to establish naturally pacified economic relations, then the law ends up losing its importance in the supervision of economic life. The private encounter between individual interests that end up converging peacefully according to the principle of the famous "invisible hand" makes it possible to justify a form of split between economy and law. This process of disconnection between the two fields is not explicit. But it does disrupt the American institutionalist tradition that articulated law, economics, and even ethics, as we shall see later.

As a natural order, the idealized market of the dominant economy can hardly be reconciled with a legal framework shaped by human choices and inscribed in a delimited spatial and temporal field. The only legal framework required for the proper functioning of the market is one that guarantees the completeness of property rights (rights of use, exclusivity, and alienability) as well as legislation that guarantees to approximate the model of pure and

---

10   Books 2 and 5 of the *Wealth of Nations*.
11   In particular, see the article by Paganelli and Schumacher (2019).
12   Maria Pia Paganelli and Reinhard Schumacher, "Do Not Take Peace for Granted: Adam Smith's Warning on the Relation between Commerce and War," *Cambridge Journal of Economics* 43, no. 3 (April 11, 2019): 785–97, https://doi.org/10.1093/cje/bey040.
13   Alfred Marshall, *Principles of Economics* (Cosimo, Inc., 1920).

perfect competition (anti-trust legislation in particular).[14] The law is therefore an instrument at the service of the economy and must not develop specific features that would take the market out of the realm of natural order.

However, law is in essence the discipline that is able to take note of the conflict of certain individual (or even collective) interests and to make a value judgment on the interests at stake. The law can privilege morality or ethics over economic efficiency by prohibiting, for example, the commodification of certain goods or services. This is the basis of the principle of the "non-patrimoniality of the human body" in the face of the advocates of "natural rights" who consider that, in the name of individual freedom, each person is free, if he or she wishes, to sell all or part of his or her body.

Coase's famous 1960 article on "the social cost problem" perfectly illustrates how recourse to legal arbitration is rejected in favor of a privately negotiated solution that is supposedly satisfactory to both parties to the negotiation.[15] This article deals with negative externalities and in particular with the issue of pollution, since a concrete case is based on the relationship between a polluter and a polluted. Economically, this type of relationship was previously treated in connection with the legal notions of victim (the polluted) and perpetrator (the polluter). This took the form of measures to prohibit or limit (by establishing quotas) the activity that caused the pollution, or by adopting taxes on the polluting activity. Coase chooses to abandon the victim-blame view and make it "a problem of reciprocal nature." He establishes a symmetry—a simulacrum of equal and powerless individuals in the model of pure and perfect competition—between polluter and polluted, which excludes a judgment on the act of polluting, which is only a consequence of the act of producing.

The economist, according to Coase, does not have to judge the right of an agent to pollute. His role is to determine how to reach an optimal level of pollution, the latter being defined not with reference to environmental standards to be respected but on the basis of a single criterion of economic efficiency (the maximization of the total gain of those involved). Moreover, Coase denies any conflict between the polluter and the polluted, since he presents them as capable of negotiating freely and reaching this optimal level of pollution naturally, smoothly, and in a mutually beneficial way. Even when, according to Coase, it is the polluted who pays the polluter to reduce his level of production and

---

14 Clotilde Champeyrache, "The Assumption of Law Neutrality: Property Rights Theory Versus Legal-Economic Nexus," Œconomia. History, Methodology, Philosophy, no. 3-3 (September 1, 2013): 391–419, https://doi.org/10.4000/oeconomia.171.

15 R. H. Coase, "The Problem of Social Cost," The Journal of Law and Economics 3 (October 1960): 1–44.

therefore pollution.[16] The erasure of the law (i.e. the rejection of the category guilty-victim) denies any dimension of conflict between the interests of the polluter and the interests of the polluted; the solution offered via private negotiation denies the violence of making the one who suffers the costs of pollution pay; finally, this reasoning denies the capacity of the law (via environmental legislation) to settle the conflict linked to pollution, to arbitrate in favor of an interest judged to be legitimate, and to protect the victim from the guilty.

The whole construction of classical thought, and even more so of the current dominant economic thought, values the so-called market economy. This is done at the cost of a bias in perceptions. Without specifically seeking to construct a pacified representation of economic relations, the idealized vision of the market is marked by irenism. The harmony of interests is presented as a systematic result of the functioning of the market. This is a naive and illusory vision of the economic world.

In addition, when violence is rarely discussed, it is done so in a Manichean way. Violence is confined to the sphere of the illegal economy with an illusory form of watertightness between the legal and illegal worlds. This is the case in the literature analyzing illegal markets in terms of protection in the tradition of Demsetz.[17] The reflection starts from the instruments used to describe the market economy and focuses on the question of illegal transactions when defined and enforceable property rights do not exist. This leads Demsetz to consider that criminals do not only provide goods and services that are prohibited by law, but that they must also ensure a form of governance in criminal markets to guarantee contracts and property rights so that, even without legal structures, the illegal market can function. Illegal markets are then characterized as markets with criminal authority, and this authority is based not on the legitimacy of law and institutions, but on violence or the credible threat of violence in case of non-compliance. Schelling's (1967) article will also maintain this connection between exacerbated violence and the illegal economy, even

---

16 According to Coasian logic, if we take two agents both using the same river that agent A pollutes by producing and that agent B uses by paying de-pollution costs for its own production, everything will depend on who owns the property rights on the said river. If agent A is the owner, it is then up to agent B, who suffers the external costs, to propose a negotiation. It is he, although polluted, who will pay for A to produce less and thus pollute less. He will do so as long as the cost is less than or equal to the gain obtained in terms of a reduction in the costs of de-pollution incurred. This reasoning is the basis of the market in pollution rights, with the difference that the polluter-pays principle has been recognized by international negotiations.

17 Harold Demsetz, "Toward a Theory of Property Rights," *The American Economic Review* 57, no. 2 (1967): 347–59.

connecting the tendency to monopolize illegal markets to the recurrent use of violence by criminal organizations.[18]

In addition to irenism (a pacified vision of the world) and Manichaeism (violence would be a specificity of the illegal world), we can also criticize the dominant thinking in economics regarding its way of apprehending the notion of violence. This notion, in addition to being on the bangs of the reflection, is also stripped of its complexity. Finally, the violence that economists talk about—a little—is reduced to its visible, even ostensible forms: to caricature (but not so much), it is basically that of criminals who, in order to enforce a contract, break arms, burn down a warehouse or kill a traitor. But violence unfolds in many ways. This is even more true in the economic field.

1.2 Conflict Theory and the Return of the Dark Side of the Economy

Recently, a minority group of economists has begun to question the pacified view of economic relations. Without questioning the importance of the market and its functioning, proponents of conflict theory point out that mainstream economists have developed a partial view of the economy. It is because of this partiality that it is important to complete it, which will make it less irenic. The idea is that there is a part of the economy that does indeed function peacefully. But there is also a part of the economy with more obscure aspects, a world that Hirshleifer—a founding member of this branch of thought—refers to as "Machiavelli's world," as opposed to "Coase's world," which is dominated by harmony and peaceful cooperation. Conflict thus returns to the field of economics and opens up a reflection that has the interest of not being Manichean: for Hirshleifer, it is fundamental to understand that there are connections between conflict and cooperation in the sense that the two are not juxtaposed but cohabit and interact. Moreover, this reflection opens a door to a better understanding of the forms that violence can take, particularly in the economic field.

As we have seen, the original economic thought (that of the Classics) and then the dominant economic thought (around the neoclassical core) have constructed an increasingly irenic representation of the world. This process has even led to the replacement of sometimes unflattering principles by others that are rewarding. Thus, Adam Smith, when he described the quest for individual interest by each person, emphasized the selfish nature of this quest.

---

18 Thomas C. Schelling, *Economics and Criminal Enterprise*, 1967.

The modeling of Pure and Perfect Competition will replace Smith's moral theory with the hypothesis of individual rationality. But this evolution is part of the same logic, that of the positive forms of the market economy: the invisible hand harmoniously and spontaneously reconciling divergent interests; the division of labor allowing massive productivity gains; the monetization of market exchanges favoring cooperation between individuals.

If the development of the market economy after the Industrial Revolution has indeed allowed economic growth, the increased interconnection of economic agents, and the transition to mass production and consumption, it is no less true that these processes of enrichment also have negative aspects that Hirshleifer calls the "dark side of the force." These include war and territorial conquest, political corruption, and crime (especially appropriation: theft, extortion, misappropriation of wealth, and undue enrichment). Vilfredo Pareto noted that human activities were partly oriented toward production and exchange (the positive side) but also toward the appropriation of the production of others (the negative side).[19,20] Taking into account this double orientation of human efforts reintroduces into the field of economic activities such as appropriation, confiscation, and, their corollary, defense, and protection in order to guard against predatory actions.

There are activities that privilege exchange and production and that favor an increase in total wealth. But some activities are driven by a spirit of predation and conflict and that aim at appropriating wealth, even without having participated in the effort to create it. For conflict theorists, it is fundamental to give this second branch its rightful place because it contributes to economic dynamics and evolution.

In the words of Jack Hirshleifer, we must add to the "Coase world" (abundantly discussed by mainstream economists) characterized by the prevalence of inter-individual cooperation via mutually beneficial private negotiations, the "Machiavellian world" dominated by conflict.

---

19 "The efforts of men are utilized in two different ways: they are directed to the production or transformation of economic goods, or else to the appropriation of goods produced by others" (quoted by Hirshleifer, 2001, p.9). It should be noted that an author of original American institutionalism such as Thorstein Veblen (1915) also mentions the idea that men are driven by contradictory instincts, with instincts that are beneficial to the group (instinct of workmanship or love of work well done; parental bent or sense of community; idle curiosity or non-utilitarian curiosity) and instincts that are harmful to the group (predatory instinct; propensity for invidious emulation with instinct of rivalry and hierarchy; self-regarding instinct).

20 Thorstein Veblen, *The Theory of the Leisure Class: An Economic Study of Institutions* (Macmillan, 1915).

Moreover, conflict theorists emphasize that these two worlds are not juxtaposed and impermeable, that Machiavelli's world is not a deviation from Coase's world, which would be the reference and the model to which to move in case of deviation. On the contrary, the two worlds are in repeated interaction. Jack Hirshleifer[21] even draws two main propositions from this (pp.11–12):

1   Cooperation, with rare exceptions, takes place in the shadow of conflict: it is to avoid a conflict that one fears (because of the costs it generates and because of the uncertainty weighing on its outcome) that one may be led to choose to cooperate;
2   When there is cooperation, it is often a conspiracy of some individuals to enter into conflict with others or to respond to an aggression of the latter.

This means that it is complicated, if not impossible, to opt systematically and exclusively for the path of cooperation. Such an assumption would be naive. Even if an individual, or even a nation, chose to privilege cooperation and invested its human and material resources exclusively in the path of production or exchange, he/she could not escape the question of conflict. Indeed, such a specialization in the Coasian way should lead to an increase in the wealth produced. However, this enrichment will arouse in other individuals/nations a desire for predation. In response to this risk of confiscation of the wealth produced, its author will be led to develop defense capacities and thus invest resources in sectors other than those strictly productive (for example, armament at the level of a nation; alarm, armor for individuals). Violence, the threat of violence, and the anticipation of the risk of being a victim of violence therefore influence economic choices, including those made by peaceful agents in the legal sphere.

There is another element of interest in conflict theory—albeit indirectly—for the problem of economists and violence. As its name suggests, the theory deals with conflict, particularly appropriation conflict, without particularly seeking to define precisely the related issue of violence. Jack Hirshleifer notes, however, that conflict is not necessarily accompanied by violence, which seems to take up the idea of violence being defined by its visibility. He illustrates this with various examples such as strikes or the initiation of legal proceedings. This last point gives a significant place to the law since the law once again becomes a tool for regulating conflicts (insofar as it defines what is authorized and what is not: for example, price competition is authorized, but competition

---

21   Jack Hirshleifer, *The Dark Side of the Force: Economic Foundations of Conflict Theory* (Cambridge University Press, 2001).

through deception is not). The law also enables the implementation of agreements reached (via enforcement).

All in all, conflict theory—which remains a marginal branch of current economic thought—has the merit of challenging an irenic vision limited to mutually advantageous exchange. It points out that many inter-individual economic relations are in reality not harmonious but rivalrous relations: the advantage obtained by one is at the expense of another. It also reminds us that even apparently peaceful exchange is likely to harbor a conflictual dimension. In this sense, conflict theory opens a door to the reintegration of violence into the field of economic reflection.

However, this gap remains fragile. The emphasis is mainly on conflicts of appropriation (of the type of theft, confiscation), particularly in a form that can be described as militarized (unless we exclude the question of violence when the conflict takes forms such as strikes or judicial solutions). It is still necessary to extend the reflection by seeking a framework that will allow us to truly ask the question of violence in the complexity of its manifestations. The question of appropriation is naturally important, but it does not exhaust the subject. Violence can also manifest itself more subtly in the form of subjection or conditioning exercised by certain agents on other agents without the coercive nature of the relationship necessarily being formally evident. This calls into question the content of the notion of economic freedom as well as the reduction of violence to its ostensible manifestations with attacks on goods and persons. Taking these elements into account invites us to turn to a school of thought marginalized by the dominant economic thought: original American institutionalism.

1.3   Original American Institutionalism: A Reflection on Power, Freedom and Coercion

Emphasis is placed on the contribution of the original institutionalist economics (OIE), as the latter allows to deal with violence not in its strictly physical (homicides, attacks, etc.) or strictly in its material dimension (racketeering, theft, destruction of equipment, etc.) but in the form of undue coercion of others. The IOE, in fact, puts the notion of power back at the heart of reasoning. John R. Commons in particular offers relevant tools for analyzing the relationship between violence and economics.

Although he does not deal directly with the question of violence, John R. Commons (1924) distinguishes between freedom "in vacuo" and freedom "in action."[22] The first corresponds to the absolute freedom at the basis of dominant economic models: every agent has at any moment the alternative between doing and not doing (working, producing, consuming ...). Freedom in action reflects reality because it is shaped by the constraints exercised by others, and by the real opportunities offered to each person economically and institutionally. This freedom therefore includes asymmetries of power between agents and allows the shift from persuasion to coercion in economic thinking to be introduced into the effective expression of will in the market. This notion and the "economic power to withhold" (intended as the capacity to deny others access to resources) shed new light on the notion of the economy of violence, which is not reduced to the sole sphere of illegality.

One of the major contributions of John R. Commons is to think of the economy as co-produced with the law. This is the thesis of the legal economic nexus, where law, economics, and ethics are permanently intertwined and in reciprocal interaction; each field being co-constructed in evolution with the others. In this sense, the idea of a natural order is completely removed. The market is a human and collective construction, determined by a legal context specific to a place and a time, and therefore called upon to evolve. This allows Commons to think of market transactions differently from the dominant irenic vision.[23] For him, market transactions bring together agents who are legally equal but who may be economically unequal. The inequality is then located in what Commons calls bargaining power. It is at this level that the possibility of moving from a pacified economy based on persuasion (via private negotiation leading to a solution considered by the parties involved to be mutually advantageous) to an economy where transactions—although formally peaceful—are in reality the result of a capacity for coercion.

The shift from persuasion to coercion is possible when one considers the notion of free will in economics. In mainstream thinking, freedom seems to be both a condition and a result of the competitive functioning of the market. By hypothesis, agents are considered free, and it is this freedom that allows them to make rational choices. At the same time, the fact that agents agree to carry out a transaction is sufficient to assume that agents were free to do so. Thus, for example, in Coase's (1960) configuration, no account is initially taken of the fact that the polluted party may be subject to pressure modifying the terms

---

22 John R. Commons, *Legal Foundations of Capitalism*, Law Books Recommended for Libraries (New York: Macmillan, 1924).
23 John R. Commons, *Institutional Economics; Its Place in Political Economy* (New York: The Macmillan Company, 1934).

of the negotiation, that he may be blackmailed[24] by the polluter (for example, threatening to increase the level of production and therefore of pollution in order to increase the clean-up costs for the polluted party and to place him in a more difficult situation for negotiating). The freedom expressed is in reality more formal than real. Well before Coase (1960), Commons had nevertheless underlined the emptiness of free will as it is represented in mainstream economics.

While free will is at the heart of the dominant economic reasoning, its content is not clearly and finely defined. The supposed equality of individuals leads one to deduce too quickly that their degrees of freedom are also equal. Yet, Commons (1924, p.69)[25] points out that this vision does not correspond to the real world and represents only a weak form of freedom inspired by Locke's thought. In fact, the free will of the market model is a binary free will, a "mere faculty of acting and not acting" (Commons, 1924, p.69):[26] at any moment, the agent is "free" to produce or not to produce, to consume or not to consume, to work or not to work, etc. The interest of this binarity is that the agent is "free" to produce or not to produce, to consume or not to consume, to work or not to work, etc. The interest of this binarity is to be able to reduce any human activity to an alternative that is easy to model. But this remains an abstract construction, with no real explanatory power for the reality of human choices and the constraints that continually shape these choices. For Commons, it is only a "will-in-vacuo" that does not take into account the fact that the free will of each person interacts with the free will of others and that these interacting free wills can be divergent and constrained.

For Commons, the free will that is expressed in markets and the economic space is what he calls "will-in-action": a free will "continually overcoming resistance and choosing between different degrees of resistance, in actual space and time" (Commons, 1924, p.69).[27] The notion of scarcity is part of institutionalist reasoning, but it is not thought of as necessarily producing harmony. The emphasis is on the constraints it imposes and the opportunities it shapes, these economic opportunities not being the same for everyone. Hence the

---

24 This criticism was addressed to Ronald Coase, who took it into account in an article published in 1988. This then gave rise to a reformulation of the problem in terms of property rights and the costs of protecting these rights (see, for example, Cheung (1970) for a development in terms of the political Coase theorem including a coercive dimension).
25 Commons, *Legal Foundations of Capitalism*.
26 Commons.
27 Commons.

free wills that are part of different fields of action, as well as the possibility of switching from persuasion to coercion:

> For the will is not an empty choosing between doing and not doing, but between different degrees of power in doing one thing instead of another. The will cannot choose nothing-it must choose something in this world of scarcity-and it chooses the next best alternative. If this alternative is a good one, then the will is free, and can be induced only by persuasion. If the alternative is a poor one, or if there is no alternative, then the will is coerced. The will chooses between opportunities, and opportunities are held and withheld by other wills which are choosing between opportunities, and these opportunities are limited by principles of scarcity.
> COMMONS, 1924, 303–4[28]

Will-in-action therefore differs from one individual to another, in particular, because not all economic agents are equal when it comes to ownership. However, still according to Commons, with the evolution of the economic system since industrialization, ownership has become a factor of power: an economic power to withhold. Individuals participating in market transactions therefore exercise a free will conditioned by the free will of other market participants. Their effective freedom is therefore also characterized by their degree of exposure (in the sense of a limit to the exercise of rights) vis-à-vis others. Asymmetries between individuals then emerge, asymmetries notably in terms of property.

For a long time, property could be defined as the exclusive holding of physical objects for the owner's private use. But industrialization and the concentration of industry from the end of the 19th century onwards changed the nature of property (Commons, 1924, pp.6–7).[29] The simple holding of property rights was transformed into the power to withhold from others what they need but do not own. This transformation in the nature of property was accompanied by a shift from "producing power" to "bargaining power" (Commons, 1924, p.21).[30] The former aims at increasing use values, the latter at increasing exchange values. But this evolution is incompatible with the "pure and perfect" market relations between owners and non-owners. It turns these relations into relations of power. The agents on the market are no longer systematically on an equal footing. The propertyless are at a disadvantage in bargaining processes

---

28 Commons.
29 Commons.
30 Commons.

vis-à-vis the owners, since the latter have the capacity "to hold back until the opposite party consents to the bargain" (Commons, 1924, p.54).[31]

The asymmetry is all the stronger because markets often involve unorganized individuals facing corporations that are able to exploit their economic power (Commons, p.269).[32] Commons illustrates this fundamental asymmetry using the relationship between employers and job seekers. Where the mainstream economy would represent a competitive labor market where suppliers and applicants meet freely, Commons points out that the employer—in effect, the firm—may or may not offer the applicant a job. The job seeker is in an inferior position in terms of bargaining power since he needs the job to secure an income. The employer can knowingly take advantage of this asymmetry to impose conditions (whether they are not prohibited by law, prohibited by law, or pending legislation). In the case studied by Commons, employers—in the initial absence of legislation prohibiting it—took advantage of bargaining to impose clauses prohibiting the individual from unionizing if hired. This clause would not have been accepted by most job seekers if they had not been forced by necessity to accept the job. As long as the state does not regulate these asymmetries, the coercive situation (in the sense that the employer imposes his conditions) can continue. Conversely, laws can be created to rebalance the bargaining power of contractors. This explains why clauses prohibiting unionization were finally prohibited in the United States, or why usury is also illegal, even though interest-bearing loans are illegal (usury corresponding to excessively high interest that takes advantage of the debtor's situation of distress).

The liberal credo advocating the free confrontation of free wills on markets tends to oppose this intervention by an authority outside the market. This is in line with the liberal logic of the market as a "natural order" and corresponds to the inability of mainstream thinking to perceive the dimension of coercion that may accompany certain transactions. For Commons and several institutionalist economists, the state is not a neutral umpire: it can and even must identify and restrict economic power by exercising the physical power of sovereignty (Dawson, 1998).[33]

---

31   Commons.
32   John Rogers Commons, "The Economics of Collective Action," *University of Wisconsin Press*, 1950, https://cir.nii.ac.jp/crid/1130282270167963648.
33   Richard Dawson, "Sovereignty and Withholding in John Commons's Political Economy 1," in *The Founding of Institutional Economics: The Leisure Class and Sovereignty.*, ed. Warren J. Samuels (London: Routledge, 1998), 47–75.

1.4 Some Illustrations

The Commonsian approach opens new perspectives in order to reintroduce—via power asymmetries and coercion—the problem of violence in the field of economics. This reintroduction is not limited to the illegal sphere; it also allows us to look at "invisible" violence. Visible violence is that which is statistically accounted for and marked by attacks on people (murder, assault and battery, threats and intimidation) and property (attacks, damage, racketeering, etc.). Broadening the scope of violence then raises the question of violence expressed specifically in the legal economic sphere and taking the form of a capacity to condition economic (or even political and social) activity.

Four illustrations follow to show the relevance of the Commonsian view in shifting the relationship between violence and economics from an unaccounted tale to a hidden force of economics.

1.4.1 Asymmetries and Economies in Transition

The state can, in common-sense logic, intervene to restore more equal access to economic opportunities. The law is a fundamental tool for framing economic transactions and for controlling the level of violence (in all its forms) in the economy. From this perspective, we can understand why phases of economic transition are particularly at risk of seeing the development of predatory, coercive, and violent behavior.

Bruno Dallago defines transition as "a set of processes and transformations required for a country to move from one economic system to another" (Dallago, 1996, p.1).[34] During this period there is usually a coordination vacuum, a period of latency during which the old system (feudal, socialist, or other) is no longer in force, but the new system is not yet fully in place. It is in this gap that opportunistic and predatory behaviors can be grafted, which can favor economic agents resorting to violence over others.

In the case of Russia's transition from the Soviet socialist system to the market economy, Volkov (2002) spoke of the development of a class of violent entrepreneurs: by this, he meant that "(…) seemingly different groups were all engaged in the same activities: they intimidated, protected, gathered information, settled disputes, gave guarantees, enforced contracts, and imposed taxes. Their similarity (…) was derived from the management of the same

---

34   Bruno Dallago, "The Market and the State: The Paradox of Transition," *Most: Economic Policy in Transitional Economies* 6, no. 4 (December 1, 1996): 1–29, https://doi.org/10.1007/BF02430928.

resource: organized violence. Hence, I called them violent entrepreneurs and their activity violent entrepreneurship" (Volkov, 2002, p.5).[35]

Sometimes this drift toward an industry of violence benefits from a form of formalization. This occurs more particularly when the transfer of the monopoly of violence to a state perceived as legitimate does not take place, or only partially. In this case, a private protection industry tends to be set up, with the potential for abuse of private violence. The use of violence then becomes an economic opportunity, even a source of income. In post-socialist transitional Russia, the number of private protection companies is soaring; nineteenth-century Sicily is characterized by the recruitment of guards—known for their violent curriculum—to protect the agricultural properties of the often-absent owners.

Sometimes the state itself resorts to the questionable use of violence for the benefit of private economic interests. It is in these terms that we can reread the history of industrialization in the United States at the end of the 19th century with the birth of industrial empires controlled by those whom the journalist Josephson called "robber barons" in 1940.[36] The monopoly that these captains of industry succeeded in establishing over natural resources (such as oil) or growth sectors (such as transportation) was often achieved at the cost of economic violence against employees (wage cuts, obstacles to unionization) and even physical violence validated by the state when the giant strikes of 1892 (Homestead Strike) and 1894 (Pullman Strike) against the deterioration of working conditions were put down in blood.

1.4.2 The Case of Non-violent Racketeering

Racketeering, especially when it is systematic and repeated over time, falls within the scope of violence: it constitutes an example of predation where racketeers take undue advantage of wealth produced by others (entrepreneurs and traders). As such, mainstream economists tend to situate it in the field of the illegal economy and to consider that it will be accompanied by violent acts (in the sense of being visible and therefore prosecuted by the forces of law and order) and denunciations by those who will be subjected to it.

However, there are many situations where racketeering is carried out without visible violence (no threatening letters, no attacks or damage to property,

---

35 Vadim Volkov, *Violent Entrepreneurs: The Use of Force in the Making of Russian Capitalism* (Cornell University Press, 2002).

36 Matthew Josephson, *The Robber Barons: The Great American Capitalists, 1861–1901* (Amereon Limited, 1940).

no physical violence against people) and without reporting it. The violence, however, falls within the scope of the unaccounted tale.

This type of racketeering is particularly observed in territories that have been under the influence of crime for a long time, as is the case in Sicily's Palermo Province. It can also be found in other territories, even though they are considered less criminogenic. For example, the Aemilia investigation that concluded in 2015 in Emilia-Romagna in northern Italy highlighted how the 'Ndrangheta, the Calabrian mafia, managed to establish itself in this bastion of legality and to racketeer local entrepreneurs without the law enforcement agencies observing an increase in the number of denunciations (see Dalla Chiesa, Cabras, 2019).[37] The racketeering system implemented mixed persuasion and coercion. Coercion corresponds to the illegal levy set up by the mafia. Persuasion is the invention of a supposedly win-win racket: the mobsters running legal businesses issued false invoices in return for extortion, making it more acceptable. The victims of the racketeering became accomplices of the racketeers by evading taxes thanks to the false invoices. But in doing so, they lost the ability to denounce the criminals since they were at fault. At the same time, the businessmen and traders who accepted this system did so in the hope that complicity with the mafia would give them access to greater economic opportunities, in particular, for the businessmen, access to public contracts obtained by the mafia through the "vote of exchange" (voto di scambio).[38]

1.4.3 Mafia Infiltration in the Legal Economy

Mafia infiltration of the legal economy illustrates how violence can take the form of economic conditioning that can go unnoticed because it appears to respect the free consent of the contracting parties. Champeyrache (2014) explains how mafiosi develop a strategy in the legal sphere based on artificial scarcity. The objective of the criminal organization is to control access to resources (material or financial) in a territory via legal enterprises.[39]

By controlling these resources, the mafia exerts power over other economic actors. They can create queues and discriminate in access to these resources

---

37 Nando Dalla Chiesa and Federica Cabras, *Rosso Mafia* (Florence-Milan: Bompiani, 2019), http://www.bompiani.it/catalogo/rosso-mafia-9788830100961.

38 By this term, the Italians refer to a corrupt relationship in which the mafia control packages of votes that they offer to politicians who accept them and who, once elected, will return the favor by providing them with advantages such as public contracts, special authorizations for urban planning, etc.

39 Clotilde Champeyrache, "Artificial Scarcity, Power, and the Italian Mafia," *Journal of Economic Issues* 48, no. 3 (September 1, 2014): 625–40, https://doi.org/10.2753/JEI0021-3624480302.

by first favoring other members of the criminal association, and then non-members by imposing conditions. Thus, in the construction sector, the mafia invests priority in the production and marketing of concrete as well as earth-moving and clearing equipment in order to be able to condition the entire production chain downstream. By controlling companies in these sectors of activity upstream, the mafia can suffocate construction sites by not delivering supplies or services on time. The situation can be unblocked when downstream contractors agree to conditions such as employing recommended persons, choosing certain suppliers, subcontracting certain activities, etc. This artificial scarcity then combines with the power to withhold identified by Commons: "Using its ownership of legal enterprises the Mafia has acquired economic power that it would not wield if it confined its activities to the illegal economic sphere. This power extends to non-Mafiosi, increasing their exposure to Mafiosi and adulterating the true meaning of their will-in-action. This economic power in criminal hands may go unnoticed because of its legal façade. It, in turn, raises the question of what the State can do and of the use of its sovereignty when confronted with the rise of a competing criminal power. If the economic power of the Mafia remains unconstrained by the physical power of the State, the Mafia will stand as a competing sovereignty because it tends *de facto* to define rules and duties and, through artificial scarcity and the capacity to withhold, to determine who is to be excluded from what, a prerogative usually in the hands of the State" (Champeyrache, 2021, p. 424).[40]

In this case, the monopoly of violence is technically no longer in the hands of the state. Yet this transfer of power, even of sovereignty, is not necessarily visible because it seems to be validated by supposedly free and voluntary economic transactions.

1.4.4 Legislation on Economic Violence

In the field of the strictly legal economy, violence can also occur. Indeed, if we link the economic dimension of violence to the de facto impossibility for certain individuals to access all or part of the economic opportunities that are theoretically offered to them, then the legal debates on abusive clauses in terms of exploitation of a situation of economic dependence fall within the scope of the relationship between violence and the economy.[41]

---

40 Clotilde Champeyrache, "A Commonsian Approach to Crime: The Mafia and the Economic Power to Withhold," *Cambridge Journal of Economics* 45, no. 3 (May 1, 2021): 411–25, https://doi.org/10.1093/cje/beab006.

41 See for example, in French case law: 'L'abus de dépendance ou la violence économique'. (Aurélien Bamdé, 20 February 2017). Available at https://aureulienbamde.com/2017/02/20/labus-de-dependance-ou-la-violence-economique/.

There is an abuse of economic dependence when a person is obliged to accept contractual conditions that he would not have accepted if he had not been in a position of dependence. We find in similar terms the reasoning of Commons on the asymmetry of free will in recruitment.

In France, several trials around the application of the principle of abuse of economic dependence have supported the jurisprudence on the subject. Above all, this has contributed to a real redefinition in the Civil Code of what violence is, with a turning point in 2018. Until then, the French Civil Code considered, in article 1140, that "Violence occurs when a party enters into a commitment under the pressure of coercion that inspires fear of exposing his person, his fortune or those of his relatives to considerable harm." Since then, the definition of defects of consent has been supplemented in article 1143 by the following situation: "Violence also occurs when a party, abusing the state of dependence in which his co-contractor finds himself toward him, obtains from him a commitment that he would not have entered into in the absence of such constraint and derives a manifestly excessive benefit from it." This article would surely have been of great interest to Commons, who was working on lawsuits in the United States and on how jurisprudence could shape economic relations and contribute to the construction of a "reasonable capitalism," which he called for. This article shows the relevance of an institutionalist rather than a mainstream approach to economics to understand the place of violence in economic reality, both in the legal and illegal spheres. It also highlights the urgency of reconnecting law and economics and moving away from the modeling abstraction and its idealized vision of a peaceful market and a pacified world in order to understand and combat forms of economies of violence.

Bibliography

Champeyrache, Clotilde. "A Commonsian Approach to Crime: The Mafia and the Economic Power to Withhold." *Cambridge Journal of Economics* 45, no. 3 (May 1, 2021): 411–25. https://doi.org/10.1093/cje/beab006.

Champeyrache, Clotilde. "Artificial Scarcity, Power, and the Italian Mafia." *Journal of Economic Issues* 48, no. 3 (September 1, 2014): 625–40. https://doi.org/10.2753/JEI0021-3624480302.

Champeyrache, Clotilde. "The Assumption of Law Neutrality: Property Rights Theory Versus Legal-Economic Nexus." *Œconomia. History, Methodology, Philosophy*, no. 3–3 (September 1, 2013): 391–419. https://doi.org/10.4000/oeconomia.171.

Cheung, Steven N. S. "The Structure of a Contract and the Theory of a Non-Exclusive Resource." *The Journal of Law & Economics* 13, no. 1 (1970): 49–70.

Chiesa, Nando Dalla, and Federica, Cabras. *Rosso Mafia*. Florence-Milan: Bompiani, 2019. http://www.bompiani.it/catalogo/rosso-mafia-9788830100961.

Coase, R. H. "The Problem of Social Cost." *The Journal of Law and Economics* 3 (October 1960): 1–44. https://doi.org/10.1086/466560.

Coase, Ronald H. "Blackmail." *Occasional Papers from the Law School, the University of Chicago* 24 (1988). https://heinonline.org/HOL/Page?handle=hein.journals/unc hoocp24&id=3&div=&collection=.

Commons, John R. *Institutional Economics; Its Place in Political Economy*. New York: The Macmillan Company, 1934.

Commons, John R. *Legal Foundations of Capitalism*. Law Books Recommended for Libraries. New York: Macmillan, 1924.

Commons, John Rogers. "The Economics of Collective Action." *University of Wisconsin Press*, 1950. https://cir.nii.ac.jp/crid/1130282270167963648.

Dallago, Bruno. "The Market and the State: The Paradox of Transition." *Most: Economic Policy in Transitional Economies* 6, no. 4 (December 1, 1996): 1–29. https://doi.org/10.1007/BF02430928.

Dawson, Richard. "Sovereignty and Withholding in John Commons's Political Economy 1." In *The Founding of Institutional Economics: The Leisure Class and Sovereignty.*, edited by Warren J. Samuels, 47–75. London: Routledge, 1998.

Demsetz, Harold. "Toward a Theory of Property Rights." *The American Economic Review* 57, no. 2 (1967): 347–59.

Dugger, William M. "Instituted Process and Enabling Myth: The Two Faces of the Market." *Journal of Economic Issues*, June 1, 1989. https://www.tandfonline.com/doi/abs/10.1080/00213624.1989.11504927.

Hirshleifer, Jack. *The Dark Side of the Force: Economic Foundations of Conflict Theory*. Cambridge University Press, 2001.

Josephson, Matthew. *The Robber Barons: The Great American Capitalists, 1861–1901*. Amereon Limited, 1940.

Marshall, Alfred. *Principles of Economics*. Cosimo, Inc., 1920.

Nooteboom, Bart. *How Markets Work and Fail, and What to Make of Them*. Edward Elgar Publishing, 2014.

Paganelli, Maria Pia, and Reinhard, Schumacher. "Do Not Take Peace for Granted: Adam Smith's Warning on the Relation between Commerce and War." *Cambridge Journal of Economics* 43, no. 3 (April 11, 2019): 785–97. https://doi.org/10.1093/cje/beyo40.

Robbins, Lionel. *An Essay on the Nature and Significance of Economic Science*. Ludwig von Mises Institute, 1935.

Schelling, Thomas C. *Economics and Criminal Enterprise*, 1967.

Veblen, Thorstein. *The Theory of the Leisure Class: An Economic Study of Institutions*. Macmillan, 1915.

Volkov, Vadim. *Violent Entrepreneurs: The Use of Force in the Making of Russian Capitalism*. Cornell University Press, 2002.

CHAPTER 2

Human Trafficking and the Economy of Violence

Louise Shelley

Human trafficking relies on violence just as slavery in the past depended on extreme force to subjugate the enslaved. But the violence associated with slavery was legal in most regions of the world as the slaves were property and did not enjoy human rights. But human trafficking is now illegal and 181 countries are signatories to the UN Protocol to Prevent, Suppress and Punish Trafficking in Persons that came into force in 2003.[1] The Protocol defines human trafficking as follows:

> The recruitment, transportation, transfer, harboring or receipt of persons, by means of the threat or use of force or other forms of coercion, of abduction, of fraud, of deception, of the abuse of power or of a position of vulnerability or of the giving or receiving of payments or benefits to achieve the consent of a person having control over another person, for the purpose of exploitation.[2]

Despite the illegality of this human exploitation, human trafficking has been identified in every country in the world[3] and individuals are often subject to acute violence whether they are trafficked for sexual or labor exploitation, as child soldiers, or placed into forced marriages. An international survey of human trafficking data indicates that violence is greater when the victims are younger.[4]

---

1 UNODC, "The UN Protocol to Prevent, Suppress, and Punish Trafficking in Persons Is the World's Primary Legal Instrument to Combat Human Trafficking," United Nations: Office on Drugs and Crime, February 23, 2023, //www.unodc.org/unodc/en/human-trafficking/protocol.html.
2 UNODC, "United Nations Convention against Transnational Organized Crime," United Nations: Office on Drugs and Crime, September 29, 2003, //www.unodc.org/unodc/en/organized-crime/intro/UNTOC.html.
3 US Department of State, Office to Monitor and Combat Trafficking in Persons, "2023 Trafficking in Persons Report," *United States Department of State* (blog), 2023, https://www.state.gov/reports/2023-trafficking-in-persons-report/.
4 Heidi Stöckl et al., "Human Trafficking and Violence: Findings from the Largest Global Dataset of Trafficking Survivors," *Journal of Migration and Health* 4 (January 1, 2021): 100073, https://doi.org/10.1016/j.jmh.2021.100073.

The problem of human trafficking is widespread, and it is expanding as more individuals are displaced annually by war, conflict, and climate change. As of May 2023, there were more than 110 million forcibly displaced people, more than at any time since data collected on this problem was initiated.[5] Furthermore, the difficulties of survival in many regions of the world with nonfunctional, dysfunctional, and corrupt governments make ever larger numbers seek to emigrate from their home countries and regions. Desperate individuals often hire smugglers to move them and their inability to pay smugglers' often exorbitant fees results in individuals becoming victims of human trafficking either in transit or on arrival.[6]

The violence experienced by victims of human trafficking is not evenly distributed. In contrast with the drug trade, the violence associated with human trafficking is not associated with criminal rivalries that often result in assaults or deaths of competitors or those who refuse to pay their debts. Rather, the violence of human trafficking is usually more focused on intimidating victims, especially women and children,[7] and their immediate families, rather than their criminal associates. But men and boys can also be subject to extreme violence as laborers and forced combatants.

The central element of trafficking is coercion and deception. Victims rarely comply immediately with the wishes of their traffickers, or they may subsequently resist. Escape attempts are brutally punished so that subsequent trafficking victims will be compliant. To coerce the victims in these situations, traffickers may retain the services of particularly violent criminals to repeatedly rape and beat women they plan to sexually traffic. Men forced to work in isolation on remote farms may be subject to extraordinary violence and those forced to work on shipping vessels at sea may find themselves killed or just thrown overboard to drown.[8,9,10]

---

5   USA for UNHCR, "Refugee Statistics," 2023, https://www.unrefugees.org/refugee-facts/statistics/.
6   UNODC, "Global Report on Trafficking in Persons," 2022, https://www.unodc.org/documents/data-and-analysis/glotip/2022/GLOTiP_2022_web.pdf.
7   UNODC, 18, 58.
8   Casetext, "U.S. v. Ramos-Ramos, File No. 1:07-CR-08," accessed March 28, 2024, https://casetext.com/case/us-v-ramos-ramos-4.
9   The Outlaw Ocean Project, "A Lawless Frontier the High Seas Are a Realm in Dire Need of Investigative Journalism," The Outlaw Ocean Project, accessed March 28, 2024, https://www.theoutlawocean.com.
10 Ian Urbina, *The Outlaw Ocean: Journeys Across the Last Untamed Frontier* (Alfred A. Knopf, 2019).

Human trafficking has distinct geographical patterns. Human trafficking differs among diverse groups. Balkan, sub-Saharan, and post-Soviet, Chinese groups all deploy different levels of violence against their victims. This chapter focuses on the violence experienced by human trafficking victims in the United States.

Diverse groups engage in human trafficking in the United States and there is also concern about the use of trafficked labor in the supply chain of commodities entering into the US. As this covert phenomenon is often hard to study systematically, the violence against trafficking victims is clearly and precisely documented in federal court cases that are prosecuted under the Trafficking Victims Protection Act.[11] These cases reveal the forms of violence used, the enforcers of the violence, and the motivation for such acts against victims. Examination of numerous court cases reveals that this violence results not from revenge, as is often the case in the drug trade but serves a distinct economic function. Violence is deployed to ensure that the victim performs the economic activity that they have been trafficked for—to sell sex, work as domestic servants for long hours in contravention of labor laws, or provide cheap labor in work conditions, often at unsafe sites that could not be staffed by legal workers.

Human trafficking is not confined to one region of the United States. Human trafficking is present in urban, suburban, and rural areas and in locales adjoining major highways in all regions of the country as calls to the US human trafficking hotline and federal human trafficking cases reveal.[12,13] Domestic servitude is often hidden in cities and suburbs. Agricultural sites where fruit is harvested, meat processing plants, egg farms, construction sites, and factories are key locales where victims are subject to violence. The more isolated the facility, the more likely that the violence can be significant and sustained against trafficking victims. Many victims do not know that a trafficking hotline exists nor have the capacity to call. Moreover, many lack faith that they could be helped by law enforcement or have access to justice.

---

11 U.S. Department of Justice, "Human Trafficking: Key Legislation," August 23, 2023, https://www.justice.gov/humantrafficking/key-legislation.

12 National Human Trafficking Hotline, "National Human Trafficking Hotline Data Report from January 1, 2021—December 31, 2021," 2023, https://humantraffickinghotline.org/sites/default/files/2023-01/National%20Report%20For%202021.docx%20%283%29.pdf.

13 Louise Shelley, Chu-Chuan Jeng, and Edward Huang, "Combating Sex Trafficking: Examining the Spatial Distribution of Hotels in Urban Areas That Facilitate Sex Trafficking in the US," *Urban Crime. An International Journal* 3, no. 1 (May 10, 2022): 128–58, https://doi.org/10.26250/heal.panteion.uc.v3i1.279.

Trafficking victims may be controlled by acute violence, psychological intimidation, and threats to their families both in the US and abroad. Many of the dehumanizing practices that were used during the Holocaust to produce passive victims are replicated by the traffickers. Trafficking victims are deprived of their identities,[14] may be moved vast distances away from their families, languages, and cultures in inhumane conditions, and are tortured to induce compliance. Some trafficked American girls are subject to violence having their arms, bodies and private parts tattooed indicating they are the possessions of the traffickers, recalling the branding of slavery in the past or that which went on in the concentration camps of World War II.[15] Illustrative of this is a Northern Virginia case that revealed that a member of the Cold Blooded Cartel, and his conspirators had several of his victims tattooed with his nickname "Boo" to prevent them from changing their pimp.[16]

Wiretaps on traffickers and interviews with investigators who have conducted surveillance of traffickers reveal that many are among the most vicious of criminals. They never identify with the suffering of their victims, recalling the brutal guards who loaded the boxcars of humans to deliver victims to the concentration camps. The discourse of traffickers recalls that of slave traders of previous centuries who referred to their commodities as "ignorant savages," meriting the brutal treatment they received.

The violence of human trafficking occurs at every stage of the process from recruitment to the work situation, the daily work environment, and even at the trial stage where criminal groups and gangs threaten possible witnesses and even their families at home. Threats to family members such as beatings, death, and destruction of homes have been executed by the transnational crime groups and gangs that are credible to the victims. For example, in 2014, Ruth Antuanet Miller, a Peruvian citizen residing in the United States, pleaded guilty to forcing undocumented women into sex trafficking. Miller was affiliated with a criminal street gang, through her boyfriend, and threatened

---

14 University of Baltimore School of Law Human Trafficking Prevention Project et al., "An Advocate's Guide to Tax Issues Affecting Victims of Human Trafficking," December 2019, https://www.htlegalcenter.org/wp-content/uploads/An-Advocates-Guide-to-Tax-Issues-Affecting-Victims-of-Human-Trafficking.pdf.

15 Annie Kelly, "'I Carried His Name on My Body for Nine Years': The Tattooed Trafficking Survivors Reclaiming Their Past," *The Guardian*, November 16, 2014, sec. Global development, https://www.theguardian.com/global-development/2014/nov/16/sp-the-tattooed-trafficking-survivors-reclaiming-their-past.

16 Casetext, "United States v. Barcus, Criminal 1:13-Cr-00095," February 9, 2022, https://casetext.com/case/united-states-v-barcus-5.

victims and their families with violence if they refused to work for her. As the statement of facts from the federal case indicates:

> Miller also informed BML [a victim who was an illegal alien in the United States] that Miller's boyfriend is from Guatemala, and if BML refused to work for Miller, Miller's boyfriend would "find" BML's family in Guatemala, which BML reasonably understood as a threat to harm her family.[17]

2.1 Violence in Recruitment

Many of the most violent traffickers are gang members whose reputation is well known. One-fifth of federally prosecuted cases of minors in the United States had gang members as traffickers.[18] Research in Virginia, a center of gang sex trafficking, found that MS-13 cliques recruit runaways and young Central Americans who have recently arrived in the US into prostitution using the gang's reputation for violence.[19] A national gang assessment confirmed this insight in a more general context asserting that women were coerced into prostitution by gang members.[20,21] Violence was also used to ensure that the girls recruited by gang members comply with their demands.[22]

There is also coercion in labor trafficking situations. Migrants being smuggled from Central America to the United States seeking to better their financial situation are captured by criminals who torture them attempting to extort money for their continued transfer to the United States.[23] Others find

---

17   Casetext, "Miller v. United States, Criminal Case No. 1:13-Cr-175," October 18, 2016, https://casetext.com/case/miller-v-united-states-267.
18   Dominique Roe-Sepowitz, "A Six-Year Analysis of Sex Traffickers of Minors: Exploring Characteristics and Sex Trafficking Patterns," *Journal of Human Behavior in the Social Environment* 29, no. 5 (July 4, 2019): 608–29, https://doi.org/10.1080/10911359.2019.1575315.
19   K. Elysse Stolpe, "MS-13 and Domestic Juvenile Sex Trafficking: Causes, Correlates, and Solutions," *Virginia Journal of Social Policy & the Law* 21 (2014): 341.
20   Shared Hope International, "Gang Sex Trafficking on the Rise," March 28, 2014, https://sharedhope.org/2014/03/28/gang-sex-trafficking-rise/.
21   National Gang Center, "2011 National Gang Threat Assessment—Emerging Trends," 2011, https://nationalgangcenter.ojp.gov/library/publications/2011-national-gang-threat-assessment-emerging-trends.
22   Justin Jouvenal, "Fairfax-Based Crips Members Charged with Recruiting Girls for Prostitution—The Washington Post," March 29, 2012, https://www.washingtonpost.com/local/crime/fairfax-based-crips-members-charged-with-recruiting-girls-for-prostitution/2012/03/29/gIQAJRx6iS_story.html.
23   Ann Norris, "Guadalupe Correa-Cabrera: Asylum Seekers and Migrants in the Western Hemisphere Face Real Threats from Human Trafficking," Council on Foreign Relations,

themselves after physical abuse in a trafficked labor situation in agriculture or other menial labor in Mexico or the United States.

The "violence specialists" retained by the traffickers are a special subset of the business, composed often of demobilized soldiers, and veterans of civil wars and regional conflicts; they are the pure thugs of organized crime networks. In a 2022 federal court case in Texas, a man was sentenced to ten years imprisonment. He had answered an online ad to break a human trafficking victim, asserting that he had previous experience in this line of work.[24]

Individual victims who resist their traffickers may be tortured. In 2010, the torturers of a mentally deficient woman forced into years as an exotic dancer in a nightclub were arrested, and several of the traffickers were subsequently sentenced to 20 years of incarceration without parole for the severe physical abuse of the woman.[25]

2.2 Violence in Keeping Victims in Sex and Labor Trafficking

In a gang-related case, Rances Ulices Amaya, an MS-13 gang member, was arrested for helping to run a juvenile prostitution business. He recruited clients and provided security at the appointments, which included carrying a machete. Amaya was accused of threatening the juveniles—who were runaways—and physically assaulting them if they did not want to have sex with the clients.[26] Cordario Marcell Uzzle, a member of the Bloods Street gang was found guilty of trafficking a minor after one of his victims was taken to the hospital as a result of his violence.[27] "According to the federal court documents, he threatened one of his victims with an unloaded gun, purposefully pinching her skin

---

May 31, 2023, https://www.cfr.org/blog/guadalupe-correa-cabrera-asylum-seekers-and-migrants-western-hemisphere-face-real-threats.

24 U.S. Attorney's Office, Northern District of Texas, "Man Sentenced to 10 Years for Offering to 'Break' Sex Trafficking Victim," March 17, 2022, https://www.justice.gov/usao-ndtx/pr/man-sentenced-10-years-offering-break-sex-trafficking-victim.

25 United States Attorney's Office, Western District of Missouri, "Woman Tortured As Slave, Victim Of Sex Trafficking And Forced Labor," September 9, 2010, https://www.justice.gov/archive/usao/mow/news2010/bagley.ind.html.

26 FBI Washington Field Office, "MS-13 Associate Sentenced to 292 Months for Sex Trafficking Teenage Runaway Girls," FBI, November 4, 2011, https://www.fbi.gov/washingtondc/press-releases/2011/ms-13-associate-sentenced-to-292-months-for-sex-trafficking-teenage-runaway-girls.

27 U.S. Attorney's Office, Eastern District of Virginia, "Bloods Gang Member Sentenced to Prison for Prostituting a Minor," June 3, 2016, https://www.justice.gov/usao-edva/pr/bloods-gang-member-sentenced-prison-prostituting-minor.

in the mechanism of the gun and warning her that he knew where her sister was."[28]

Psychological manipulation and drugs[29] are important tools by which the pimps may keep control over their victims, forcing the women to be totally subservient and relinquish all of their earnings to their pimps. But physical violence is also used. Federal cases have documented the violence against trafficked women. Illustrative of this is "Prostitutes endured beatings with belts, baseball bats, or 'pimp sticks' (two coat hangers wrapped together). The pimps also punished their prostitutes by kicking them, punching them, forcing them to lay naked on the floor and then have sex with another prostitute while others watched, or 'trunking' them by locking them in the trunk of a car to teach them a lesson."[30]

Violence is also deeply associated with the abuses of farm workers who work on remote farms. One of the first major US labor trafficking cases in 1997 involved serious violence against over 400 male and female farm workers in Florida and South Carolina over an extended period.[31,32,33] Some of the workers had legally entered the country on temporary work permits and therefore it was their isolation rather than their legal vulnerability that made them particularly susceptible to their traffickers' violence. The traffickers were each sentenced to 15 years in federal prison on slavery, extortion, and firearms charges, amongst others. The workers "were forced to work 10–12 hour days, 6 days per week, for as little as $20 per week, under the watch of armed guards. Those who attempted escape were assaulted, pistol-whipped, and even shot."[34] A similar

---

28 Yulia Krylova and Louise Shelley, "Criminal Street Gangs and Domestic Sex Trafficking in the United States: Evidence from Northern Virginia," *Crime, Law and Social Change* 80, no. 3 (October 1, 2023): 307–28, https://doi.org/10.1007/s10611-023-10088-9.

29 Anthony Marcus et al., "Conflict and Agency among Sex Workers and Pimps: A Closer Look at Domestic Minor Sex Trafficking," *The Annals of the American Academy of Political and Social Science* 653, no. 1 (May 1, 2014): 225–46, https://doi.org/10.1177/0002716214521993.

30 Marcus et al.

31 John Bowe, "Nobodies," April 13, 2003, https://www.newyorker.com/magazine/2003/04/21/nobodies.

32 John Bowe, *Nobodies: Modern American Slave Labor and the Dark Side of the New Global Economy*, 1st ed (New York: Random House, 2007), https://www.yourcloudlibrary.com.

33 US Department of Justice, "Miguel Flores and Associate Sentenced to 15 Years For Enslaving Migrant Workers," November 14, 1997, https://www.justice.gov/archive/opa/pr/1997/November97/482cr.htm.html.

34 Coalition of Immokalee Workers, "Slavery in the Fields and the Food We Eat," n.d., https://ciw-online.org/Resources/tools/general/10Slavery%20in%20the%20Fields.pdf.

case of Mexican farm workers in Florida between 2015 and 2017 also included threats to family members at home.[35]

2.3 Trafficking Victims Subjected to Violence by Customers and Law Enforcement

Sex trafficking victims may experience violence from customers and law enforcement as well as their traffickers. Workers at massage parlors, almost entirely from Asia, experience violence at the hands of customers and bosses, as well as police and undercover officers.[36] Although this problem is not sufficiently studied, advocates who work with women employed at massage parlors report that many experienced verbal, sexual, and physical abuse, often associated with racism.[37] This problem was brought into public view with the killing of 8 people (6 of whom were Asian) by a lone gunman at two Atlanta spas in 2021.[38]

Women who sell sex in other locales may also experience significant violence. A study in Baltimore found that 78% of women selling sex reported lifetime abusive police encounters, and 41% reported daily or weekly encounters of any type. In the previous three months, 22% experienced client-perpetrated violence.[39]

---

35 Office of Public Affairs, US Department of Justice, "Owner of Farm Labor Contracting Company Pleads Guilty in Racketeering Conspiracy Involving the Forced Labor of Mexican Workers," September 27, 2022, https://www.justice.gov/opa/pr/owner-farm-labor-contracting-company-pleads-guilty-racketeering-conspiracy-involving-forced.

36 Kelsey Vlamis, "The Atlanta Spa Shootings Revealed the Most Dangerous Threat Massage-Parlor Workers Face Each Day on the Job," Yahoo News, March 24, 2021, https://uk.news.yahoo.com/atlanta-spa-shootings-were-emblematic-070829113.html.

37 Angie Hsu, "Part of the Massage Industry Is Built on Hate Crimes against Asian Women—The Washington Post," March 22, 2021, https://www.washingtonpost.com/outlook/2021/03/22/illegal-massage-business-asian-women/.

38 Derek Hawkins et al., "What We Know about the Victims of the Atlanta Shootings," Washington Post, March 21, 2021, https://www.washingtonpost.com/nation/2021/03/20/atlanta-shooting-victims/.

39 Katherine H. A. Footer et al., "Police-Related Correlates of Client-Perpetrated Violence Among Female Sex Workers in Baltimore City, Maryland," American Journal of Public Health 109, no. 2 (February 2019): 289–95, https://doi.org/10.2105/AJPH.2018.304809.

2.4 Under What Circumstances Is Violence Greatest?

The violence against human trafficking victims is greatest when they are not compliant with the demands of their traffickers. The cases discussed in this chapter focus particularly on labor trafficking and sex trafficking, particularly of minors. The victims in these cases are young, often uninformed of their rights, and in the case of irregular migrants or temporary farm workers, they often lack the language skills or the capacity to access assistance as they are living and working in remote locales. Moreover, many are afraid to have contact with law enforcement because they do not have long-term status in the United States.

There is a high demand for the service of smugglers or temporary guest worker permits in the United States for individuals from Central America and Mexico. Traffickers know that there is a continuous supply of people they can economically exploit. Therefore, the traffickers know that abusing present-day workers will not curtail the future recruitment of other victims.

Violence may be especially vicious when individuals labor in farms, and food processing facilities or are entrapped in homes as victims of domestic servitude. Yet the violence is not limited to locales where individuals are less visible. Those forced to sell sex may be subjected to violence, in more public locales such as hotels where 80% of the federally prosecuted sex trafficking cases are identified.[40,41]

2.5 Economies of Violence and Human Trafficking

Trafficking is a criminal offense where humans are turned into commodities. To maximize the extraction of revenue from their exploitation, traffickers often use violence and sometimes even extreme violence to maximize the compliance and output of those who are exploited.

Deploying violence occurs with all forms of trafficking but the profits differ depending on the sector of the economy in which they are exploited. The profits are often higher in the area of sex trafficking, but the profits derived from

---

40   Louise Shelley, "Human Trafficking and Responsible Leadership," in *Responsible Leadership* (Routledge, 2022) 279–294.
41   Kate Hodal, "Major Global Hotel Brands Accused of Profiting from Sex Trafficking," *The Guardian*, December 11, 2019, sec. Global development, https://www.theguardian.com/global-development/2019/dec/11/major-global-hotel-brands-accused-of-profiting-from-sex-trafficking.

this business depend on the clientele that are served. Therefore, sex-trafficked individuals serving a more affluent clientele may generate more proceeds for the traffickers. Those exploited within homes and subjected to violence, provide their employers more domestic service than they could afford if they paid market rates. Yet having a compliant worker resulting from violence perpetrated against the servant does not yield more than personal economic benefits. Those who are coerced into manual labor in agriculture, lawn servers, food processing plants, and other sectors are allowing their employers to be more competitive in the domestic and global economy.

The United States is predominantly a service economy, with two-thirds of the economy based on the sale of services. However, the United States is deeply involved in the global commodities market as its agricultural products are sold globally, and the United States is the largest importer of goods in the world. Therefore, the United States is all too often the recipient of goods produced by forced and trafficked labor. This is especially true with fish obtained through IUU fishing which represents approximately one-third of the wild-caught fish in the United States.[42,43] Many cotton products are imported from China where production is heavily concentrated in the west in areas where Uighurs are forced to produce cotton and cotton products.[44] Much of the chocolate consumed in the country contains chocolate produced by child labor.[45,46] These three products are just three illustrations of the diverse products produced by child and forced labor that link the US to the larger global commodities market. To give an illustration of the diversity of problematic products, the United States government keeps an extensive list of the types of products that

---

42 Oceana, "Americans Overwhelmingly Support Ending Illegal Fishing and Seafood Fraud, Poll Finds," Oceana USA, January 28, 2021, https://usa.oceana.org/press-releases/americans-overwhelmingly-support-ending-illegal-fishing-and-seafood-fraud-poll-finds/.

43 Louise I. Shelley, *Dark Commerce: How a New Illicit Economy Is Threatening Our Future* (Princeton University Press, 2018), https://doi.org/10.2307/j.ctv346n56.

44 Adrian Zenz, "How Beijing Forces Uyghurs to Pick Cotton," *Foreign Policy* (blog), April 18, 2024, https://foreignpolicy.com/2023/05/16/china-xinjiang-uyghurs-cotton-forced-labor/.

45 Government of Côte d'Ivoire et al., "CLCCG Report: 2010–2020 Efforts to Reduce Child Labor in Cocoa," n.d., https://www.dol.gov/sites/dolgov/files/ILAB/reports/CLCCG-Ten-Year-Report.pdf.

46 Peter Whoriskey and Rachel Siegel, "Hershey, Nestle and Mars Won't Promise Their Chocolate Is Free of Child Labor," Washington Post, June 5, 2019, https://www.washingtonpost.com/graphics/2019/business/hershey-nestle-mars-chocolate-child-labor-west-africa/.

are produced by child and forced labor. This list is used to raise awareness and prevent entry of these products into the United States.[47]

2.6 Responses to Human Trafficking

The United States has numerous activities to address the violence associated with human trafficking both in the United States and internationally. The responses involve federal and local governments, businesses, and civil society. The Trafficking Victims Protection Act has consistently included significant budgets for assistance programs both in the United States and abroad to help victims and provide training for law enforcement.[48] Many other pieces of federal legislation that address human trafficking ensure that supply chains are free of forced or child labor as well as goods made by trafficked individuals. Legal provisions ensure that federal grants and contracts are not staffed with forced or trafficked labor.[49]

The TVPA's successes are most evident in the victims' assistance areas as victims are served by residential, medical, and psychological programs as well as by hotlines. These programs as well as others run by non-governmental organizations throughout the country are key in assisting victims and fighting trafficking. NGOs, religious,[50] non-denominational, and community-based organizations dedicated to fighting trafficking are now functioning in all regions of the country.[51,52] The opening of shelters for victims in many locales in the United States has brought services and support to victims that did not exist until the passage of the TVPA.

Victims of human trafficking, if they agree to cooperate with law enforcement, are eligible for T-visas. For minors, there is no requirement to cooperate

---

47 US Department of Labor, "2022 List of Goods Produced By Child Labor Or Forced Labor," 2022, https://www.dol.gov/sites/dolgov/files/ILAB/child_labor_reports/tda2021/2022-TVPRA-List-of-Goods-v3.pdf.
48 Anthony M. DeStefano, *The War on Human Trafficking: U.S. Policy Assessed* (Rutgers University Press, 2007).
49 American Bar Association, "Human Trafficking Legislation," accessed March 28, 2024, https://www.americanbar.org/groups/human_rights/human-trafficking/trafficking-legislation/.
50 Shayne Moore, Sandra Morgan, and Kimberly McOwen Yim, *Ending Human Trafficking: A Handbook of Strategies for the Church Today* (InterVarsity Press, 2022).
51 U.S. Department of Homeland Security, "Victim Support Pamphlet for NGOs, Faith-Based and Community Groups | Homeland Security," May 16, 2023, https://www.dhs.gov/blue-campaign/materials/pamphlet-victim-support-ngo-and-faith-based.
52 HEAL Trafficking, "Non-Governmental Organizations," HEAL Trafficking: Health, Education, Advocacy, Linkage, accessed March 28, 2024, https://healtrafficking.org/non-governmental-organizations/.

with law enforcement. But the willingness to cooperate in an investigation all too rarely results in an actual investigation, this is especially true in labor cases which represent a significant percentage of T-visas granted.[53]

The T-visa itself is also underused. Only 5000 can be issued each year, but only in 2022 did the number of T-visas granted total 3,000 for the first time. Law enforcement's failure to follow up on the insights from T-visa applications helps explain the fact that labor trafficking cases represented less than 3% of the new trafficking cases in 2022.[54]

The number of actual prosecutions by the federal government was very small. 2021 data reveal that only 203 traffickers were convicted, a decline from previous pre-pandemic years.[55] The preponderance of cases involved sex rather than labor trafficking. The paucity of labor trafficking cases shows the failure of the US government to prioritize this problem. Only 55 defendants were charged in forced labor cases in 2021.[56]

Civil law is an increasingly important tool for trafficking survivors in their fight for justice against powerful individuals and companies such as hotels and hotel chains, locales where they have been subjected to violence. Employers that have intimidated workers or failed to protect workers from violence have been increasingly sued by trafficking victims.[57,58,59] Using civil law provides survivors of labor trafficking, who rarely see their cases prosecuted by the

---

53 Reference to T-visa: note that T-visas are awarded to minors and their cooperation is not necessary; Madeline Sloan, "T Visas Protect Victims of Human Trafficking and Strengthen Community Relationships," Police Executive Research Forum, www.policeforum.org/assets/TVisas.pdf; Presentation at the International Conference on Human Trafficking Research, Creighton University, May 28–30, 2019, www.creighton.edu/geo/creightonglobalinitiative/20182019program; Discussions with lawyers at Ayuda.

54 Analysis based on data on page 2 of the Federal Human Trafficking Report: Lindsey Lane, "2022 Federal Human Trafficking Report (FHTR)," 2023, https://traffickinginstitute.org/wp-content/uploads/2023/06/2022-Federal-Human-Trafficking-Report-WEB-Spreads_compressed.pdf.

55 Office to Monitor and Combat Trafficking in Persons, United States Department of State, "2022 Trafficking in Persons Report," *United States Department of State* (blog), 2022, 575 https://www.state.gov/reports/2022-trafficking-in-persons-report/.

56 Lindsey Lane, Angela Gray, and Alicen Rodolph, "2021 Federal Human Trafficking Report," 2022, https://traffickinginstitute.org/wp-content/uploads/2022/06/2021-Federal-Human-Trafficking-Report-Web.pdf.

57 Bernice Yeung, "Should Hotel Chains Be Held Liable for Human Trafficking?" The New Yorker, July 26, 2023, https://www.newyorker.com/news/a-reporter-at-large/should-hotel-chains-be-held-liable-for-human-trafficking.

58 Sarah Meo and Louise Shelley, "Sex Trafficking and Hotels: Why There Is a Need for Effective Corporate Social Responsibility," Global Policy Journal, November 11, 2021, https://www.globalpolicyjournal.com/blog/11/11/2021/sex-trafficking-and-hotels-why-there-need-effective-corporate-social-responsibility.

59 Shelley, "Human Trafficking and Responsible Leadership," 279–294.

federal government, a legal tool to address their exploitation.[60] Since 2003, US courts have awarded over $265,009,824 in civil damages and settlements in 539 cases in federal courts across the country. This statement predates the hundreds of millions paid by Deutsche Bank and JP Morgan in their settlements related to the Jeffrey Epstein case and his abuse of minors. The majority of the cases in 2021 were for sex trafficking (51.9%) but labor was a close second at 46.8% of all cases.[61] Three-quarters of those who initiated civil suits in forced labor cases were individuals who had entered the US on legal visas (392 of the 539 cases) and then were abused by their employers.[62]

One of the most original approaches to controlling human trafficking originated in California with its Transparency in Supply Chain Act[63] that came into force in 2012 and requires that large "retailers and manufacturers provide consumers with information regarding their efforts to eradicate slavery and human trafficking from their supply chains, and educate consumers on how to purchase goods produced by companies that responsibly manage their supply chains."[64] Unfortunately, this law has no enforcement authority against companies that have trafficked laborers within their supply chains. But the passage of this law has forced many large retailers and producers to be more proactive and attentive to their supply chains.

Under the Biden administration, there has been the introduction of the Uyghur Forced Labor Protection Act in late 2021 that places great pressure on businesses to ensure that they do not have substances produced by enslaved Uyghurs in China in their supply chains.[65] This has placed a significant responsibility on the US Customs service to monitor imports.[66] Ironically at the same time, there have been many more trafficked minors and unaccompanied

---

60 Merrick M. Black, "Using Civil Litigation to Combat Human Trafficking: Federal Human Trafficking Civil Litigation: 2021 Data Update," 2022, 19, https://htlegalcenter.org/wp-content/uploads/Civil-Litigation-2021-Data-Update.pdf.
61 Black, 5–6.
62 Black, 18.
63 Benjamin Thomas Greer and Jeffrey G. Purvis, "Corporate Supply Chain Transparency: California's Seminal Attempt to Discourage Forced Labour," *The International Journal of Human Rights* 20, no. 1 (January 2, 2016): 55–77, https://doi.org/10.1080/13642987.2015.1039318.
64 State of California, Department of Justice, "The California Transparency in Supply Chains Act," accessed March 28, 2024, https://oag.ca.gov/SB657.
65 US Department of Homeland Security, "Uyghur Forced Labor Prevention Act," October 16, 2023, https://www.dhs.gov/uflpa.
66 https://www.expeditionhacks.com/bring-down-counterfeiting-2023 addressed the implementation of the Uyghur forced labor law.

minors who have crossed the border in the States and are now working in conditions of forced labor within the US. This has been possible because there has been a reduction in legal protections for minors working in many states of the United States. The violence perpetrated against these workers, often migrant children, or American minorities, is rarely addressed or prosecuted in the US.

The response to human trafficking has included the cooperation of the government, the business community, and civil society. Illustrative of this has been the proactive response of the financial community to assist in the rapid detection of sex trafficking. In the financial community, in particular, banks collect large amounts of data on credit, debit card, and ATM withdrawals. Key indicators of human trafficking have been created by bankers following discussions with law enforcers as well as insights obtained from interviewing trafficking victims. Applying Artificial Intelligence and other forms of advanced data analytics, bankers and some other financial institutions in different parts of the US have been able to detect "red flags" for human traffickers in real time through their data mining. During a Super Bowl in Minnesota, a major sporting event, 94 human traffickers were arrested in about a week.[67] The dissemination of best practices has been achieved by the cooperation of the financial community with civil society.[68,69]

There are financial benefits in both the business world and the consumer world from the use of trafficked and forced labor. Workers' compliance with this exploitation is often achieved through the use of violence. Therefore, as in the past, the application of violence often has many beneficiaries from the legitimate economy.

---

67   Evan Sparks, "At Super Bowl, U.S. Bank Tackles Human Trafficking," ABA Banking Journal, January 30, 2019, https://bankingjournal.aba.com/2019/01/at-super-bowl-u-s-bank-tackles-human-trafficking/.
68   Thomson Reuters Foundation, "Banks Alliance Against Trafficking," accessed March 28, 2024, https://www.trust.org/banks-alliance/.
69   "Testimony of Barry M. Koch, esq., Cams, CFCS before the House Financial Services Committee Subcommittee on National Security, International Development and Monetary Policy," March 25, 2021, https://democrats-financialservices.house.gov/uploadedfiles/barry_koch_testimony.pdf.

Bibliography

American Bar Association. "Human Trafficking Legislation." Accessed March 28, 2024. https://www.americanbar.org/groups/human_rights/human-trafficking/trafficking-legislation/.

Black, Merrick M. "Using Civil Litigation to Combat Human Trafficking:Federal Human Trafficking Civil Litigation: 2021 Data Update," 2022. https://htlegalcenter.org/wp-content/uploads/Civil-Litigation-2021-Data-Update.pdf.

Bowe, John. *Nobodies: Modern American Slave Labor and the Dark Side of the New Global Economy*. 1st ed. New York: Random House, 2007. https://www.yourcloudlibrary.com.

Casetext. "Miller v. United States, Criminal Case No. 1:13-Cr-175," October 18, 2016. https://casetext.com/case/miller-v-united-states-267.

Casetext. "United States v. Barcus, Criminal 1:13-Cr-00095," February 9, 2022. https://casetext.com/case/united-states-v-barcus-5.

Casetext. "U.S. v. Ramos-Ramos, File No. 1:07-CR-08." Accessed March 28, 2024. https://casetext.com/case/us-v-ramos-ramos-4.

Coalition of Immokalee Workers. "Slavery in the Fields and the Food We Eat," n.d. https://ciw-online.org/Resources/tools/general/10Slavery%20in%20the%20Fields.pdf.

DeStefano, Anthony M. *The War on Human Trafficking: U.S. Policy Assessed*. Rutgers University Press, 2007.

FBI Washington Field Office. "MS-13 Associate Sentenced to 292 Months for Sex Trafficking Teenage Runaway Girls." FBI, November 4, 2011. https://www.fbi.gov/washingtondc/press-releases/2011/ms-13-associate-sentenced-to-292-months-for-sex-trafficking-teenage-runaway-girls.

Footer, Katherine H. A., Ju Nyeong, Park, Sean T. Allen, Michele R. Decker, Bradley E. Silberzahn, Steve, Huettner, Noya, Galai, and Susan G. Sherman. "Police-Related Correlates of Client-Perpetrated Violence Among Female Sex Workers in Baltimore City, Maryland." *American Journal of Public Health* 109, no. 2 (February 2019): 289–95. https://doi.org/10.2105/AJPH.2018.304809.

Government of Côte d'Ivoire, Government of Ghana, U.S. Department of Labor, and International Chocolate and Cocoa Industry. "CLCCG Report: 2010-2020 Efforts to Reduce Child Labor in Cocoa," n.d. https://www.dol.gov/sites/dolgov/files/ILAB/reports/CLCCG-Ten-Year-Report.pdf.

Greer, Benjamin Thomas, and Jeffrey G. Purvis. "Corporate Supply Chain Transparency: California's Seminal Attempt to Discourage Forced Labour." *The International Journal of Human Rights* 20, no. 1 (January 2, 2016): 55–77. https://doi.org/10.1080/13642987.2015.1039318.

Hawkins, Derek, Tim, Craig, Paulina, Villegas, and Meryl, Kornfield. "What We Know about the Victims of the Atlanta Shootings." *Washington Post*, March 21, 2021. https://www.washingtonpost.com/nation/2021/03/20/atlanta-shooting-victims/.

HEAL Trafficking. "Non-Governmental Organizations." HEAL Trafficking: Health, Education, Advocacy, Linkage. Accessed March 28, 2024. https://healtrafficking.org/non-governmental-organizations/.

Hodal, Kate. "Major Global Hotel Brands Accused of Profiting from Sex Trafficking." *The Guardian*, December 11, 2019, sec. Global development. https://www.theguardian.com/global-development/2019/dec/11/major-global-hotel-brands-accused-of-profiting-from-sex-trafficking.

Hsu, Angie. "Part of the Massage Industry Is Built on Hate Crimes against Asian Women—The Washington Post," March 22, 2021. https://www.washingtonpost.com/outlook/2021/03/22/illegal-massage-business-asian-women/.

John, Bowe. "Nobodies," April 13, 2003. https://www.newyorker.com/magazine/2003/04/21/nobodies.

Jouvenal, Justin. "Fairfax-Based Crips Members Charged with Recruiting Girls for Prostitution—The Washington Post," March 29, 2012. https://www.washingtonpost.com/local/crime/fairfax-based-crips-members-charged-with-recruiting-girls-for-prostitution/2012/03/29/gIQAJRx6iS_story.html.

Kelly, Annie. "'I Carried His Name on My Body for Nine Years': The Tattooed Trafficking Survivors Reclaiming Their Past." *The Guardian*, November 16, 2014, sec. Global development. https://www.theguardian.com/global-development/2014/nov/16/sp-the-tattooed-trafficking-survivors-reclaiming-their-past.

Krylova, Yulia, and Louise, Shelley. "Criminal Street Gangs and Domestic Sex Trafficking in the United States: Evidence from Northern Virginia." *Crime, Law and Social Change* 80, no. 3 (October 1, 2023): 307–28. https://doi.org/10.1007/s10611-023-10088-9.

Lane, Lindsey. "2022 Federal Human Trafficking Report (FHTR)," 2023. https://traffickinginstitute.org/wp-content/uploads/2023/06/2022-Federal-Human-Trafficking-Report-WEB-Spreads_compressed.pdf.

Lane, Lindsey, Angela, Gray, and Alicen, Rodolph. "2021 Federal Human Trafficking Report," 2022. https://traffickinginstitute.org/wp-content/uploads/2022/06/2021-Federal-Human-Trafficking-Report-Web.pdf.

Marcus, Anthony, Amber, Horning, Ric, Curtis, Jo, Sanson, and Efram, Thompson. "Conflict and Agency among Sex Workers and Pimps: A Closer Look at Domestic Minor Sex Trafficking." *The Annals of the American Academy of Political and Social Science* 653, no. 1 (May 1, 2014): 225–46. https://doi.org/10.1177/0002716214521993.

Meo, Sarah, and Louise, Shelley. "Sex Trafficking and Hotels: Why There Is a Need for Effective Corporate Social Responsibility." Global Policy Journal, November 11,

2021. https://www.globalpolicyjournal.com/blog/11/11/2021/sex-trafficking-and-hotels-why-there-need-effective-corporate-social-responsibility.

Moore, Shayne, Sandra, Morgan, and Kimberly McOwen, Yim. *Ending Human Trafficking: A Handbook of Strategies for the Church Today*. InterVarsity Press, 2022.

National Gang Center. "2011 National Gang Threat Assessment—Emerging Trends," 2011. https://nationalgangcenter.ojp.gov/library/publications/2011-national-gang-threat-assessment-emerging-trends.

National Human Trafficking Hotline. "National Human Trafficking Hotline Data Report from January 1, 2021—December 31, 2021," 2023. https://humantraffickinghotline.org/sites/default/files/2023-01/National%20Report%20For%202021.docx%20%283%29.pdf.

Norris, Ann. "Guadalupe Correa-Cabrera: Asylum Seekers and Migrants in the Western Hemisphere Face Real Threats from Human Trafficking." Council on Foreign Relations, May 31, 2023. https://www.cfr.org/blog/guadalupe-correa-cabrera-asylum-seekers-and-migrants-western-hemisphere-face-real-threats.

Oceana. "Americans Overwhelmingly Support Ending Illegal Fishing and Seafood Fraud, Poll Finds." Oceana USA, January 28, 2021. https://usa.oceana.org/press-releases/americans-overwhelmingly-support-ending-illegal-fishing-and-seafood-fraud-poll-finds/.

Office of Public Affairs, US Department of Justice. "Owner of Farm Labor Contracting Company Pleads Guilty in Racketeering Conspiracy Involving the Forced Labor of Mexican Workers," September 27, 2022. https://www.justice.gov/opa/pr/owner-farm-labor-contracting-company-pleads-guilty-racketeering-conspiracy-involving-forced.

Office to Monitor and Combat Trafficking in Persons, United States Department of State. "2022 Trafficking in Persons Report." *United States Department of State* (blog), 2022. https://www.state.gov/reports/2022-trafficking-in-persons-report/.

Roe-Sepowitz, Dominique. "A Six-Year Analysis of Sex Traffickers of Minors: Exploring Characteristics and Sex Trafficking Patterns." *Journal of Human Behavior in the Social Environment* 29, no. 5 (July 4, 2019): 608–29. https://doi.org/10.1080/10911359.2019.1575315.

Shared Hope International. "Gang Sex Trafficking on the Rise," March 28, 2014. https://sharedhope.org/2014/03/28/gang-sex-trafficking-rise/.

Shelley, Louise. "Human Trafficking and Responsible Leadership." In *Responsible Leadership*, 279–94. Routledge, 2022.

Shelley, Louise I. *Dark Commerce: How a New Illicit Economy Is Threatening Our Future*. Princeton University Press, 2018. https://doi.org/10.2307/j.ctv346n56.

Shelley, Louise, Chu-Chuan, Jeng, and Edward, Huang. "Combating Sex Trafficking: Examining the Spatial Distribution of Hotels in Urban Areas That

Facilitate Sex Trafficking in the US." *Urban Crime. An International Journal* 3, no. 1 (May 10, 2022): 128–58. https://doi.org/10.26250/heal.panteion.uc.v3i1.279.

Sparks, Evan. "At Super Bowl, U.S. Bank Tackles Human Trafficking." ABA Banking Journal, January 30, 2019. https://bankingjournal.aba.com/2019/01/at-super-bowl-u-s-bank-tackles-human-trafficking/.

State of California, Department of Justice. "The California Transparency in Supply Chains Act." Accessed March 28, 2024. https://oag.ca.gov/SB657.

Stöckl, Heidi, Camilla Fabbri, Harry Cook, Claire Galez-Davis, Naomi Grant, Yuki Lo, Ligia Kiss, and Cathy Zimmerman. "Human Trafficking and Violence: Findings from the Largest Global Dataset of Trafficking Survivors." *Journal of Migration and Health* 4 (January 1, 2021): 100073. https://doi.org/10.1016/j.jmh.2021.100073.

Stolpe, K. Elysse. "MS-13 and Domestic Juvenile Sex Trafficking: Causes, Correlates, and Solutions." *Virginia Journal of Social Policy & the Law* 21 (2014): 341.

"Testimony of Barry M. Koch, esq., Cams, CFCS before the House Financial Services Committee Subcommittee on National Security, International Development and Monetary Policy," March 25, 2021. https://democrats-financialservices.house.gov/uploadedfiles/barry_koch_testimony.pdf.

The Outlaw Ocean Project. "A Lawless Frontier the High Seas Are a Realm in Dire Need of Investigative Journalism." The Outlaw Ocean Project. Accessed March 28, 2024. https://www.theoutlawocean.com.

Thomson Reuters Foundation. "Banks Alliance Against Trafficking." Accessed March 28, 2024. https://www.trust.org/banks-alliance/.

United States Attorney'Office, Western District of Missouri. "Woman Tortured As Slave, Victim Of Sex Trafficking And Forced Labor," September 9, 2010. https://www.justice.gov/archive/usao/mow/news2010/bagley.ind.html.

University of Baltimore School of Law Human Trafficking Prevention Project, University of Baltimore Low-Income Taxpayer Clinic, The Human Trafficking Legal Center, and Ropes & Gray LLP. "An Advocate's Guide to Tax Issues Affecting Victims of Human Trafficking," December 2019. https://www.htlegalcenter.org/wp-content/uploads/An-Advocates-Guide-to-Tax-Issues-Affecting-Victims-of-Human-Trafficking.pdf.

UNODC. "Global Report on Trafficking in Persons," 2022. https://www.unodc.org/documents/data-and-analysis/glotip/2022/GLOTiP_2022_web.pdf.

UNODC. "The UN Protocol to Prevent, Suppress, and Punish Trafficking in Persons Is the World's Primary Legal Instrument to Combat Human Trafficking." United Nations: Office on Drugs and Crime, February 23, 2023. //www.unodc.org/unodc/en/human-trafficking/protocol.html.

UNODC. "United Nations Convention against Transnational Organized Crime." United Nations: Office on Drugs and Crime, September 29, 2003. //www.unodc.org/unodc/en/organized-crime/intro/UNTOC.html.

Urbina, Ian. *The Outlaw Ocean: Journeys Across the Last Untamed Frontier*. Alfred A. Knopf, 2019.

U.S. Attorney's Office, Eastern District of Virginia. "Bloods Gang Member Sentenced to Prison for Prostituting a Minor," June 3, 2016. https://www.justice.gov/usao-edva/pr/bloods-gang-member-sentenced-prison-prostituting-minor.

U.S. Attorney's Office, Northern District of Texas. "Man Sentenced to 10 Years for Offering to 'Break' Sex Trafficking Victim," March 17, 2022. https://www.justice.gov/usao-ndtx/pr/man-sentenced-10-years-offering-break-sex-trafficking-victim.

US Department of Homeland Security. "Uyghur Forced Labor Prevention Act," October 16, 2023. https://www.dhs.gov/uflpa.

U.S. Department of Homeland Security. "Victim Support Pamphlet for NGOs, Faith-Based and Community Groups | Homeland Security," May 16, 2023. https://www.dhs.gov/blue-campaign/materials/pamphlet-victim-support-ngo-and-faith-based.

U.S. Department of Justice. "Human Trafficking: Key Legislation," August 23, 2023. https://www.justice.gov/humantrafficking/key-legislation.

US Department of Justice. "Miguel Flores And Associate Sentenced to 15 Years For Enslaving Migrant Workers," November 14, 1997. https://www.justice.gov/archive/opa/pr/1997/November97/482cr.htm.html.

US Department of Labor. "2022 List of Goods Produced by Child Labor or Forced Labor," 2022. https://www.dol.gov/sites/dolgov/files/ILAB/child_labor_reports/tda2021/2022-TVPRA-List-of-Goods-v3.pdf.

US Department of State, Office to Monitor and Combat Trafficking in Persons. "2023 Trafficking in Persons Report." *United States Department of State* (blog), 2023. https://www.state.gov/reports/2023-trafficking-in-persons-report/.

USA for UNHCR. "Refugee Statistics," 2023. https://www.unrefugees.org/refugee-facts/statistics/.

Vlamis, Kelsey. "The Atlanta Spa Shootings Revealed the Most Dangerous Threat Massage-Parlor Workers Face Each Day on the Job." Yahoo News, March 24, 2021. https://uk.news.yahoo.com/atlanta-spa-shootings-were-emblematic-070829113.html.

Whoriskey, Peter, and Rachel, Siegel. "Hershey, Nestle and Mars Won't Promise Their Chocolate Is Free of Child Labor." Washington Post, June 5, 2019. https://www.washingtonpost.com/graphics/2019/business/hershey-nestle-mars-chocolate-child-labor-west-africa/.

Yeung, Bernice. "Should Hotel Chains Be Held Liable for Human Trafficking?" The New Yorker, July 26, 2023. https://www.newyorker.com/news/a-reporter-at-large/should-hotel-chains-be-held-liable-for-human-trafficking.

Zenz, Adrian. "How Beijing Forces Uyghurs to Pick Cotton." *Foreign Policy* (blog), April 18, 2024. https://foreignpolicy.com/2023/05/16/china-xinjiang-uyghurs-cotton-forced-labor/.

CHAPTER 3

The Economy of Violence in Afghanistan 2001–2021

David Izadifar

3.1 American Military Intervention and the Fall of the Taliban

3.1.1 *Background*

The decision of the United States to intervene militarily in Afghanistan in 2001 was a direct response to the September 11, 2001, attacks perpetrated by al-Qaeda (AQ) on American soil, resulting in the loss of nearly 3000 lives. After a prompt investigation, US intelligence agencies discovered that Afghanistan was providing shelter to Osama bin Laden and serving as a base for the al-Qaeda training camps, the group responsible for the attacks.

Seldom before had a conflict achieved such a broad consensus. Unity prevailed not just among the 19 North Atlantic Treaty Organization (NATO) member states, but also within the Organization of American States. In addition, the United States strategically aligned itself with an existing coalition that had been striving to topple the Taliban since the mid-1990s. This coalition comprised India, Iran, and Russia, joined by the indigenous Northern Alliance insurgency within Afghanistan.[1] Russia publicly backed the anti-terrorism effort, effectively lending its approval to the operation. While China refrained from overt opposition, Beijing abstained from vocalizing any objections. Notably, Pope John Paul II recognized the rightful self-defense stance of the United States.[2]

On September 12, 2001, the United Nations Security Council unanimously adopted Resolution 1368, recognizing the inherent right to individual or collective self-defense as enshrined in the UN Charter.[3] As early as September 18, 2001, the United Nations Security Council (UNSC) called on the Taliban to

---

1 James Dobbins, "Negotiating with Iran: Reflections from Personal Experience," *The Washington Quarterly* 33, no. 1 (January 1, 2010): 149–62, https://doi.org/10.1080/01636600903424833.
2 Jean-Pierre Perrin, "How the Americans Lost Afghanistan," Politique Internationale, 2022, https://politiqueinternationale.com/revue/n174/article/comment-les-americains-ont-perdu-lafghanistan.
3 United Nations Security Council, "Resolution 1373 (2001)," September 28, 2001, https://www.unodc.org/pdf/crime/terrorism/res_1373_english.pdf.

comply with Resolution 1333, which demanded the extradition of Osama bin Laden.[4]

Although the UNSC didn't explicitly mandate the military campaign in Afghanistan, following the 9/11 attacks, the United States garnered swift international support for its self-defense and subsequent retaliatory actions under the UN Charter.[5] Notably, despite reservations from the UN, on September 28, 2001, following Resolution 1373,[6] NATO authorized intervention in Afghanistan. Conversely, the International Security Assistance Force (ISAF) mission received full authorization from the UN Security Council.

Operation Enduring Freedom (OEF) in Afghanistan, commencing on October 7, 2001, sought to dismantle the Taliban regime and counteract the pervasive influence of al-Qaeda. The military campaign garnered backing from traditional American allies, and Japan also made some contributions. However, the United States assumed the main responsibility for the operation. On the ground, the U.S. opted to collaborate with the Northern Alliance, which comprises several anti-Taliban factions, including numerous Sunni groups with ideological ties to Salafism, as well as Shia groups linked to the Islamic Republic of Iran's ideology. Additionally, some of these factions received financial support from foreign countries, particularly from the Islamic Republic of Iran and Pakistan. Many of these factions were helmed by warlords. i.e. non-state actors, some with charisma, all with military legitimacy arising from the Soviet-Afghan War (1979–1989), who, due to the weakness or absence of the State, played a political role without political legitimacy.[7] In sum, as around 6,000 local commanders emerged in the 1980s, they replaced local disputes with a full-fledged war in the countryside. Widespread violence became the main political dynamic. Insecure conditions led to the rise of a 'specialists in violence' class. Local elites sought protection from militia leaders, initially providing resources to jihadi and rebel commanders, evolving into strategic alliances and even intermarriages.[8]

Operation Enduring Freedom put an end to the Taliban regime as Afghanistan had just emerged from 23 years of civil conflict. Amid the turmoil in Afghanistan, certain sectors flourished in an economy of violence,

---

4 United Nations Security Council.
5 Arabella Lang and Ben Smith, "The Legal Basis for the Invasion of Afghanistan," March 28, 2024, https://commonslibrary.parliament.uk/research-briefings/sn05340/.
6 UN Security Council, "Resolution 1368 (2001)," September 12, 2001, https://digitallibrary.un.org/record/448051.
7 Antonio Giustozzi, *Empires of Mud: Wars and Warlords in Afghanistan* (Oxford University Press, 2012).
8 Giustozzi.

exploiting weakened State structures. The multiple stages of the civil conflicts eroded central authority, leading to the dominance of warlords and militias controlling different regions. The rise of the Taliban further shaped this landscape, incorporating warlords into their ranks. This economy of violence involved activities like opium cultivation, smuggling, and collaboration with militant groups on an international scale. Meanwhile, the Taliban's disregard for the country's welfare exacerbated social disparities and poverty.[9] The US and its allies intervened in Afghanistan when the country's first significant crop export was illegal narcotics, an integral part of the economy of violence.

While the liberation of Afghanistan from the clutches of the Taliban in 2001 owed much to American firepower, the ground operations, and the actual seizure of power were chiefly orchestrated by the United Islamic and National Front for the Salvation of Afghanistan, commonly referred to as the Northern Alliance.

The Northern Alliance was composed of six prominent groups:[10]

1. *Jamiat-e Islami*: Comprising mainly Tajik and Sunni members, this faction was led by Burhanuddin Rabbani.
2. *Hezb-e Wahdat-Islami*: Led by Mohammad Mohaqiq and Karim Khalili, this group represented the Hazara and Shia communities.
3. *Junbish-e Islami*: Mainly consisting of Uzbek and Sunni members, this faction was led by Abdul Rashid Dostum.
4. *The Eastern Shura*: Predominantly composed of Pashtun and Sunni members, Abdul Qadir led this faction.
5. *Harakat-e Islami*: Led by Muhammad Asef Mohseni, this faction was primarily made up of Hazara and Shia members.
6. *Partisans of the National Liberation Movement of Afghanistan (Nimruz Front)*: Representing Baluch and Sunni groups, General Haji Karim Brahui led this faction in the Nimruz Province.

Notably, Hamid Karzai, who ascended to the presidency of Afghanistan in the aftermath of the Taliban's downfall, conducted diplomatic missions as an envoy for the Northern Alliance.

---

9 Conrad Schetter, "Afghanistan's Economy of Violence," *Center for Development Research, University of Bonn*, February 9, 2002, https://www.zef.de/fileadmin/user_upload/N09-2-2002-eng.pdf.

10 Mohammad Javad Aghajari and Morteza Karimi, "The Role of Regional Players in the State-Building Process of Afghanistan During the Taliban Era and Post-Taliban Period," *Islamic Azad University* 8, no. 30 (September 30, 2014): 57–104.

These factions trace their lineage back to the Mujaheddin, who battled the Soviet army from 1979 to 1989 and later fought against the communist regime during the Afghan civil war from 1989 to 1992. Commanded by Ahmad Shah Massoud until his assassination by AQ on September 9, 2001, the alliance remained a significant force during its duration.

Moreover, a cohort of warlords hailing from Pashtun tribes, who had previously espoused support for the Taliban cause, opportunistically defected or deserted the battle lines when the tide shifted. In this context, it is worth noting that these Pashtun tribes entertained aspirations of participating in power-sharing arrangements upon the culmination of the protracted conflict. In the wake of the Taliban's demise, these diverse factions coalesced to form Afghan governments, emerging as pivotal actors in the administration of the country until 2021.

Following the capture of Kabul in 2001, an assortment of influential power brokers emerging from the country's conservative class, who had actively contributed with their respective armies to the overthrow of the Taliban regime, seized the opportunity to consolidate their authority in strategically significant regions throughout the country. Their limited grasp of governance principles and their disregard for ethical leadership marred their tenure. These officials treated the land, viewed as divinely entrusted, as their personal domain, and citizens as mere subjects. This culminated in a wave of oppressive measures, land confiscations, and the unjust victimization and torture of countless innocent individuals. These officials functioned autonomously, unaffected by central government directives, and were beholden solely to their respective factions.

Corruption spread rapidly as warlords and newcomers invested their profits in gaining political influence. Development aid programs worsened the situation, fueling corruption and intensifying competition over resources. The escalating insecurity across the country left Afghans caught between the Taliban and international forces, compelling them to choose sides, ultimately eroding community cohesion.[11]

3.1.2 *Bonn Conference: Establishment of a Transitional Government*

The inception and composition of the Bonn conference (November 27–December 5, 2001) can be ascribed to the cogitations of two influential figures: Lakhtar Brahimi, the United Nations Secretary-General Special

---

11   Thomas Ruttig, "Afghanistan's War Economy," Rosa Luxemburg Stiftung, September 23, 2022, https://www.rosalux.de/en/news/id/47021/afghanistans-war-economy.

Representative in Afghanistan, and Zalmay Khalilzad, a trusted advisor to Donald Rumsfeld. Subsequently appointed as George W. Bush's special envoy to Afghanistan in December 2001, Khalilzad assumed a paramount role in shaping US policy in Afghanistan, effectively serving as a *de facto* senior advisor to two Afghan presidents over two decades. This pivotal conference led to the establishment of the Bonn Agreement.

Under the Bonn Agreement, an international force also was established under the auspices of the United Nations Assistance Mission in Afghanistan (UNAMA) to foster stability in the country. NATO assumed command of the International Security and Assistance Force, marking a watershed moment as the organization embarked upon its maiden expedition beyond the confines of the North Atlantic region. Comprising contingents from approximately fifty nations, including eight non-NATO members, the strength of the ISAF swelled from 5,000 troops in 2003 to 130,000 troops by 2010.[12]

The Bonn Conference convened a convergence of four Afghan factions: the Northern Alliance, representing a tapestry of factions; the Peshawar Group, comprising Afghan refugees residing in Pakistan; the Rome Group, acting as proxies for former King Mohammed Zaher Shah; and the "Cyprus Group," standing in for a cohort of Afghan exiles based in Iran.

In preparation for the Bonn Conference, Lakhtar Brahimi and James Dobbins separately met with representatives of certain regional states, including Iran and Pakistan, and beyond, notably Russia and Turkey—countries invited to the Bonn Conference.

Brahimi's visits revealed various peace-focused groups, including the dominant Northern Alliance. In the absence of the Taliban, the UN proposed consolidating these processes, uniting Pashtun, Cyprus, Rome, and Northern Alliance groups, but faced limitations.[13]

In mid-November, Dobbins secured global backing for the conference. Despite initial resistance from Pakistan, ISI director Lt. Gen. Ehsan ul-Haq proposed Karzai. Aligned with Russia and India, the Iranian delegation supported Karzai over King Zahir. Dobbins, as the US envoy, solidified commitments, indicating a consensus for Karzai as the future president of the interim Afghan authority.

---

12   UNHCR, "Afghanistan 10 Years after Soviet Pull-Out," UNHCR India, February 12, 1999, https://www.unhcr.org/in/news/briefing-notes/afghanistan-10-years-after-soviet-pull-out.

13   Geoffrey Hayes and Mark Sedra, *Afghanistan: Transition under Threat* (Wilfrid Laurier Univ. Press, 2009).

At the Bonn Conference, the Northern Alliance, led by figures such as Qasim Fahim, Yunus Qanuni, and Dr. Abdullah Abdullah, backed Karzai as an interim president. Despite internal divisions, their support held weight due to territorial control. Abdullah voiced concerns that a Northern Alliance leader might deepen political divisions in Afghanistan.[14,15]

At the Bonn Conference, Professor Abdul Sattar Sirat, nominated by the Rome Group, initially emerged as the choice for interim government leadership. However, an erroneous assessment by the Group led to withdrawal requests from the international community, recognizing the absence of necessary consensus.[16]

As a result of the conference, an interim government led by Hamid Karzai emerged. Capitalizing on his nomination by the representatives of the Loya Jirga (a Pashtun term for an assembly), he then assumed governance of Afghanistan through a universal suffrage election in 2004. In 2009, he was once more elected, but this election was marred by low turnout, corruption, and fraud, which significantly characterized and eroded the credibility of the results.[17]

In 2001, Afghanistan had emerged from 23 years of devastating conflict, leading to a massive exodus of millions of Afghans, including many technocrats and members of the bourgeoisie from the past.[18] The war spawned a new class of businessmen in Afghanistan: former Mujahideen from the 1980s who controlled districts or provinces. Often labeled warlords, they earned income through activities tied to the violence-based economy, including extortion at checkpoints, taxing farmers, narcotics trade, illegal land seizures, and other crimes. Hamid Karzai, from the start, strengthened their power by creating a patronage network, complicating national unity and stable state-building.

The transitional choices made by the international community, encompassing the problematic acceptance of power brokers for immediate military advantage and their instrumentalization as political tools, played a significant role in engendering and perpetuating a culture of criminality and corruption

---

14 Rory McCarthy and Ewen MacAskill, "King's Aide Is Favourite to Be next Leader," *The Guardian*, December 3, 2001, sec. World news, https://www.theguardian.com/world/2001/dec/03/afghanistan.ewenmacaskill1.
15 *A Special Interview with James Dobbins, the Former US Representative in Afghanistan*, 2022, https://www.youtube.com/watch?v, DmV7woqu9xo.
16 *A Special Interview with James Dobbins, the Former US Representative in Afghanistan*.
17 Julian Borger and Kate Connolly, "Evidence of Fraud as Hamid Karzai Passes Threshold in Afghan Poll," *The Guardian*, September 8, 2009, sec. World news, https://www.theguardian.com/world/2009/sep/08/hamid-karzai-afghan-election-fraud.
18 UNHCR, "Afghanistan 10 Years after Soviet Pull-Out".

in post-2001 Afghanistan. Consequently, the nascent Afghan State assumed the characteristics of a "Predatory State" whereby rulers leaned upon rents and client networks as the bedrock of their power and personal interests.[19] Throughout its embryonic stage, the Afghan State primarily subsisted on rents as opposed to tax revenues, governing through personalized ties and patronage networks while repressing or isolating individuals who failed to align with the established network.[20] Furthermore, given the heavy reliance on direct foreign money inflows and support from external powers, Afghan leaders seldom engaged in substantive consultations or negotiations with indigenous forces concerning state-building policies and objectives.

The urgent reforms necessary for establishing a meritocratic State apparatus were shunned, leaving the governance framework crippled. Gradually, these webs of corruption unfurled, spreading like dark shadows over the political landscape, tarnishing the reputation of the entire class of leaders, and casting a cloud of mistrust upon the central state and government.[21]

3.2 Ministers' Appointments under Hamed Kazai and Ashraf Ghani

The appointment of ministers under the administrations of Hamid Karzai and Ashraf Ghani underscores the central role of political patronage as the practical foundation of the economies of violence. This system allowed influential individuals to not only preserve their positions of power but also to capitalize on the ongoing conflict and engage in various illicit economic activities.

3.2.1 Interim Government

With Karzai designated as "Chairman" of the Interim Administration on December 22, 2001, he moved forward to assemble a 30-member cabinet. In this interim cabinet's composition, roughly half of the positions were assigned to the Northern Alliance, while the Rome group secured eight positions. Notably, these included figures associated with private militias or former Mujahidin figures.[22]

---

19 S. Yaqub Ibrahimi, "Afghanistan's Political Development Dilemma: The Centralist State Versus a Centrifugal Society," *Journal of South Asian Development* 14, no. 1 (April 1, 2019): 40–61, https://doi.org/10.1177/0973174119839843.
20 Ibrahimi.
21 Serge Michailof, "The Failure of Nation Building," in *Afghanistan: Autopsy of a Disaster 2001–2021—What Lessons for the Sahel?* (Gallimard, 2022), 82–108.
22 Staff, "The Afghan Interim Government: Who's Who," *The Guardian*, December 6, 2001, sec. World news, https://www.theguardian.com/world/2001/dec/06/afghanistan1.

The cabinet had a diverse ethnic composition, including seven Hazara ministers, 10 Pashtuns, 12 Tajiks, and three Uzbeks. Qanuni, Fahim, and Abdullah from the Shuray-e Nizar secured key positions, not only due to their Northern Alliance affiliation but also as a reward for supporting Hamid Karzai during the Bonn Conference.

In 2003, a pivotal moment arose when President Karzai removed Yunus Qanuni from the position of Minister of the Interior, placing Ali Ahmad Jalali at the helm. This strategic shift set the stage for a transformative period as Jalali, accompanied by his team, had launched an ambitious plan aimed at reshaping the contours of provincial governance and security commands.

At its core, these proposed reforms were poised to fortify the bedrock of governance. Yet, this paradigm shift was met with resistance from factions within the Panjshir Valley. Reacting to the proposed reforms, these groups propagated a counter-narrative, utilizing the dissemination of strategic propaganda to assert that the Ministry of Interior was sidelining the Mujahidin. Their perspective rested on the premise that the only authentic forms of jihad were those rooted in Panjshir, Parwan, and their specific struggles while discrediting the legitimacy of others' contributions.

As the transitional phase unfolded, the reform measures assumed greater significance. This materialized in the establishment of proactive provincial collaboration teams, each empowered to chart a dynamic vision for reconstruction efforts within their respective provinces. This marked the inception of the Provincial Reconstruction Team (PRT). However, the trajectory was marked by tensions between the PRT and Karzai appointees, and even President Karzai himself.

Amid these pivotal developments, President Karzai fostered connections with fellow compatriots who had shared his experiences in Pakistan, resulting in their appointment to pivotal governmental roles. One illustration was the appointment of Jan Muhammad Khan as the governor of Uruzgan Province. Khan's tenure was marred by the employment of oppressive methods. Subsequently, he faced allegations of orchestrating the assassination of prominent figures within the province.

Similarly, Sher Muhammad Akhundzada, known for his involvement in corrupt practices and smuggling activities, assumed the role of governor in Helmand Province. In 2005, US and Afghan narcotics agents conducted a raid on Akhundzada's offices, revealing the presence of nine tons of opium. Despite his resistance, international pressure compelled President Karzai to remove Akhundzada from the governor's position.[23]

3.2.2 Minister Appointments under Karzai (2004–2014)

Following his 2004 election victory, Hamid Karzai skillfully crafted a diverse administration that navigated the demands of influential groups, including the international community. This strategic move not only afforded him greater independence in shaping the government but also empowered him to prioritize technocrats over former Mujahideen in appointments, despite external pressures. Despite efforts to create an inclusive government, some of these appointments faced public disapproval due to concerns over their backgrounds and alleged involvement in violence.

For instance, Ghulam Jelani Popal, a close associate of Karzai, played significant roles in finance and governance, while Dr. Ahmad Mushahid, representing a dissatisfied faction from the northern Takhar Province, led administrative reforms. Ubaidullah Ramin became the Minister of Agriculture with the intervention of an Afghan American business entrepreneur (Ehsanullah Bayat) and the endorsement of Zalmay Khalilzad, who was the US Ambassador to Afghanistan at the time. Dr. Rangin Dadfar Spanta assumed the position of National Security Advisor, a role facilitated and supported by Karzai's influential brother, Qayum.[24] Similarly, Rahim Wardak, known for his loyalty to Karzai, was appointed as Minister of Defense, and Khodaidad Hazara, close to the British envoys in Afghanistan, was appointed as the Minister of Counter-Narcotics. Karzai pursued these actions to reduce the influence of political parties and break the monopoly of power held by specific groups, including the Panjshiri circle and the Northern Alliance.

Furthermore, in the endeavor to combat narcotics, Karzai not only exhibited a lack of resolute action but also cultivated concerning connections with individuals associated with drug trafficking or production. This network allegedly extended to his family members, including his half-brother Ahmad Wali Karzai. This intricate situation escalated tensions between Karzai and international forces. Concurrently, the Provincial Reconstruction Teams encountered obstacles while harmonizing their endeavors with local governments, encountering resistance, and nurturing a prevailing atmosphere of skepticism.

---

23   Craig Whitlock, "Consumed by Corruption," Washington Post, December 9, 2019, https://www.washingtonpost.com/graphics/2019/investigations/afghanistan-papers/afghanistan-war-corruption-government/.

24   Qayum played a significant role in influencing ministerial and key appointments across various cabinets during both of Karzai's terms.

Another pattern emerged where certain individuals were appointed to ministerial or significant roles primarily as a reward for their loyalty. Both Ashraf Ghani and Hamid Karzai employed such practices. Those who aided them in winning elections through fraudulent means or influence were reciprocated. This was evident in the case of Ghulam Faruq Wardak, who was appointed as the Director of the Joint Election Management Bodies Secretariat (a collaboration between the UN and Afghan Government) by the President. Wardak organized the initial voter registration process during the 2004 presidential election. In recognition of his contribution to Karzai's victory, Wardak was promoted to the positions of Cabinet Secretary and Director General of the Office of Administrative Affairs. Another individual closely associated with Karzai was Sayed Hussein Anwari, who commanded respect within Shia factions. He was initially appointed as the governor of Kabul and subsequently assumed the same position in Herat.

Zia ul-Haq Amarkhil serves as another illustration of such promotions. Initially appointed by President Ghani to lead the Independent Election Commission Secretariat, he resigned in 2014 amid allegations of fraud during the 2014 runoff presidential election. Accusations included planning ballot stuffing, with audio recordings supporting these allegations being made public. Although he briefly left the country, Amarkhil returned following assurances from President Karzai. Instead of facing legal consequences, he was appointed as a Senior Advisor on Public and Political Affairs to President Ashraf Ghani, and later assumed the position of governor of Nangarhar in 2020. During his governorship, Amarkhil's involvement in corruption came to light. He was accused of embezzling significant sums, particularly from customs revenues in the province, with an estimated monthly embezzlement of \$40,000.[25]

This intricate web of appointments also created tensions. Karzai, wielding influence, pressured ministers hindering his control. An example is Ali Ahmad Jalali, the former Interior Minister, whose anti-corruption efforts were undermined by his deputy, Zarar Ahmad Muqbil, encouraged by Karzai.

---

25   Kate Clark and Roxanna Shapour, "The Khalid Payenda Interview (1): An insider's view of politicking, graft and the fall of the Republic," Afghanistan Analysts Network—English, September 27, 2021, https://www.afghanistan-analysts.org/en/reports/economy-development-environment/the-khalid-payenda-interview-1-an-insiders-view-of-politicking-graft-and-the-fall-of-the-republic/.

3.2.3 Power Struggles and Political Dynamics: Abdullah Abdullah's Role and Ethnocentrism in Ghani's Afghan Governments

After the 2014 and 2020 presidential elections, Dr. Abdullah Abdullah contested alleged electoral fraud. In 2014, negotiations led to a power-sharing agreement with Ghani, recognizing him as the winner but allowing Abdullah to nominate a council member. In the 2020 election, an agreement acknowledged Ghani's victory but empowered Abdullah to lead the peace council, with some team members joining the government.[26] These arrangements, however, didn't mark a significant departure from Afghanistan's patronage system.

George Packer—a thoughtful chronicler of Afghanistan—portrayed Ghani as a "visionary technocrat." However, Packer also underscored a significant hindrance to Ghani's governance—his elitist disposition and lack of political acumen. Ghani's track record revealed strained relationships across the board, as he alienated key groups including the parliament, influential warlords, and the political establishment beyond the Pashtun community.[27] In response, Ghani opted to establish a close-knit circle of advisors to navigate these challenges.

Due to Afghanistan's intricate web of ethnic and tribal affiliations, where allegiance typically gravitates toward one's kin or group, Ghani's leadership was marked by a cautious and inward-focused approach.

Amid escalating concerns, Ghani's administration was shaped by the formidable influence of a dynamic duo: advisors Hamdullah Mohib and Fazel Mahmood Fazly, both originating from Eastern Afghanistan, echoing Ghani's own roots.

Mohib, a freshly minted Ph.D. holder in engineering in his early 30s, initially served as Afghanistan's ambassador to the United States, smoothly transitioning into the pivotal role of Ghani's national security advisor. Meanwhile, Fazly, the Head of the President's Administrative Office and Swedish citizen, practiced as a family doctor in Sweden until 2017.[28] His rapid rise to a critical position in Afghanistan added a unique dimension to the collaboration, often colloquially referred to as the "three-man republic"—a trio with no military background or experience in security, yet tasked with managing a country at

---

26 Abdul Qadir Sediqi and Hamid Shalizi, "Afghan President and Rival Strike Power-Sharing Deal after Months of Feuding," *Reuters*, May 17, 2020, sec. World, https://www.reuters.com/article/idUSKBN22T09H/.

27 George Packer, The Governing Style Of Ashraf Ghani, The Departing Afghan President, interview by Don Gonyea, August 15, 2021, https://www.npr.org/2021/08/15/1027962001/the-governing-style-of-ashraf-ghani-the-departing-afghan-president.

28 Elisabeth Braw, "The Afghan Collapse: An Insider's Account," CEPA, August 23, 2022, https://cepa.org/article/the-afghan-collapse-an-insiders-account/.

war.[29] In addition, the two advisors wielded considerable influence over personnel and budgetary decisions at various government levels.[30] This centralization of power led to the politicization of the military and the appointment of unqualified political loyalists to crucial positions, especially originating from the Pashtun ethnic group.[31] This trend persisted until the fall of Kabul in August 2021.

3.2.4 Corruption Undermining Ministerial Appointments in Afghan Parliament

According to the Afghanistan 2004 Constitution, the Parliament wielded the authority to inquire about Ministers if proposed by at least 20% of its members. In cases where the explanations provided by the Ministers proved unsatisfactory, a no-confidence vote could be considered, requiring explicit, direct, and convincing reasons, with approval needed from the majority of all members of the Parliament.[32]

Corruption plagued Parliament, with MPs having dubious backgrounds—some engaged in criminal activities like drug production or trafficking, and others with ties to insurgent groups. The vote of confidence turned into an opportunity for parliamentarians to seek financial incentives or engage in bribery from ministerial candidates. General Nur-ul-Haq Ulumi, a former MP and Minister of Interior, exposed MPs accepting bribes to favor specific candidates. Using covert methods, they discreetly marked ballots with colored pens as signs of loyalty. Some accepted favors and regular payments, while others succumbed to upfront sums. Covertly taken pictures of previous votes highlighted the extent of deceit in the process.[33]

The willingness of some candidates for ministerial positions to pay exorbitant amounts, sometimes over $1 million (USD), to secure votes of confidence

---

29 Jennifer Brick Murtazashvili, "The Collapse of Afghanistan," *Journal of Democracy* 33, no. 1 (2022): 40–54.

30 John F. Sopko and David H. Young, "The Factors Leading to the Collapse of the Afghan Government And Its Security Forces" (Special Inspector General for Afghanistan Reconstruction, March 2, 2023), https://www.sigar.mil/pdf/speeches/SIGAR_John_Sopko_David_Young_Berlin_Speech_2023-03-02.pdf.

31 Reuters, "Leaked Memo Fuels Accusations of Ethnic Bias in Afghan Government," *Reuters*, September 21, 2017, sec. World, https://www.reuters.com/article/idUSKCN1BW147/.

32 Islamic Republic of Afghanistan, "Afghanistan 2004 Constitution, Article 92," accessed March 28, 2024, https://www.constituteproject.org/constitution/Afghanistan_2004.

33 Kate Clark, "How to become a minister: bribe the parliament (Updated)," Afghanistan Analysts Network—English, June 30, 2010, https://www.afghanistan-analysts.org/en/reports/political-landscape/how-to-become-a-minister-bribe-the-parliament-updated/.

of parliamentarians undoubtedly led them to expect a favorable return on their investment from holding a ministerial post.[34]

3.3 The Landscape of Governance in Post-Taliban Afghanistan

3.3.1 *Power Dynamics, Corruption, and the Perpetual Cycle of Violence in Afghan Governance*

3.3.1.1 Shaping Post-Taliban Afghanistan: The Northern Alliance-US Partnership and Government Influences

The alliance between Northern Alliance and US forces in 2001 significantly influenced post-Taliban governance, leading to key aligned individuals securing prominent government positions with US support.

A noteworthy instance of this influence occurred during a meal at Karzai's palace, where the former Afghan president shared his concerns with General John Abizaid, who was leading the US Central Command at that time. The president expressed reservations about the US support for certain warlords, who were causing challenges for his government. In response, General Abizaid sought to foster political accommodation by emphasizing that these warlords were viewed as allies in the broader mission, stating, "They are one of us, just as you are one of us."[35] It is worth clarifying that Karzai, like many Afghan Americans, used the term "*warlord*" primarily to refer to strongmen affiliated with the Northern Alliance, while Pashtun warlords were often referred to as "*tribal elders*" or "*influential leaders*."

The 2004 Afghan Constitution mandated the presidential appointment of provincial governors with Wolesi Jirga's approval, while the Ministry of Interior played a significant role in the process by selecting and recommending potential candidates for the governor positions. In practice, during the two decades of the presence of international forces in Afghanistan, the President maintained exclusive authority in appointing governors.

In the aftermath of the Bonn Conference, the initial appointment of 32 provincial governors suggested that a significant number of these appointees were identified as militia commanders, warlords, or strongmen. This trend extended

---

34 Jelena Bjelica, "Lost in Procedure: How a corruption case in the Afghan parliament was (not) dealt with," Afghanistan Analysts Network—English, January 4, 2018, https://www.afghanistan-analysts.org/en/reports/political-landscape/lost-in-procedure-how-a-corruption-case-in-the-afghan-parliament-was-not-dealt-with/.

35 Mujib Mashal, "After Karzai," *The Atlantic*, June 23, 2014, https://www.theatlantic.com/magazine/archive/2014/07/after-karzai/372294/.

to the ranks of district governors as well, with smaller militia commanders occupying these positions.[36]

As previously mentioned, between 2002 and 2004, the Jamiat-e-Islami group wielded substantial influence in key positions throughout the country.

3.3.1.2 Continued Influence of Militia Commanders and Warlords

Following the 2004 presidential election, Karzai's approach to governance continued to be characterized by an inclusive but informal network of tribal leaders and other powerbrokers, often neglecting the former government apparatus. While this tactic allowed him to consolidate power and weaken potential rivals, it hindered the establishment of stable institutions and a modern democratic government. Most of these appointees were able to regain control over territories they had previously lost to the Taliban between 1996 to 2001. Upon returning after years of absence to their respective home provinces, these individuals resumed their criminal activities, now benefiting from official appointments facilitated by the interim presidency supported by the international community.

Across the entire nation, these powerbrokers treated both citizens and public lands as personal possessions, relegating people to mere subjects instead of active participants, and resulting in profound oppression. This prevailing attitude gave rise to the confiscation of land, arbitrary arrests targeting dissenters or rival groups, extrajudicial killings, and a multitude of other criminal practices.

Widespread land seizures in Afghanistan, orchestrated by influential figures—whether official or non-official—vividly illustrate the consequences of economies fueled by violence. These land grabs had devastating consequences for returning Afghan refugees, as criminal elements took control of their properties. Efforts to reclaim the land often led to physical abuse and wrongful imprisonment, leaving the refugees in dire straits. A notable incident occurred in 2003 when influential individuals bulldozed 30 homes in Kabul's Sherpur neighborhood, displacing over 250 people from land historically owned by the Ministry of Defense and seizing it for themselves.[37]

Ahmad Wali Karzai (AWK), the half-brother of Hamid Karzai, was also implicated in land appropriation. A noteworthy episode revolved around the land in Kandahar Province's Daman District. The land was forcibly taken, with

---

36 Antonio Giustozzi, *Koran, Kalashnikov and Laptop: The Neo-Taliban Insurgency in Afghanistan* (Hurst, 2007).

37 Huma Saeed, *Transitional Justice and Socio-Economic Harm: Land Grabbing in Afghanistan* (Taylor & Francis, 2022).

armed loyalists, some posing as police officers, acting under AWK's direction and employing tractors. Following this unlawful seizure, AWK attempted to sell the land. In response, villagers protested and brought the matter to President Karzai's attention. An envoy was dispatched to verify their claim using title documents. Nevertheless, Ahmad Wali Karzai publicly contested their rights to the land.[38]

Employing force against rivals, individuals sought to control drug routes. Sher Mohammad Akhundzada's appointment as Helmand governor exemplifies ties between major players in the violence-based economy and the Karzai family, lasting until 2005 when a US raid found tons of opium at his compound.[39,40] Following Sher Mohammad's dismissal, President Karzai made strategic appointments that endorsed the Akhundzada family, appointing Sher Mohammad's brother, Amir Mohammad Akhundzada, as Deputy to a newly appointed governor in Helmand. Simultaneously, Karzai not only protected Sher Mohammad from prosecution, even in the wake of the discovery of drugs in his offices but also appointed him as a senator in the Meshrano Jirga. This move occurred despite Sher Mohammad publicly confessing to influencing approximately 3,000 of his armed men to join the Taliban after his removal as the governor of Helmand.[41]

Following the 2004 elections, President Karzai rewarded Ghulam Farooq Wardak for his loyalty and support. Wardak had prior ties to Hekmatyar's Hezb-e Islami (HIG), a former insurgent group with governmental influence until 2018. In 2005, Karzai appointed Wardak as the Secretary to the Council of Ministers and Director-General of the Office of Administrative Affairs. During his tenure, Wardak's influence led to significant shifts in governor appointments, resulting in heightened insecurity across the country.

3.3.1.3 Navigating Afghanistan's Governance Dilemmas

In the northeast, Faruq Wardak strategically appointed Hezb-e Islami-affiliated governors with Pashtun ties, enabling them to exploit their positions

---

38 Stephen Carter and Kate Clark, "No Shortcut to Stability: Justice, Politics and Insurgency in Afghanistan," December 15, 2010, https://policycommons.net/artifacts/612958/no-shortcut-to-stability/1592607/.

39 Antonio Giustozzi and Noor Ullah, "'Tribes' and Warlords in Southern Afghanistan, 1980–2005," Monograph (London, UK: Crisis States Research Centre, London School of Economics and Political Science, September 2006), http://www.crisisstates.com.

40 ANI, "Ex-Afghan Governor Admits to Helping Taliban," *The Indian Express* (blog), November 21, 2009, https://indianexpress.com/article/news-archive/print/exafghan-governor-admits-to-helping-taliban/.

41 ANI.

for personal gain, often misappropriating funds. This inadvertently fueled the resurgence of former Taliban members, resulting in heightened Taliban attacks in the Northeast post-2006. Wardak's influence endured until the fall of the previous regime, and he has since returned to Kabul, collaborating with the Taliban.

After taking office in 2014, the second president, Ashraf Ghani, saw regional powerbrokers, especially non-Pashtuns in the north, as obstacles to his modern state and technocratic goals.[42] Ghani's attempts to diminish the influence of these "warlords" had unintended consequences, creating a power vacuum in the Northern region, which worsened security. The Taliban exploited this situation, gaining control over districts, even in previously stable provinces, such as Balkh or Takhar.

President Ghani faced challenges in removing governors, such as Atta Mohammad Nur in Balkh Province and Abdul Karim Khudam in Samangan. These governors resisted their removal due to political affiliations and tribal or ethnic ties. Despite resistance, Ghani replaced them with Pashtun loyalists, triggering protests and violence in the two provinces. Paradoxically, Ghani appointed Pashtun warlords, such as Gul Agha Sherzai, to key positions, raising questions about his stance on warlords within his administration. Therefore, theecometeration remained largely unchanged from the time of Karzai's presidency. Corruption persisted, with almost all governors and customs directors engaging in illicit activities. The former Afghan Minister of Finance, Khalid Payenda, voiced his exasperation, lamenting the scarcity of upright governors. Despite efforts to crack down on corruption, tainted officials often sought refuge in a blame game, rationalizing their actions by highlighting the involvement of others in similar wrongdoing. This widespread corruption even seeped into the realm of bribing the police, provincial councils, members of parliament, and shockingly, even the Taliban, in exchange for protection.[43]

3.3.2   *Ministry of Interior*
3.3.2.1   Constitution of the Afghan Police Following the Security Sector Reform (SSR)

The abrupt overthrow of the Taliban lacked a well-thought-out plan for post-conflict law enforcement. This created a void filled by private militias, eroding the central government's authority and laying the groundwork for Afghanistan's

---

42   John F. Sopko and David H. Young, "The Factors Leading to the Collapse of the Afghan Government and Its Security Forces".
43   Clark and Shapour, "The Khalid Payenda Interview (1)".

violent economies. The absence of a robust police force allowed these militias to wield considerable power.

Overall, the Afghan National Police (ANP) served as the overarching police institution in the country, including various specialized security forces including the Afghan Uniformed Police (AUP), responsible for routine policing tasks, the Afghan Border Police (ABP), the Afghan National Civil Order Police (ANCOP), and the Counter Narcotic Police of Afghanistan (CNPA). To support counterinsurgency operations, the US authorized in 2006 the establishment of the Afghanistan National Auxiliary Police (ANAP) as a tactical response to the escalating Taliban insurgency in southern Afghanistan. ANAP comprised more than 11,000 village youths from the six Southern provinces.[44] After undergoing a condensed ten-day training program, these individuals were provided with uniforms and firearms and aimed at manning checkpoints and performing community policing duties, thus allowing the ANP to focus on counterinsurgency operations. However, the recruitment process for the ANPA relied on provincial governors, leading to concerns of factional control and manipulation, as recruits were often affiliated with local power brokers and tribal militias. Despite assurances of thorough vetting, it was suspected that some ANPA members had ties to the Taliban, compromising the force's effectiveness. Additionally, the creation of the ANPA was seen as reversing the efforts made under the UN-led Disband Illegally Armed Groups (DIAG) program in 2005, which aimed to disarm and demobilize local militias associated with powerful warlords. The ineffectiveness of ANPA led to the disbandment of the force in May 2008.

3.3.3 Empowering the Afghan National Defense and Security Forces

Over two decades, a significant investment of approximately $90 billion was allocated by the United States (US), in collaboration with NATO and the Afghan government, to support the advancement of the Afghan National Defense and Security Forces (ANDSF).[45] The ANDSF, including the Afghan National Army, Afghan Air Force, and Afghan National Police, received extensive assistance in the form of training, guidance, and mentorship from both military and civilian personnel. Moreover, the US equipped the ANDSF with a wide range of resources, including weapons, aircraft, vehicles, and advanced technology.

---

44 Robert Perito, *Afghanistan's Police: The Weak Link in Security Sector Reform*, Special Report (United States Institute of Peace) (Washington, D.C.: United States Institute of Peace, 2009), http://library.usip.org/articles/1012419.1131/1.PDF.

45 John F. Sopko and David H. Young, "The Factors Leading to the Collapse of the Afghan Government and Its Security Forces".

The overarching objective was to develop an independent and self-sufficient force capable of effectively countering internal and external security threats in Afghanistan.[46]

The situation with the Afghan National Defense and Security Forces was marred by significant corruption, particularly regarding the existence of "ghost soldiers" within the ranks—individuals who were either deceased, deserted, or never existed. In two decades, the Afghan National Police witnessed remarkable growth. Back in 2003, no national police force existed. Fast forward to April 2021, and the number surged significantly, with 118,628 serving in the national police.[47] The last finance minister of Ashraf Ghani indicated that the reported numbers of soldiers and personnel, totaling 120,000 and 300,000, respectively, were greatly exaggerated. According to his assessment, there were at best around 40,000 to 50,000 actual personnel, with the rest being "ghosts" on the payroll.[48]

3.3.4 Challenges in Establishing an Efficient Police Force in Afghanistan: NATO Internal Divisions

The endeavor to establish a robust and capable police force in Afghanistan was fraught with a myriad of intricate challenges. Central to these difficulties was the discord that emerged between the United States and Germany, along with the complex division of responsibilities among NATO allies. The United States advocated for a more militarized approach to police training, emphasizing the need for swift action, while Germany favored a gradual and comprehensive methodology that prioritized institutional capacity building.

Counternarcotics efforts in Afghanistan encountered significant hurdles. The UK adopted the ambitious goal of eradicating poppy cultivation within a decade.[49] This initial enthusiasm of the United Kingdom was tempered by a lack of understanding of the intricate dynamics of the drug industry and an overly optimistic outlook. The British implemented an eradication program intending to compensate farmers whose poppy crops were destroyed. However, certain provincial representatives of the Ministry of Agriculture,

---

46 John F. Sopko and David H. Young.
47 Bryan Bender and Paul Mcleary, "The $88 Billion Gamble on the Afghan Army That's Going up in Smoke," POLITICO, August 13, 2021, https://www.politico.com/news/2021/08/13/afghan-army-pentagon-504469.
48 Clark and Shapour, "The Khalid Payenda Interview (1)".
49 SIGAR, "Counternarcotics: Lessons from the U.S. Experience in Afghanistan" (SIGAR, June 2018), https://www.sigar.mil/pdf/lessonslearned/SIGAR-18-52-LL-Executive-Summary.pdf.

in collaboration with other corrupt officials, embezzled the farmers' rightful compensation. As a result, the farmers were left without any means to recover their losses, adding to the already challenging situation they faced. Moreover, the emerging Afghan central State struggled to extend its influence beyond major urban centers, impeding the effectiveness of counternarcotics initiatives. Compounding these challenges was the appointment of individuals with questionable backgrounds, including allegations of corruption and involvement in the opiate trade, to key positions. As eradication efforts intensified, they inadvertently contributed to instability, providing an opportunity for the Taliban to exploit the grievances of local communities who bore the brunt of these measures.[50]

The divergent strategies pursued by different US government agencies further complicated counternarcotics efforts. The Pentagon displayed limited interest in addressing the drug issue, while the State Department advocated for an eradication policy based on its experience in Colombia. This divergence within the US government hindered the implementation of a cohesive and effective counternarcotics strategy.[51] From 2004 onwards, the Americans, having initially delegated the counter-narcotics mission to their British ally, reestablished their authority over this mission. Crop destruction emerged as a contentious issue within counternarcotics initiatives. Disagreements arose regarding the selection of target areas and the method of crop destruction, particularly the controversial use of herbicides. These disagreements not only fractured the US government internally but also strained relationships between the US government, the Afghan government, the International Security Assistance Force (ISAF), the UK government, and other coalition allies. The predominance of a force-oriented approach in this policy, at the expense of other strategies like alternative development, yielded thus only limited success at best.

US support for drug-linked powerbrokers deepened international disputes. Criminals continued operations if they aided intelligence efforts, sustaining both al-Qaeda and the Taliban. Racketeers in conflict zones helped capture al-Qaeda members. This criminal impunity fueled resentment and legitimized militant groups as champions of a supposed just social order. The appointment

---

50   Shehryar Fazli, "Narcotics Smuggling in Afghanistan: Links between Afghanistan and Pakistan," June 2022, https://globalinitiative.net/wp-content/uploads/2022/06/narcotics-smuggling-in-afghanistan-paper.pdf.

51   Anthony Armiger, "United Against Drugs? Divergent Counternarcotic Strategies of US Government Agencies in Afghanistan," SSRN Scholarly Paper (Rochester, NY, January 15, 2015), https://papers.ssrn.com/abstract=2721586.

of Matiullah Khan as the chief of the Highway Police Unit in Uruzgan, along with his intricate relationships with NATO, NGOs, and other actors, vividly demonstrates the divisions prevailing within the international community and the far-reaching ramifications for security dynamics. Operating under the governance of his uncle, Jan Mohammad Khan (JMK),[52] Matiullah Khan commanded a series of squads that tragically perpetrated targeted assassinations against resilient farmers who valiantly resisted the relinquishment of their lands, daughters, or herds to the clutches of the Taliban.[53]

To facilitate their deployment in Uruzgan, the Dutch military contingent, acting within the NATO framework, laid down a pivotal condition—the removal of JMK from his position as governor. In response to mounting pressure from NATO, the Netherlands, the European Union, and UNAMA, President Karzai ultimately ousted JMK from office in 2006. Relations between Dutch forces and Matiullah Khan remained strained and limited due to his associations with drug traffickers and collaboration with Taliban insurgents, all while commanding his own private army. However, this privately commanded force, enjoying the trust and support of NATO and US special forces, provided Matiullah Khan with lucrative opportunities to accumulate substantial wealth by ensuring the protection of critical NATO convoys navigating treacherous terrains from Kandahar to Trinkot in central Uruzgan. In this particular case, NATO found itself compelled to secure its convoys at the cost of enriching a criminal figure, who, in turn, exacerbated insecurity. Paradoxically, without the prevailing insecurity, Matiullah Khan would not have been contracted by NATO in the first place. His company charged each NATO cargo truck $1,200 for safe passage, or $800 for smaller ones. His income might be $2.5 million a month.[54]

This scenario is not unique among private military contractors enlisted by NATO or the US in Afghanistan. An illustrative case involves the Watan Group, led by two of Hamid Karzai's cousins, which clinched a highly lucrative multimillion-dollar contract with the US military. Nevertheless, a

---

52 Jan Mohammad Khan was a prominent member of the Popalzai tribe (the same tribe as Karzai) and closely associated with the Karzai family. He was assassinated.
53 Christoph Reuter, "Le Seigneur de l'autoroute," *Vice* (blog), December 10, 2009, https://www.vice.com/fr/article/8gyn4v/warlord-of-the-highway-226-v3n12.
54 Dexter Filkins, "With U.S. Aid, Warlord Builds Afghan Empire," *The New York Times*, June 5, 2010, sec. World, https://www.nytimes.com/2010/06/06/world/asia/06warlords.html.

comprehensive inquiry exposed the company's complicity in an unlawful protection scheme, channeling funds to sustain insurgent operations.[55]

In the meantime, the Taliban executed a captivating display of strategic maneuvering, adopting the roles of modern-day Robin Hoods. They allocated a portion of their ill-gotten gains to uplift the local population, thereby fostering reciprocal bonds of loyalty. The shadow government established by the Taliban adeptly filled the void created by disillusionment, offering essential public services such as the establishment of madrassas and administering an alternative justice system to address grievances. This skillful exploitation tapped into deep-seated resentment toward the corrupt and ineffectual judicial apparatus imposed during the protracted presence of international forces in Afghanistan. Simultaneously, warlords associated with the Taliban embarked on infrastructure ventures, emulating the visionary endeavors of figures like Haji Juma Khan, who was arrested for drug trafficking by the DEA in 2008 and invested in the construction of vital roads and hospitals.

Disillusionment permeated the southern communities. In a 2010 interview, a Taliban combatant elucidated his decision to join the group, vividly recounting an incident where an American general (referring to General McNeill, Chief ISAF between 2002 and 2003) warmly embraced Jan Mohammad Khan. This was despite Khan and his armed men forcing the local population of Uruzgan Province into opium cultivation and mistreating women. The incident solidified his belief that external actors were colluding with criminals rather than genuinely supporting the Afghan people. Driven by this disenchantment, he made the decision to join the Taliban, determined to confront and resist foreign forces in Helmand.[56]

The outcome of these policies, pursued by both the international community and Afghan governments in the realm of drug control, can be encapsulated in a striking statement: during two decades, Afghanistan's opium production skyrocketed by a staggering factor of 30, making up a colossal 85% of global production in 2020, as reported by the UNODC.[57] This has catapulted the nation into a prominent position as a major player in the worldwide heroin

---

55 National Defense University, "Traffickers and Truckers: Illicit Afghan and Pakistani Power Structures with a Shadowy but Influential Role," *The Journal of Complex Operations*, October 19, 2017.

56 Two interviews were conducted with a member of Nurzai tribe engaged with Taliban in Helmand, October 2009 and January 2010.

57 UNODC, "Booklet 3—Drug Market Trends: Opioids, Cannabis," United Nations: Office on Drugs and Crime, 2021, //www.unodc.org/unodc/en/data-and-analysis/wdr-2021_booklet-3.html.

market, while witnessing the emergence of thriving industries in hashish and methamphetamine production.

3.3.5 Negative Consequences of Patronage in the Police Force's Appointment Process

After the 2004 presidential elections in Afghanistan, President Karzai, despite the introduction of security sector reform (SSR) in 2005, deliberately avoided its implementation and dismissed a merit-based approach for appointing officials. Instead, he chose to reshuffle officials with ties to armed groups, some with limited education but considerable influence in their respective provinces. This decision persisted despite strong objections from the international community, leading to the reassignment of these individuals to crucial positions.

The appointment of senior officials in the Afghan government was heavily influenced by political affiliations, international recommendations, personal connections with high-ranking authorities, local powerbrokers, and parliamentary intervention. This system, entrenched by a longstanding patronage network, resulted in short-lived tenures for individuals without such connections. Those appointed as chief provincial or district police during this period extended their influence by capitalizing on private conflicts, perpetuating a cycle of violence.[58]

Due to the system of patronage, qualified individuals outside established networks faced limited opportunities for advancement, hindering the overall effectiveness of government institutions, notably in their efforts to combat criminal activities or address other illicit interests associated with local powerholders. There were instances where these officers faced physical attacks orchestrated by the very strongmen they sought to challenge.

On the flip side, there were instances where the stronger faction eliminated competitors in a province, notably observed in Kandahar. A fierce rivalry unfolded among the three Durrani tribes—Alokozai, Barakzai, and Popalzai, prominently involving Ahmad Wali Karzai.

During Ahmad Wali Karzai's tenure, he wielded significant control as the de facto governor, chief police, and mayor in Kandahar. Officials from the Barakzai and Alokozai tribes faced the persistent risk of losing their positions as governors or chief police officers in the province, leading to occasional physical confrontations. In a notable incident in April 2010, Khan Muhammad

---

58   Adam Baczko, "Juger en situation de guerre civile. Les cours de justice Taleban en Afghanistan (2001–2013)," *Politix* 104, no. 4 (2013): 25–46, https://doi.org/10.3917/pox.104.0025.

Mujahid, the Kandahar chief of police from the Alokozai tribe, formerly associated with Jamiat-e Islami, was killed by a suicide bomber posing as a police officer. Although the Taliban was publicly blamed for the incident, speculation arose regarding Ahmad Wali Karzai's potential involvement in the assassination. Importantly, Mujahid had been previously removed from his position in Kandahar in 2005, reportedly under the influence of Ahmad Wali Karzai.[59]

3.3.6 Trading Positions: The Impact of Financial Transactions on Key Police Appointments

An additional avenue for obtaining these positions arose through the practice of outright purchasing, wherein select individuals engaged in financial transactions with influential stakeholders such as the Minister of the Interior, parliamentarians, the presidential office, and others. The financial costs associated with acquiring a position were contingent upon the perceived profitability of the position and the candidates' expectations of potential earnings and whether the price of the position is worth the investment. Prospective candidates displayed diligent efforts in initiating negotiations or engaging in monetary transactions to secure their desired positions. It is indisputable that those who resorted to purchasing positions had to resort to unscrupulous means, including the misappropriation of public funds and forging alliances with criminal entities, or even delving into illicit undertakings, all in an effort to maximize their investment returns.

During the pay and rank reform, revelations from the police selection panel raised concerns among mid- and senior-ranking officers about potential dismissals. Subsequently, these officers faced pressure from the Minister's office to pay for new appointments. For instance, a northern border chief revealed that in 2007, he paid a substantial $150,000 to then-Minister of Interior Zarar Muqbil for a one-year position. Notably, the Minister's office falsely claimed to this "Jihadi officer" that his reappointment application was rejected by the international community due to his criminal record. In reality, Zarar Muqbil warned that securing the position would require a higher payment than in 2007. With these appointments, police corruption surged to unprecedented levels. This was starkly evident in a 2018 SIGAR audit, which estimated, for instance, fuel theft at over $154.4 million US, and potentially even more. The audit exposed damning allegations against Brig. Gen. Abdul Karim Fayeq, the

---

59   Baczko.

former provincial police chief in Kapisa Province, accusing him of orchestrating the theft of 60,000 gallons of government fuel intended for Afghan troops.[60]

3.3.7 The International Community's Role in Appointing Officials

After the Bonn Conference, the international community's involvement in recommending candidates introduced an external element into the decision-making process, potentially prioritizing geopolitical interests over local expertise. From 2002 onwards, the interventions of the UN, the EU, NATO, and Western embassies in the appointment or rejection of specific candidates for crucial positions within the Afghan security forces became a regular occurrence. Following the 2009 presidential election, the influence of the UN and its affiliated agencies on the Afghan government and its president significantly waned.

The overall lack of expertise among international actors, particularly among military personnel, coupled with the high turnover rates, posed significant challenges in developing a comprehensive understanding of the intricate social dynamics and context in Afghanistan. Additionally, as the security situation in the country worsened, strict security measures imposed on the international community limited their interactions and engagement with Afghans and hindered the international actors' ability to gain insights into the ground realities and perspectives of the Afghan people. This had further an impact on their decision-making processes, potentially compromising the effectiveness of their interventions and efforts in addressing the complex challenges faced by Afghanistan.

In addition, the pursued objectives and approaches of the international actors often varied. Some actors placed a higher emphasis on the immediate interests of their forces in Afghanistan, sometimes overlooking the potential long-term consequences of their decisions. Therefore, they tended to favor candidates who aligned with their own agenda, regardless of their professionalism or even criminal background. In contrast, other actors took a more nuanced approach, considering factors such as expertise, professionalism, and a clean background as important criteria in promoting effective governance and stability.

The military, particularly the United States, demonstrated for example a preference for candidates who possessed English proficiency and displayed a

---

60 SIGAR, "Why the Afghan Security Forces Collapsed" (SIGAR, February 2023), https://www.sigar.mil/pdf/evaluations/SIGAR-23-16-IP.pdf.

flexible disposition to comply with their plans and conditions. This preference sometimes overlooked the candidates' competencies, complex backgrounds, and past transgressions, leading to the selection of individuals who were more compliant than qualified.

A case that exemplifies this discrepancy in perception is the enigmatic figure of Assadullah Khalid, who held significant positions in the Afghan government, including head of the National Directorate of Security (NDS), Minister of Tribal and Border Affairs, Governor of Kandahar Province, Governor of Ghazni Province, and Minister of Defense. He was affiliated with the Islamic Dawah Organisation of Afghanistan and considered a loyalist of former President Hamid Karzai.

Khalid skillfully nurtured strong relationships with his American mentors, advisors, and military counterparts. However, testimonials from Canadian officials who closely collaborated with Khalid during his tenure in Kandahar, where Canadian forces were deployed, suggested his direct involvement in acts of torture, his leadership of a covert criminal network, his utilization of private prisons, and his complicity in targeted assassinations.[61] Rumors circulating within the corridors of the Ministry of Interior and the international community also hinted at Khalid's involvement in orchestrating the assassination of a pregnant French aid worker in Ghazni Province in 2005.

Khalid's influence expanded significantly as he allegedly established an extensive drug trafficking network spanning from the northern to the southern regions of the country. Despite numerous reports on his controversial actions, they didn't impede his ascent; rather, he was subsequently promoted to the key position of heading the National Directorate of Security (Afghanistan intelligence agency).

3.4 Ministry of Defense

3.4.1 *Background*

Under the guidance of the UN-mandated ISAF, the initial effort to build an Afghan army aimed to recruit and train a 600-member unit, carefully selected to reflect diverse ethnic backgrounds, encompassing the majority of Afghanistan's 33 provinces at that time. This ambitious program proved fleeting. Subsequently, establishing the first four battalions posed significant

---

61 "Special Committee on the Canadian Mission in Afghanistan: Number 015, 2nd session, 40th Parliament," November 18, 2009, https://www.ourcommons.ca/DocumentViewer/en/40-2/AFGH/meeting-15/evidence.

challenges for the Coalition forces., which encountered recruitment obstacles, leading to a meager personnel count. After training, a concerning pattern emerged—many quickly deserted, returning to their original militias, lured by substantially higher pay. The nascent Afghan force, diverse yet unorganized, found itself disconnected from a well-established command structure capable of genuinely representing the nation's ethnic diversity. Meanwhile, a cohesive plan for integrating or demobilizing scattered illegal armed forces remained absent, and critical actions against various spoilers were lacking.

After the US troop withdrawal in 2021, President Biden projected the Afghan war's staggering cost at over $2 trillion, encompassing substantial allocations for both military operations and reconstruction. Notably, SIPRI's analysis identifies a substantial $72.7 billion in military aid between 2001 and 2020, primarily originating from the Department of Defense, channeled through key mechanisms such as the Afghanistan Security Forces Fund (ASFF) and Train and Equip Fund. Furthermore, the Department of State contributed an additional $564 million in military aid through diverse funding avenues.

In 2001, the country had just emerged from over two decades of devastating civil war, leaving the central state heavily reliant on a turbulent economy driven by violence, a dynamic that often favored the emerging class of businessmen and warlords, regardless of their ethnic background. The once-dominant feudal lords had been replaced by the authority of Mujahidin commanders and their armed forces. In such an intricate context, the central state faced a formidable challenge in regaining control over the entire territory. Not only was the disarmament of militias crucial, but providing viable alternatives to former combatants was equally indispensable for ensuring lasting peace and security. This transformative process aimed to replace the dominance of militias with the stability of state institutions, paving the path for peaceful competition in the quest for power. The strategic objective behind these efforts was the launch of the Disarmament, Demobilization, and Reintegration (DDR) program.

3.4.2 *Disarmament, Demobilization, and Reintegration & Disarmament of Illegal Armed Groups*

Navigating the intricacies stemming from the 2001 Bonn agreement proved to be a challenging endeavor, largely due to the vehement resistance posed by militia leaders against the explicit inclusion of the DDR process. Notably, prominent figures like Marshal Fahim, who held the position of Minister of Defense at the time, advocated for the integration of their militias into the Afghan National Army. Nevertheless, the UNAMA/US plan, bolstered by donor support, emerged as the chosen course of action, resulting in the establishment of the Afghan National Army with restricted militia involvement, all guided by the UNDP's Afghan New Beginnings Programme (ANBP).[62]

Within Afghanistan, the DDR initiative took root in 2003 with the primary goal of diminishing the influence wielded by mid-level commanders through the facilitation of combatant disarmament. The initial phase prioritized voluntary disarmament, offering essentials such as clothing, sustenance, and vocational training. Curiously, some former combatants, including those associated with human rights violations, transitioned into security roles.

By 2006, the DDR program achieved the disbandment of 62,326 combatants leading to a decrease in militia strength and the recovery of a substantial amount of heavy weaponry. Nonetheless, these achievements were accompanied by a significant financial burden, surpassing $100 million.[63] The DDR process exhibited a preference for high and mid-ranking militia commanders, with reported manipulation in combatant lists. This led to disproportionate financial benefits for these commanders. Regions under Shuray-e Nezar control, like Kabul and Kunduz, accounted for 56% of processed militiamen, while the remaining regions made up just 33%, highlighting regional disparities.[64]

Following this phase, the subsequent Disarmament of Illegal Armed Groups (DIAG) aimed to address illicit armed groups. However, this initiative faced criticism for its inadequate screening of candidates with militia affiliations. A portion of the collected weapons was found to be outdated, dating back to the Second World War. This complexity grew due to concerns about a resurgent Taliban and commanders being rearmed by coalition forces without sufficient human rights scrutiny, shortly after disarmament.[65] This has given rise to a significant dilemma: on one hand, the endeavor to establish proficient state institutions in an enduringly fragile state, and on the other hand, the challenge of combating terrorism or insurgency by reequipping local militias.[66]

---

62 Simonetta Rossi and Antonio Giustozzi, "Disarmament, Demobilisation and Reintegration of Ex-Combatants (DDR) in Afghanistan: Constraints and Limited Capabilities," Monograph (London, UK: Crisis States Research Centre, London School of Economics and Political Science, June 2006), http://www.crisisstates.com.
63 Patricia Gossman, "Transitional Justice and DDR: The Case of Afghanistan," June 2009, https://www.ictj.org/sites/default/files/ICTJ-DDR-Afghanistan-ResearchBrief-2009-English.pdf.
64 Rossi and Giustozzi, "Disarmament, Demobilisation and Reintegration of Ex-Combatants (DDR) in Afghanistan".
65 Gossman, "Transitional Justice and DDR: The Case of Afghanistan".
66 Deedee Derksen, "The Politics of Disarmament and Rearmament in Afghanistan," United States Institute of Peace, May 20, 2015, https://www.usip.org/publications/2015/05/politics-disarmament-and-rearmament-afghanistan.

3.4.3 Appointment in the MoD

Just like its counterpart in the Ministry of the Interior, Jamiat-e Islami became a dominant force within the Ministry of Defense as it achieved significant victories against the Taliban. The late Marshal Fahim, hailing from Panjshir and the chief commander of the military council of Shuray-e Nizar, was appointed as the first Minister of Defense, exerting considerable influence over the nascent Afghan army. Consequently, it was expected that notable challenges would arise in the initial selection of generals to lead the fledgling Afghan army. Out of the hundred generals appointed by Marshal Qasim Fahim during the interim administration, an overwhelming majority—around 90%—hailed from the relatively confined Panjshir Valley, which later became a designated province.[67] This initial imbalance already indicated the complex nature of efforts to establish an inclusive and representative Afghan army.

Throughout the two decades, the appointment of officers to key positions had often been tainted by political interference or individuals connected to criminal or mafia groups, and patronage networks. Additionally, the Ministry of Defense faced a pervasive trend of pay-for-appointment, particularly within departments that yielded significant revenues, such as finance, logistics, construction, procurement, and supplies. These departments were deeply embroiled in extensive corrupt practices, particularly concerning contracts for essential items like food and other supplies, among other matters. This corruption had extensive consequences in combating the Taliban.

Accounts from Afghan soldiers indicated that they confronted significant hardships including insufficient resources, ill-fitting uniforms, and strategic disadvantages in their battle against the Taliban. This predicament resulted in a dire struggle for essential sustenance. Those positioned in remote regions endured even more grueling circumstances, occasionally isolated from primary bases and receiving meager supplies.[68]

Amid these conditions, soldiers' motivation to defend the country declined, particularly when their leaders were embroiled in scandals affecting their working conditions. Corruption thrived due to favoritism networks in the Ministry of Defense, combined with armed faction infiltration in the army, undermining its integrity and endangering young recruits. Illicit activities, like drug

---

67 International Crisis Group, "A Force in Fragments: Reconstituting the Afghan National Army," May 12, 2010, https://www.crisisgroup.org/asia/south-asia/afghanistan/force-fragments-reconstituting-afghan-national-army.
68 Alijani Ershad, "'We Haven't Eaten for Days': Afghan Soldiers Suffer amid Widespread Corruption," The Observers—France 24, February 18, 2020, https://observers.france24.com/en/20200218-afghanistan-corruption-rations-soldiers-army-eat.

trafficking, cast a troubling shadow over the police and the army. Some senior military commanders prioritized the interests of their backers over the long-term institutional strength of the Afghan National Army. Notably, Brigadier General Abdul Samad Habibi, responsible for army recruitment in Mazar-e-Sharif in 2013, was caught driving an official Ministry of Defense vehicle loaded with 20 kg of heroin.[69] This incident unquestionably also raised grave concerns about the integrity of the recruitment process, casting a persistent shadow of doubt over the effectiveness of the selection and vetting procedures.

In 2002, Marshal Fahim appointed General Bismillah Muhammadi as the ANA's Chief of Staff. By 2005, President Karzai moved Fahim to the role of First Vice President and appointed General Abdul Rahim Wardak as the Minister of Defense. Wardak, linked to the Mahaz-e Milliy-e Islami Afghanistan faction, made a series of appointments, predominantly of Pashtun individuals with close ties to him or his associates. This created additional divisions within the ministry, with one group led by Uzbeks under Lieutenant General Hamayoun Fauzi and another by Hazaras under Lieutenant General Baz Mohammad Jawhari. These appointments further complemented the existing followers of Bismillah Khan.[70] In essence, this alteration in leadership resulted in the continuation of the existing patronage network, albeit manifesting as multiple distinct groups.

Adding to the complexity was the withdrawal of ISAF forces from Afghanistan by the close of 2014. The subsequent NATO mission, titled the Resolute Support Mission (RSM), set out to "assist Afghan institutions and security forces in developing the capacity to defend Afghanistan and sustainably protect its citizens." This mission was governed by the principles of "train, advise, and assist."[71] Amid this critical situation, Karzai and Abdullah engaged in a competition to place their loyalists in key ministry positions, rather than seeking compromise. Under Ashraf Ghani's presidency, tensions re-emerged between him and Abdullah, particularly regarding appointment and advancement policies and the influence of provincial powerbrokers in official roles within the security apparatus. The interference of politicians, senior officials, and intermediaries in military career progress not only weakened the operational

---

69 Fazul Rahim, "Top Afghan General Caught Transporting Heroin in Truck: Officials," NBC News, July 1, 2015, https://www.nbcnews.com/news/world/top-afghan-general-caught-transporting-heroin-truck-n385041.
70 Pamela Brown, "Analysis of the Afghan Defense Appointments" (Institute for the Study of War, 2010), https://www.jstor.org/stable/resrep07865.
71 NATO, "Resolute Support Mission in Afghanistan (2015–2021)," NATO, May 30, 2022, https://www.nato.int/cps/en/natohq/topics_113694.htm.

effectiveness of the military and police, who were embroiled in an unrelenting war, but also undermined their morale and willingness to fight. Merit didn't always determine advancement; connections to powerful figures did.

The 2019 presidential elections were tainted by allegations of fraud, igniting a fresh political crisis between Ghani and Abdullah. This tumultuous period found resolution in May 2020, when Ghani and Abdullah inked a power-sharing accord. According to this arrangement, Ghani would retain the presidency, while Abdullah would lead peace negotiations with the Taliban once initiated. As a result, Abdullah relinquished control over ministerial and authoritative appointments, ceding the reins to Ghani and his two protégés, Fazly and Mohib. Subsequently, Ghani took a hands-on approach, personally handpicking every commander with the rank of brigadier general and above. During this time, the Afghan military underwent a notable leadership turnover, wherein newly appointed commanders had limited opportunity to showcase their capabilities. In addition, the National Security Council's interference compounded the issue, relegating the minister of defense and army leadership to mere figureheads without the authority to appoint or dismiss. In an intriguing twist of fate, power found its cozy abode within the office of the National Security Advisor, a role that might seem somewhat perplexing given Mohib's rather unconventional academic background in the realm of virtual reality entertainment and communications.[72] It's almost as if his Ph.D. dissertation on virtual reality was a fitting precursor for navigating the labyrinth of Afghan military affairs. One might even say it's akin to having an orchestra conductor who specializes in heavy metal rock music.

One-sided negotiations between the United States and the Taliban marginalized the Kabul government. Additionally, Ghani's assertive demeanor and his detachment from ground realities transformed him into a leader disconnected from the nation's pulse. He frequently reacted negatively to unfavorable news, leading his advisors to manipulate information about the security situation before presenting it to him. Furthermore, during his second term, Ghani occasionally replaced Northern Alliance generals with officers trained in the United States, intensifying the divisions within the military, which included former jihadists, U.S.-trained personnel, and those educated during the Soviet era or under the Soviet proxy regime in Kabul.

---

72 John F. Sopko and David H. Young, "*The factors leading to the collapse of the Afghan government and its security forces: Remarks before the 1st Committee of Inquiry (Afghanistan) in the 20th Electoral Term*," German Bundestag Statement, SIGAR Lessons Learned Program, March 2, 2023.

As districts fell to the Taliban and their proximity to Kabul increased, Ghani's actions remained out of sync. While the Taliban advanced, he persisted in urban planning meetings and appointed new loyalist figures. As the situation grew dire, corruption within the security sector reached alarming heights unveiling a stark disparity between reported and actual numbers. The Afghan National Army fell far short of its claimed strength of 120,000 soldiers, and the aggregate size of the Afghan National Security Forces failed to surpass 300,000 personnel.[73] Equally, the proclaimed 4-to-1 numerical advantage of the ANSF over the Taliban, as asserted by Afghan authorities, was a stark departure from reality.

This deception secured inflated financial support from the United States. Monetary resources, ammunition, and provisions intended for distribution to the troops were intercepted and stolen before reaching their intended destinations on the ground. The ammunition and other vital equipment were illicitly sold within the clandestine market, eventually falling into the hands of the Taliban.[74]

On the ground, soldiers from disadvantaged regions endured extended frontline stints without rotation, while those with connections found refuge in Kabul, diverting their salaries to other channels, and inflicting financial hardships on their families.

In the weeks leading up to the fall of Kabul, the condition of the Afghan army became increasingly precarious. Indications that it would take six months for the army to recover hinted at a shortage of available soldiers. Recruitment was difficult, and the number of casualties surged—approximately 350 soldiers were lost or severely injured each day, amounting to around 10,000 soldiers every month.[75] Additionally, the funds intended for local commanders and other militia leaders to jointly defend the territory alongside Afghan security forces were largely misused in Kabul. In the context shared by a former Finance Minister, certain individuals exploited the situation, receiving extra funds during emergencies. This led to a scenario where a significant portion of the money didn't reach those directly involved in the fighting. For instance, only a fraction of the allocated funds reached individuals engaged in conflict.[76]

---

73 Clark and Shapour, "The Khalid Payenda Interview (1)".
74 Abdul Basit, "Why Did the Afghan Army Disintegrate so Quickly?," August 17, 2021, https://www.aljazeera.com/opinions/2021/8/17/why-did-the-afghan-army-disintegrate-so-quickly.
75 Clark and Shapour, "The Khalid Payenda Interview (1)".
76 Clark and Shapour.

Over two decades, the Afghan government's military struggled against the relentless Taliban advance, exposing errors from the international community and Afghan leaders. The military's widespread involvement in the economy of violence further weakened the fragile national army, leaving soldiers ill-equipped and impacting front-line forces. From 2001 to 2021, nearly 92,000 ANSF members and 47,000 civilians made the ultimate sacrifice.[77] Afghanistan, known as the "graveyard of empires," unfolded as a tragic narrative for its people.

3.5 Judiciary

3.5.1 Challenges to Judicial Independence and Rule of Law in Afghanistan's Constitutional Order

The fall of the Taliban in 2001 presented hope for a new constitutional order in Afghanistan, aiming for democracy and the rule of law. The 2004 Constitution established a system of separation of powers between the executive, legislative, and judicial branches, intended as checks and balances, however, the President held a combination of powers previously exercised by the King and the Prime Minister under the Constitution of 1964.[78]

The National Assembly, with two chambers, served as the highest legislative organ representing the people. Its powers included ratifying and abrogating laws, approving the state budget, endorsing development programs, ratifying international treaties, and deciding on high-level appointments. The judiciary consisted of the Supreme Court, Courts of Appeal, and Primary Courts. The Supreme Court had nine members appointed by the president and endorsed by the National Assembly, with judges receiving lifetime financial security under specific conditions.[79] The court system eventually comprised three main branches serving districts, provinces, and national appeals. In addition, the legal system included several specialized courts, such as anti-corruption

---

77   Susannah George, "4,000 Afghan Security Forces Dead, 1,000 Missing in Final Battles against Taliban, Former Official Says," Washington Post, December 29, 2021, https://www.washingtonpost.com/world/2021/12/30/afghanistan-security-forces-deaths/.
78   Rainer Grote, "Separation of Powers in the New Afghan Constitution," *The Max Planck Institute for Comparative Public Law and International Law*, May 2015, https://zaoerv.de/64_2004/64_2004_4_a_897_916.pdf.
79   Mehdi J. Hakimi, "The Judiciary and the Rule of Law in Afghanistan," SSRN Scholarly Paper (Rochester, NY, December 1, 2021), https://papers.ssrn.com/abstract=3987775.

courts, serious crimes courts, and courts with related prosecution units handling gender-based violence cases.

However, the institutional design suffered significant flaws, weakening the separation of powers. The president had undue influence over judicial appointments, and the Supreme Court's jurisdiction for judicial review was ambiguous, leading to conflicts with other bodies. Under Karai, the president capitalized on constitutional gaps to expand his power. For instance, the Constitution did not clarify who appoints members of the Independent Electoral Commission (IEC), responsible for overseeing elections. Exploiting this ambiguity, the president issued a decree granting himself the authority to make these appointments.[80] Thus, all the heads of the IEC were individuals closely connected to the two successive presidents.

Despite efforts by the House of Representatives to pass a law requiring parliamentary approval for IEC members, the president vetoed it and appointed the members unilaterally. This allowed the president to consolidate more authority, highlighting the need for clearer constitutional provisions.

The judiciary had thus faced challenges in establishing itself as an independent branch due to both a weak constitutional structure and historical deficiencies in institutional capacity within the judiciary.[81]

The executive branch regularly interfered with judicial proceedings and sanctions, eroding the judiciary's independence. Moreover, poor security and direct threats targeted judges, while the public perceived a lack of judicial neutrality due to the bench's proximity to the executive.

These factors led to a significant gap between the official rules (*de jure*) and their actual implementation (*de facto*) in Afghanistan, which eroded the rule of law and judicial independence. Furthermore, the 2004 constitution weakened the judiciary by creating exceptions to its jurisdiction, especially in cases involving ministers. This allowed the executive to disregard rules applicable to the security forces even more freely.

In 2007, for example, Haji Abdul Zahir Qadeer, a self-proclaimed general and known Jihadist, was appointed as head of the border police for the North and North-West regions despite lacking relevant experience. He had connections to prominent Jihadi figures and political associates linked to Karzai.

---

80   Sayed Reza Hussaini, "Constitutional Design as the Primary Cause of a Political Tragedy: A Case Study of Afghanistan's 2004 Constitution" 105, no. 3 (2021), https://www.wlv.ac.uk/media/departments/marketing-and-communications/(2022)-7-WLJ-3.pdf.

81   Farid Hamidi and Aruni Jayakody, "Separation of Powers under the Afghan Constitution: A Case Study," Refworld, March 2015, https://www.refworld.org/reference/countryrep/areu/2015/en/104992.

During his tenure, Haji Zahir and his team were caught transporting over 120 kg of heroin in an official border patrol vehicle, leading to the arrest of six individuals, including Haji Zahir and his closest associate. However, Haji Zahir was never prosecuted and immediately released from custody, facilitated by Attorney General Sabit, who shared the same province as Haji Zahir, and with the endorsement of President Hamid Karzai.[82] In 2009, shortly after his re-election, President Karzai ordered the release of the five individuals implicated in drug smuggling as compensation for Zahir's support for Karzai's re-election in 2009.

Under President Ghani's rule, the landscape of justice remained unchanged, mirroring the footsteps of his predecessor, with the judiciary weakened by selective exceptions to its jurisdiction. In February 2021, a peaceful protest in the serene backdrop of Behsud, Wardak Province, turned into a tragic event as unarmed civilians lost their lives.[83] The suspension of Wardak Province's Chief of Police offered a glimmer of hope for further investigation, yet the path taken veered away from justice. Instead of prosecuting the responsible police chief, Ghani's decision led to a transfer to Laghman Province, leaving a bittersweet taste of concern among the public.

3.5.2 The Disconnect between International Approaches and Local Realities

In approaching Afghanistan, the international community treated it as a blank legal canvas and introduced foreign legal concepts, overlooking Afghan legal traditions. To truly promote the rule of law, it is essential to engage with the local foundations of legitimate legal order, which often stem from non-state authority, and enjoy support from credible domestic partners, including high-level State officials.[84] From 2002 to 2006, Italy took on the role of the judiciary sector's "lead nation," while the United States emerged as the most influential international actor, largely surpassing other donors in financial contributions. However, within the US, Individual agencies pursued their own programmatic priorities without adequate coordination, resulting in a lack of cohesion and consistency in their approach.[85,86]

---

82   Confidential interview with high level Afghan military source.
83   TOLOnews, "Maidan Wardak Police Chief Suspended Over Behsud Incident," TOLOnews, February 8, 2021, https://tolonews.com/afghanistan-169852.
84   Geoffrey Swenson, "Why U.S. Efforts to Promote the Rule of Law in Afghanistan Failed," International Security 42, no. 1 (July 1, 2017): 114–51, https://doi.org/10.1162/ISEC_a_00285.
85   Swenson.
86   James Dobbins et al., "The Beginner's Guide to Nation-Building" (RAND Corporation, January 11, 2007), https://www.rand.org/pubs/monographs/MG557.html.

During the revision of the Criminal Procedure Code from 2004 to 2006, the international community disregarded the existing 1975 Penal Code and 1977 Criminal Procedure Code, opting instead to create an entirely new code influenced by the Italian system. This new code not only conflicted with Afghan law but also covered only a fraction of the 1977 Afghan Criminal Procedure Code. Similarly, in the field of constitutional law, an American professor provided training to Afghan prosecutors based on the US case, overlooking the intricacies of the Afghan constitution.[87] As a result, significant disparities arose between the specific needs of Afghan jurists and the short three-week courses conducted by an American professor, highlighting the lack of synchronization between the imported legal systems and the Afghan legal context, which hindered effective and coherent justice reform efforts in the country.

In 2010, the international community prioritized establishing a proper judicial system due to the return of the Taliban, which made rural areas inaccessible. However, rural courts faced numerous challenges, and finding qualified judges became arduous due to ongoing insecurity. As a result, the government's judicial system remained concentrated in urban areas. Therefore, political entrepreneurs took advantage of this legal vacuum, as regime courts favored them, allowing them to expedite cases with the use of bribes and their influential connections. For the general population, legal proceedings became perilous and financially burdensome, with high corruption costs involved. Trials often turned into auctions, with sometimes bribes exceeding the actual value of the dispute, especially in emotionally charged cases like land and family matters.[88] Notably, after fleeing during the civil war in 1992, Kabul pharmacist Nader Naderi returned to find his family home seized by a local commander and rented out for $10,000 annually. His legal efforts to regain the property failed, leading to frustration and bribery. The justice minister eventually ordered the house's return, but Naderi had to pay an additional $4,000 in bribes, totaling around $11,000.[89]

Failure to pay bribes frequently resulted in legal cases remaining unresolved. Take, for instance, the case of Farooq Farani, who returned in 1997 to discover a stranger occupying his home. Seven years passed, and the matter of house

---

87 Adam Baczko, *La Guerre Par Le Droit–Les Tribunaux Taliban En Afghanistan*–CNRS Editions, 2021, https://www.cnrseditions.fr/catalogue/relations-internationales/la-guerre-par-le-droit/.
88 Baczko, "Juger en situation de guerre civile".
89 Paul Watson, "In Afghanistan, Money Tips the Scales of Justice," Los Angeles Times, December 18, 2006, https://www.latimes.com/archives/la-xpm-2006-dec-18-fg-justice18-story.html.

ownership remained in limbo as Mr. Farani steadfastly rejected the bribes sought by a judge, culminating in a legal impasse. This situation entailed a convoluted process involving intermediaries, ultimately resulting in the house title being attainable for $25,000; half its market value.[90]

The irregular inflow of funds into Afghanistan's legal system disrupted the entire process from the formulation of laws to the application of verdicts. This gave rise to unintended consequences: the imposition of external laws by Western embassies marginalized the role of the parliament, the lack of coordination in financial allocations led to a judicial system plagued by favoritism toward powerful figures including warlords, and the involvement of the US military in promoting customary institutions undermined the legitimacy of official ones.[91] Some donors drafted laws based on their representatives' expertise, while others focused on laws related to the "war on terror." This ad hoc approach created legal bodies with vague jurisdictions, causing issues with efficiency and coherence in Afghanistan's legal system. Ineffective initiatives prompted donors to overhaul certain systems under Western pressure. As a result, the legislative complexity hinders the effective implementation of laws and efforts to combat corruption and other problems.[92]

3.5.3 Appointment in the Judiciary

Under the Constitution, the judiciary was designated as an independent organ of the state, encompassing the Supreme Court, Courts of Appeal, and Primary Courts. The Supreme Court consisted of nine members, appointed by the president, and confirmed by the National Assembly. Notably, the judges of the Supreme Court were promised lifetime financial security under specific conditions upon completion of their terms.[93]

During the entirety of the Coalition forces' tenure in Afghanistan, the nation grappled with glaring examples of political interference and favoritism that overshadowed the transparency of judicial appointments. Apprehensions of undue influence emanating from armed factions, members of parliament, ministers, and other influential figures left an indelible mark on the system's credibility. A 2007 report from the Anti-Corruption Resource Center unveiled

---

90 Dexter Filkins, "Bribes Corrode Afghans' Trust in Government," January 1, 2009, https://www.nytimes.com/2009/01/02/world/asia/02kabul.html.

91 Adam Baczko, "Les effets pervers de l'exportation du droit dans des guerres civiles. L'intervention militaire en Afghanistan (2001–2014)," *Droit et société* 110, no. 1 (2022): 131–49, https://doi.org/10.3917/drs1.110.0131.

92 Baczko.

93 Hakimi, "The Judiciary and the Rule of Law in Afghanistan".

manipulations within the Supreme Court, leading to the appointment of judges ill-equipped for their responsibilities. Estimates suggested that a mere 20% of these appointments exhibited genuine competence and suitability for their esteemed roles.[94]

Like police or military appointments, the positions of judges but also most vital administrative roles further succumbed to the influence of commercial interests. This spawned a prevailing ideology of "state deconstruction" rather than the pursuit of State-Building, which ultimately led to the State's decline[95] and fall in 2021. This trajectory was unrelated to Afghan culture or any historical aversion to the State. The Afghan judicial system was thus marred by corruption, nepotism, and bribery. Confidence in the system was low, as anti-corruption efforts had limited impact, and judges enjoyed impunity. Nepotism exacerbated conflicts in land and marital disputes, leading to prolonged litigation.

Former Supreme Justice Fazl Hadi Shinwari (a *madrasa* graduate linked to Saudi-backed jihadist Abdul Rasul Sayyaf, leader of Ittehad-e Islami of Afghanistan) was appointed by Karzai in 2002. Shinwari at his turn appointed several unqualified individuals, leading to a judiciary filled with corrupt and incompetent judges. After Shinwari, Karzai appointed Abdul Salam Azimi as Chief Justice at a time when Afghans were turning to Taliban courts for swift results. Despite the latter's efforts to initiate reforms, Shinwari's legacy persisted, with many of his appointees remaining in their positions since 2006.[96] However, the judge transfer system, under Shinwari or Azimi's influence, became susceptible to favoritism, prompting some judges to leave their positions to avoid being assigned to insecure or undesirable locations.[97]

---

94 Marie Chêne, "Tackling Judicial Corruption in Afghanistan," U4 Anti-Corruption Resource Centre, September 12, 2007, https://www.u4.no/publications/tackling-judicial-corruption-in-afghanistan.pdf.

95 Fontanarava Clément, "Les Taliban ont-ils gagné la guerre par le droit ? Une conversation avec Adam Baczko," *Le Grand Continent* (blog), November 11, 2021, https://legrandcontinent.eu/fr/2021/11/11/les-taliban-ont-ils-gagne-la-guerre-par-le-droit-une-conversation-avec-adam-baczko/.

96 International Crisis Group, "Reforming Afghanistan's Broken Judiciary," November 17, 2010, https://www.refworld.org/reference/countryrep/icg/2010/en/76505.

97 Shoaib Timory, "Judicial Independence in Afghanistan: Legal Framework and Practical Challenges," *Afghanistan Research and Evaluation Unit Organization* (blog), February 21, 2021, https://areu.org.af/publication/2102/.

3.5.4 *The Permeating Culture of Impunity and Corruption*

Within the corridors of power, well-connected elites, including ministers, judges, and governors, eluded justice, evading consequences for corruption and criminal activities. The 2010 Kabul Bank scandal starkly exposes the weaknesses in Afghanistan's justice system. Influential figures like Mahmud Karzai allegedly embezzled nearly $980 million, triggering the bank's collapse and impacting over 5% of Afghanistan's GDP. Despite extensive investigations, only $180 million of the fraudulent loans were recovered by October 2012, leaving the perpetrators untouched by justice.

Even individuals like Sher Muhammad Akhundzada, connected to narcotic cases or assisting the Taliban, managed to escape thorough investigations, leaving justice-seeking efforts incomplete. Such individuals were even rewarded with promotions, exemplifying the gravity of the systemic issues.

In the realm of narcotics cases, a high conviction rate combined with lenient possession thresholds flooded Afghan prisons with minor traffickers, overshadowing the pursuit of the most serious offenders. Major traffickers, often tied to the political elite, appeared untouchable, further undermining the efficacy of the judiciary. In this landscape, criminals easily procured their freedom through bribes to the police or judiciary, while covert arrangements with judges offered a reliable escape from accountability. The justice system's inefficiency and corruption normalized crime, perpetuating an economy of violence, where wrongdoers could act with impunity.

3.6 Insurgents and Terrorist Organizations: Other Actors of the Economy of Violence

Throughout the presence of international forces in Afghanistan, the economy of violence thrived. It was sustained not only by corrupt authorities, warlords and criminals, and influential figures engaged in illicit activities but by insurgent groups like the Taliban, the long-standing Hezb-e-Islami Afghanistan led by Gulbuddin Hekmatyar, as well as al-Qaeda and later Daesh from 2013 onwards. These groups actively participated in perpetuating this economy of violence, deriving a significant portion of their income from various criminal enterprises and the illicit economy.

According to the May 2020 report by the United Nations Security Council's Sanctions Committee, the Taliban's annual revenue ranged from $300 million

(USD) to over $1.5 billion.⁹⁸ A critical development in the Taliban's financial network was the successful consolidation of power by Mullah Yaqoob, the son of the former Taliban emir Mullah Omar. In 2016, Yaqoob established a financial committee to maximize revenue and strengthen his bid for leadership within the group. Since then, he rapidly rose through the ranks, ecomeng deputy leader and eventually assuming the powerful role of military chief. Under his leadership, the Taliban's revenue reached $1.6 billion in 2019. Income sources included mining ($464 million), drug trafficking ($416 million), foreign countries and individuals ($240 million), exports ($240 million), taxes ($160 million), and real estate ($80 million)⁹⁹ not just in Afghanistan but also in neighboring Pakistan and possibly other countries.¹⁰⁰

3.6.1 *Kidnapping for Ransom*

A notable source of income for terrorist organizations in Afghanistan stemmed from the abduction of hostages, primarily targeting Western captives, but also extending to Afghan businessmen and various other individuals. The exact ransoms paid for the release of each hostage were shrouded in secrecy, with the nations involved frequently disavowing their participation in such transactions.

An illustrative example took place in July 2007, when 23 South Korean missionaries were abducted by the Taliban while traveling between Kandahar and Kabul. Two hostages were later executed. The South Korean government officially denied paying any ransom for the release of the remaining 21 missionaries, while the Taliban claimed to have received a substantial $20 million ransom from the South Korean government asserting that these funds would be used to procure additional weapons and carry out more suicide attacks.¹⁰¹

---

98   UNSC, "*Analytical Support and Sanctions Monitoring Team*," United Nations Security Council, May 2020.
99   Hanif Sufizada, "The Taliban Are Megarich—Here's Where They Get the Money They Use to Wage War in Afghanistan," The Conversation, December 8, 2020, http://theconversation.com/the-taliban-are-megarich-heres-where-they-get-the-money-they-use-to-wage-war-in-afghanistan-147411.
100 Frud Bezhan, "Exclusive: Taliban's Expanding 'Financial Power' Could Make It 'Impervious' To Pressure, Confidential Report Warns," September 16, 2020, https://www.rferl.org/a/exclusive-taliban-s-expanding-financial-power-could-make-it-impervious-to-pressure-secret-nato-report-warns/30842570.html. RFE/RL obtained a confidential document from NATO, and the information was subsequently reported by RFE/RL.
101 "Taliban Say S.Korea Paid over $20 Mln Ransom," *Reuters*, September 1, 2007, https://www.reuters.com/article/idUSCOL317931/.

The payment of ransoms had far-reaching implications beyond the financing of terrorists. It involved the intricate participation of diverse actors within the economy of violence, assuming the role of intermediaries between terrorist organizations and local leaders. These intermediaries, while facilitating the release of hostages, cunningly secured a share of the ransom as a commission for their pivotal role.

Furthermore, the grim realm of hostage captivity frequently unveiled a chilling collaboration between criminal syndicates and terrorist groups. The initial abductors would pass their captives to the second party, thereby perpetuating the interplay between organized crime and terrorism.

The release of hostages witnessed the involvement of additional actors. The notorious security firm Watan, owned by the cousins of the former president Karzai, audaciously offered its services to orchestrate the liberation of a Western hostage demanding an exorbitant ransom.[102] Similarly, a foreign private security company was enlisted to ensure the safe retrieval of a journalist working for a prestigious American newspaper, demanding extravagant remuneration for their intricate undertaking.

In a series of incidents involving Western hostages held by terrorist or insurgent groups, the captors would leverage their captives' plight to negotiate the release of their fellow fighters detained by the Afghan government. One case of particular controversy was that of an Italian journalist, along with his Afghan interpreter and driver, ensnared in the province of Helmand in 2007. Despite the limitations imposed on humanitarian workers, who typically lack the mandate to intervene in abduction cases, the Italian government employed an Italian NGO.[103] This prisoner swap for the Italian journalist was reluctantly carried out by Karzai after Romano Prodi, the Italian Minister of Foreign Affairs at the time, threatened to withdraw Italian forces from Afghanistan if the journalist was not released.

The Italian government paid a hefty ransom to secure the release of the Italian journalist. In a controversial twist, the released prisoners included five senior Taliban commanders, among them the infamous Mullah Dadullah Akhund, known for his extreme violence, including beheading captives. Despite this, the journalist's interpreter and driver fell victim to the Taliban,

---

102   In one case, according to a confidential source, the release of a Western hostage abducted in 2008, an attempt was made by the head of Watan to act as an intermediary, requesting a substantial sum of $2 million.

103   "Kidnapped Italian Journalist Freed in Afghanistan," *Reuters*, August 9, 2007, https://www.reuters.com/article/idUSSP42965/.

paying the ultimate price, while the journalist endured two weeks of captivity before finally regaining freedom.[104]

With the increasing insecurity, the persistent specter of abduction rendered it a near-impossible endeavor across vast swathes of the country. Therefore, the arduous task of reconstruction suffered profound setbacks, while international aid organizations found their operations severely curtailed. To navigate the perilous terrain, NGOs were compelled to forge partnerships with local organizations, each possessing varying degrees of expertise, to sustain the critical provision of assistance amid the prevailing challenges. The kidnapping industry aggravated the monitoring capacity of the international community to ensure its aid wasn't being diverted.

3.6.2   *Justifications of Drugs Related Incomes*

The Mujahideen have instrumentalized Islam to rationalize their participation in the economy of violence, particularly in drug production and trafficking while in theory, the marketing and sale of all categories of drugs by any means and for any purpose, is formally prohibited under Muslim law in both peacetime and conflict.[105] These prohibitions find no mention in the two primary sources of Islamic law (*fiqh*), namely the Quran and the Sunna, nor within the sharia as established in the 9th century. The absence of such explicit proscriptions can be attributed to a simple fact: drug trafficking simply did not exist during that era.

It was only later that prohibitions were introduced, as secondary sources of law were developed through the qiyas, a method of rigorous and systematic reasoning guided by the rules of analogy. This method was employed by Muslim jurists to determine legal solutions when the Quran and Sunnah texts provided no direct guidance on a specific issue.[106]

Nonetheless, Islamic jurisprudence offers strategies to circumvent this, known as "*al-hayal.*" The term, which translates to "cunning," refers to the legal tactics that can be devised to navigate the law regarding a specific prohibition,[107] all in the service of "*maslaha*," signifying an absolute interest, benefit,

---

104   Ron Synovitz, "Afghanistan: Kabul Admits Exchanging Taliban Members For Hostage," March 20, 2007, https://www.rferl.org/a/1075376.html.
105   Felicitas Opwis, "*Maṣlaḥa* and the Purpose of the Law: Islamic Discourse on Legal Change from the 4th/10th to 8th/14th Century," in *Maṣlaḥa and the Purpose of the Law* (Brill, 2010), https://brill.com/display/title/12932.
106   Kojiro Nakamura, "IBN Mada's Criticism of Arabic Grammarians," *Orient* 10 (1974): 89–113, https://doi.org/10.5356/orient1960.10.89.
107   Interview with anthropologist Dr Mohammed Fall Ould Bah, Secretary General of the Centre d'Etude et de Recherche sur l'Ouest Saharien (CEROS) in Nouakchott, October 2018.

or ultimate necessity in a context of exigency.[108] *Maslaha* is employed to legitimize decisions that might seem contradictory to the teachings and essence of the Quran, hadiths, and sharia. The construction of *maslaha* is facilitated through "*istislah*," a series of mechanisms utilized by legal experts to identify the optimal solution to a problem within a given context. It's essential to note that this method is merely an instrument for interpreting Islamic law and not an independent source of law itself.[109]

The formalization of this system occurred during the 1979–1989 war in Afghanistan, as it aimed to establish local financial resources to support the jihad against Soviet troops. Mawlawi Ajab Gul, a Pashtun hailing from Kunduz Province, along with other religious leaders, including Mullah Muhammad Nassim Akhundzada, who had family ties to opium production and trafficking, played a pivotal role. In 1981, they issued a fatwa that not only legalized poppy cultivation but also actively encouraged its commercialization.[110] To authorize this activity, the Council of Ulemas invoked a *maslaha* justifying the establishment of opium trafficking as an absolute necessity in order to create funds for the fight against the Soviet enemy:

> We have an obligation to increase opium cultivation and we have an obligation to sell it in order to finance our holy war against Russian non-believers.[111]

3.6.3 Revenues from Narcotics

After the Americans reassumed control of the counter-narcotics mission in 2004, they shifted their focus to highlight the critical connection between terrorism and drug trafficking. The Taliban's revenue sources from narcotics have been a subject of varying estimates ranging widely between $40 million to $400 million annually.[112] Various reports have shed light on the extent of the Taliban's involvement in the narcotics trade. According to SIGAR, about

---

108   Phone interview with Abdallah Annas, September 2019. Mehran Tamadinfar, *Islamic Law and Governance in Contemporary Iran: Transcending Islam for Social, Economic, and Political Order* (Lexington Books, 2015).
109   Mehran Tamadonfar, *Islamic Law and Governance in Contemporary Iran: Transcending Islam for Social, Economic, and Political Order* (Lexington Books, 2015).
110   With regards to Mawlawi Ajab Gul, sources: Muhammad Hussain Shahryar, Political Affairs Officer, UNAMA, November 08, 2016; and Abdullah Anas, 15 November 2016; Steven Fantigrossi, "Afghan Narcoterrorism: The Problem, Its Origins, and Why International Law Enforcement Should Fight It," *Syracuse University, Honors Capstone Projects*, n.d., 2015.
111   *Ibid.*
112   Fazli, "Narcotics Smuggling in Afghanistan: Links between Afghanistan and Pakistan".

60% of the Taliban's revenues come from narcotics. USFOR-A estimated that in 2017, 20% of the total revenue from the domestic narcotics trade ended up in Taliban hands, which resulted'from profits from direct ownership, transportation, and protection fees, licensing fees to drug traffickers, and taxing the harvest.[113] In a June 2019 report, the UNSC cited figures from Afghan authorities, suggesting that despite the decline in poppy production, the Taliban's primary income source remained the international narcotics trade, generating approximately $400 million for the group.[114]

The opium trade and tax collection on opium production have a significant monetary impact, with the UNODC estimating that the amount collected was around $29 million in total taxes in 2018. Notably, at least $3 million directly benefited the Taliban. However, interpreting these figures requires caution. Nonetheless, it is evident that a substantial portion of these taxes likely ended up with either the Taliban or local powerbrokers in the regions where poppy cultivation is prevalent.[115] Apart from taxing the opium trade, the Taliban also levied taxes on heroin laboratories and profited from traders involved in smuggling illicit drugs. Additionally, they were known to facilitate logistics for drug syndicates.

In its 2012 report, the UNSC however emphasized that the widely held belief that the poppy economy in Afghanistan was the primary funding source for the Taliban needed careful examination. While it did generate substantial funds and financed a significant portion of the insurgency in major poppy-growing provinces, the revenues from the drug trade proved inadequate to cover the expenses associated with insurgent activities in other regions. Although the Taliban's share of the poppy trade was significant in absolute terms, it constituted a relatively small percentage of their overall funding. This observation suggests that the Taliban did not actively prioritize exploiting this potential revenue source.[116]

---

113 SIGAR, "Counternarcotics: Lessons from the U.S. Experience in Afghanistan".
114 UN Secretary-General, "The Situation in Afghanistan and Its Implications for International Peace and Security: Report of the Secretary-General," January 28, 2022, https://digitallibrary.un.org/record/3956568.
115 UNODC, "Afghanistan Opium Survey 2019. Socio-Economic Survey Report: Drivers, Causes and Consequences of Opium Poppy Cultivation.," Report (Vienna: United Nations Office on Drugs and Crime, February 2021), https://www.unodc.org/documents/crop-monitoring/Afghanistan/20210217_report_with_cover_for_web_small.pdf.
116 UN Secretary-General, "The Situation in Afghanistan and Its Implications for International Peace and Security: Report of the Secretary-General," December 6, 2012, https://digitallibrary.un.org/record/740267.

3.6.4 Financial Support from Drug Lords

According to the UNSC June 2019 report, the Taliban's entanglement in the narcotics trade in Afghanistan revealed a multifaceted relationship with criminal entities, showcasing distinct patterns of engagement. The first type of relationship was characterized by a mutualistic alliance, wherein the Taliban leverages pre-existing networks of narcotics traffickers to bolster its financial resources. Notably, drug barons such as Abdul Habib Alizai and Lahore Jan adopted a strategic approach by entrusting the management of their illicit enterprises and money laundering endeavors to third parties. This method allowed the Taliban to maintain a level of detachment from direct criminal activities while benefiting from the proceeds generated through the narcotics trade, ultimately serving as a lucrative revenue stream for the group. Conversely, the second type of cooperation involved a more overt collaboration between the Taliban and influential Afghan drug lords. Within this category, prominent figures like Hajji Juma Khan and Hajji Azizullah Alizai play a pivotal role by actively funding the Taliban's operations through the financial gains accrued from their direct involvement in the illegal narcotics trade. These vital patrons provide critical financial support to the Taliban's activities, which range from insurgency operations to broader organizational expenses.[117]

Similarly, drug lord Haji Bashir Noorzai had close ties with the Taliban[118] and received protection for his drug operations in exchange for supporting the group. He was apprehended by the DEA in 2005 in New York while attempting to evade US intelligence seeking information on Mullah Omar, Osama Bin Laden, and drug production. Subsequently, he received a life sentence in 2009 for conspiring to import over $50 million worth of heroin into the US and other countries.[119]

In July 2022, Mullah Yaqoob Mujahid, the son of Mullah Omar and the current Taliban Minister of Defense conducted a secret diplomatic mission to Doha to negotiate Noorzai's release with US representatives. The proposed deal involved exchanging Noorzai for an American who had been held captive by the Taliban since 2020. Upon his arrival in Kabul, Noorzai was warmly

---

117 UN Secretary-General, "The Situation in Afghanistan and Its Implications for International Peace and Security: Report of the Secretary-General," February 27, 2015, https://digitallibrary.un.org/record/789285.
118 Al Jazeera Staff, "US-Taliban Prisoner Swap: Who Are Mark Frerichs, Bashir Noorzai?," September 19, 2022, https://www.aljazeera.com/news/2022/9/19/us-taliban-prisoner-swap-who-are-mark-frerichs-bashir-noorzai.
119 Al Jazeera Staff.

welcomed by Amir Khan Muttaqi, the current Taliban Minister of Foreign Affairs.[120]

3.6.5 Additional Financial with Holdings

The Taliban's financial operations went beyond opium taxation, including a diverse range of revenue streams.[121] They acquired significant resources through a highly profitable taxation system, especially as they expanded their control over major trade routes and border crossings. By imposing taxes on various goods, farmers, and traders, they bolstered their financial strength, effectively ensuring compliance from Afghan traders traveling through their controlled areas.

Extortion had been a major financial lifeline for the Taliban, covering up to 70% of their operational expenses and, in certain regions, surpassing opium revenue.[122] The Haqqani network, lacking access to opium, heavily depended on extortion and kidnappings as their primary income sources. Notably, they imposed a tax ranging from approximately $135 to $400 dollars on skilled expatriate workers from the Wasiri community in the Arab states of the Persian Gulf.[123]

The Taliban leveraged taxes on Western-funded development and infrastructure projects, such as roads, schools, and clinics, to secure a steady income. Another lucrative source was taxing truckers supplying international forces across Afghanistan, resulting in significant annual profits. Furthermore, the group exploited revenue generation from services offered by the Afghan government, like billing electricity consumers in various regions, yielding over a million annually.[124]

3.6.6 Taliban's Involvement in the Mining Sector

In 2010, Afghanistan's mineral reserves, valued at over $900 billion, were identified by the United States Geological Survey (USGS).[125] These reserves included

---

120   Kazim Ehsan, "Taliban's Pablo Escobar: Who Is Haji Bashir Noorzai?," KabulNow, October 13, 2023, https://kabulnow.com/2023/06/talibans-escobar-who-is-haji-bashir-noorzai/.
121   Dawood Azami, "Afghanistan: How Do the Taliban Make Money?," December 22, 2018, https://www.bbc.com/news/world-46554097.
122   *Terrorisme et Insurrection: Évolution Des Dynamiques Conflictuelles et Réponses Des États*, 1st ed. (Presses de l'Université du Québec, 2013), https://doi.org/10.2307/j.ctv18pgs08.
123   *Terrorisme et Insurrection*.
124   Dawood Azami, "Afghanistan".
125   Adrienne Bober, "How Lapis Lazuli Turned One Afghan Mining District to the Taliban," *New Security Beat* (blog), August 25, 2016, https://www.newsecuritybeat.org/2016/08/lapis-lazuli-turned-afghan-mining-town-taliban/.

copper, iron, gold, and more than one million metric tons of rare earth elements.[126] Considered vital for the country's economic growth, these resources attracted interest from various parties, including insurgent groups, and were estimated to potentially yield up to $2 billion in annual tax revenue for the central government. The mining sector became the Taliban's second-largest revenue source nationally, despite contributing less than 1% to the state budget.

In 2014, illegal mining in Afghanistan involved a web of actors tied to the economy of violence, including government representatives, criminal networks, and insurgency groups. According to Global Witness, the mining zones of Deodara and Kuran wa Munjan in Badakhshan Province alone contributed a staggering $20 million to various armed groups. These estimates, though conservative, revealed the significant financial impact of illegal mining. Out of the $20 million, approximately $18 million was channeled to Commander Malek and informal armed groups associated with him.[127] Additionally, both the Taliban and armed groups allegedly linked to Zulmai Mujadid, a former member of the Afghan Lower House of Parliament and a loyal supporter of Hamid Karzai, received over $1 million each.[128]

The Taliban's involvement in the extractive sector can be categorized into three main types: direct extraction in areas under their control, extortion tactics in mining operations, and acting as "service providers" for unauthorized mining activities. These activities enable them to accumulate substantial profits and control access to valuable resources, impacting Afghanistan's economy and governance:[129]

1. Direct control of certain areas: The Taliban extracted natural resources, such as onyx marble in Helmand's southern part, smuggled it globally with forged documents, and earned substantial profits.

---

126 Raphaël Danino-Perraud, "Les ressources minérales dans le développement de l'Afghanistan," GeoStrategia—L'agora stratégique 2.0, February 13, 2018, https://www.geostrategia.fr/les-ressources-minerales-dans-le-developpement-de-lafghanistan/.
127 "Full Report: War in the Treasury of the People: Afghanistan, Lapis Lazuli and the Battle for Mineral Wealth," Business & Human Rights Resource Centre, June 4, 2016, https://www.business-humanrights.org/en/latest-news/full-report-war-in-the-treasury-of-the-people-afghanistan-lapis-lazuli-and-the-battle-for-mineral-wealth/.
128 "Full Report".
129 UNSC, "Eleventh report of the Analytical Support and Sanctions Monitoring Team submitted pursuant to resolution 2501 (2019) concerning the Taliban and other associated individuals and entities constituting a threat to the peace, stability and security of Afghanistan," *United Nations Security Council*, 27 May, 2020 https://www.securitycouncilreport.org/atf/cf/%7B65BFCF9B-6D27-4E9C-8CD3-CF6E4FF96FF9%7D/s_2020_415_e.pdf.

2. Extortion in unstable regions: In areas with weaker Taliban control, they extorted payments from individuals involved in mining, like in Kuran wa Munjan District for lapis-lazuli. They offered protection and secure mining operations in exchange for money.
3. "Service providers" for illegal mining: Local Taliban groups acted as facilitators for unlicensed mining operations, preventing government intervention. They received a share of the revenue and charged fees for transporting illegally extracted precious stones, potentially yielding millions of dollars annually.[130]

3.6.7 *Zakat, Riba Duties, and External Donations*

Over the course of two decades of international presence in Afghanistan, external financial support played a prominent role, with contributions coming from wealthy individuals. Private citizens from Pakistan and several Arab countries in the Persian Gulf, including Saudi Arabia, the United Arab Emirates, and Qatar, were considered the largest individual contributors to the Taliban. Funding for terrorist organizations in Afghanistan indirectly originates from significant amounts of money collected through *zakat* and *riba* duties. These financial resources are meant to fulfill a duty of solidarity and provide development aid to conflict-ridden countries, particularly those with a Muslim majority. These funds are occasionally funneled to terrorist groups through non-profit organizations (NPOs). Numerous NPOs operate under multiple aliases, exemplified by the al-Haramain Islamic Foundation, which has been identified under 26 different spellings and configurations.[131] The UN Security Council listed the Al-Haramain Foundation Afghanistan branch in 2004 for its ties to AQ and the Taliban, providing financial and logistical support. It was associated with the Saudi-based al-Haramain Islamic Foundation, a global funder of AQ.[132]

---

130 UNSC, "Report of the Analytical Support and Sanctions Monitoring Team on specific cases of cooperation between organized crime syndicates and individuals, groups, undertakings and entities eligible for listing under paragraph 1 of Security Council resolution 2160 (2014)," *United Nations Security Council*, February 2, 2015, https://www.securitycouncilreport.org/atf/cf/%7B65BFCF9B-6D27-4E9C-8CD3-CF6E4FF96FF9%7D/s_2015_79.pdf.
131 Nimrod Raphaeli, "Islamic Banking—A Fast-Growing Industry," *American Civil Entities Union*, September 23, 2004, https://www.aclu.org/wp-content/uploads/legal-documents/ACLURM002789.pdf.
132 United Nations Security Council, "Al-Haramain: Afghanistan Branch," March 14, 2022, https://www.un.org/securitycouncil/sanctions/1267/aq_sanctions_list/summaries/entity/al-haramain%3A-afghanistan-branch.

This external funding significantly impacted the dynamics of terrorism in Afghanistan and beyond, highlighting the challenges in addressing and mitigating such illicit financial flows.

3.6.7.1 The Role of Zakat in Financing Extremist Activities

Zakat which translates to almsgiving in Arabic plays a pivotal role in financing extremist activities. Donations can be made through various channels, including mosques, trusted individuals, specialized organizations, or government committees. However, the discrete nature of zakat payments can lead to transparency issues, as the exact amounts donated by individuals might not be fully disclosed to the community, allowing room for misuse or diversion of funds by terrorist organizations and other actors of the economy of violence like some of the warlords as Abdul Rasul Sayyaf, a former MP.

Each year, the practice of *zakat* generates huge amounts of money: as a vast majority of Muslims throughout the world comply with this duty,[133] it is estimated that the annual *zakat* donations amount to $12 billion in Saudi Arabia alone.[134] Powerful local NPOs collect part of these donations either directly or via transfers to Islamic banks. In either case, tracking these transactions is difficult both for the regulatory bodies of the countries where the transactions take place and for the international institutions in charge of tracking terrorist financing. Furthermore, according to the rules of Islamic finance, once a banking operation is completed, all evidence is destroyed, and it is impossible to trace it back.[135]

3.6.7.2 Islamic Banking and Its Role in Financing Extremist Activities

While these organizations have their own direct fundraising channels, they also benefit from the financial manna generated by the increasing number of "Islamic banks." Based on the Koranic prohibition of interest (*riba*), many institutions have developed since the 1970s to promote a form of Islamic economy, a third way between capitalism and socialism. For each Islamic bank, a supervisory religious council comprising *ulema* ensures that operations are legal in Islam. The first of its kind, the Islamic Development Bank was established in 1975 as an interstate bank whose capitalization was determined by the Saudi regime. Two other major banking groups emerged, each with an international network of institutions (banks, insurance companies, investment companies): the Dar al-Mal al-Islami group founded in 1981 by Prince

---

133 United Nations Security Council.
134 United Nations Security Council.
135 United Nations Security Council.

Muhammad al-Faisal (founder of Faisal banks in Sudan and Egypt) and the AI-Baraka group founded in 1982 by Saudi businessman, the deceased Saleh Abdullah Kamel, the billionaire founder and chairman of the banking and real estate conglomerate Dallah Albaraka Group.[136] Some elements of the Islamic banking network may have been involved in the transfer and/or laundering of money intended for terrorist organizations

In addition to traditional financial activities, these banks generate two types of funds illustrating the proximity between the financial and charitable sectors. They have their own *zakat* funds deducted from depositors' accounts, and they reconvert some funds considered illicit under Islam into charitable works. Indeed, in a financial system where interest-bearing loans are dominant, they are led to conduct transactions with interest. In order to comply with the prohibition of *riba* and to maintain Islamic legitimacy, the religious supervisory council requires that funds derived from interest be converted to charity.

3.6.7.3 Extent of External Donations to Taliban

A classified US intelligence report estimated that in 2008, the Taliban received $106 million from foreign sources, particularly from Gulf states. In 2021, US counter-terrorism estimated that $60 million was offered annually to the Taliban by citizens from Saudi Arabia, Pakistan, Qatar, and Iran.[137] Furthermore, they accused the States in these countries of providing the Taliban with up to $500 million annually.[138] Nevertheless, the report acknowledges that verifying these figures is complicated due to the use of payment methods that evade any form of control by donor countries.[139] Many of these donations to the Taliban originated from charitable organizations and private trusts located in the Afghanistan Center for Research and Policy Studies estimated these donations to be around $150 to $200 million annually.

In reality, the external donors of the Taliban and other insurgency or terrorist groups in Afghanistan played a role in the resurgence and empowerment of actors within the economy of violence. The substantial financial support received by these actors endowed them with the means to execute a greater number of attacks and perpetrate atrocities with heightened efficiency. This

---

136 Abdullah Shihri, "Billionaire Saudi Banking Tycoon Dead at 79, Family Says," AP News, May 19, 2020, https://apnews.com/general-news-e6f60cc2d3be814129f4f4f6f0642004.
137 Dawood Azami, "Afghanistan".
138 Dawood Azami.
139 Michel Santi, "L'argent Des Talibans," August 22, 2021, https://www.latribune.fr/opinions/tribunes/l-argent-des-talibans-890961.html.

influx of resources bolstered their operational capabilities, enabling them to expand their influence and unleash havoc with intensified impact.

3.7 Regional Influence in the Economy of Violence

3.7.1 *Background*

In the intricate narrative of Afghanistan's state-building efforts following the fall of the Taliban in 2001, the roles assumed by both regional and global players can be classified into three distinct tiers, each marked by a unique level of influence and resonance. Taking a prominent stance were the primary actors—Iran, Pakistan, and Russia—exerting substantial influence and molding the core narrative. Simultaneously, secondary actors like the European Union and Japan subtly interwove their contributions into the unfolding fabric. On a broader scale, the periphery introduced the United States, Saudi Arabia, India, and China, each contributing their distinct shades to the evolving tableau.[140]

The intricate interplay of Afghanistan's geopolitical, economic, social, and ethnic complexities set the stage, responding to the magnetic forces stemming from both regional and global dynamics. This symphony of influence and interaction elegantly converges to create a sophisticated masterpiece, emblematic of the nuanced interplay between Afghanistan and its diverse spectrum of stakeholders.

Pakistan, India, and Iran exerted substantial influence during Afghanistan's two-decade international engagement. Yet, it is crucial to recognize that the impact of other nations, including China, Saudi Arabia, Qatar, UAE, and Russia, on Afghanistan's conflict-ridden landscape should not be underestimated.

In this complex context, Pakistan, India, and Iran navigated a rich interplay of cultural dynamics and linguistic diversity, embracing Pashtun, Persian, Urdu, and Hindi as eloquent Indo-European elements. This interaction extended to social dynamics, economic significance, political repercussions, and deep-seated ethnic bonds. Woven over centuries, these elements collectively compose a compelling tapestry of shared history.

---

140 Mohammad Javad Aghajari and Morteza Karimi, "The Role of Regional Players in the State-Building Process of Afghanistan During the Taliban Era and Post-Taliban Period (in Persian)," International Relation Studies, Vol. 8, Number 30, September 30, 2014, Page 57–104, https://prb.ctb.iau.ir/article_515652.html.

3.7.2   *Afghanistan and Pakistan: A Geopolitical Dance*
In Afghanistan's complex history, the economy of violence is fueled by geopolitical interests, with Pakistan playing a major perpetuating role. Since the 1970s, it has supported Afghan factions, escalating involvement during the Soviet invasion (1979–1989). Through the Inter-Services Intelligence (ISI), Pakistan aided the mujahideen and served as a key US ally in facilitating American assistance to Afghan fighters.

Since 1994, the ISI has wielded its influence over the Afghan Taliban by providing sanctuaries, assistance, and even corrective measures for those straying from their directives.[141] This strategic interplay has empowered the ISI with substantial leverage to mold the contours of Taliban strategies. Notably, during the Taliban's rule from 1996 to 2001, Pakistan stood among a handful of nations formally recognizing their authority. Guided by this paramount goal, Islamabad's tactics are consistently geared toward preventing Afghanistan from falling into a pro-India sphere. Whether through a politically neutral Afghan government or alignment with Pakistan's interests, Islamabad seeks to singularly channel its focus onto its relationship with India. As articulated by a former Taliban minister, the substantial support extended by the ISI to the Taliban is driven by strategic considerations largely aligned with their own interests. This complex interconnection is intimately linked to a shared concern, specifically, the longstanding Kashmir issue. Therefore, it is justifiable to claim that the deep-seated intricacies of the Afghan situation stem from the enduring rivalry between Pakistan and India, a rivalry that exerts a substantial influence on the dynamics of the region.[142]

As international forces intervened in Afghanistan in 2001, the US aimed to secure Pakistan's assistance for logistical and border control needs, along with aiding anti-Taliban factions.

Pakistan faced a pivotal choice: whether to support American antiterrorism measures. Pakistan's financial reliance on international institutions hindered resistance. Former Pakistani president Musharraf's September 19, 2001, announcement marked Pakistan's alignment with the US and disassociation from the Taliban, positioned as safeguarding national interests against an anti-Pakistani Kabul government.[143] Despite outwardly aligning with the US,

---

141   Matt Waldman, "The Sun in the Sky: The Relationship Between Pakistan's ISI and Afghan Insurgents," June 2010, https://www.files.ethz.ch/isn/117472/dp%2018.pdf.
142   Waldman.
143   Gilles Dorronsoro, "La Grande Illusion. Bilan de La Politique Afghane Du Pakistan," Les études du CERI, December 31, 2014, 84, pp.30 http://sciencespo.fr/ceri/en/content/la-grande-illusion-bilan-de-la-politique-afghane-du-pakistan.

Pakistan engaged in a "double game," simultaneously aiding the Taliban while collaborating with international efforts. This involved offering safe havens, financial backing, and training to the Taliban.¹⁴⁴ Notably, Pakistan provided crucial sanctuaries to the Taliban, who had been ousted from power. These sanctuaries were strategically positioned in Pakistan's tribal areas bordering Afghanistan, historically attracting mujahidin and foreign fighters associated with Al-Qaeda, as well as locally radicalized militants. The Taliban leadership established councils in various Pakistani cities, including Quetta in the Balochistan Province, Peshawar, and Miranshah in the Khyber Pakhtunkhwa Province.

The ISI's deep ties with the Taliban were exposed in a leaked 2012 NATO report, based on 27,000 interrogations of 4,000 detainees. It revealed extensive Pakistani government support for Taliban attacks on coalition forces and the Afghan government, hinting at direct manipulation. The report also disclosed the familiarity of Pakistani officials and the ISI with the residences of top Taliban leaders, including Nasiruddin Haqqani, located near the ISI headquarters in Islamabad.¹⁴⁵

In the intricate dance of support from Pakistan to the Taliban, the threads of assistance were deliberately woven into a nuanced fabric, making the identification of direct sources elusive. This support, contributing to an unsettling "economy of violence," diverted foreign aid originally intended to counterterrorism, redirecting it to militant groups, fostering drug trafficking, and subtly influencing peace negotiations. The resulting instability echoed not only within Afghanistan but resonated across the broader region, notably in Pakistan, where the seeds of violence-driven economic activities found fertile ground, adding a poignant layer to the geopolitical narrative.

Since 2001, Pakistan has navigated the Afghan crisis with a nuanced blend of diplomacy and a dual military strategy, supported financially by the U.S. Driven by its persistent conflict with India, Pakistan sought strategic depth in Afghanistan. Its intricate ties with terrorism stemmed from internal conflicts linked to the feud with India. Historically tolerating Afghan instability, Pakistan then recognized the imperative of regional stability. Pursuing peace, Pakistan desired a nuanced Taliban return, subtly stirring Afghan discontent.

---

144 Dorothée Vandamme, "Afghanistan : pourquoi le Pakistan a un rôle important dans l'arrivée au pouvoir des talibans," lejdd.fr, September 16, 2021, https://www.lejdd.fr/International/afghanistan-pourquoi-le-pakistan-a-un-role-important-dans-larrivee-au-pouvoir-des-talibans-4066894.

145 "Pakistan Helping Afghan Taliban—Nato," BBC News, January 31, 2012, sec. Asia, https://www.bbc.com/news/world-asia-16821218.

China's support to Pakistan to counter India added complexity, fueling societal resentment in Afghanistan.

3.7.3 *India*

India strategically places Afghanistan in its innermost foreign policy circle due to historical and educational ties.

Ousted during the Taliban's rise, India maintained post-2001 involvement through investments, avoiding direct confrontation with Pakistan. Rapidly reopening diplomatic relations, India contributed to Afghan development funds, signed a 2011 strategic partnership agreement, and increased military cooperation post-2008. Strategically, India aimed to counter Chinese and Pakistani influence in the northwest while securing economic interests. Leveraging the Chabahar port in Iran, India aimed to enhance regional connectivity, bypassing Pakistan and gaining access to resources and markets in Iran and Central Asia.

India's strategic push to expand influence in Afghanistan, countering both Pakistani and Chinese sway, added intricate layers to the situation, with far-reaching consequences for Afghanistan and the broader regional landscape of conflict-driven economies. Notably, Indian intelligence operatives were active on the ground, exemplified by the targeted assassination of Mr. Laghmani, the deputy chief of intelligence, with alleged ties to the Indian intelligence service. This incident unfolded just a month before the Taliban orchestrated an attack on the Indian ambassador in Afghanistan in November 2009, underlining the complex web of geopolitical maneuvering and covert operations in the region.

3.7.4 *Islamic Republic of Iran (IRI)*

Iran's role in Afghanistan evolved in the past decade. Initially supporting Shiite groups and the Sunni-led Rabbani government, tensions arose when the Taliban seized Kabul in 1996. Relations soured further in 1998 after the Taliban intentionally killed Iranian diplomats in Mazar-e Sharif. However, in 2001, Iran became a committed contributor to post-Taliban reconstruction. During Iran's "golden era" of support (2002–2007), it provided over half a billion dollars for Afghanistan's recovery initiatives.[146]

Beyond the realm of financial aid, Iran extended a compassionate embrace to the multitude of Afghans who sought refuge from the protracted conflict that had ravaged their homeland since 1979. Notably, over 1.5 million undocumented

---

146 Bruce Koepke, *Iran's Policy on Afghanistan: The Evolution of Strategic Pragmatism* (SIPRI, 2013), https://www.sipri.org/publications/2013/irans-policy-afghanistan-evolution-strategic-pragmatism.

Afghan migrant workers found their place within Iran's workforce, emerging as a lifeline for families and communities across Afghanistan.[147] The remittances they sent back served as a crucial support pillar for vital aspects of life, including through illicit channels, favoring human and drug trafficking operations from one side of the border to the other.

In anticipation of a prolonged international presence in Afghanistan surpassing the initially projected timeline, Iran's strategic outlook underwent a significant transformation. As early as October 2003, when ISAF's mandate expanded to cover all provinces, Iran started viewing the presence of foreign military forces near its borders as a direct security challenge. This prompted Iran to adopt a strategic approach aimed at undermining the United States' objectives. Following the Kabul-Washington Security Agreement of 2014 permitted a portion of US military forces to remain in Afghanistan beyond the conclusion of the international mission in 2014, Iran tactfully adopted a nuanced stance, strategically supporting the Afghan government but at the same time assisting actors associated with the "economy of violence," such as the Taliban and pro-IRI political and armed groups in Afghanistan as a countermeasure to US policy. This approach, though not as extensive as its support for anti-American Shiite groups in Iraq, experienced periodic upswings, particularly during moments of escalated tensions between Iran and the United States.[148] This calculated involvement can be seen as a deliberate utilization of violence as a tool to further strategic objectives, within the broader context of geopolitical maneuvering.

During this period, a significant incident came to the fore, spotlighting Iran's assertive actions. The Iranian navy detained 15 British marines from two patrol boats after intercepting a cargo ship in the Persian Gulf. In parallel, between 2007 and 2009, reports multiplied regarding the inflow of Iranian weaponry into regions under Taliban control within Afghanistan. This phenomenon coincided with Iran's unveiling of a new policy framework. Afghan security forces reported a substantial seizure of a 10-ton cache of weapons in the Ghurian District of Herat Province, positioned near the border with Iran.[149]

---

147 Bruce Koepke.
148 Seid Ahmad Fateminejad and Seyed Mojtaba Alawi, "Explaining Afghanistan's National Security with Respect to the US-Iran Conflict (2001–2021) (in Persian)," *Iranian Research Letter of International Politics* 11, no. 2 (March 21, 2023), https://doi.org/10.22067/irlip.2022.72753.1162.
149 Ron Synovitz, "Afghanistan: U.S. Worried Iran Sending Chinese Weapons To Taliban," *Radio Free Europe/Radio Liberty* (RFE/RL), September 14, 2007, https://milnewstbay.pbworks.com/f/IRN-CHN-WPNS-TALIBAN-14SEPT07.pdf.

Iran's endorsement of the peace process in 2010, exemplified by diplomatic engagements with Taliban delegations, underscored its ambitions to play a decisive role in shaping Afghanistan's path toward reconciliation. However, this commitment has not deterred Tehran from continuing its decision to assist insurgents linked to the Taliban or HIG as well as other armed groups in opposition to coalition forces within Afghanistan.

The Islamic Republic of Iran adopted a nuanced strategy in Afghanistan, distinguishing itself from both India and Pakistan. This approach involved balancing support for the Afghan government and actively engaging in the country's reconstruction while discreetly providing backing to insurgents and warlords associated with the Islamic Republic.

Iran's primary objectives were the cessation of NATO's presence, specifically, the withdrawal of American forces from Afghan soil, coupled with the pursuit of consensus among Afghanistan's diverse factions and the establishment of a friendly government in Kabul. Therefore, Iran's support for the Taliban and various warlords should not be misinterpreted as a validation of Pakistan's growing influence.

Bibliography

A Special Interview with James Dobbins, the Former US Representative in Afghanistan, 2022. https://www.youtube.com/watch?v=DmV7woqu9xo.

Abdul, Basit. "Why Did the Afghan Army Disintegrate so Quickly?," August 17, 2021. https://www.aljazeera.com/opinions/2021/8/17/why-did-the-afghan-army-disintegrate-so-quickly.

Abdullah, Shihri. "Billionaire Saudi Banking Tycoon Dead at 79, Family Says." AP News, May 19, 2020. https://apnews.com/general-news-e6f60cc2d3be814129f4f4f6f0642004.

Adam, Baczko. *La Guerre Par Le Droit—Les Tribunaux Taliban En Afghanistan—CNRS Editions*, 2021. https://www.cnrseditions.fr/catalogue/relations-internationales/la-guerre-par-le-droit/.

Adrienne, Bober. "How Lapis Lazuli Turned One Afghan Mining District to the Taliban." *New Security Beat* (blog), August 25, 2016. https://www.newsecuritybeat.org/2016/08/lapis-lazuli-turned-afghan-mining-town-taliban/.

Aghajari, Mohammad Javad, and Morteza, Karimi. "The Role of Regional Actors in the Process of Afghanistan State-Building during Taliban and Post-Taliban." (2015): 57–104.

Al Jazeera, Staff. "US-Taliban Prisoner Swap: Who Are Mark Frerichs, Bashir Noorzai?," September 19, 2022. https://www.aljazeera.com/news/2022/9/19/us-taliban-prisoner-swap-who-are-mark-frerichs-bashir-noorzai.

Alijani, Ershad. "'We Haven't Eaten for Days': Afghan Soldiers Suffer amid Widespread Corruption." The Observers—France 24, February 18, 2020. https://observers.france24.com/en/20200218-afghanistan-corruption-rations-soldiers-army-eat.

ANI. "Ex-Afghan Governor Admits to Helping Taliban." *The Indian Express* (blog), November 21, 2009. https://indianexpress.com/article/news-archive/print/exafghan-governor-admits-to-helping-taliban/.

Armiger, Anthony. "United Against Drugs? Divergent Counternarcotic Strategies of US Government Agencies in Afghanistan." SSRN Scholarly Paper. Rochester, NY, January 15, 2015. https://papers.ssrn.com/abstract=2721586.

Baczko, Adam. "Juger en situation de guerre civile. Les cours de justice Taleban en Afghanistan (2001–2013)." *Politix* 104, no. 4 (2013): 25–46. https://doi.org/10.3917/pox.104.0025.

Baczko, Adam. "Les effets pervers de l'exportation du droit dans des guerres civiles. L'intervention militaire en Afghanistan (2001–2014)." *Droit et société* 110, no. 1 (2022): 131–49. https://doi.org/10.3917/drs1.110.0131.

BBC News. "Pakistan Helping Afghan Taliban—Nato." January 31, 2012, sec. Asia. https://www.bbc.com/news/world-asia-16821218.

Bender, Bryan and Paul, Mcleary. "The $88 Billion Gamble on the Afghan Army That's Going up in Smoke." POLITICO, August 13, 2021. https://www.politico.com/news/2021/08/13/afghan-army-pentagon-504469.

Bjelica, Jelena. "Lost in Procedure: How a corruption case in the Afghan parliament was (not) dealt with." Afghanistan Analysts Network—English, January 4, 2018. https://www.afghanistan-analysts.org/en/reports/political-landscape/lost-in-procedure-how-a-corruption-case-in-the-afghan-parliament-was-not-dealt-with/.

Borger, Julian, and Kate, Connolly. "Evidence of Fraud as Hamid Karzai Passes Threshold in Afghan Poll." *The Guardian*, September 8, 2009, sec. World news. https://www.theguardian.com/world/2009/sep/08/hamid-karzai-afghan-election-fraud.

Braw, Elisabeth. "The Afghan Collapse: An Insider's Account." CEPA, August 23, 2022. https://cepa.org/article/the-afghan-collapse-an-insiders-account/.

Brown, Pamela. "Analysis of the Afghan Defense Appointments." Institute for the Study of War, 2010. https://www.jstor.org/stable/resrep07865.

Bruce, Koepke. *Iran's Policy on Afghanistan: The Evolution of Strategic Pragmatism*. SIPRI, 2013. https://www.sipri.org/publications/2013/irans-policy-afghanistan-evolution-strategic-pragmatism.

Business & Human Rights Resource Centre. "Full Report: War in the Treasury of the People: Afghanistan, Lapis Lazuli and the Battle for Mineral Wealth," June 4,

2016. https://www.business-humanrights.org/en/latest-news/full-report-war-in-the-treasury-of-the-people-afghanistan-lapis-lazuli-and-the-battle-for-mineral-wealth/.

Carter, Stephen, and Kate, Clark. "No Shortcut to Stability: Justice, Politics and Insurgency in Afghanistan," December 15, 2010. https://policycommons.net/artifacts/612958/no-shortcut-to-stability/1592607/.

Clark, Kate, and Roxanna, Shapour. "The Khalid Payenda Interview (1): An insider's view of politicking, graft and the fall of the Republic." Afghanistan Analysts Network—English, September 27, 2021. https://www.afghanistan-analysts.org/en/reports/economy-development-environment/the-khalid-payenda-interview-1-an-insiders-view-of-politicking-graft-and-the-fall-of-the-republic/.

Clark, Kate. "How to become a minister: bribe the parliament (Updated)." Afghanistan Analysts Network—English, June 30, 2010. https://www.afghanistan-analysts.org/en/reports/political-landscape/how-to-become-a-minister-bribe-the-parliament-updated/.

Clément, Fontanarava. "Les Taliban ont-ils gagné la guerre par le droit ? Une conversation avec Adam Baczko." *Le Grand Continent* (blog), November 11, 2021. https://legrandcontinent.eu/fr/2021/11/11/les-taliban-ont-ils-gagne-la-guerre-par-le-droit-une-conversation-avec-adam-baczko/.

Dawood, Azami. "Afghanistan: How Do the Taliban Make Money?," December 22, 2018. https://www.bbc.com/news/world-46554097.

Deedee, Derksen. "The Politics of Disarmament and Rearmament in Afghanistan." United States Institute of Peace, May 20, 2015. https://www.usip.org/publications/2015/05/politics-disarmament-and-rearmament-afghanistan.

Dexter, Filkins. "Bribes Corrode Afghans' Trust in Government," January 1, 2009. https://www.nytimes.com/2009/01/02/world/asia/02kabul.html.

Dobbins, James, Seth G. Jones, Keith, Crane, and Beth Cole, DeGrasse. "The Beginner's Guide to Nation-Building." RAND Corporation, January 11, 2007. https://www.rand.org/pubs/monographs/MG557.html.

Dobbins, James. "Negotiating with Iran: Reflections from Personal Experience." *The Washington Quarterly* 33, no. 1 (January 1, 2010): 149–62. https://doi.org/10.1080/01636600903424833.

Dorothée, Vandamme. "Afghanistan : pourquoi le Pakistan a un rôle important dans l'arrivée au pouvoir des talibans." lejdd.fr, September 16, 2021. https://www.lejdd.fr/International/afghanistan-pourquoi-le-pakistan-a-un-role-important-dans-larrivee-au-pouvoir-des-talibans-4066894.

Ehsan, Kazim. "Taliban's Pablo Escobar: Who Is Haji Bashir Noorzai?" KabulNow, October 13, 2023. https://kabulnow.com/2023/06/talibans-escobar-who-is-haji-bashir-noorzai/.

Fantigrossi, Steven. "Afghan Narcoterrorism: The Problem, Its Origins, and Why International Law Enforcement Should Fight It." *Syracuse University, Honors Capstone Projects*, n.d., 2015.

Fateminejad, Seid Ahmad, and Seyed, Mojtaba Alawi. "Explaining Afghanistan's National Security with Respect to the US-Iran Conflict (2001–2021) (in Persian)." *Iranian Research Letter of International Politics* 11, no. 2 (March 21, 2023). https://doi.org/10.22067/irlip.2022.72753.1162.

Fazli, Shehryar. "Narcotics Smuggling in Afghanistan: Links between Afghanistan and Pakistan," June 2022. https://globalinitiative.net/wp-content/uploads/2022/06/narcotics-smuggling-in-afghanistan-paper.pdf.

Fazul, Rahim. "Top Afghan General Caught Transporting Heroin in Truck: Officials." NBC News, July 1, 2015. https://www.nbcnews.com/news/world/top-afghan-general-caught-transporting-heroin-truck-n385041.

Filkins, Dexter. "With U.S. Aid, Warlord Builds Afghan Empire." *The New York Times*, June 5, 2010, sec. World. https://www.nytimes.com/2010/06/06/world/asia/06warlords.html.

Frud, Bezhan. "Exclusive: Taliban's Expanding 'Financial Power' Could Make It 'Impervious' To Pressure, Confidential Report Warns," September 16, 2020. https://www.rferl.org/a/exclusive-taliban-s-expanding-financial-power-could-make-it-impervious-to-pressure-secret-nato-report-warns/30842570.html.

George, Packer. The Governing Style Of Ashraf Ghani, The Departing Afghan President, August 15, 2021. https://www.npr.org/2021/08/15/1027962001/the-governing-style-of-ashraf-ghani-the-departing-afghan-president.

Gilles, Dorronsoro. "La Grande Illusion. Bilan de La Politique Afghane Du Pakistan." Les études du CERI, December 31, 2014. http://sciencespo.fr/ceri/en/content/la-grande-illusion-bilan-de-la-politique-afghane-du-pakistan.

Giustozzi, Antonio, and Noor, Ullah. "'Tribes' and Warlords in Southern Afghanistan, 1980–2005." Monograph. London, UK: Crisis States Research Centre, London School of Economics and Political Science, September 2006. http://www.crisisstates.com.

Giustozzi, Antonio. *Empires of Mud: Wars and Warlords in Afghanistan*. Oxford University Press, 2012.

Giustozzi, Antonio. *Koran, Kalashnikov and Laptop: The Neo-Taliban Insurgency in Afghanistan*. Hurst, 2007.

Gossman, Patricia. "Transitional Justice and DDR: The Case of Afghanistan," June 2009. https://www.ictj.org/sites/default/files/ICTJ-DDR-Afghanistan-ResearchBrief-2009-English.pdf.

Grote, Rainer. "Separation of Powers in the New Afghan Constitution." *The Max Planck Institute for Comparative Public Law and International Law*, May 2015. https://zaoerv.de/64_2004/64_2004_4_a_897_916.pdf.

Hakimi, Mehdi J. "The Judiciary and the Rule of Law in Afghanistan." SSRN Scholarly Paper. Rochester, NY, December 1, 2021. https://papers.ssrn.com/abstract=3987775.

Hamidi, Farid, and Aruni, Jayakody. "Separation of Powers under the Afghan Constitution: A Case Study." Refworld, March 2015. https://www.refworld.org/reference/countryrep/areu/2015/en/104992.

Hayes, Geoffrey, and Mark, Sedra. *Afghanistan: Transition under Threat*. Wilfrid Laurier Univ. Press, 2009.

Hussaini, Sayed Reza. "Constitutional Design as the Primary Cause of a Political Tragedy: A Case Study of Afghanistan's 2004 Constitution" 105, no. 3 (2021). https://www.wlv.ac.uk/media/departments/marketing-and-communications/(2022)-7-WLJ-3.pdf.

Ibrahimi, S. Yaqub. "Afghanistan's Political Development Dilemma: The Centralist State Versus a Centrifugal Society." *Journal of South Asian Development* 14, no. 1 (April 1, 2019): 40–61. https://doi.org/10.1177/0973174119839843.

Imbert, Louis. "Scandale étouffé à la Kabul Bank." Le Monde diplomatique, November 1, 2011. https://www.monde-diplomatique.fr/2011/11/IMBERT/46928.

International Crisis Group. "A Force in Fragments: Reconstituting the Afghan National Army," May 12, 2010. https://www.crisisgroup.org/asia/south-asia/afghanistan/force-fragments-reconstituting-afghan-national-army.

International Crisis Group. "Reforming Afghanistan's Broken Judiciary," November 17, 2010. https://www.refworld.org/reference/countryrep/icg/2010/en/76505.

Islamic Republic of Afghanistan. "Afghanistan 2004 Constitution, Article 92." Accessed March 28, 2024. https://www.constituteproject.org/constitution/Afghanistan_2004.

Lang, Arabella, and Ben, Smith. "The Legal Basis for the Invasion of Afghanistan," March 28, 2024. https://commonslibrary.parliament.uk/research-briefings/sn05340/.

Marie, Chêne. "Tackling Judicial Corruption in Afghanistan." U4 Anti-Corruption Resource Centre, September 12, 2007. https://www.u4.no/publications/tackling-judicial-corruption-in-afghanistan.pdf.

Mashal, Mujib. "After Karzai." *The Atlantic*, June 23, 2014. https://www.theatlantic.com/magazine/archive/2014/07/after-karzai/372294/.

McCarthy, Rory, and Ewen MacAskill. "King's Aide Is Favourite to Be next Leader." *The Guardian*, December 3, 2001, sec. World news. https://www.theguardian.com/world/2001/dec/03/afghanistan.ewenmacaskill1.

Michailof, Serge. "The Failure of Nation Building." In *Afghanistan: Autopsy of a Disaster 2001–2021—What Lessons for the Sahel?*, 82–108. Gallimard, 2022.

Michel, Santi. "L'argent Des Talibans," August 22, 2021. https://www.latribune.fr/opinions/tribunes/l-argent-des-talibans-890961.html.

Murtazashvili, Jennifer Brick. "The Collapse of Afghanistan." *Journal of Democracy* 33, no. 1 (2022): 40–54.

Nakamura, Kojiro. "IBN Mada's Criticism of Arabic Grammarians." *Orient* 10 (1974): 89–113. https://doi.org/10.5356/orient1960.10.89.

NATO. "Resolute Support Mission in Afghanistan (2015–2021)." NATO, May 30, 2022. https://www.nato.int/cps/en/natohq/topics_113694.htm.

Opwis, Felicitas. *"Maṣlaḥa* and the Purpose of the Law: Islamic Discourse on Legal Change from the 4th/10th to 8th/14th Century." In Maṣlaḥa *and the Purpose of the Law*. Brill, 2010. https://brill.com/display/title/12932.

Perito, Robert. *Afghanistan's Police: The Weak Link in Security Sector Reform*. Special Report (United States Institute of Peace). Washington, D.C.: United States Institute of Peace, 2009. http://library.usip.org/articles/1012419.1131/1.PDF.

Perrin, Jean-Pierre. "How the Americans Lost Afghanistan." Politique Internationale, 2022. https://politiqueinternationale.com/revue/n174/article/comment-les-ame ricains-ont-perdu-lafghanistan.

Peters, G. Traffickers and truckers: Illicit Afghan and Pakistani power structures with a shadowy but influential role, Washington, DC: PRISM, 2017.

Raphaël, Danino-Perraud. "Les ressources minérales dans le développement de l'Afghanistan." GeoStrategia—L'agora stratégique 2.0, February 13, 2018. https://www.geostrategia.fr/les-ressources-minerales-dans-le-developpement-de-lafghanistan/.

Raphaeli, Nimrod. "Islamic Banking—A Fast-Growing Industry." *American Civil Entities Union*, September 23, 2004. https://www.aclu.org/wp-content/uploads/legal-documents/ACLURM002789.pdf.

Reuter, Christoph. "Le Seigneur de l'autoroute." *Vice* (blog), December 10, 2009. https://www.vice.com/fr/article/8gyn4v/warlord-of-the-highway-226-v3n12.

Reuters. "Kidnapped Italian Journalist Freed in Afghanistan." August 9, 2007. https://www.reuters.com/article/idUSSP42965/.

Reuters. "Leaked Memo Fuels Accusations of Ethnic Bias in Afghan Government." *Reuters*, September 21, 2017, sec. World. https://www.reuters.com/article/idUSKCN1BW147/.

Reuters. "Taliban Say S.Korea Paid over $20 Mln Ransom." September 1, 2007. https://www.reuters.com/article/idUSCOL317931/.

Ron, Synovitz. "Afghanistan: Kabul Admits Exchanging Taliban Members For Hostage," March 20, 2007. https://www.rferl.org/a/1075376.html.

Rossi, Simonetta, and Antonio, Giustozzi. "Disarmament, Demobilisation and Reintegration of Ex-Combatants (DDR) in Afghanistan: Constraints and Limited Capabilities." Monograph. London, UK: Crisis States Research Centre, London School of Economics and Political Science, June 2006. http://www.crisisstates.com.

Ruttig, Thomas. "Afghanistan's War Economy." Rosa Luxemburg Stiftung, September 23, 2022. https://www.rosalux.de/en/news/id/47021/afghanistans-war-economy.

Saeed, Huma. *Transitional Justice and Socio-Economic Harm: Land Grabbing in Afghanistan*. Taylor & Francis, 2022.

Schetter, Conrad. "Afghanistanís Economy of Violence." *Center for Development Research, University of Bonn*, February 9, 2002. https://www.zef.de/fileadmin/user_upload/N09-2-2002-eng.pdf.

Secretary-General, UN. "The Situation in Afghanistan and Its Implications for International Peace and Security: Report of the Secretary-General," December 6, 2012. https://digitallibrary.un.org/record/740267.

Secretary-General, UN. "The Situation in Afghanistan and Its Implications for International Peace and Security: Report of the Secretary-General," February 27, 2015. https://digitallibrary.un.org/record/789285.

Secretary-General, UN. "The Situation in Afghanistan and Its Implications for International Peace and Security: Report of the Secretary-General," January 28, 2022. https://digitallibrary.un.org/record/3956568.

Sediqi, Abdul Qadir, and Hamid, Shalizi. "Afghan President and Rival Strike Power-Sharing Deal after Months of Feuding." *Reuters*, May 17, 2020, sec. World. https://www.reuters.com/article/idUSKBN22T09H/.

SIGAR. "Counternarcotics: Lessons from the U.S. Experience in Afghanistan." SIGAR, June 2018. https://www.sigar.mil/pdf/lessonslearned/SIGAR-18-52-LL-Executive-Summary.pdf.

SIGAR. "Why the Afghan Security Forces Collapsed." SIGAR, February 2023. https://www.sigar.mil/pdf/evaluations/SIGAR-23-16-IP.pdf.

Sopko, John F and David H. Young. "The Factors Leading to the Collapse of the Afghan Government and Its Security Forces." Special Inspector General for Afghanistan Reconstruction, March 2, 2023. https://www.sigar.mil/pdf/speeches/SIGAR_John_Sopko_David_Young_Berlin_Speech_2023-03-02.pdf.

"Special Committee on the Canadian Mission in Afghanistan: Number 015, 2nd session, 40th Parliament," November 18, 2009. https://www.ourcommons.ca/DocumentViewer/en/40-2/AFGH/meeting-15/evidence.

Staff. "The Afghan Interim Government: Who's Who." *The Guardian*, December 6, 2001, sec. World news. https://www.theguardian.com/world/2001/dec/06/afghanistan1.

Sufizada, Hanif. "The Taliban Are Megarich—Here's Where They Get the Money They Use to Wage War in Afghanistan." The Conversation, December 8, 2020. http://theconversation.com/the-taliban-are-megarich-heres-where-they-get-the-money-they-use-to-wage-war-in-afghanistan-147411.

Susannah, George. "4,000 Afghan Security Forces Dead, 1,000 Missing in Final Battles against Taliban, Former Official Says." Washington Post, December 29, 2021. https://www.washingtonpost.com/world/2021/12/30/afghanistan-security-forces-deaths/.

Swenson, Geoffrey. "Why U.S. Efforts to Promote the Rule of Law in Afghanistan Failed." *International Security* 42, no. 1 (July 1, 2017): 114–51. https://doi.org/10.1162/ISEC_a_00285.

Synovitz, Ron. "Afghanistan: U.S. Worried Iran Sending Chinese Weapons To Taliban." *Radio Free Europe/Radio Liberty (RFE/RL)*, September 14, 2007. https://milnewstbay.pbworks.com/f/IRN-CHN-WPNS-TALIBAN-14SEPT07.pdf.

Tamadonfar, Mehran. *Islamic Law and Governance in Contemporary Iran: Transcending Islam for Social, Economic, and Political Order*. Lexington Books, 2015.

Terrorisme et Insurrection: Évolution Des Dynamiques Conflictuelles et Réponses Des États. 1st ed. Presses de l'Université du Québec, 2013. https://doi.org/10.2307/j.ctv18pgso8.

Timory, Shoaib. "Judicial Independence in Afghanistan: Legal Framework and Practical Challenges." *Afghanistan Research and Evaluation Unit Organization* (blog), February 21, 2021. https://areu.org.af/publication/2102/.

TOLO news. "Maidan Wardak Police Chief Suspended Over Behsud Incident." TOLO news, February 8, 2021. https://tolonews.com/afghanistan-169852.

UN Security Council. "Resolution 1368 (2001)," September 12, 2001. https://digitallibrary.un.org/record/448051.

UNHCR. "Afghanistan 10 Years after Soviet Pull-Out." UNHCR India, February 12, 1999. https://www.unhcr.org/in/news/briefing-notes/afghanistan-10-years-after-soviet-pull-out.

United Nations Security Council. "Al-Haramain: Afghanistan Branch," March 14, 2022. https://www.un.org/securitycouncil/sanctions/1267/aq_sanctions_list/summaries/entity/al-haramain%3A-afghanistan-branch.

United Nations Security Council. "Resolution 1373 (2001)," September 28, 2001. https://www.unodc.org/pdf/crime/terrorism/res_1373_english.pdf.

UNODC. "Afghanistan Opium Survey 2019. Socio-Economic Survey Report: Drivers, Causes and Consequences of Opium Poppy Cultivation." Report. Vienna: United Nations Office on Drugs and Crime, February 2021. https://www.unodc.org/documents/crop-monitoring/Afghanistan/20210217_report_with_cover_for_web_small.pdf.

UNODC. "Booklet 3—Drug Market Trends: Opioids, Cannabis." United Nations : Office on Drugs and Crime, 2021. //www.unodc.org/unodc/en/data-and-analysis/wdr-2021_booklet-3.html.

Waldman, Matt. "The Sun in the Sky: The Relationship Between Pakistan's ISI and Afghan Insurgents," June 2010. https://www.files.ethz.ch/isn/117472/dp%2018.pdf.

Watson, Paul. "In Afghanistan, Money Tips the Scales of Justice." *Los Angeles Times*, December 18, 2006. https://www.latimes.com/archives/la-xpm-2006-dec-18-fg-justice18-story.html.

Whitlock, Craig. "Consumed by corruption." *Washington Post* 9 (2019).

CHAPTER 4

Mapping the Politics of Water and the Hidden Violence of the Legal Economy through the Small-scale Water Providers of Metro Manila

Nazia Hussain

Joining the conversation on water syndicates in Metro Manila, Cathy,[1] a diminutive woman in her 30s, and a housewife mother of two explains, 'I sell water from my piped connection. I also sell cookies. Some may call me a syndicate, but I am only helping neighbors. I am not the only one doing so. Just look at every other street corner. We are all doing it. But the police can arrest us at any minute. They arrested my brother, put him in jail, and fined him.' Cathy is referencing the National Water Crisis Act of 1995—the law that stipulates imprisonment and fines for selling water without consent from authorities. Thus far, she has evaded arrest.

Alan is a water provider in another informal settlement. Unlike Catherine, selling water is his primary source of livelihood. His business is also more complicated. Tapping water mains in some places where they exist, and piped connections of other residents of the community who are lucky to have them, Alan sells water to a sizable number of households. His trusted lieutenants collect weekly dues, punishing those who are unable to pay by cutting off the water supply. 'I am no bigshot. I just sell water to make a living and help them. If their houses caught fire, they would not have water to quench the blaze! They depend on me,' he says. However, times are getting harder for Alan. He faces competition from a more powerful group of water providers that carries out violence-for-hire and is untouchable on account of favorable relationships with local government officials. They demand cuts from Alan's business proceeds. If he doesn't deliver regularly, they promise to kill him. Alan highlights his predicament and contrasts his workings with theirs. 'I am the last hope standing between them and the community. I am

---

1 The names of water providers have been changed to maintain anonymity.

just trying to make a living. These people operate with impunity. I don't know how long I can stand against them!' Despite the power he wields over residents of the community by selling water, Alan seems afraid, shriveling at the prospects of a violent end.

Michael thinks of himself as an entrepreneur. Previously a community organizer, his water business caters to the needs of at least a thousand households in urban poor communities in the outlying informal settlements of Metro Manila. 'I do nothing illegal, see?' He says as he points out pipelines connecting official mains from one of the concessionaires to customer households. The pipelines are on riverbeds, which are public land, and thus legal and available to the public. 'My problem-solving techniques may entail bribing government or concessionaire officials, but if I do not provide these hapless people living under bridges, no one else will,' he says.

Edna, on the other hand, looks down upon the workings of sellers like Michael. She has been able to organize a water cooperative in her community with the help of a local NGO and like-minded residents. 'Our organization is registered and legitimate as per government rules and Manila Water (private concessionaire). We do not have to resort to shady dealings ... But running this (organization) is not easy either,' she explains.

∴

It is small-scale providers that sell water to urban poor communities in Metro Manila. The quality may be substandard, supply irregular, and prices higher than those purchasing water directly from private concessionaires. The threat of physical violence in cases like Alan and his competitors, or financial losses for communities as they spend substantial portions of their incomes on water are significant aspects. In urban settlements in Metro Manila, Cathy, Michael, and Alan and his competitors may be referred to as 'syndicates'. Unlike cooperatives, which are endorsed by Maynilad and Manila Water—private concessionaires responsible for water provision, and the Metropolitan Waterworks and Sewerage System (MWSS), the government institution responsible for oversight—syndicates are deemed to operate illegally.

These notes from the field illustrate not only that the terrain of water governance includes state (MWSS) and non-state players (Manila Water, Maynilad, small-scale water providers), but also the ways these players and economies are related through dynamics of power and violence. The power to legitimize or criminalize players rests with the state and private concessionaires, even if they may not be able or willing to provide water to urban poor communities. Violence and the threat of violence accompany these processes, whether among small-scale providers, in urban communities, or in the capacity and will of the state to criminalize spaces, activities, and individuals. Intersecting these dynamics is the fact that unless they organize into cooperatives, residents of informal settlements are not allowed to access water through private concessionaires. Uncertainty of securing access, heavy financial costs in purchasing water, governmentality conditioning communities[2] to earn legal access to water, and deep connections between water access and land tenure are part of the waterscapes of Metro Manila.

Accounts from around the world suggest that these realities are not unique to Metro Manila. Policy discussions on water supply credit poor government capacity and performance that makes the workings of small-scale providers possible (OECD, 2011;[3] World Bank, 2019).[4] This functionalist lens rests on normative assumptions of coherence of the state as a unified and complete project, distinct boundaries between formal (legal) and informal (illegal) that come about through neutral processes, and perfect competition of market economies that does not disadvantage any groups. However, anthropological and postcolonial readings of the state point out the inherently political nature of inscribing an activity legal or illegal, the power of which lies with the state. A functionalist approach also assumes an apolitical role in market economies. Yet, as perspectives from urban political ecology suggest, market dynamics contribute to, if not deepen, and shape uneven waterscapes.[5,6] It is

---

2 Thomas Lemke, "An Indigestible Meal? Foucault, Governmentality and State Theory," *Distinktion: Journal of Social Theory* 8, no. 2 (January 1, 2007): 43–64, https://doi.org/10.1080/1600910X.2007.9672946.
3 OECD, *Water Governance in OECD Countries: A Multi-Level Approach* (Paris: Organisation for Economic Co-operation and Development, 2011), https://www.oecd-ilibrary.org/environment/water-governance-in-oecd-countries_9789264119284-en.
4 Dustin Garrick et al., "Informal Water Markets in an Urbanising World: Some Unanswered Questions," Text/HTML, World Bank, 2019, https://documents.worldbank.org/en/publication/documents-reports/documentdetail/358461549427540914/Informal-Water-Markets-in-an-Urbanising-World-Some-Unanswered-Questions.
5 Erik Swyngedouw, "The Political Economy and Political Ecology of the Hydro-Social Cycle," *Journal of Contemporary Water Research & Education* 142, no. 1 (2009): 56–60, https://doi.org/10.1111/j.1936-704X.2009.00054.x.
6 Maria Rusca et al., "An Interdisciplinary Political Ecology of Drinking Water Quality. Exploring Socio-Ecological Inequalities in Lilongwe's Water Supply Network," *Geoforum* 84 (August 1, 2017): 138–46, https://doi.org/10.1016/j.geoforum.2017.06.013.

these structural contexts in which small-scale providers sell water, and urban communities manage to access a resource central to human existence. It is necessary then to further investigate how these contexts are shaped, and the effects they may have on individual and collective behavior including that of water vendors and urban communities.

This chapter is a study of processes that shape contexts in which water providers like Michael, Alan, Cathy, and Edna operate. Using the workings of water providers as a lens, the chapter addresses the following questions: what makes it possible for small-scale providers to sell water in urban poor communities? What role is played by the state and market economy processes in facilitating or constraining their workings? How are these dynamics contributing to economies of violence? Instead of a top-down perspective, this study adopts a relational approach by placing these players concerning legal/formal economies, spaces, state players, and private concessionaires. In raising these questions, this study attempts to explore the underlying dynamics of power and politics that shape urban water supply.

Secondary and primary sources (survey of 800 urban poor households; 9 focus group discussions; 70 semi-structured interviews of small-scale providers, community organizers, an NGO working on water issues, and government officials at varying levels; and field site visits during 2019, 2020, and 2022) help to address these questions. The remaining chapter is organized as follows. The remaining chapter presents a brief literature review, followed by findings, and discussion.

4.1 Going beyond Functionalist and Apolitical Explanations of Urban Water Supply: A Brief Review

The divide between apolitical and political explanations runs deep in discussions on urban water supply in developing countries. Keeping in view that access to clean and affordable water is not universally available, and that climate change and population pressures risk contributing to depleting water resources, understanding differences in the conceptualization of the problem is necessary.

With a persisting dichotomy between formal and informal,[7] policy framings tend to focus mostly on functional aspects of water supply. The problem lies

---

7   Malini Ranganathan, "Rethinking Urban Water (In)Formality," 2016, 1–18, https://doi.org/10.1093/oxfordhb/9780199335084.013.23.

in the failure of formal governments to extend municipal infrastructures and provide water to all residents. Especially in informal settlements, where the state is unable to implement its writ, small-scale providers serve the needs of residents.[8] The problem, thus, is ineffective state governance. Policy solutions based on this conceptualization suggest privatization and corporatization of the water sector to encourage competition, improve efficiency, and weaken the hold of politics and corruption in water management. Formalizing informal water economies by regulating the workings of small-scale providers has also been encouraged, suggesting a shift from perceiving them as stop-gap solutions to entrepreneurial efforts.[9,10,11,12,13,14]

Despite the fact that these conceptualizations attempt to sidestep the politics of water governance, outcomes remain political. Access to water remains unequal within cities, between urban and rural areas, and among countries. By 2021, a quarter of the world's population, an estimated two billion people, were unable to use safely managed drinking water.[15] Some suggest that even the successes of extending water access around the world are overestimated; they need to be examined beyond 'superficial' considerations of quality, regularity, and affordability.[16] Moreover, the gains that were supposed to be made

---

8   "UN World Water Development Report 2019—Leaving No One Behind," 2019, https://www.unesco.org/en/wwap/wwdr/2019.
9   Tova María Solo, Eduardo Perez, and Steven Joyce, "Constraints in Providing Water and Sanitation Services to the Urban Poor," *Office of Health, Bureau for Research and Development, USAID*, March 1993, https://pdf.usaid.gov/pdf_docs/Pnabn953.pdf.
10 Cyrus Njiru, "Utility-Small Water Enterprise Partnerships: Serving Informal Urban Settlements in Africa," *Water Policy* 6, no. 5 (October 1, 2004): 443–52, https://doi.org/10.2166/wp.2004.0029.
11 K. Eales, "Partnerships for Sanitation for the Urban Poor: Is It Time to Shift Paradigm?" (Delft, The Netherlands: IRC International Water and Sanitation Centre, 2008).
12 David Schaub-Jones, "Harnessing Entrepreneurship in the Water Sector: Expanding Water Services through Independent Network Operators," *Waterlines* 27, no. 4 (2008): 270–88.
13 Garrick et al., "Informal Water Markets in an Urbanising World".
14 UN-Habitat and UNICEF, "Interim Technical Note on Water, Sanitation and Hygiene for COVID-19 Response in Slums and Informal Urban Settlements," Humanitarian UNICEF, May 2020, https://aa9276f9-f487-45a2-a3e7-8f4a61a0745d.usrfiles.com/ugd/aa9276_df4ca ca1767d4a80849c9713c6cf3eb4.pdf.
15 WHO, UNICEF, World Bank, "State of the World's Drinking Water: An Urgent Call to Action to Accelerate Progress on Ensuring Safe Drinking Water for All," October 24, 2022, https://www.who.int/publications-detail-redirect/9789240060807.
16 Victoria A. Beard and Diana Mitlin, "Water Access in Global South Cities: The Challenges of Intermittency and Affordability," *World Development* 147 (November 1, 2021): 105625, https://doi.org/10.1016/j.worlddev.2021.105625.

through an enhanced role of the private sector in water provision also did not bear dividends,[17,18] leading to re-municipalization in some cases.

Political readings of water supply go beyond functional explanations. This diverse literature questions the centrality of Western normative ideas about infrastructure, urban theories, and the state in conversations on water supply in the rest of the world. It suggests that neutral notions of the state, governance, infrastructure, and urban water supply mask geographies of inequities and dynamics of power shaping them. Questions of criminalization or legalization, public-private partnerships, logic of governance involving governments, water providers, corporations, and communities, and unequal water access, all become processes infused with politics. How are these theoretical constructs connected with the exercise of power and the production of inequality? What perspectives are needed to ground these themes in historical, cultural, political, social, and economic contexts and lived realities of ordinary people? These and other such concerns are the focus of scholarship on urban political ecology,[19,20,21,22] studies of infrastructure,[23,24,25,26] urban theories from the

---

17 R. Ahlers, K. Schwartz, and V. Perez Guida, "The Myth of 'Healthy' Competition in the Water Sector: The Case of Small Scale Water Providers," *Habitat International* 38 (April 1, 2013): 175–82, https://doi.org/10.1016/j.habitatint.2012.06.004.

18 Rhodante Ahlers et al., "Unleashing Entrepreneurs or Controlling Unruly Providers? The Formalisation of Small-Scale Water Providers in Greater Maputo, Mozambique," *The Journal of Development Studies* 49, no. 4 (April 1, 2013): 470–82, https://doi.org/10.1080/00220388.2012.713467.

19 Nik Heynen, Maria Kaika, and Erik Swyngedouw, "Urban Political Ecology: Politicizing the Production of Urban Natures," in *In the Nature of Cities* (Routledge, 2005).

20 Matthew Gandy, "Landscapes of Disaster: Water, Modernity, and Urban Fragmentation in Mumbai," *Environment and Planning A: Economy and Space* 40, no. 1 (January 1, 2008): 108–30, https://doi.org/10.1068/a3994.

21 Michelle Kooy and Karen Bakker, "Splintered Networks: The Colonial and Contemporary Waters of Jakarta," *Geoforum*, Placing Splintering Urbanism, 39, no. 6 (November 1, 2008): 1843–58, https://doi.org/10.1016/j.geoforum.2008.07.012.

22 Mary Lawhon, Henrik Ernstson, and Jonathan Silver, "Provincializing Urban Political Ecology: Towards a Situated UPE Through African Urbanism," *Antipode* 46, no. 2 (2014): 497–516, https://doi.org/10.1111/anti.12051.

23 Rhodante Ahlers et al., "Informal Space in the Urban Waterscape: Disaggregation and Co-Production of Water Services," *Water Alternatives* 7 (February 5, 2014): 1–14.

24 Michelle Kooy, "Developing Informality: The Production of Jakarta's Urban Waterscape," *Water Alternatives* 7 (February 1, 2014): 35–53.

25 Kathryn Furlong and Michelle Kooy, "Worlding Water Supply: Thinking Beyond the Network in Jakarta," *International Journal of Urban and Regional Research* 41, no. 6 (2017): 888–903, https://doi.org/10.1111/1468-2427.12582.

26 Margreet Zwarteveen et al., "Engaging with the Politics of Water Governance," *WIREs Water* 4, no. 6 (2017): e1245, https://doi.org/10.1002/wat2.1245.

Global South,[27,28,29,30,31,32] and postcolonial and anthropological readings of the state.[33,34,35]

From the vantage point of understanding the dynamics of water governance that includes multiple players (governments, corporations, and small-scale providers), the question then becomes not only of functionality but the politics behind it. For instance, how is the responsibility to provide water distributed and what may it signify for state-society relations? How is authority related to water shared in a polity, especially considering histories of governance? Who may be held accountable when it comes to water provision? What is the logic behind illegality and informality? What is the nature of relationships among state, market, and citizens in a society? What are the loci of inequities in a society as well as the dynamics that may entrench them over time?

These questions may lend insights in whether the work of small-scale providers runs parallel to state control, or if it may be formative of state-making experiences, including in postcolonial contexts. Similarly, such a shift of the lens could direct attention to the effects of public-private-community collaborations on state-society relations, investigate such policies in terms of governmentality and lived experiences of populations, and provide clues to persisting

---

27 Ananya Roy, "Urban Informality: Toward an Epistemology of Planning," *Journal of the American Planning Association* 71, no. 2 (June 30, 2005): 147–58, https://doi.org/10.1080/01944360508976689.
28 D. Asher Ghertner, "Analysis of New Legal Discourse behind Delhi's Slum Demolitions," *Economic and Political Weekly* 43, no. 20 (2008): 57–66.
29 Liza Weinstein, "Mumbai's Development Mafias: Globalization, Organized Crime and Land Development," *International Journal of Urban and Regional Research* 32, no. 1 (2008): 22–39, https://doi.org/10.1111/j.1468-2427.2008.00766.x.
30 Ananya Roy, "The 21st-Century Metropolis: New Geographies of Theory," *Regional Studies* 43, no. 6 (July 1, 2009): 819–30, https://doi.org/10.1080/00343400701809665.
31 Ananya Roy, "Slumdog Cities: Rethinking Subaltern Urbanism," *International Journal of Urban and Regional Research* 35, no. 2 (2011): 223–38, https://doi.org/10.1111/j.1468-2427.2011.01051.x.
32 Liza Weinstein, "Demolition and Dispossession: Toward an Understanding of State Violence in Millennial Mumbai," *Studies in Comparative International Development* 48, no. 3 (September 1, 2013): 285–307, https://doi.org/10.1007/s12116-013-9136-9.
33 Thomas Blom Hansen, "Sovereigns beyond the State: On Legality and Authority in Urban India," in *Sovereign Bodies* (Princeton University Press, 2009), 169–91, https://doi.org/10.1515/9781400826698.169.
34 Christian Lund, "Twilight Institutions: Public Authority and Local Politics in Africa," *Development and Change* 37, no. 4 (2006): 685–705, https://doi.org/10.1111/j.1467-7660.2006.00497.x.
35 Jean-Pierre Olivier de Sardan and Tom Herdt, *Real Governance and Practical Norms in Sub-Saharan Africa: The Game of the Rules*, 2015, https://doi.org/10.4324/9781315723365.

inequalities related to water. The following section explores some of these themes in Metro Manila, Philippines.

4.2 Case Study: Informal Water Supply in Metro Manila

In 1997, MWSS, the government institution responsible for water delivery, and Maynilad and Manila Water, the two private concessionaires, signed concessions agreements to mark the privatization of water in Metro Manila. The regulatory office of MWSS-RO (Metropolitan Waterworks and Sewerage System Regulatory Office) was created to monitor the performance of the two concessionaires. Privatization of water in Metro Manila was one of the largest such schemes carried out in Asia.

On the metrics of reducing non-revenue water through pilferage and increasing the number of piped connections, both concessionaires have reported significant progress.[36] According to the 2015 population census, at least 90% of households have piped access (Figure 4.1).

Yet, while the rest of the city has experienced dividends, urban poor households have not fared well. They pay more despite earning low wages, combine multiple sources to fulfill needs and experience daily shortages. A deeper look reveals that households have access to water through the help of cooperatives, neighbors, individuals, and groups. Some of these players have been characterized as syndicates, a term denoting the illegality of operations. Drawing on primary data, the remaining section explains these themes in more detail.

4.2.1 *Paying More for Less: Ground Realities for Urban Poor Communities*

Responses from an urban poor household survey (n = 800)[37] and focus group discussions (n = 9) with urban poor groups illustrate uncertainty and desperate water needs of communities.

---

[36] Maynilad, responsible for the western zone, reduced non-revenue water from 66.20% in 1997 to 38.67% in 2013, and increased the number of connections from 449,000 in 1997 to 1129,000 in 2013. Manila Water, responsible for the eastern zone, reduced non-revenue water from 45.43% in 1997 to 12.35% in 2013, and increased the number of connections from 311,000 in 1997 to 922,000 in 2013. Statistics available at the MWSS-RO website: https://ro.mwss.gov.ph/consumer-policies-procedures-guidelines/non-revenue-water/.

[37] Hussain, Nazia, Chaves, Carmeli, & Gonzales, Ricky. (2021). Survey on Understanding the Challenges of Accessing Water in Metro Manila [Data set]. Zenodo. https://doi.org/10.5281/zenodo.5166508.

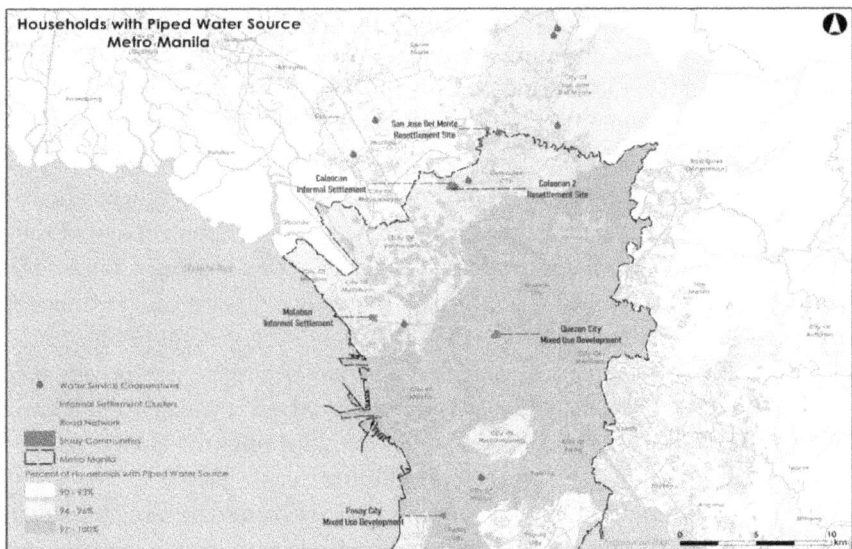

FIGURE 4.1   Households with piped water source[a]
a Compiled by Carmeli Chaves, Kenneth Punay and Nazia Hussain (2021). Data sources: Households with piped water and informal settlements population (Philippines Census of Population and Housing 2015); informal settler clusters as of 2015 (University of the Philippines Planning and Development Research Foundation), water cooperatives as of 2020 (Philippines Cooperative Development Authority), and study communities (Household Survey 2021)

The household survey population comprised six urban poor communities.[38] These communities were either a part of Metro Manila (Pasay, Caloocan, Malabon, Quezon City), or adjacent to Metro Manila (San Jose del Monte). The

---

38 The criteria for selecting study sites included the following: / People self-identified themselves as a community. Each site had community leaders and community-based organizations including home-owner associations and water cooperatives. In one community, two urban poor advocacy organizations were additional players. These communities were selected not only because they fit the study criteria but also because of access facilitated by community organizers and the Institute for Popular Democracy (IPD), a Metro Manila-based NGO that has been working on water issues for a long time. (i) Communities comprised urban poor households and lived in and around Metro Manila. (ii) For exploring whether challenges to access water were connected to housing, the survey population included people living in informal settlements, resettlement sites, and a community comprising renters, informal settlers, and those paying amortization dues. (iii) To capture as detailed a picture as possible, the survey included a variety of informal water providers.

sampling frame consisted of members of water cooperatives and housing associations identified by community representatives working with an NGO in five communities and in the case of Quezon City, members of urban poor advocacy organizations identified by a community organizer. Systematic random sampling ensured an unbiased representation of the study population.

Survey responses paint a granular picture.[39] Although significant households live below the poverty line, they spend substantial percentages of their income on water (Table 4.1). In doing so, families forgo buying other budget items or limit their consumption (e.g., two meals a day instead of three) so that they can purchase water. On the other hand, the general population of Metro Manila with individual piped connections from the two private concessionaires, Maynilad and Manila Water, pay fixed rates, which are still lower (Maynilad Water—PHP 36.24/cubic meter) than the amount paid least by survey households (Pasay City—PHP 40.34/cubic meter).

Not only do communities pay more, but they also cannot rely on one steady source of water. This results in combining multiple sources used for drinking and non-drinking purposes (bathing, washing, etc.) based on the quality. If the water smells, it is unfit for drinking unless boiled. These strategies also reveal patterns of consumption—compared to non-piped households, households with piped connections consume more water. For those who do not have individual piped connections, purchasing from other sources is not only expensive, but the quality of water is also not reliable. Individual piped connections remain the golden benchmark—those with piped dwellings find water less expensive than their less fortunate counterparts.

Despite these efforts, nearly 87% of households experience daily shortages (Figure 4.2). Within this majority, there is variation in experiencing shortages among different sources of water. Households depending on piped-to-neighbor connections and water delivery from alternative sources such as kiosks, small-time vendors, etc. suffer the most. Respondents attributed these shortages to a lack of money to buy water and pay bills. Households must pay bills to cooperatives and individual providers. If they cannot pay the bill, access to water is disconnected. Purchasing from other sources including kiosks, refilling stations, or small-scale vendors is the next best option. Sometimes, households may not have enough money to buy water either.

---

39 The survey focused on the following themes: \ (i) How do households seek access to water? (ii) What challenges do they face in accessing water? (iii) Do households experience water shortages in everyday lives? (iv) What are coping strategies in times of water shortages? (v) Who or what influences provision of and access to water?

TABLE 4.1 Urban communities—a profile

Community	Housing tenure	Occupation	Average monthly household income (PHP)[a]	Poor (%)	Income spent on water (%)
Caloocan 2 (resettlement site)	Amortizing house and/or lot (94.16%)	Construction, factory work, driver	11,507.30	62%	4.24%
San Jose del Monte (resettlement site)	Amortizing house and/or lot (86.14%)	Vending, operating market stall, factory work	12,896.10	39%	12.19%
Pasay (mixed-use development)	Rent house/room (41.80%)	Housekeeping/domestic work, construction, personal care service	10,236.26	85%	10.78%
Caloocan 1 (informal settlement)	Own house, on rent-free lot without consent of owner (77.10%)	Selling/vending, factory/warehouse, home-based enterprise, construction	10,727.85	80%	6.19%
Malabon (informal settlement)	Own house, on rent-free lot without consent of owner (84.69%)	Operating market stall, factory work, home-based enterprise	8,103.26	91%	9.16%
Quezon City (mixed-use development)	Rent house/room (51.35%)	Selling/vending, construction, home-based enterprise	10,800.00	90%	9.53%

a poverty threshold for metro manila in 2018 was php 11,951 (roughly us$1.5 per capita/day)

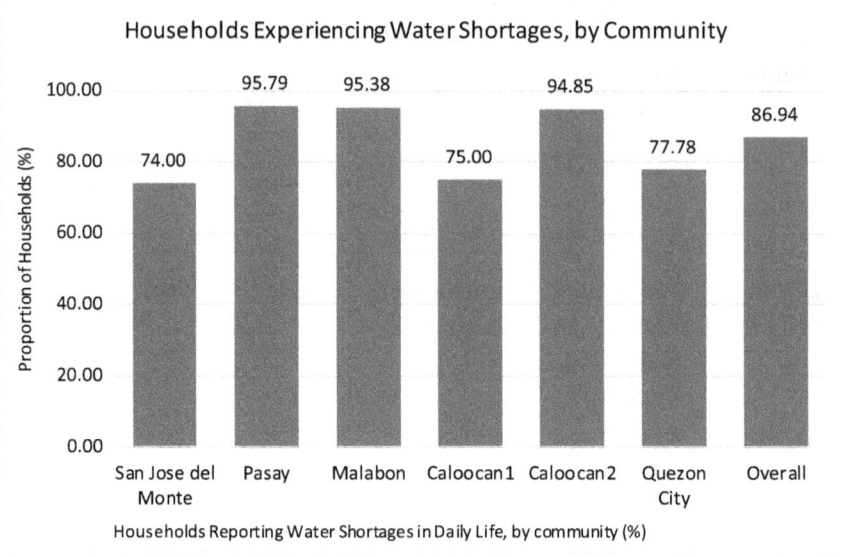

FIGURE 4.2 Households experiencing water shortages (percentage)

Numbers only tell part of the story. Open-ended responses (Figure 4.4), focus group discussions, and field site visits (Figure 4.3) reveal stories of struggle and deep concern about the availability of water for daily needs. Coping strategies include measures such as storing rainwater, reducing consumption, recycling water for multiple uses, and figuring out various ways that households may afford water (Figure 4.5).

While these broad themes highlight the range of available options, open-ended responses provide a window into experiences of deep insecurity. For instance, people end up visiting extended families living elsewhere in the city to use water, go without it when they cannot pay, wake up in the middle of the night (when water flow may be strong) to do laundry, etc. The quality of water may be so poor that people need to boil it before use. In semi-structured interviews, community members recounted how their lives are conditioned around access to water. For instance, some housewives explained how their bathing needs are served around meeting times with their itinerant worker husbands. Others talked about getting up in the early hours of the morning or standing in queues during the late hours of the night to collect water, foregoing spending time with family to follow the schedule set by a syndicate leader or a neighbor. The central theme could be summed up in a common refrain—'No money, no water!'

FIGURE 4.3 An informal settlement

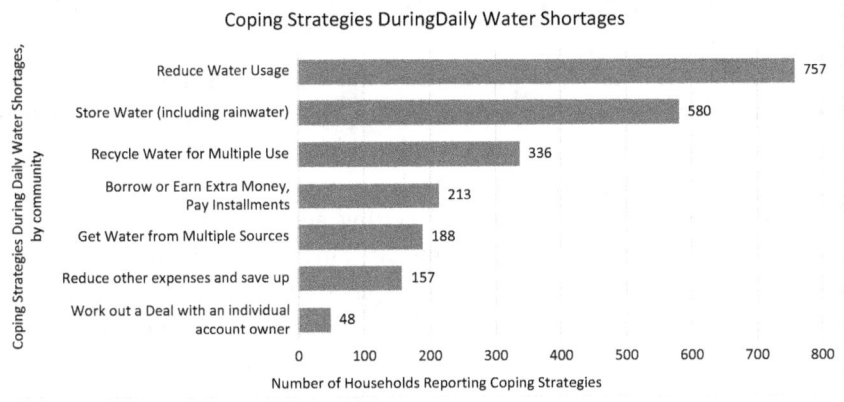

FIGURE 4.4 Coping strategies during daily water shortages

FIGURE 4.5   Storing water in an informal settlement

It is within these contexts of need that small-scale providers sell water in Metro Manila. A functional explanation would credit the lack of capacity of successive governments and private concessionaires to provide water to urban communities, as well as the absence of state authority in these spaces. A political reading suggests otherwise.

4.2.2   *Small-Scale Water Providers of Metro Manila: Cooperatives and Syndicates*

Although there is a variety of water sellers, this study focuses on the two defining categories of cooperatives and syndicates. The two represent the flipside of the same coin—cooperatives are considered legal 'informal' providers; syndicates are deemed illegal 'informal' providers.

Both illustrate self-help means of getting access to water, an aspect of service provision that has roots in history. Since colonial times, successive governments left the poor to find ways to get access to water. Before the construction of infrastructure in 1882, shallow wells often contaminated by used water, rainwater in poorly constructed water tanks, ditches surrounding the fortified city filled with stagnant water, and the Pasig River were primary sources for low-income populations.[40,41]

Conditions did not change substantially after independence. Those living in low-income settlements along garbage dumps, waterways, and other such land were poorly served by the MWSS. By 1994, the MWSS supplied water to only two-thirds of the population; supply was intermittent on an average of 16 hours each day.[42] A survey conducted in 1995 revealed that poor people depended on vendors for low quality and paid far more than their wealthier compatriots. Since this was an expensive option, many chose to buy even poorer quality water from neighbors.[43] As this study's findings illustrate, things have not changed considerably for urban poor communities after privatization, except with the formation of water cooperatives.

4.2.2.1   Cooperatives

Under pro-poor schemes introduced by private concessionaires and facilitated by local government units and non-governmental organizations (NGOs), cooperatives are organizations of community members living in informal or resettlement sites. They are registered organizations that sign agreements with concessionaires. From the standpoint of functionality, cooperatives provide a simple solution to providing water in informal settlements. Since extending infrastructure to informal settlements would legitimize these spaces, concessionaires refrain from issuing individual piped connections. Cooperatives fill this gap by allowing concessionaires to install mother meters, bear the costs of infrastructure installation and repair, and collect water dues on behalf of the concessionaires.

However, organizing a cooperative is not easy. Assembling a group of people who work pro-bono to collect dues, ensure regular supply, garner the support of communities, raise money for start-up costs, and navigate local power geographies shaped by dynamics among government officials, politicians, and strongmen is a stressful endeavor. Communities cannot come together on their

---

40 L. Mervin Maus, *An Army Officer on Leave in Japan: Including a Sketch of Manila and Environment, Philippine Insurrection of 1896–7, Dewey's Battle of Manila Bay and a Description of Formosa* (Chicago: A.C. McClurg & Co., 1911).

41 Xavier Huetz de Lemps, "Waters in Nineteenth Century Manila," *Philippine Studies* 49, no. 4 (2001): 488–517.

42 Mark Dumol, *The Manila Water Concession: A Key Government Official's Diary of the World's Largest Water Privatization* (World Bank Publications, 2000).

43 Estrella M. Maniquis, "IDRC Reports: Water Policy in Manila," December 1996, https://idl-bnc-idrc.dspacedirect.org/server/api/core/bitstreams/3693570f-6d8b-4062-bb14-67d2e46fc36d/content.

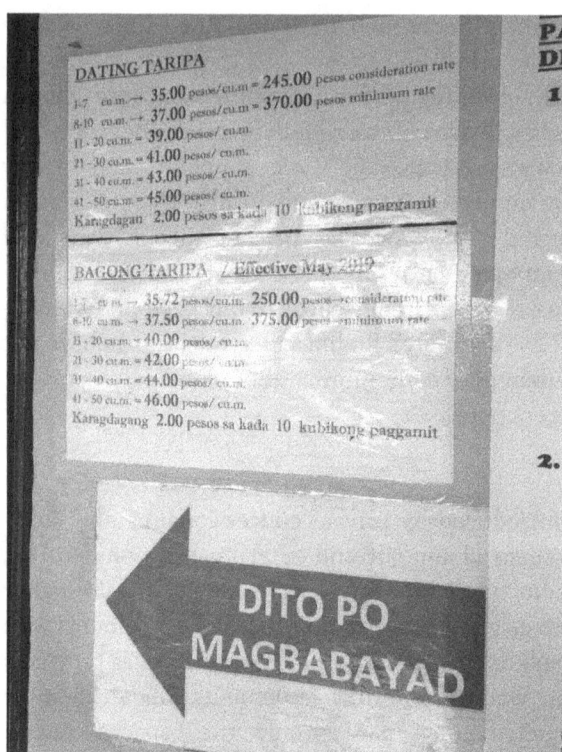

FIGURE 4.6 Cooperative-set prices for water supply

own, raise revenue for initial costs, and figure out myriad legal steps to get the organization registered without the help of external players like NGOs. Once a cooperative has come into being, the next task is to ensure compliance in ensuring that residents of the community make regular payments (Figures 4.6 and 4.7), or else the account holder is penalized by disconnecting the water supply. In focus groups with cooperative members, many shared about the difficulties in forming their organization, tensions, and competition within communities during the process, and bitter contests over leadership in some cases. Moreover, the decision-making process when it comes to solving day-to-day challenges entails consultation with board members of the cooperative and may run into conflicts among members and resentments within communities.

From the lens of functionality, cooperatives may be perceived as governance players. It is through their everyday workings that they ensure access to water and embody the spectral presence of the state and concessionaires. It is also cooperatives that face accountability from communities if the water supply runs into problems. Despite their hybrid nature, cooperatives are dependent

FIGURE 4.7 Members of a water cooperative

on the state and concessionaires for regularization as well as access to water. Their legitimacy stems from serving as a connective tissue between the formal and the seemingly informal spaces. Since they work in partnership with the concessionaires, they are considered superior to those working outside of the zones of coverage, highlighting 'differentiation in informality.'[44]

4.2.2.2   Syndicates

Syndicates illustrate a different phenomenon. Unlike syndicates associated with housing that represent organized groups,[45] water syndicates are diffuse in form. From the standpoint of the law, anyone selling water, from housewives to community organizers to individuals employing the threat of violence against communities or competitors may be deemed a syndicate. Under the National Crisis Water Act of 1995, selling pilfered water is a crime that can result in arrest

---

44   Deborah Cheng, "The Persistence of Informality: Small-Scale Water Providers in Manila's Post-Privatisation Era," *Water Alternatives* 7 (February 1, 2014).

45   P. Parnell and S. Kane, *Crime's Power: Anthropologists and the Ethnography of Crime* (Springer, 2003).

and imposition of fines.[46] Yet, they are representative of everyday illegality that is widely known but tacitly overlooked, not only by households but other players including NGOs, government officials, and community leaders. The threat of violence against competitors is also part of the story; at times, the fear of violence deters others (for instance, developers and community organizers) from disrupting the workings of these water providers in any manner. Relations with low-level government functionaries may also make some of these providers seem powerful to their competitors.

The workings of these players vary from one to the next, depending on the scale of their operations and connections with communities, government officials at varying levels, and political capital. For instance, piped-to-neighbor vendors are ordinary people trying to make ends meet. They may be criminalized easily. Cathy, the housewife selling water and cookies is afraid of getting arrested like her brother. In 2015, the arrests came about on the complaint of the concessionaire, which noted rampant illegal tapping of water mains in an informal settlement. The issue was raised with the *barangay*[47] officials. As a result, the city police conducted surveillance, collected evidence, and arrested individuals. Sellers like Cathy and her brother are not anomalies—selling water to neighbors is a pervasive occurrence.

Michael, a community organizer, on the other hand, is a powerful player. With his background in community organizing, he runs his water business efficiently, laying down pipelines on public land (riverbeds) to connect them with the mains laid out by the private concessionaires (Figure 4.8). He serves almost a thousand households in different communities; his lieutenants collect water dues from residents and terminate supply in case of non-payment. Michael bribes local government officials and connects with community notables to make inroads in water supply in a particular community. 'Sometimes, I bribe

---

46 Section 8 of the law states on 'anti-pilferage': / It is hereby declared unlawful for any person to: (a) Destroy, damage or interfere with any canal, raceway, ditch, lock, pier, inlet, crib, bulkhead, dam, gate, service, reservoir, aqueduct, water mains, water distribution pipes, conduit, pipes, wire benchmark, monument, or other works, appliance, machinery, buildings, or property of any water utility entity, whether public or private; (f) Use or receive the direct benefit of water service with knowledge that diversion, tampering, or illegal connection existed at the time of that use, or that the use or receipt was otherwise without the authorization of the water utility; (g) Steal or pilfer water meters, main lines, pipes and related or ancillary facilities; (h) Steal water for profit or resale; (i) Knowingly possess stolen or tampered water meters; and (j) Knowingly or willfully allow the occurrence of any of the above.

47 Smallest administrative unit.

FIGURE 4.8 Laying down water pipelines on public land

even those who did not ask for it, just to ensure that nothing slows down my operation. I am doing nothing illegal', he points out.

Providers like Alan have soft agreements with residents with piped supply who allow their water connections to be used for pilfering and selling of water to other residents lacking individual connections.

The entrepreneur in turn sells water to other residents of the community. Sellers like Alan may also directly tap water mains illegally to sell water to residents (Figure 4.9).

Despite the unsavory nature of these arrangements, residents of a community may help to conceal the workings of illegal water delivery in the community from outsiders. Since living in an informal settlement prevents them from securing legal piped connections unless they form a cooperative, residents are left on their own to devise ways to get access to water. In one informal settlement, water arrangements were explained as follows by a community leader:

> 48 households with individual piped connections allow the entrepreneur to pilfer water in return for payment. They also connect secondary pipes with the neighboring houses who pay directly to the household entrepreneur. In 124 households with sub-meters, there are two ways of water

FIGURE 4.9 Tapping legal water connections

provision (i) households provide water to neighbors with illegal submeters and collect payment from them. In doing so, they service at least 44 households. (ii) providers like Alan 'jump' (tap) main pipes illegally, supply water to customer households and collect payment from at least 80 households. An estimated 65% of households in the submeter category are either illegally sharing water through illegal sub-meters or through 'jumper' connections.

In this informal settlement, residents feared small-scale providers. Local government officials also overlooked their activities since the provision of water was fiercely contested by competing players and had resulted in violence in the past. Competition could deprive residents of affordable water as well as subject them to unpredictable workings and threats of violence perpetrated by water providers. Amy, a community organizer, for instance, expressed fears of

Alan's competition taking over the area. 'They are friends with the mayor and work as hired killers. Alan is our last hope (in preventing these providers from operating in the community).' Competition among these players, thus, may contribute to competition over resources, creating 'artificial scarcity.'[48]

While it may be easy to consider these players as belonging to water syndicates, the term masks the political nature of their dealings as well as their roots in communities and ideological leanings. One provider, for instance, was a community organizer with a history of working with the Communist Party of the Philippines. Aligned with the leftist ideology, this organizer was once a part of the 'Sparrow Unit', the hit squad of the Communist party that became known for killing government officials and suspected government agents in the 1980s during the dictatorship of President Marcos.[49] Similarly, players like Michael are community organizers and not merely water providers; in addition to selling water, Michael continues to engage with other community organizers and NGOs on issues of relevance to urban poor communities.

A commonality shared between cooperatives and syndicates is that there is little oversight in the day-to-day when it comes to setting prices and disconnecting access to water on account of non-payment. Models of decision-making vary from one type of player to the next. Cooperatives set prices with the concurrence of the board of directors of their organization, while individual entrepreneurs may do so based on their calculus of profit-making. Access to water is ensured on payments of bills, with connections cut off after warnings. Since water providers are often based in communities, they may regulate the behaviors of residents through close observation.

From the lens of postcolonial scholarship, water sellers falling under the rubric of syndicates could be deemed 'informal sovereigns'[50] that carry out functions associated with the state but do not attempt to subvert state sovereignty. Ranganathan (2014, p.90)[51] in the case study of water mafias of Bangalore characterizes them as 'formative of the post-colonial state rather than existing apart from it'. These framings not only praise open meanings and

---

48   Clotilde Champeyrache, "A Commonsian Approach to Crime: The Mafia and the Economic Power to Withhold," *Cambridge Journal of Economics* 45, no. 3 (May 1, 2021): 411–25, https://doi.org/10.1093/cje/beab006.
49   Justus M. Van Der Kroef, "The Philippine Vigilantes: Devotion and Disarray," *Contemporary Southeast Asia* 10, no. 2 (1988): 163–81.
50   Thomas Blom Hansen and Finn Stepputat, "Sovereignty Revisited," *Annual Review of Anthropology* 35, no. Volume 35, 2006 (October 21, 2006): 295–315, https://doi.org/10.1146/annurev.anthro.35.081705.123317.
51   Malini Ranganathan, "'Mafias' in the Waterscape: Urban Informality and Everyday Public Authority in Bangalore," *Water Alternatives* 7 (April 2, 2014): 89–105.

interpretations behind these processes but also how they need to be analyzed in relation to the workings of the law and the state. Such an approach may help to understand what makes the workings of these players possible, and how these dynamics are contributing to economies of violence.

4.3 The Politics of Water and Hidden Violence of the Legal Economy

Situating cooperatives and syndicates in larger contexts lends insights into the relationship between the state and urban poor, and the role of market economies and the state in the governance and planning of Metro Manila. It is within these discursive and physical spaces that water access and supply take place.

Functional explanations of water supply in informal settlements characterize them as spaces where the state is unable to extend its imprint. A historical reading of the state illustrates however that the spaces occupied by the poor have been 'othered' and criminalized systematically over time.[52] During the Spanish rule, a classless society became bifurcated into upper classes (Filipino chieftains inducted into administration and given privileges) and lower classes. These class distinctions became stratified during the American period of colonization in which rights were only given to Filipinos who affirmed loyalty to American laws, education, and rule. These social and political divisions became entrenched within the urban fabric of Manila during American rule. Designed as a defensible city, American schools, commercial establishments, government offices, and a concentration camp populated Manila. The city was protected not only by walls but laws that divided 'civilized' colonizers from 'savages' Filipinos, law-observing from criminals, rebels from incarcerated comrades, and educated from the illiterate.[53] Not only have these divisions persisted over time, but state laws have also successively criminalized the urban poor. For instance, in 1975, President Marcos criminalized squatting

---

52   Christopher N. Magno and Philip C. Parnell, "The Imperialism of Race: Class, Rights and Patronage in the Philippine City," *Race & Class* 56, no. 3 (January 1, 2015): 69–85, https://doi.org/10.1177/0306396814542922.

53   These laws prohibited Filipinos from forming or joining any organization or nationalist movement., considered people not belonging to any concentration camps or marked villages as bandits and enemies of the state, prohibited the display of Philippine flags and other symbols not approved by the United States. Chris Magno, "Policing Poverty and the Criminalization of the Poor," January 1, 2014, p.32 https://www.academia.edu/113710632/Policing_Poverty_and_the_Criminalization_of_the_Poor.

with a presidential decree, affecting at least a third of the urban population at the time.⁵⁴

Over the years, the disciplining of the urban poor has continued to take place by successive governments, resulting in the precariousness of their daily existence and the deepening of class divides. The poor are perceived as a 'morally inferior impoverished class' (Kusaka, 2017, p.11),⁵⁵ and their needs are 'unworthy of recognition and consideration by the state' (Hutchison, 2007, p.854).⁵⁶ Within the context of urban planning, the needs of the urban poor continue to be out of sync with the world-class visions of Metro Manila.⁵⁷⁵⁸ These spatial transformations are also increasing political divides between the urban poor and the rest, contributing not only to contention over the 'right to the city but also over the right to speak and be heard' (Garrido 2019, p.12).⁵⁹ The precarity of the urban poor when it comes to water, then, is not only related to governance as exercised by private entities but planning of urban space and the nature of state-society relations.

It is within these contexts that privatization of water took place in the Philippines. After the end of the Marcos era, international institutions including the World Bank encouraged the democratic administration of President Corazon Aquino to privatize government-owned industries and utilities to ensure efficient service provision extricated from political influence and poor performance of bureaucracy. By 1997, then-President Fidel Ramos privatized the MWSS. The policy illustrated what has been covered in governance literature as the state losing monopoly over policy processes to international and national private economic actors on the one hand, and parts of the civil society on the other.⁶⁰ These interventions were considered innovative ways to

---

54 Magno and Parnell, "The Imperialism of Race".
55 Wataru Kusaka, *Moral Politics in the Philippines: Inequality, Democracy and the Urban Poor* (NUS Press, 2017).
56 Jane Hutchison, "The 'Disallowed' Political Participation of Manila's Urban Poor," *Democratization* 14, no. 5 (December 1, 2007): 853–72, https://doi.org/10.1080/1351034070 1635696.
57 Gavin Shatkin, "Colonial Capital, Modernist Capital, Global Capital: The Changing Political Symbolism of Urban Space in Metro Manila, the Philippines," *Pacific Affairs* 78, no. 4 (December 1, 2005): 577–600, https://doi.org/10.5509/2005784577.
58 Morgan Mouton and Gavin Shatkin, "Strategizing the For-Profit City: The State, Developers, and Urban Production in Mega Manila," *Environment and Planning A: Economy and Space* 52, no. 2 (March 1, 2020): 403–22, https://doi.org/10.1177/0308518X19840365.
59 Marco Z. Garrido, *The Patchwork City: Class, Space, and Politics in Metro Manila* (University of Chicago Press, 2019).
60 F. Matthews, "Governance and State Capacity," in *The Oxford Handbook of Governance, Levi-Faur, David (Ed.)* (2012, n.d.), https://www.google.co.in/books/edition/The_Oxford_Handbook_of_Governance/9nAWEAAAQBAJ?hl=en&gbpv=1.

produce systems of 'good governance' with the help of civil society and economic actors in urban contexts.[61]

It was hoped that these interventions would empower democracy and enhance effective governance, but critical readings point out the democratic deficit of these measures.[62] These developments, in which the inclusion of civil society actors in governance does not enable distribution unless they become employable welfare subjects, have unfolded differently in the Philippines and much of the Global South.[63] In these contexts, formal welfare states have not existed previously, unlike in the Global North—instead, people have relied on familial and community networks.[64]

Ideological in nature,[65] governance reforms involving the privatization of water through corporate control[66][67] have led to various types of violence in countries around the world. The guiding motives for market-led water companies are related to productivity or price increases, both of which pose knotty problems—productivity may result from capital and technology-intensive efforts leading to a reduction in labor, while price hikes may contribute to social unrest.[68]

For instance, the privatization of water in Cochabamba, Bolivia led to increased prices by the private company in a bid to secure returns. Long neglected by the state, and outraged at drastic increases in water tariffs,

---

61   Frank Moulaert et al., "Introduction: Social Innovation and Governance in European Cities: Urban Development Between Path Dependency and Radical Innovation," *European Urban and Regional Studies* 14, no. 3 (July 1, 2007): 195–209, https://doi.org/10.1177/09697 76407077737.

62   Erik Swyngedouw, "Governance Innovation and the Citizen: The Janus Face of Governance-beyond-the-State," *Urban Studies* 42, no. 11 (October 1, 2005): 1991–2006, https://doi.org/10.1080/00420980500279869.

63   Koki Seki, *Ethnographies of Development and Globalization in the Philippines: Emergent Socialities and the Governing of Precarity* (Routledge, 2020).

64   Seki.

65   Karen J. Bakker, "A Political Ecology of Water Privatization," *Studies in Political Economy*, March 1, 2003, https://www.tandfonline.com/doi/abs/10.1080/07078552.2003.11827129.

66   Bakker.

67   Rhodante Ahlers, "Fixing and Nixing: The Politics of Water Privatization," *Review of Radical Political Economics* 42, no. 2 (June 1, 2010): 213–30, https://doi.org/10.1177/04866 13410368497. A detailed discussion on privatization is not within the remit of this chapter. However, it is important to note that privatization of water should be seen beyond the narrow view of corporate control. States and multilateral financial institutions facilitate and steer the process of privatization.

68   Erik Swyngedouw, "Dispossessing H2O: The Contested Terrain of Water Privatization," *Capitalism Nature Socialism* 16, no. 1 (March 1, 2005): 81–98, https://doi.org/10.1080/1045 575052000335384.

residents of Cochabamba protested peacefully at first. The killing of a young man during the protests led almost 100,000 people into the streets. It also brought together farmers, coca growers, and peri-urban residents who had been protesting over the passage of a law that threatened farmers' water supplies.[69] The resulting Cochabamba war was 'the first water war in the 21st century' (Ahlers 2010, p.213).[70] In South Africa, the government policy developed by private water companies and the World Bank led to cutting off water supply for those who could not pay full costs.[71] It led to millions of people sourcing water from polluted rivers and lakes, which in turn led to South Africa's worst cholera outbreak.[72] In the Colombian Caribbean, the privatization of water has contributed to the degradation of natural systems and the exclusion of social groups, further heightened by development models that sideline local practices supporting ecosystems.[73]

In Metro Manila, innovative pro-poor schemes introduced by private concessionaires and the state reflect a democratic deficit. Instead of empowering communities, they have shifted the responsibility of water access to urban communities that need to organize, raise revenue, and bear risks to be able to earn access to legal sources of water. In conversations with members of cooperatives in informal and resettlement sites and open-ended survey responses, the realization on the part of respondents was that water security was only possible through self-help. One could argue that such pro-poor schemes could be perceived as exercises in governmentality[74]—conditioning communities to get their act together or face the consequence of acquiring water through means beyond the pale of endorsed informality. This lack of faith in the government and concessionaires reflects not only that pro-poor schemes do not always empower communities, but also that urban residents have accepted

---

69   Susan Spronk and Jeffery R. Webber, "Struggles against Accumulation by Dispossession in Bolivia: The Political Economy of Natural Resource Contention," *Latin American Perspectives* 34, no. 2 (March 1, 2007): 31–47, https://doi.org/10.1177/0094582X06298748.
70   Ahlers, "Fixing and Nixing".
71   Jacques Pauw, "The Politics of Underdevelopment: Metered to Death—How a Water Experiment Caused Riots and a Cholera Epidemic," *International Journal of Health Services* 33, no. 4 (October 1, 2003): 819–30, https://doi.org/10.2190/KF8J-5NQD-XCYU-U8Q7.
72   Pauw.
73   Johana Herrera Arango, Juan Antonio Senent-De Frutos, and Elías Helo Molina, "Murky Waters: The Impact of Privatizing Water Use on Environmental Degradation and the Exclusion of Local Communities in the Caribbean," *International Journal of Water Resources Development* 38, no. 1 (January 2, 2022): 152–72, https://doi.org/10.1080/07900627.2021.1931052.
74   LEMKE, "An Indigestible Meal?".

their desperate realities. It is important, however, to consider that such self-help efforts and lack of access to basic rights of water (and housing) have roots in the history of state-society relations.

With privatization, the urban poor have lost more space. Privatization has contributed to further weakening of state-society relations in terms of accountability. Under the Water Code of 1975, urban populations do not have water rights,[75] but now with privatization, there is no accountability. Since they cannot provide water to informal settlements on account of not having the right of way, concessionaires cannot be blamed. The government, in turn, places the responsibility of water provision on concessionaires. This game of musical chairs played out during pervasive shortages in 2019 resulting from historic low water levels in the Angat and La Mesa dams, the two sources of water for Metro Manila that led to popular outrage, which in turn was directed by the government toward the concessionaires.[76] During this period, however, the urban poor were not allowed to participate in the public spectacle of outrage,[77] denoting their absence when it comes to being included in the state-citizenship discourse.

Urban poor communities get access to water within these contexts, resorting to everyday illegality including buying and selling water to neighbors, and depending on providers selling them water from illegally tapped mains. They pay more to get access to often what is poor-quality water, which is neither adequate in quantity for daily needs nor available on a regular basis. Moreover, the boundaries between legality and illegality are continuously disrupted through the selective formalization of informal providers (cooperatives) by concessionaires and the state.[78] As well, while a resident may have a legal piped connection, they may sell water to neighbors, an illegal action. However, it is not only a transaction among neighbors as Cathy pointed out; it also reflects how

---

75   Issued in 1976 by President Ferdinand Marco as Executive Order 1067, the Water Code states that all waters are under the control of the state, and authorities must approve uses of water. It allows municipalities to apply and obtain rights on behalf of users. However, unlike rural users who may apply for water permits to acquire ground or surface water, urban users are not afforded such rights. Sarah I. Hale, "Water Privatization in the Philippines: The Need to Implement the Human Right to Water," *Pacific Rim Law & Policy Journal* 15 (2006): 765.

76   "Duterte threatens water concessionaires: Gov't can take over if water crisis happens," CNN *Philippines,* October 28, 2019, https://www.cnnphilippines.com/news/2019/10/28/panelo-duterte-maynilad-manila-water-shortage-crisis.html (accessed January 4, 2022).

77   Paolo Romero, "Congress to Probe Water Shortage," Philstar.com, accessed March 29, 2024, https://www.philstar.com/headlines/2019/03/14/1901351/congress-probe-water-shortage.

78   Cheng, "The Persistence of Informality".

urban communities resort to social networks in times of need.[79] Yet, it is easy to criminalize urban poor communities under the National Water Crisis Act of 1995 which awards fines and imprisonment for selling water without consent from authorities. Unless they find a way to raise revenue for start-up costs, manage to assemble an organization, and at times, go against local political players and strongmen, they are always on the wrong side of the law.

One may contend that in these economies of violence, which disrupt clear-cut boundaries of legality and illegality, concessionaires and the state are as much a part as syndicates. This chapter has made the case to go beyond functional explanations of water supply to make sense of the politics of water and the hidden violence of the legal economy of water provision. It may help to understand the dynamics of vulnerability experienced in everyday lives by ordinary people and to push for meaningful conversations on ensuring equitable access to water.

Especially considering that water shortages resulting from the increasing movement of people to cities and climate change are imposing burdens on governments and populations alike, it is necessary to outline contexts and mechanisms in the formal and (in) formal realm that entrench geographies of inequity.

Bibliography

Ahlers, R., K. Schwartz, and V. Perez Guida. "The Myth of 'Healthy' Competition in the Water Sector: The Case of Small Scale Water Providers." *Habitat International* 38 (April 1, 2013): 175–82. https://doi.org/10.1016/j.habitatint.2012.06.004.

Ahlers, Rhodante, Frances, Cleaver, Maria, Rusca, and Klaas, Schwartz. "Informal Space in the Urban Waterscape: Disaggregation and Co-Production of Water Services." *Water Alternatives* 7 (February 5, 2014): 1–14.

Ahlers, Rhodante, Valeria Perez, Güida, Maria, Rusca, and Klaas, Schwartz. "Unleashing Entrepreneurs or Controlling Unruly Providers? The Formalisation of Small-Scale Water Providers in Greater Maputo, Mozambique." *The Journal of Development Studies* 49, no. 4 (April 1, 2013): 470–82. https://doi.org/10.1080/00220388.2012.713467.

Ahlers, Rhodante. "Fixing and Nixing: The Politics of Water Privatization." *Review of Radical Political Economics* 42, no. 2 (June 1, 2010): 213–30. https://doi.org/10.1177/0486613410368497.

---

79 Seki, *Ethnographies of Development and Globalization in the Philippines.*

Bakker, Karen J. "A Political Ecology of Water Privatization." *Studies in Political Economy*, March 1, 2003. https://www.tandfonline.com/doi/abs/10.1080/07078 552.2003.11827129.

Beard, Victoria A., and Diana Mitlin. "Water Access in Global South Cities: The Challenges of Intermittency and Affordability." *World Development* 147 (November 1, 2021): 105625. https://doi.org/10.1016/j.worlddev.2021.105625.

Champeyrache, Clotilde. "A Commonsian Approach to Crime: The Mafia and the Economic Power to Withhold." *Cambridge Journal of Economics* 45, no. 3 (May 1, 2021): 411–25. https://doi.org/10.1093/cje/beab006.

Cheng, Deborah. "The Persistence of Informality: Small-Scale Water Providers in Manila's Post-Privatisation Era." *Water Alternatives* 7 (February 1, 2014).

Dumol, Mark. *The Manila Water Concession: A Key Government Official's Diary of the World's Largest Water Privatization*. World Bank Publications, 2000.

Eales, K. "Partnerships for Sanitation for the Urban Poor : Is It Time to Shift Paradigm?" Delft, The Netherlands: IRC International Water and Sanitation Centre, 2008.

Furlong, Kathryn, and Michelle, Kooy. "Worlding Water Supply: Thinking Beyond the Network in Jakarta." *International Journal of Urban and Regional Research* 41, no. 6 (2017): 888–903. https://doi.org/10.1111/1468-2427.12582.

Gandy, Matthew. "Landscapes of Disaster: Water, Modernity, and Urban Fragmentation in Mumbai." *Environment and Planning A: Economy and Space* 40, no. 1 (January 1, 2008): 108–30. https://doi.org/10.1068/a3994.

Garrick, Dustin, E, O'Donnell, Matthew, Scott Moore, N, Brozovic, and Thomas, Iseman. "Informal Water Markets in an Urbanising World : Some Unanswered Questions." Text/HTML. World Bank, 2019. https://documents.worldbank.org/en/publicat ion/documents-reports/documentdetail/358461549427540914/Informal-Water -Markets-in-an-Urbanising-World-Some-Unanswered-Questions.

Garrido, Marco Z. *The Patchwork City: Class, Space, and Politics in Metro Manila*. University of Chicago Press, 2019.

Ghertner, D. Asher. "Analysis of New Legal Discourse behind Delhi's Slum Demolitions." *Economic and Political Weekly* 43, no. 20 (2008): 57–66.

Hale, Sarah I. "Water Privatization in the Philippines: The Need to Implement the Human Right to Water." *Pacific Rim Law & Policy Journal* 15 (2006): 765.

Hansen, Thomas Blom, and Finn, Stepputat. "Sovereignty Revisited." *Annual Review of Anthropology* 35, no. Volume 35, 2006 (October 21, 2006): 295–315. https://doi.org/10 .1146/annurev.anthro.35.081705.123317.

Hansen, Thomas Blom. "Sovereigns beyond the State: On Legality and Authority in Urban India." In *Sovereign Bodies*, 169–91. Princeton University Press, 2009. https: //doi.org/10.1515/9781400826698.169.

Herrera Arango, Johana, Juan Antonio, Senent-De Frutos, and Elías Helo, Molina. "Murky Waters: The Impact of Privatizing Water Use on Environmental Degradation and the Exclusion of Local Communities in the Caribbean." *International Journal of Water Resources Development* 38, no. 1 (January 2, 2022): 152–72. https://doi.org/10.1080/07900627.2021.1931052.

Heynen, Nik, Maria, Kaika, And Erik, Swyngedouw. "Urban Political Ecology: Politicizing the Production of Urban Natures." In *In the Nature of Cities*. Routledge, 2005.

Hutchison, Jane. "The 'Disallowed' Political Participation of Manila's Urban Poor." *Democratization* 14, no. 5 (December 1, 2007): 853–72. https://doi.org/10.1080/13510340701635696.

Kooy, Michelle, and Karen, Bakker. "Splintered Networks: The Colonial and Contemporary Waters of Jakarta." *Geoforum*, Placing Splintering Urbanism, 39, no. 6 (November 1, 2008): 1843–58. https://doi.org/10.1016/j.geoforum.2008.07.012.

Kooy, Michelle. "Developing Informality: The Production of Jakarta's Urban Waterscape." *Water Alternatives* 7 (February 1, 2014): 35–53.

Kusaka, Wataru. *Moral Politics in the Philippines: Inequality, Democracy and the Urban Poor*. NUS Press, 2017.

Lawhon, Mary, Henrik, Ernstson, and Jonathan, Silver. "Provincializing Urban Political Ecology: Towards a Situated UPE Through African Urbanism." *Antipode* 46, no. 2 (2014): 497–516. https://doi.org/10.1111/anti.12051.

Lemke, Thomas. "An Indigestible Meal? Foucault, Governmentality and State Theory." *Distinktion: Journal of Social Theory* 8, no. 2 (January 1, 2007): 43–64. https://doi.org/10.1080/1600910X.2007.9672946.

Lemps, Xavier Huetz de. "Waters in Nineteenth Century Manila." *Philippine Studies* 49, no. 4 (2001): 488–517.

Lund, Christian. "Twilight Institutions: Public Authority and Local Politics in Africa." *Development and Change* 37, no. 4 (2006): 685–705. https://doi.org/10.1111/j.1467-7660.2006.00497.x.

Magno, Chris. "Policing Poverty and the Criminalization of the Poor," January 1, 2014. https://www.academia.edu/113710632/Policing_Poverty_and_the_Criminalization_of_the_Poor.

Magno, Christopher N., and Philip C. Parnell. "The Imperialism of Race: Class, Rights and Patronage in the Philippine City." *Race & Class* 56, no. 3 (January 1, 2015): 69–85. https://doi.org/10.1177/0306396814542922.

Maniquis, Estrella M. "IDRC Reports: Water Policy in Manila," December 1996. https://idl-bnc-idrc.dspacedirect.org/server/api/core/bitstreams/3693570f-6d8b-4062-bb14-67d2e46fc36d/content.

Matthews, F. "Governance and State Capacity." In *The Oxford Handbook of Governance*, Levi-Faur, David (Ed.). 2012, n.d. https://www.google.co.in/books/edition/The_Oxford_Handbook_of_Governance/9nAWEAAAQBAJ?hl=en&gbpv=1.

Maus, L. Mervin. *An Army Officer on Leave in Japan: Including a Sketch of Manila and Environment, Philippine Insurrection of 1896–7, Dewey's Battle of Manila Bay and a Description of Formosa*. Chicago: A.C. McClurg & Co., 1911.

Moulaert, Frank, Flavia, Martinelli, Sara, González, and Erik, Swyngedouw. "Introduction: Social Innovation and Governance in European Cities: Urban Development Between Path Dependency and Radical Innovation." *European Urban and Regional Studies* 14, no. 3 (July 1, 2007): 195–209. https://doi.org/10.1177/09697 76407077737.

Mouton, Morgan, and Gavin, Shatkin. "Strategizing the For-Profit City: The State, Developers, and Urban Production in Mega Manila." *Environment and Planning A: Economy and Space* 52, no. 2 (March 1, 2020): 403–22. https://doi.org/10.1177 /0308518X19840365.

Njiru, Cyrus. "Utility-Small Water Enterprise Partnerships: Serving Informal Urban Settlements in Africa." *Water Policy* 6, no. 5 (October 1, 2004): 443–52. https://doi .org/10.2166/wp.2004.0029.

OECD. *Water Governance in OECD Countries: A Multi-Level Approach*. Paris: Organisation for Economic Co-operation and Development, 2011. https://www.oecd-ilibrary.org /environment/water-governance-in-oecd-countries_9789264119284-en.

Olivier de Sardan, Jean-Pierre, and Tom, Herdt. *Real Governance and Practical Norms in Sub-Saharan Africa: The Game of the Rules*, 2015. https://doi.org/10.4324/978131 5723365.

Parnell, P., and S. Kane. *Crime's Power: Anthropologists and the Ethnography of Crime*. Springer, 2003.

Pauw, Jacques. "The Politics of Underdevelopment: Metered to Death—How a Water Experiment Caused Riots and a Cholera Epidemic." *International Journal of Health Services* 33, no. 4 (October 1, 2003): 819–30. https://doi.org/10.2190/KF8J-5NQD -XCYU-U8Q7.

Ranganathan, Malini. "'Mafias' in the Waterscape: Urban Informality and Everyday Public Authority in Bangalore." *Water Alternatives* 7 (April 2, 2014): 89–105.

Ranganathan, Malini. "Rethinking Urban Water (In)Formality," 1–18, 2016. https://doi .org/10.1093/oxfordhb/9780199335084.013.23.

Romero, Paolo. "Congress to Probe Water Shortage." Philstar.com. Accessed March 29, 2024. https://www.philstar.com/headlines/2019/03/14/1901351/congress-probe -water-shortage.

Roy, Ananya. "Slumdog Cities: Rethinking Subaltern Urbanism." *International Journal of Urban and Regional Research* 35, no. 2 (2011): 223–38. https://doi.org/10.1111/j.1468 -2427.2011.01051.x.

Roy, Ananya. "The 21st-Century Metropolis: New Geographies of Theory." *Regional Studies* 43, no. 6 (July 1, 2009): 819–30. https://doi.org/10.1080/00343400701809665.

Roy, Ananya. "Urban Informality: Toward an Epistemology of Planning." *Journal of the American Planning Association* 71, no. 2 (June 30, 2005): 147–58. https://doi.org/10.1080/01944360508976689.

Rusca, Maria, Akosua, Boakye-Ansah, Alex, Loftus, Giuliana, Ferrero, and Pieter, van der Zaag. "An Interdisciplinary Political Ecology of Drinking Water Quality. Exploring Socio-Ecological Inequalities in Lilongwe's Water Supply Network." *Geoforum* 84 (August 1, 2017): 138–46. https://doi.org/10.1016/j.geoforum.2017.06.013.

Schaub-Jones, David. "Harnessing Entrepreneurship in the Water Sector: Expanding Water Services through Independent Network Operators." *Waterlines* 27, no. 4 (2008): 270–88.

Seki, Koki. *Ethnographies of Development and Globalization in the Philippines: Emergent Socialities and the Governing of Precarity*. Routledge, 2020.

Shatkin, Gavin. "Colonial Capital, Modernist Capital, Global Capital: The Changing Political Symbolism of Urban Space in Metro Manila, the Philippines." *Pacific Affairs* 78, no. 4 (December 1, 2005): 577–600. https://doi.org/10.5509/2005784577.

Solo, Tova María, Eduardo, Perez, and Steven, Joyce. "Constraints in Providing Water and Sanitation Services to the Urban Poor." *Office of Health, Bureau for Research and Development*, USAID, March 1993. https://pdf.usaid.gov/pdf_docs/Pnabn953.pdf.

Spronk, Susan, and Jeffery R. Webber. "Struggles against Accumulation by Dispossession in Bolivia: The Political Economy of Natural Resource Contention." *Latin American Perspectives* 34, no. 2 (March 1, 2007): 31–47. https://doi.org/10.1177/0094582X06298748.

Swyngedouw, Erik. "Dispossessing H2O: The Contested Terrain of Water Privatization." *Capitalism Nature Socialism* 16, no. 1 (March 1, 2005): 81–98. https://doi.org/10.1080/1045575052000335384.

Swyngedouw, Erik. "Governance Innovation and the Citizen: The Janus Face of Governance-beyond-the-State." *Urban Studies* 42, no. 11 (October 1, 2005): 1991–2006. https://doi.org/10.1080/00420980500279869.

Swyngedouw, Erik. "The Political Economy and Political Ecology of the Hydro-Social Cycle." *Journal of Contemporary Water Research & Education* 142, no. 1 (2009): 56–60. https://doi.org/10.1111/j.1936-704X.2009.00054.x.

UN-Habitat and UNICEF. "Interim Technical Note on Water, Sanitation and Hygiene for COVID-19 Response in Slums and Informal Urban Settlements." Humanitarian UNICEF, May 2020. https://aa9276f9-f487-45a2-a3e7-8f4a61a0745d.usrfiles.com/ugd/aa9276_df4caca1767d4a80849c9713c6cf3eb4.pdf.

"UN World Water Development Report 2019—Leaving No One Behind," 2019. https://www.unesco.org/en/wwap/wwdr/2019.

Van Der Kroef, Justus M. "The Philippine Vigilantes: Devotion and Disarray." *Contemporary Southeast Asia* 10, no. 2 (1988): 163–81.

Weinstein, Liza. "Demolition and Dispossession: Toward an Understanding of State Violence in Millennial Mumbai." *Studies in Comparative International Development* 48, no. 3 (September 1, 2013): 285–307. https://doi.org/10.1007/s12116-013-9136-9.

Weinstein, Liza. "Mumbai's Development Mafias: Globalization, Organized Crime and Land Development." *International Journal of Urban and Regional Research* 32, no. 1 (2008): 22–39. https://doi.org/10.1111/j.1468-2427.2008.00766.x.

WHO, UNICEF, World Bank. "State of the World's Drinking Water: An Urgent Call to Action to Accelerate Progress on Ensuring Safe Drinking Water for All," October 24, 2022. https://www.who.int/publications-detail-redirect/9789240060807.

Zwarteveen, Margreet, Jeltsje S. Kemerink-Seyoum, Michelle Kooy, Jaap Evers, Tatiana Acevedo Guerrero, Bosman Batubara, Adriano Biza, et al. "Engaging with the Politics of Water Governance." *WIREs Water* 4, no. 6 (2017): e1245. https://doi.org/10.1002/wat2.1245.

CHAPTER 5

Illicit Urban Economies: The Toll of Local and Global Illegalities in the Making of Cities

Arturo Alvarado

5.1 The Problem

Global illicit activities are significant components of the world economy, causing serious issues for people, economic actors, and governments as well. Illicit activities distort the articulation of the public sector and represent a heavy toll on individuals and communities. However, our understanding of how these transgressive activities are embedded within urban contexts, as well as the impact on regional and national territories, remains limited. This chapter aims to estimate the scale and impacts of local and transnational transgressions, by comparing two major urban centers in Latin America, São Paulo in the south and Mexico City in the North. We aim to contribute to the existing literature on city making, by shedding light on the destructive role of illicit global activities. Additionally, we will present some examples of economies of violence endured by/impact the lives of millions of people.

Cities are places where multiple forms of law transgressions take place in mixed environments, making it difficult to discern the extent of destruction that illegal actors produce. To provide a more precise approach to this topic, our interpretation will be based on Bauer (2022: 6–7),[1] who characterizes illicit economy as … "all (individual and group) actions or behaviors leading to a benefit in terms of power and/or financial gains to the detriment of another person, organization or institution." The economies of violence can be either financial or economic gains (Bauer, 2022: 5),[2] and might be motivated by the lure of gain and/or the establishment of power relations. And … "the harm endured by another person or entity following the perpetuated action, which resulted in a financial gain, being physical/moral/psychological, remains a common denominator qualifying the latter act as "violent" (Bauer, 2022: 6).[3]

---

1 Alain Bauer, "Special Issue: Economies of Violence," *International Journal on Criminology* 9, no. 2 (April 1, 2022), https://doi.org/10.18278/ijc.9.2.1.
2 Bauer.
3 See the definition of the economies of violence in the Introduction of this book.

Cities concentrate resources, abilities, and power. Metropolitan regions are pivotal drivers of regional and national economies. For example, the São Paulo Metropolitan Region has nearly 22 million inhabitants. It is the world's fourth most populous urban entity and the biggest in the Americas. It contributes to nearly 15% of Brazil's wealth (see Table 5.1). São Paulo alone produces more wealth than Uruguay, Paraguay and Bolivia combined. Mexico City has a metropolitan area with nearly 22 million inhabitants and contributes to 10% of the national economy. Both urban areas also contribute simultaneously to global illicit activities. These transgressive activities are nested in the urban productive and distributive spheres and the effects they have in their economies reach regional, national, and transnational territories.

Estimating the revenues generated by illicit economies is a complex and yet unfulfilled task. While various international organizations and national institutions have attempted to measure the underground economy, no reasonable estimates of illicit economic outputs in urban areas have been obtained. For instance, for Ciudad de México, the informal economy is often used as a proxy, accounting for nearly 45% of the city's GDP, and 33% of its workforce in informality. In certain cases, estimated losses suffered by victims are used as a proportion of illicit income. It is common to say that for every formal activity, there are informal and illicit practices. Cities are built by these dimensions, as well as with the citizens' perception of the phenomena.[4] We can observe that markets fulfill consumers' demands and interact with one another, forming a complex web of relations among actors. Therefore, cities serve as spaces and networks where all actors concur as producers, consumers, or regulators in legal, formal, informal, irregular, or illegal activities.

There are claims that both economies cater to customer satisfaction. For sure, illegal activities can represent a large part of individuals' and families' income. Some scholars consider that crime activities provide employment and social mobility opportunities, particularly for the urban poor (Feltran, 2019:1),[5] or at the very least offer *"a minimum level of economic citizenship"* (Beckert and Dewey, 2017: 14).[6] City governments often acknowledge the legitimacy of self-employment and some informality as a survival strategy for the more

---

4 Teresa Pires do Rio Caldeira, *Cidade de muros: crime, segregação e cidadania em São Paulo* (Editora 34, 2000).
5 Gabriel Feltran, "(Il)Licit Economies in Brazil: An Ethnographic Perspective: Economias (i) Lícitas No Brasil: Uma Perspectiva Etnográfica," *Journal of Illicit Economies and Development* 1, no. 2 (June 4, 2019): 145–54.
6 Jens Beckert and Matías Dewey, *The Architecture of Illegal Markets: Towards an Economic Sociology of Illegality in the Economy* (Oxford University Press, 2017).

disadvantaged individuals, often serving as the basis of political patronage and clientelism. However, it is crucial to understand that crime is a violent and destructive behavior, far more than the infringement of laws. It harms individuals, groups, and communities, and destroys environments and economies. Crimes increase power asymmetries, exacerbate inequalities and discrimination, erode human rights, deteriorate democratic governments, and distort public spaces. It limits access to basic services and often imperils liberties.

We need to understand how and to what extent illicit activities impact urban societies' economies, as well as how the interaction between criminal actors, victims, and authorities shapes the urban framework and local governance structures. The interaction emerges from everyday licit and illicit, encompassing creative, destructive, and reactive practices. They are nested in urban space. Cities run with this problem, finding ways to cope, survive, innovate, integrate, transform, or be destroyed. Governments do the same, producing both welfare and damage.

5.2   Measuring Illicit Activities in Urban Contexts

Illegal activities refer to actions or transactions that violate public regulations set by a State Authority. It can refer to the illegal production, distribution, transaction, or consumption of a product, activity, and/or service. A public regulatory system is key to both legal and illegal markets. Urban violence is a broader category that encompasses a broader range of acts, including infringement of laws, such as aggressions, homicides, assaults, robberies, as well as stealing and pirating either by individuals, groups, or criminal organizations.

For the characterization of illegal markets, in addition to Bauer (2022, above) we follow Beckert and Wehinger's (2013)[7] proposal, as "arenas of regular exchange of goods or services for money under conditions of competition and in which the product itself or its production, exchange, or consumption violate legal stipulations" (Beckert and Wehinger 2013 quoted in Beckert & Dewey, 2017:2).[8] However, it is worth noting that some transactions or parts of it are legal and taken within the bounds of the law.[9] One author defines an action

---

7   Jens Beckert and Frank Wehinger, "In the Shadow: Illegal Markets and Economic Sociology," *Socio-Economic Review* 11, no. 1 (January 1, 2013): 5–30, https://doi.org/10.1093/ser/mws020.
8   Beckert and Dewey, *The Architecture of Illegal Markets*.
9   There are fuzzy legal regulations, blurred lines of transactions and gray areas where certain illegal products or services can enter the legal market. In certain areas of the cities some actors operate infringing liberties and opportunities to all actors; they impose social and

TABLE 5.1 Demographic, economic and social characteristics of Sao Paulo and Ciudad de Mexico

Metric	Sao Paulo	Ciudad de Mexico
Metropolitan population c.2020	21,138,247	21,804,000
City population (2020–2021)	12,396,372	9,209,944
Extension (sqKms)	1.521	1.494
Population Density (Po/km2) 2020	7.803	6.163
Housing Units (2020)	4,107,161	2,756,319
Unemployment (2022)	9.25	5.25
Informality (% employment in informal sector)	42.6	46.1
Main activities (terciarization)	Service, commerce, trade, industry, financial services, manufacturing	Services, commerce, trade, government services, financial services, transportation, tourism
City contribution to national GDP (% 2019, 2020)	10%	15.80%
City Budget (2020)	13,935,238,590,00 USD (68,900,000,000 BR)	13,610,692,078,50 USD (238,975,000,000 MXP)
Budget as % GDP (2020)	34% (State)	15,8 (2020)
HDI x City 2021	0.806	0.83
GINI Index (national, 2020)	48.9	45.4
Salary Minimum Wage 2022–2023	8,30 USD (42,8 R$ – 2022)	11,52 USD (207,44 MXP)
Income- Salary (monthly average, 2022)	229,7 USD	241,85 USD
Average Income form population (Year 2022)	R$ 83,349 (16,456 USD)	72,000 MXP (3,692 USD)

political constraints. Telles (2010: 2, 12) argues that empirical studies find it difficult to come up with clear distinctions between the lines of the legal and the illicit.

TABLE 5.1   Demographic, economic and social characteristics of Sao Paulo and Ciudad de Mexico (*cont.*)

Metric	Sao Paulo	Ciudad de Mexico
Poverty index (Mexico: IBN) / levels / poverty line (Sao Paulo incomeless than US Dls 5,5 ppp) 2020	57 % (16,8% extreme poverty)	36,2 % (4,3% extreme poverty)
Average cost of living (average monthly individual cost in 2022 USD)	1,316,3 USD (6,783 R$)	1,455,3 USD (29,254 MXN)
Ranking of cost of living – country	2nd for Brazil / Ranked 177 out of 232 in world cities	1St for Mexico / Ranked 176 out of 23 in world cities

as legal if that action complies with sanctioned norms "it does not violate any state-sanction norms." (Beckert and Dewey, 2017:11, quoting Mayntz, 2017).[10] But there are many loopholes in regulation.

Both legal and illicit activities follow the rules of economic exchange in the capitalist system, and face the same challenges confronted by firms: harsh competition, high costs of market entry, asymmetries of information, transaction costs, difficulties in enforcing contracts (particularly transgressions, modes of conflict resolution). However, conducting illicit actions may present for its actors more barriers to accessing credit or property through the legal system.[11] As a consequence, to access similar goods, criminal actors rely on alternative means for reinforcing transactions, such as corruption, arbitration, socially shared rules, alternative threats, violent threats, or by building a reputation (Beckert and Dewey, 2017:15).

To solve some of the aforementioned problems and avoid competition from others and punishment from the state, we hypothesize that illicit actors adopt

---

10   Beckert and Dewey, *The Architecture of Illegal Markets*.
11   Philippe Steiner and Marie Trespeuch, eds., *Marchés contestés : Quand le marché rencontre la morale, Marchés contestés : Quand le marché rencontre la morale*, Socio-logiques (Toulouse: Presses universitaires du Midi, 2014), https://books.openedition.org/pumi/8079.

the strategy of firms. This notion has also been attached to the development of organized crime. As markets become more competitive and better regulated by authorities and other enforcers, they tend to develop corporate rules. Thus, we hypothesize that illicit actors in urban settings adapt to competition and a complex regulatory landscape shaped by public and private agents.[12]

The question that follows is: what is the role of the state? The state plays multifaceted roles, among them: enforcing rules (formal and informal), coordinating actors, and according to Beckert and Dewey, "reducing uncertainty and stabilizing markets. They do that through securing property rights, setting standards, and regulating firms' governance structures" (see Beckert and Dewey 2017: p.17, citing Mayntz). This helps to understand how the coordination of exchanges differs under the conditions of illegality. It is important to note that the State is not the sole source of rules although it provides the legal infrastructure for the market and selectively prosecutes market participants (Beckert and Dewey 2017: pp 9 &.17). But this might be controversial because States provide the infrastructure for both licit and illicit economies. In any event, the idea of selective enforcement is central and provides a two-sided character. Informal rules are also enforced by society, firms, or groups of criminals; even illegally by government actors (Beckert and Dewey: 9). The social organization of illegal markets is influenced not only by the different roles of the State (Beckert and Dewey, 2017:17, quoting Beckert and Wehinger 2013), but also by the utilization of state institutions and regulations by both licit and illicit actors to advance their interests.

In urban and rural settings, the question of the legitimacy of transgressive actions, as they can "enjoy high social acceptance," is essential (Beckert and Dewey: 12). This raises ongoing debates about the rule of law and the legitimacy of both legal and illegal actions. Social conventions about what is legal or not are crossed by class, income, location, and preferences for regulation. Illicit markets provide goods and services to groups or personas that might otherwise be unable to access them and might improve their quality of life. But we don't support the argument that participating in illicit markets can produce citizenship.

This discussion leads to debates over the monopoly of legal regulations by the state and onto the debate about sovereignty and the cities' monopoly of coercion. We argue that cities might not possess a monopoly on legal

---

12   Fligstein (2001) distinguishes between four different types of rules structuring markets: property rights, the governance structure (companies or firms), rules of exchange, and "'market actors' cognitive understanding of the operation of the market, or "conceptions of control"." (Quoted in Beckert and Dewey, 2017, 17 and ss.).

regulations. The claim that city actors must possess a monopoly of legal regulations does not apply to all areas of the city (as some States effectively claim the monopoly of the law). We cannot argue that all legal or illicit actions are legitimate or even consensual. There are legal actions that can be perceived as illegitimate, like "legal" police violence. Some illicit markets are socially and government-tolerated and even legitimate for some people, but this doesn't solve the problem of violent destruction and the loss of welfare for the victims. Social welfare turns out to be sub-optimal by the destructive thrust of illegal actors.

We argue therefore that cities operate and facilitate a plurality of normative, traditional, and legal regulations. Some of these regulations are created by the city and others come from the State, from diverse societal actors, or illicit practices, either local or global. Cities work not only with formal rules but with several other conventions and procedures that emerge as reputed and repetitive arrangements through a series of confrontations and negotiations. An example is the political negotiations in illicit land occupations. Illicit actions give rise to their own regulations. These multiple normative regimes and the different sets of laws and regulations operate in cities, often competing, contradicting, and overlapping with each other.

What are these regimes and how are they implemented? Feltran (2020)[13] proposes four regulatory systems operating in cities and we will build our framework based on this set. The first set of norms comes from the public legal system of rules and regulations, which are complex and often contradictory. The second are regulations imposed or negotiated with police organizations, sometimes unjust and illegal.[14] The third can be an authority with symbolic, religious authority, like church pastors. The fourth is a set of multiple rules issued by criminal actors. Some are equated to gang or street rules, while others evolve into powerful and complex regulations, particularly when a city gang achieves coercive and regulatory authority in a territory. Criminal organizations can solve conflicts among inhabitants, impose their own social rules, or negotiate with public actors (like the PCC in São Paulo).[15] Most of them are arbitrary everyday socio-economic and political activities.

---

13 Gabriel Feltran, "The Entangled City: Crime as Urban Fabric in São Paulo," in *The Entangled City* (Manchester University Press, 2020), https://www.manchesterhive.com/display/9781526151377/9781526151377.xml.
14 Police not only impose a socio spatial order, but interact with private illegal actors against citizens. Violence regulation is a field sometimes in dispute, sometimes shared or co-produced with police and non-legal actors.
15 The Primeiro Comando da Capital, PCC, is a criminal organization formed in São Paulo's prisons during the 1990s. Originally was a prisoner's protection association (an

The fifth set of rules is created by powerful informal associations (and their bosses), although they are not criminal organizations. Examples are some merchant's associations and private security firms in Mexico City with territorial control of public and private spaces where they operate, and power to interact with local governments. Together with them, there are several vigilante associations, and certain political or partisan organizations with the power to impose some local order. In certain neighborhoods, residents' associations tend to monitor and regulate the behavior of their members and limit external intrusion.

A sixth set of regulations is composed either of traditional practices (*Weber*) or informal unwritten rules of traditions (*"usos y costumbres"*), embodied in indigenous authorities and their communities in Mexico City as they hold power over land use in the city. The last one, a seventh regime is gender-based and racialized. Consists of a set of rules applied in private and public spaces, like the informal street and mobility rules imposed by and enforced by men against women.

Each regime might also be accompanied by coercive rules to oversee compliance and control behavior. They overlapped as (territorially based) private monopolies. They form a complex tapestry of socio-territorial governance that shapes exchanges within cities.

Each one of the regulations has different grades of use, consent, and legitimacy; in turn, it produces numerous disputed, negotiated, or hybrid forms of socio-territorial governance. These social and normative orders are embedded in legal and illegal markets and provide the basis for transgression. Transgressions are the more dynamic changing forces in cities, and crime is the

---

"hermandade do crime"), to defend inmates from punishing abusive practices of jail guardians. It evolved into a network in various Sao Paulo State Jails and the neighborhoods where prisoners resided (including their families) and, a few years later, into a major criminal organization controlling crime in the city, particularly drug trafficking and the market of illegal weapons, but also serving as supporting platform for bank robberies and cargo theft. Analyst proposed that PCC has become the main criminal controller of violence in several cities, specifically of homicides and by establishing urban control in the territories of influence. Today is the largest criminal organization in Brazil and has groups active in Paraguay and Bolivia. Membership is voluntary trough a *"baptism,"* and once "brothers" they have to pay a monthly fee. Money collected is used to support prisoners, their families and finance criminal enterprises. It is estimated that PCC has around 29 thousand members. The building blocks of the organization are *"sintonias"* in each prison and neighborhood. *See:* https://www.ipa-brasil.org & *Paes y Dias, (2018)*. These authors consider that PCC is a consequence of decades of erroneous security policies. It is the largest criminal organization operating in the city and in the country.

example used in this work. It transforms citizens and government positions and actions, and its capacities to confront or eradicate them.

Therefore, the idea of the rule of law as a universal regulation does not apply to all areas of the cities. Their authorities cannot claim to have a monopoly on legal regulations. Of course, it is the prerogative of state actors (bureaucrats, politicians, police) to claim what is regular and what is illegal. But many other actors can manage conflicts, illegalities, and violence.[16,17,18,19,20,21] Sometimes social, traditional, or illegal actors are the ones that allow business to run, as well as independent of government and, in certain situations, city bureaucrats. It is notably the case with informal vendors, selling either legal, pirate, counterfeit, smuggled, or stolen products.

Governance in illicit markets turns regulatory and enforcement practices into an arena of dispute. This is why illicit markets appear as areas out of the control of the state. Activities are embedded within the legal and formal market. It is a social space structured by sellers, buyers' intermediaries, public and social enforcers, and sometimes communities. This creates a market for violence[22,23,24] used by all actors. Authorities for instance also use these informal rules to deal with illicit actors.

Local markets' authorities apply selective enforcement of economic rules on property, contracts, deals, etc., because they have different interests, priorities, and perceptions of the issues at hand. Additionally, the enforcement of laws is influenced by underlying political, electoral, and social causes and the core of the urban economies of violence, including corruption, clientelism, negotiation, concession, or pure coercion. Compliance with sanctioned norms becomes complicated. Thereupon, a group of perpetrators will reap the

---

16 Vera Telles, "A Cidade Nas Fronteiras Do Legal e Ilega," 2010, https://www.academia.edu/106442253/A_cidade_nas_fronteiras_do_legal_e_ilega.
17 Feltran, "The Entangled City".
18 Feltran, "(Il)Licit Economies in Brazil".
19 Caldeira, *Cidade de muros*.
20 Benjamin Lessing, "Criminal Governance in Latin America in Comparative Perspective: Introduction to the Special Edition," *Dilemmas: Revista de Estudos de Conflito e Controle Social* 15 (September 12, 2022): 1–10, https://doi.org/10.4322/dilemas.v15esp4.52896.
21 Beckert and Dewey, *The Architecture of Illegal Markets, pp 9*.
22 Gabriel de Santis Feltran, "Fronteiras de tensão: política e violência nas periferias de São Paulo," in *Fronteiras de tensão: política e violência nas periferias de São Paulo*, 2011, 360–360, https://pesquisa.bvsalud.org/portal/resource/pt/biblio-1079927.
23 Feltran, "The Entangled City, pp 174".
24 Feltran, "(Il)licit economies in Brazil".

benefits, either in terms of power or monetary gains, to the detriment of other citizens, organizations, or institutions.

5.3 The Literature on the Topic

The topic of illicit activities in urban contexts has been widely studied across various academic disciplines, including, Economics, Geography, Sociology, Political Science, Anthropology, Law, Public Health, Security Studies, Policing, and Urban Studies.

There is not a single explanation for the illicit behavior. Studies delve into various explanatory factors of transgressions (from individuals, groups, gangs, or organizations, like protection rackets or criminal associations inside the government). Its behavior can be explained by theories of relative deprivation; opportunity structures, inadequate government (or society) surveillance, weak social cohesion or social disorder, or socioeconomic conditions associated with illegalities.[25,26,27,28] Criminal governance in urban settings is a rare topic in academic research.[29] The distribution of crime is not random but is often associated with specific socio-spatial dimensions in the urban territory, similar to enforcement patterns. Additionally, organized criminal groups, mafias, and corruption rackets intervene in the territories (Tables 5.3, 5.3b and 5.4).

Methodologically, research in the field tends to adopt micro-level, qualitative approaches, emphasizing rich and in-depth case studies. There are also quantitative and macro-level works, like the analysis of homicides.[30,31,32,33]

---

25 Sérgio Adorno, Camila Dias, and Marcelo Nery, "A Cidade e a Dinâmica Da Violência," 2016, 381–410.
26 Carlos J. Vilalta, José G. Castillo, and Juan A. Torres, "Delitos Violentos En Ciudades de América Latina," 2016, https://dds.cepal.org/redesoc/portal/publicaciones/ficha/?id=4409.
27 Mario Díaz (2018) *Distribución diferencial del delito en la Ciudad de México*.
28 J. Fernández (2021) *Controles sociales y eficacia colectiva en la localización geográfica de la violencia*.
29 Lessing, "Criminal Governance in Latin America in Comparative Perspective".
30 Maria Fernanda Tourinho Peres et al., "Queda dos homicídios no município de São Paulo: uma análise exploratória de possíveis condicionantes," *Revista Brasileira de Epidemiologia* 14 (December 2011): 709–21, https://doi.org/10.1590/S1415-790X2011000400 017, pp 709.
31 Fabio Boucault Tranchitella et al., "Homicide Occurrence in Different Regions of the City of São Paulo and Its Risk Rate According to Male Gender between 2000 and 2014: An Analysis of 11.981 Cases," *Medicina Legal de Costa Rica* 38, no. 2 (December 2021), pp 105.
32 Arturo Alvarado et al., *Vidas truncadas: El exceso de homicidios en la juventud de América Latina, 1990–2010. Los casos de Argentina, Brasil, Colombia y México* (El Colegio de Mexico AC, 2015).
33 Mario Díaz (2018) *Distribución diferencial del delito en la Ciudad de México*.

Ethnographic approaches are prevalent (Feltran, 2019:2),[34] while comparative works are fewer.

The literature diverges in basic assumptions and conceptual meaning. There is a wide and deep problematization of the state capacity, in particular, its absence, its limitation that allows the emergence of illicit markets, on law obedience, and the lack of the monopoly of coercion and limited sovereignty.[35,36] And some new studies are trying to make comparisons between several-different illicit markets, like textile, markets, antiques, drugs, environmental and traffic of species or protection rackets markets.[37] Some urban studies explore the spatiality of violence and its relation to the built environment as well as to the presence or absence of the failure of the state (Davis, 2020: 749),[38] and some to a combination of violent factors that build the cities.[39,40]

The study of criminal organizations and prisons is a growing field (either gang or organized criminal groups).[41,42,43,44,45,46,47] But, to improve our understanding of organized criminality we need a more comprehensive orientation. This broader orientation seeks to explain action driven by ambition and opportunity, by planned systematic behavior, going beyond the integration of

---

34 Feltran, "(Il)Licit Economies in Brazil".
35 Enrique Desmond Arias, ed., "Constellations of Governance: Theoretical Approaches to Micro-Level Armed Regimes," in *Criminal Enterprises and Governance in Latin America and the Caribbean* (Cambridge: Cambridge University Press, 2017), 19–38, https://doi.org/10.1017/9781316650073.002.
36 Lessing, "Criminal Governance in Latin America in Comparative Perspective".
37 Beckert and Dewey, *The Architecture of Illegal Markets*.
38 Diane E. Davis, "Urban Violence and the Spatial Question: The Built Environmental Correlates of (In)Security in Latin American Cities," in *The Oxford Handbook of the Sociology of Latin America*, ed. Xóchitl Bada and Liliana Rivera-Sánchez (Oxford University Press, 2021), 0, https://doi.org/10.1093/oxfordhb/9780190926557.013.41.
39 Caldeira, *Cidade de muros*.
40 Teresa PR Caldeira, "Peripheral Urbanization: Autoconstruction, Transversal Logics, and Politics in Cities of the Global South," *Environment and Planning D: Society and Space* 35, no. 1 (February 1, 2017): 3–20, https://doi.org/10.1177/0263775816658479.
41 Mario Pavel Díaz, "Inseguridad y Narcomenudeo En La Ciudad de México: Distribución Diferenciada y Correlativos Asociados," Sociológica México, 2022, http://www.sociologicamexico.azc.uam.mx/index.php/Sociologica/article/view/1704.
42 Bruno Paes Manso and Camila Nunes Dias, *A Guerra: a ascensão do PCC e o mundo do crime no Brasil* (Editora Todavia S.A, 2018).
43 Gabriel Feltran (2018). *Irmãos: Uma história do PCC*.
44 Camila Caldeira Nunes Dias, "Da pulverização ao monopólio da violência: expansão e consolidação do Primeiro Comando da Capital (PCC) no sistema carcerário paulista" (text, Universidade de São Paulo, 2011), https://doi.org/10.11606/T.8.2011.tde-13062012-164151.
45 Manso and Dias, *A Guerra*.
46 Lessing, "Criminal Governance in Latin America in Comparative Perspective".
47 Daniel Veloso Hirata, "Sobreviver na adversidade: entre o mercado e a vida" (text, Universidade de São Paulo, 2010), https://doi.org/10.11606/T.8.2010.tde-03032011-122251.

criminal actors from below, such as corruption and illicit actions by the economic and political elite. These include construction and real estate companies. In Mexico City, there has been a long debate about the role of housing companies in illegal activities.

5.4 Main Questions for This Chapter

The hypothesis inquires on the extent to which crime affects various aspects of everyday social, economic, and political urban life. The main research questions are therefore: To what extent does crime affect everyday life in urban economic, social, and political arenas? How violence is central in the governing systems of these cities? Who governs in the city?

Illicit actions and illicit city-making involve a wider range of actors than typically portrayed in existing literature. Illicit actions are not limited to the urban poor (typically blamed) but involve the upper middle classes, the wealthier sectors of cities, and the more powerful individuals and corporations. All of them transgress rules and appropriate, manipulate, or destroy the built environment to benefit themselves. Illicit city-making is driven by ambition and pursued by individuals or corporations. Theories related to illicit actions, relative deprivation, opportunities, or governance, offer insight into the commonalities of illicit global capitalism and move beyond parochial narratives (Robinson, 2014: 58.[48] For a broader comparative framework see Marques, 2024).[49] However, to fully understand the dynamics of city-making, additional transgressive actors such as narcotic traffickers, counterfeits, pirates, architects, and firms must be considered. And contrary to some scholarly discussions, city-making is not synonymous with crime-making. It is part of a complex web of interactions among different actors engaging in both legal and illegal actions. The collective outcome often deviates from the expected result. Illicit markets in urban contexts operate in response to market competition involving both illicit and legal actors. They adapt, create, and affect the regulatory system.

---

[48] Jennifer Robinson, "Introduction to a Virtual Issue on Comparative Urbanism," *International Journal of Urban and Regional Research* n/a, no. n/a, accessed March 29, 2024, https://doi.org/10.1111/1468-2427.12171.

[49] Eduardo Marques, "Comparative Strategies on and in Latin-American Cities," in *The Routledge Handbook of Comparative Global Urban Studies* (Routledge, 2023).

Both examined metropolises in this study share several commonalities. They are profoundly unequal, and segregated and host several violent actors, despite being powerful and resourceful. Additionally, they boast the largest public security apparatus in their respective countries and arguably the entire region (Table 5.2). At the same time, they also support participatory processes in governance, including security.

These factual observations provide the basis for one of the arguments of the present chapter. These bureaucracies navigate through a set of complex regulations encompassing both the legal order as well as other "normative regimes" all while engaging in territorial control disputes over the city. Consequently, this opens opportunities for discretion and the selective application of the law. Although both city authorities have formal control over the police, they don't respond to citizens, leading to significant consequences for accountability, legal behavior, and the relationship with inhabitants. Moreover, both cities grapple with major problems of police violence, which fosters citizen distrust toward authorities and drives them to seek alternative informal arrangements when they confront crime.

Urban governance entails navigating between law-abiding citizens and transgressors. Cities cannot always assert a monopoly or legal regulations or control different normative regimes. In many instances, they cannot claim the monopoly of coercion. City sovereignty is not like state sovereignty and no single entity can claim that prerogative, either. Cities are shaped by private coercive oligopolies as well as illicit oligopolies, which include corporations, police, cartels, neighbors, and partisan and vigilante groups. These complexities require a rethinking of conventional ideas regarding the link between crime and the state. We must see the city beyond the state. The study also analyzes the role and capacity of urban governments to combat crime and examines the consequences of these actions for city governance. It is necessary to move beyond the unidimensional concept of the state's monopoly on coercion.[50]

---

50 The idea of city making as Organized Crime might sound similar to Tilly's idea for the state (1985). But the process of negotiating among actors or seeking protection from the state by criminal organizations is different. But not all the process occurs as proposed. Certainly, as some scholars argue, all actors "seek to establish territorial sovereignty based on their capacity to monopolize violence" (Müller y Weegels, 2022: 230) and try to obtain legitimacy. We argue that city making is a complex process of governance, and it is more than a coordination process. It is a power competition that might produce a balance, it can result in equilibria, among the public and private actors, each one of them with different individual and collective interests, goals and heterogeneous preferences over public policies. Some of these policies are proposed by governments, others by citizens

5.5 Method

This exploratory chapter assesses the impact of illicit activities on the sociospatial configuration of the city. The use of a comparative approach between two cities aims to provide a better understanding of how global illicit economies influence them. It will also allow us to explore the different causal configurations of the relationship between illicit markets and governance. We shall also analyze the illicit pressures that criminals exert in the cities as well as the different effects they have on authorities' policies and the citizens.

Latin America as a region has a distinctive geopolitical position (Robinson, 2014: 61)[51], and a distinctive type of urbanization.[52] In this chapter, we will ask whether or not illicit city-making constitutes a particular urbanization in two Megapolises, Mexico City and the Metropolitan Region of São Paulo which share common urbanistic patterns and exhibit similar trends of violence.[53]

We analyze two megalopolises: Mexico City, in Mexico, with a metropolitan area that includes more than 50 municipalities within three federal states that sums up 17% of the national population; and the Metropolitan Region of São Paulo, in Brazil, which includes 7 municipalities, a major industrial region of the country (ABC) and 10% of National Population. They have some common patterns, are grounded in the region, and exhibit similar trends of violence.[54]

The study focuses on the types of illicit practices and the forms that illegal actors take in the cities. We describe the types and forms of illicit transgressions, the actors associated with it, the different illegal and legal markets that emerge due to it, the routes of traffic passing through the cities created by it,

---

or by illegal actors. These are dynamics of domination and resistance. Each actor develops its best possible strategy in public-urban arenas. Instead of considering the result as coherent, governance is a contradictory and disputed outcome. Conflicts happen in several scales from micro territorial encounters between citizens and authorities, to mezzo, metropolitan and global scales.

51   Robinson, "Introduction to a Virtual Issue on Comparative Urbanism".
52   Hélène Rivière d'Arc, "Une radiographie de la violence dans les métropoles du Sud : le cas de São Paulo," *Revue internationale et stratégique* 112, no. 4 (2018): 149–57, https://doi.org/10.3917/ris.112.0149.
53   Arturo Alvarado, "Urbicide, Violence, and Destruction Against Cities by Criminal Organizations," in *Urbicide: The Death of the City*, ed. Fernando Carrión Mena and Paulina Cepeda Pico (Cham: Springer International Publishing, 2023), 603–35, https://doi.org/10.1007/978-3-031-25304-1_30.
54   Alvarado.

and the government and community reactions. We will distinguish which illicit actions are caused by local factors, and others that come from global causes.

The cases we compare are similar in their urban processes, comparable in the illicit components, relatively diverse in the participation of its citizens and completely contrasting in the government reactions and the results produced by the interaction of criminal actors, government, and citizens. Both cases have common patterns of delinquency, but criminal organizations diverge, and this probably produces two different types of governance arrangements. In one case, São Paulo, there is a debate on whether the outcome is a hybrid regime called criminal governance between the government and a monopolistic criminal actor, the Primeiro Comando da Capital, PCC. In stark contrast, Mexico City experiences the presence and competition of several, local, regional, and transnational criminal organizations (see Table 5)., and another type of contentious, fragmented governance has emerged, where no criminal actor dominates, neither at micro nor urban scales. The Mexican and Brazilian governments have manufactured different responses to crime, according to their own perception of the problem and the pressure from communities and corporations, with stronger and tougher policies against crime than Mexico City.

Our examples are nested into two national states that are also major drivers of the economy in the region and are affected by global crime trends, like narcotraffic and other major transnational crimes that affect the configuration of the city, and its social and political arrangements. Both cities have strong infrastructure development, and strong bureaucratic governments. Policy implementation in each city varies by political coalitions, citizens perceptions and demands, by institutional developments as dependent on past events. Hence, each city offers an opportunity to test our hypothesis on the impact of illicit actions in everyday life. However, we argue that in the end, neither of them can be claimed as governed by crime.

Measurement of illicit activities is conducted using parametric and nonparametric dimensions, including the quality of services and living (Table 5.1); the intensity of violence (Table 5.2), the size of the government and its security apparatus (Table 5.3), and the varieties of illicit organizations (Table 5.4). Data comes from public sources.

5.6   Cases of Study

Mexico City is the largest urban concentration in the North, with a population of nearly twenty-two million in an extensive metropolitan area spanning three states and 50 municipalities. It's the political and financial capital of the country. Mexico City contributes to 15% of the country's GDP and has the biggest state public budget after the federation.[55] It's a hub for several illicit activities, and there is evidence of the presence of several criminal organizations with operations at regional and transnational scales, like the Sinaloa Cartel, Cartel de Jalisco Nueva Generación (CJNG), and several medium and small mafia-like gangs, like La Unión.[56]

São Paulo, on the other end, is situated mainly in its municipality but its metropolitan área extends to more than 39 municipalities. Its population is nearly twenty-two million people. It is the fourth largest city in the world. Its contribution to Brazil's GDP is about 10.8%. It is considered the financial capital of the country and is home to several national and international corporations and technological and media firms. It is considered a global city due to its international connections, its infrastructures, and its global economic role.[57]

The history of the cities is a process of occupation, division, exclusion, and in certain cases integration of irregular and illicit settlements. It is a story of growing illicit economic markets. Both metropolises share similarities in terms of inequalities. They both have a large informal sector in their economies (between 42 and 46%). Both are among the more dynamic urban centers of the region with relatively higher employment rates and income levels than other cities, but still with enormous wealth disparities and high levels of poverty.[58] They are major players in the economic and political arenas of their countries and regions. They also have a better average income and life quality than other cities and have deep contrasts in health, education, and access to public services (both cities are hubs of education in their regions).

---

55   There are some basic legal regulations in the cities of study. On the one hand, for São Paulo there are two important legal institutions: *Estatuto da Cidade*, voted in 2011 and the *Strategic Master Plan* of SP adopted by municipal law 14.430/2002. We can add *"Certificados de Potencial Additional de Construcao"* and *"Zona Especial de Interesse Social".* And for Mexico City, there is a State Constitution from 2018 and several federal regulations for urban growth. Also, the national Constitutions contain basic rules.

56   Mexico City hosts several small gangs and mafias, as well as chapters or sections or franchises of the biggest Mexican criminal transnational organizations. For instance, Cártel Jalisco Nueva Generación, CJNG, ambushed García Harfuch, Secretary of Public Security in early 2020, as a result of the government's effort to undermine and destroy their presence in the city. Other groups, like La Familia, use the territory for economic transactions. The Cartel de Sinaloa uses the city as a place for large monetary transactions and to expand its drug operations. For instance, the government arrested 14 Sinaloa members in Mexico City on July 18TH. 2022 to dissolve one cell of drug distribution in the city.

57   BBC (2009) proposed that São Paulo will be the 6th. richest world city.

58   Both cities have the higher cost of living in Latin America.

São Paulo has had strong segregation produced by class-driven practices; one is the building of fortified enclaves, with consequences for privatization of security and vigilantism, that forces other forms of segregation with the emergence of shantytowns, *cortiços* and vertical favelas (abandoned buildings).[59] The latter are large peripheral urbanizations occupied by underprivileged classes in either irregular or illicit manner, i.e. by invasion, clandestine urbanizations (*fraccionamientos*), or other forms of public and social land irregular or illicit occupation.[60] In Mexico City occupation of land by "colonias," irregular neighborhoods, and clandestine real estate projects, also followed autoconstruction with irregular or illicit access to basic goods, water, sanitation, health, education, and poor access to public services and mobility. This illicit urbanization is also built on patronage and clientelism. These factors are the basis of the concentration of wealth as well as extreme social exclusion, where the poor and disadvantaged are criminalized. It is the foundation-platforms for several forms of violence and illegalities, as this "infrastructure for violence is the assembly line of many violent actions, among them homicides."[61]

According to Adorno and Salla (2007), crime in Brazil and São Paulo started increasing at the end of the 1970s under the dictatorship and kept growing throughout the transition to democracy.[62] It coincided with policies of structural changes enforced by states and cities, like decentralization, liberalization, the opening of global trade, des-industrialization, and prevarication of labor. Homicide rates increased at the time, together with the increase of crime fear from citizens. This transformation was parallel with new waves of crime that became part of a trend of global illicit activities, like narcotraffic, money laundering, human trafficking, counterfeiting, and arms trafficking. Together with petty crime and other modalities of interpersonal or collective violence, they aggregate illicit activities. It affected the public sector, with corruption, racketeering, and other illicit practices, with the involvement of police and other public officials in crime organizations.

---

59   In São Paulo, *Cortiços* are collective housing complexes (tenements) illegally subdivided into family units where services are shared, usually for lease. *Favelas* are irregular or illicit territorial settlements with no clear property rights (Slums). Some urbanizations are extended throughout several blocks in large communities, while others are vertical, like downtown high-rises occupied by families.
60   Rivière d'Arc, "Une radiographie de la violence dans les métropoles du Sud".
61   Peres et al., "Queda dos homicídios no município de São Paulo," pp 709–11.
62   Sérgio Adorno and Fernando Salla, "Criminalidade organizada nas prisões e os ataques do PCC," *Estudos Avançados* 21 (December 2007): 7–29, https://doi.org/10.1590/S0103-401420 07000300002.

Citizens reacted in different manners in each city. Some parts supported the creation of vigilantism, promoting private security and paramilitaries. Middle and upper classes rushed to create secure, isolated, neighborhoods, secluded from the rest of the inhabitants. It transformed middle and upper classes behaviors.[63] The government responded by increasing police presence, promoting selective detentions, and arbitrary and violent reactions, particularly against young poor residents, which in turn increased human rights violations, and an upsurge in the prison population. This in turn led to the rise of punishing practices against inmates in overpopulated prisons and to the rebellion that ended in the tragic massacre of 111 persons in Carandiru Jail, in 1992.[64] Many authors connect the origins of the Primeiro Comando da Capital-PCC to this process and the unbearable living conditions in prisons, as the PCC devised as a prisoner's defensive organization which in the long run expanded its membership to several prisons and certain neighborhoods.[65][66][67] PCC achieved in three decades a quasi-monopoly of illicit activities in Brazil, and a hegemonic control of entire portions of Sao Paulo's territory, imposing its dictates to citizens and authorities.

Mexico City has experienced an increase in crime and episodes of political violence since the middle of the 1990s. Early violence was associated with common crime, rather than drug trafficking or the presence of illicit organizations. By the beginning of the 20th century, a left-wing coalition got into government and implemented reforms to enhance control over police action and plan a reduction of crime. Its strategy produced effective results by 2012 but was then abandoned. Following that, another wave of crime occurred which was aggravated by the cartelization of violence. There have been confrontations between government and criminal groups, particularly in the 2020s, but not a single criminal group has been able to control the urban territory, as it happened in several other regions of the country. Today the organized criminal economy is the main driver of other illicit activities in the region, generating crimes like extortion, kidnapping, and drug trafficking.

---

63   Caldeira, *Cidade de muros*.
64   Thirty years after the tragedy and after several attempts to bring justice to the victims, the Bolsonaro government granted indult to defendants, producing a new controversy and impunity. See: Fernanda Mena, *Folha de São Paulo*, May 20, 2023.
65   Adorno and Salla, "Criminalidade organizada nas prisões e os ataques do PCC".
66   Camila Caldeira Nunes Dias, "PCC: Hegemonia Nas Prisões e Monopólio Da Violência-NEV USP," 2013, https://nev.prp.usp.br/publicacao/pcc-hegemonia-nas-prisoes-e-monopolio-da-violencia/.
67   Feltran, "Fronteiras de tensão".

Over the course of three decades, profound social transformations have taken place in the profile of the two cities, either accentuating the internal heterogeneity between sectors of urban territory or integrating others. Criminal organizations emerged and became a determinant factor in the proliferation of the illicit economy as well as a constitutive part of urbanization, either in confrontation with authorities or sometimes in collusion with them.

Today, their metropolitan areas have major ports, roads, and airports for the distribution of goods. Puerto Santos is connected to São Paulo together with some large distribution centers in the city, for instance to a wholesale center in the territory like *Centrais de Abastecimento* and other informal markets, like *Rua 25 de março* as well as Brazil and *Santa Ifigênia* downtown.[68] Mexico City has the most dynamic international airport in the country, the largest two goods perishables and goods distribution centers in the country (*Central de Abastos*), and more than four wholesale and retail markets in different neighborhoods. Each city hosts the largest affluent malls in the richest and most highly specialized zones. On the other side are very poor and precarious centers of commerce. But we can find both legal and illicit practices in both areas.

Moreover, both urban areas are strongly policed, often compelling violent practices. They are confronted with a systemic challenge to impose a rule of law, particularly from organized crime that disputes the territorial control and sovereignty of areas in the city. They are affected both by local crime and by certain types of global illicit activities. In a previous article we analyze the differential territorial impact of crime and social reactions (See Adorno and Alvarado, 2022). Factors such as inequality, segregation, and socio-spatial accumulation of deprivations are present in these cities and are associated with different expressions of violence.

5.7   Analysis of the Data

We use public records on crime and some reports from surveys on illicit activities. Government information about illicit activities comes mainly from confiscations, seizures during the transportation of the products (by air, trucks, mail), detention, or as a result of capturing gangs. Data has to be used with some caution. It is necessary to take into consideration that definitions of crime in each country and city have strong variations. Penal and regulatory codes are

---

68   Carlos Freire da Silva, "Das calçadas às galerias: mercados populares do centro de São Paulo" (text, Universidade de São Paulo, 2014), https://doi.org/10.11606/T.8.2014.tde-31032 015-105012.

different. Data there needs to be contextualized and harmonized with global data on crime. Data of public registries in each country have different measurements which are also not always compatible. Global registries concentrate on six major activities: narcotraffic, money laundering, corruption, human trafficking (with several related crimes, like sexual and organ trafficking), counterfeiting, and arms trafficking. Each one of these categories includes several illicit actions that are caused by local factors, while others have a connection to international illicit flows and are globalized. For instance, cocaine trafficking or forged goods are manufactured in one country, transported, and then altered in selling markets in both cities.[69] There is also a "gray zone" of not clearly defined illicit actions based on disparities in the enforcement of laws and regulations according to specific contextual and even conjunctural conditions.

It is usually taught that merchandise in informal and clandestine markets has an illegal origin, but that is not the case for several products, such as used or -discontinued- garments. Not all merchandise sold in formal stores are legal. There are numerous examples of big department stores selling merchandise that had infringed innumerable customs rules, like stores selling textiles in Mexico City and luxury garments in São Paulo, and which were raided because of tax evasion and their owners jailed for counterfeit (but not for infringing legal rights and patents of the merchandise). Brazil has a $2.3-billion-a-year

---

69   The greatest forged goods are articles of leather, like handbags produced in Asia and sold in other countries. Most of the goods have an origin in one country, then shipped to other nations via complex trade routes in order to cover their tracks. Some are legal in the country of origin and become illicit in the route of commerce. So, there it is not easy to find what exactly is the illicit product (or its components). They are mixed, interweaved in both markets. And producers and "owners" of the firm are not easily traced. The example of a stolen car or truck in any city followed by Feltran (2019; see also Denyer Willis, 2015) helps understand only one part of the global chain of illicit firms. Besides, police will only capture products at selling points or during distribution, but not in production (not the global chain). Other more complex problems emerge in the market of property rights-patents or licenses. On the issue of drugs, the Andean countries are the producers while our cities are consumers. For firearms, in Mexico City the great majority are purchased in the U.S. In São Paulo various arms are smuggled. According to Aguirre and Muggah (2020: 727) more than 80% of the weapons seized in São Paulo consist of revolvers and pistols, with assault rifles making less than 2%. Brazil is a producer of firearms but in certain cases illicit guns came from Paraguay or from government warehouses. There are indications that PCC is controlling weapon trafficking for the use of their members, particularly the most powerful ones. In Mexico small arms are available at many markets. The rate for firearms homicides was 19 per 100,000 in 2019; and in Brasil 60 per 100,000. That means more that 70% were gun related homicides (Aguirre and Muggah, 2020: 720).

luxury goods market, the largest in Latin America and São Paulo accounts for 755 of the market.[70]

The research we conducted presented the different types of illicit activities occurring locally and globally. Certain products or services might be legal components while others are illegal or involve the circumvention of regulations. We provide 13 categories of products and some illicit services, showing the cities can be the nest of many transgressions as well as the residency of many actors. Sometimes the activity is merely selling or trading illicit products. Other times there are some components of the product that are legal, while others are added and curb some regulation; in certain cases, possession is legal, like marihuana in Mexico City, but selling is forbidden, notably manufacturing and selling unauthorized or pirated soda products.

Another image of the issue at hand is provided in victimization surveys. Mexico has a time series of victimization surveys but unfortunately, only a couple are available for São Paulo, particularly from 2018. One important factor that arises from these types of surveys is the calculation of unreported crime (Table 5.3). For instance, only 43% of victims of property crimes in São Paulo (robbery, house burglary) are registered while 80% of car thefts are registered. Likewise, in Mexico City, 42% of surveyed people were victims of robbery.[71] Overall in Mexico, the unreported victimizations are near 93%.[72] (INEGI, 2023). We analyze multiple forms of victimization suffered by inhabitants in spaces, public and private.[73]

Table 5.1 presents essential data of both cities. The large majority of their territory is densely occupied by low-income people; the majority of land and housing has a history of irregular urbanization. Until recently large proportions were illicit in Mexico City. Even though the provision of basic services is formally established (Table 5.2), there are strong pockets of the territory suffering

---

70 Todd Benson, "Brazil's 'temple of Luxury' Becomes Symbol of Excess," *The New York Times*, July 16, 2005, sec. Business, https://www.nytimes.com/2005/07/16/business/worldbusiness/brazils-temple-of-luxury-becomes-symbol-of-excess.html.
71 For Sao Paulo, we have used the 2018 survey. Also: Brazilian Forum of Public Security, 2020. And Nery, et.al. 2019.
72 INEGI (2023), *Encuesta Nacional de Victimización y Percepción sobre Seguridad Pública*, [En línea] 2018–2023.
73 Measurement of crime in each city varies according to legal definitions, standards of measurement and publications of (timely) reports. There are some striking differences among each city, not only in the data described above, but for instance in events like gun possession, which goes practically uncontrolled in Mexico City. Other striking differences are in certain scores, like the delinquency rate, as well as in perception of insecurity. São Paulo had a steep reduction of insecurity in the last years of more than 30 percentage points.

a lack of basic public services. They are often low quality and infrequent, notably drinkable water. Both cities have the largest low-income areas and the widest areas of deprived housing in the country. Nine percent of Sao Paulo is occupied by *favelas*; the largest and most populated *favelas* in the country, notably the ones named Sapopempa, Paraisópolis or Heliópolis; the last one comprising 200,000 inhabitants in São Paulo. For Mexico City, the eastern and northeast parts of the urban area have similar social and housing conditions. For instance, Sierra Santa Catarina and Xalpa in Alcaldía Iztapalapa, as well as Cuatepec and Tlaxpango in the northern mountains; and metropolitan municipalities' cities like *Ciudad Solidaridad, Ciudad Nezahualcóyotl* or *Ecatepec* share high concentration of poor housing areas and strong segregation.[74]

There are some contrasts in the patterns of land use and redevelopments in both cities, for instance in Downtown areas. While Sao Paulo still has several extremely poor housing areas downtown (like the so-called vertical favelas), Mexico City has been upgrading the area with a strong gentrification phenomenon arising (see Moctezuma, 2021; Alba, 2015).[75]

Income is another important category to consider in the cities. Average income is low by all standards, especially when taking into account that both places are the most expensive living spaces in their countries. The minimum wage is very low in both cities: 8 USD a day for São Paulo and 11 USD for Mexico (for 2024 in Mexico it will be 14 USD, https://www.gob.mx/conasami), and wealth distribution measured by the *Gini* index is strongly concentrated (See Table 5.1 for the adjusted data and sources. Also, Inegi, 2023). This economic condition adds instability in places since strong disparities in living conditions might lead to social tensions.

---

[74] Rosa María Rubalcava, Martha Schteingart, and Jaime Ramírez, *Ciudades Divididas: Desigualdad y Segregación Social En México* (Colegio de Mexico, 2012), https://www.jstor.org/stable/j.ctt14jxr3p.

[75] In a previous study we assembled a sociospatial configuration of both metropolises according to better or worse conditions of living, segregation, inequality and violence (measured by homicides). The variables for both cities were drinking water and sanitation coverage, materials for construction, public services (connection to the city and garbage collection), employment, income levels (proportion of high-income heads of families and low population density), security and violence-measured by homicides (See Adorno and Alvarado, 2022 Dilemas). The classification in Mexico was associated with the division of the city in 16 jurisdictions (and they were sub-classified in 6 groups: 1) high, 2) medium high, 3) medium, 4) medium low, 5) low and 6) very low – the last two the strata accumulate the worst socio spatial conditions (See maps).

5.8 Further Classification of the Metropolis

For São Paulo we use the classification of Nery, De Souza, and Adorno (2019: 8)[76] that divides the city into eight areas, from very high-quality areas with low levels of violence and strong presence of government, to other neighborhoods with lower quality of public services and levels of violence above the average. Central São Paulo, for instance, is a consolidated area that combines good commercial and public service activities, urbanization with high population density, a high proportion of owner-occupier households, a high proportion of verticalization, good levels of sanitary and hygienic conditions and a high proportion of literate, high-income heads of households. There are lower levels of homicides in the area (2019: 8 y ss). Middle and upper classes are segregated and clustered into a walled city (Caldeira, 2000, 1996).[77,78] In contrast, neighborhoods with relatively greater needs tend to have low-quality public services, and higher levels of violence and they solve their necessities through networks of interpersonal relationships or cooperation.

Mexico City is also a strongly segregated city, consistently divided between rich and poor neighborhoods, with very few mixed areas. High-end neighborhoods tend to be situated and clustered in four *Alcaldías* in the West. But some neighborhoods are mixed, there is porosity and communication between residents, and public services tend to be evenly distributed (Rubalcava and Schteingart, 2012: 81).[79] They have lower levels of violence. Neighborhoods are also divided by a variety of local citizens' participatory associations that influence the relationship with authorities and the provision of services. Homicides are also distributed following socio-spatial conditions and can be divided into five groups, associating urban conditions, social orders, and the presence of policing.[80,81,82]

---

76   Marcelo Batista Nery, Altay Alves Lino de Souza, and Sergio Adorno, "Os padrões urbano-demográficos da capital paulista," *Estudos Avançados* 33 (December 2, 2019): 5–36, https://doi.org/10.1590/s0103-4014.2019.3397.002.
77   For Caldeira (2000) segregation patterns erode accessibility, free movements of circulation and equality, corroding public spaces with the walls as constitutive social and physical divides. Also, Rolnik (2015) notes the strong contrast between neighborhoods.
78   Teresa P. R. Caldeira, "Building up Walls: The New Pattern of Spatial Segregation in São Paulo," *International Social Science Journal* 48, no. 147 (1996): 55–66, https://doi.org/10.1111/j.1468-2451.1996.tb00056.x.
79   Rubalcava, Schteingart, and Ramírez, *Ciudades Divididas*.
80   Arturo Alvarado Mendoza, *El Tamaño Del Infierno. Un Estudio Sobre La Criminalidad En La Zona Metropolitana de La Ciudad de México* (El Colegio de Mexico AC, 2012).
81   Mario Díaz (2018) *Distribución diferencial del delito en la Ciudad de México*. Tesis (Doctorado en Sociología) El Colegio de México, Ciudad de México.
82   José Fernández (2021). "Violencia en la Ciudad de México: Controles sociales y eficacia colectiva en la localización geográfica de la violencia". PhD diss.

Those in the very low sections with high levels of violence are located in the eastern and northern areas of the city.

Basic indicators for quality of life and public services, housing, and quality of services are similar in both metropolises. For São Paulo, Water and sanitation (sewage) and garbage collection are fully covered in the urban areas, but there are pockets where public services are lacking.[83] The distribution of services strongly varies according to the neighborhood areas and quality of housing. Life expectancy in Mexico City is near 76 years, while for São Paulo is 79 years but the fertility rate is higher for Mexico. Infant mortality remains high, and formal education levels vary strongly inside the city. Both cities have seen improvements in the provision of education to their citizens.[84]

In terms of urban mobility, Mexico City has longer average displacement times compared to São Paulo, even though its urban infrastructure is wider. (Nava, 2021). The average cost of transportation related to basic (low) income inhabitants is still high, and more expensive in São Paulo, in contrast with the strong subsidies in Mexico City.[85,86]

The maps provide an overview of the trends of illicit activities in São Paulo and Mexico City. Let's start with homicide trends, since they are commonly used as indicators of overall violence as well as an indication of the presence of criminal organizations. Both cities have a relatively low occurrence of homicides compared to other cities within each country as well other metropolitan regions in the continent,[87] since the regional (i.e., Latin America) average in 2018 was a rate of 16.92 homicides per one hundred population. There has been a trend of a small reduction in the homicide rate in recent years in both cities. The causes underlying these trends differ between cities.

In certain places, the trend is linked either to the presence of criminal actors or to police violence. Several studies of homicides in both countries claim that their evolution is strongly linked to criminal organizations' activities and to their capacity to control the territory against other gangs. In the case of Mexico City, there are some cases related to conflicts between and inside gangs. They are distributed around areas of drug distribution, but there are still several

---

83 Nery, Souza, and Adorno, "Os padrões urbano-demográficos da capital paulista".
84 INEGI (2023), *Encuesta Nacional de Victimización y Percepción sobre Seguridad Pública*, [En línea] 2018–2023.
85 Nery, Souza, and Adorno, "Os padrões urbano-demográficos da capital paulista".
86 INEGI (2023), *Encuesta Nacional de Victimización y Percepción sobre Seguridad Pública*, [En línea] 2018–2023.
87 Alvarado, "Urbicide, Violence, and Destruction Against Cities by Criminal Organizations".

ILLICIT URBAN ECONOMIES 179

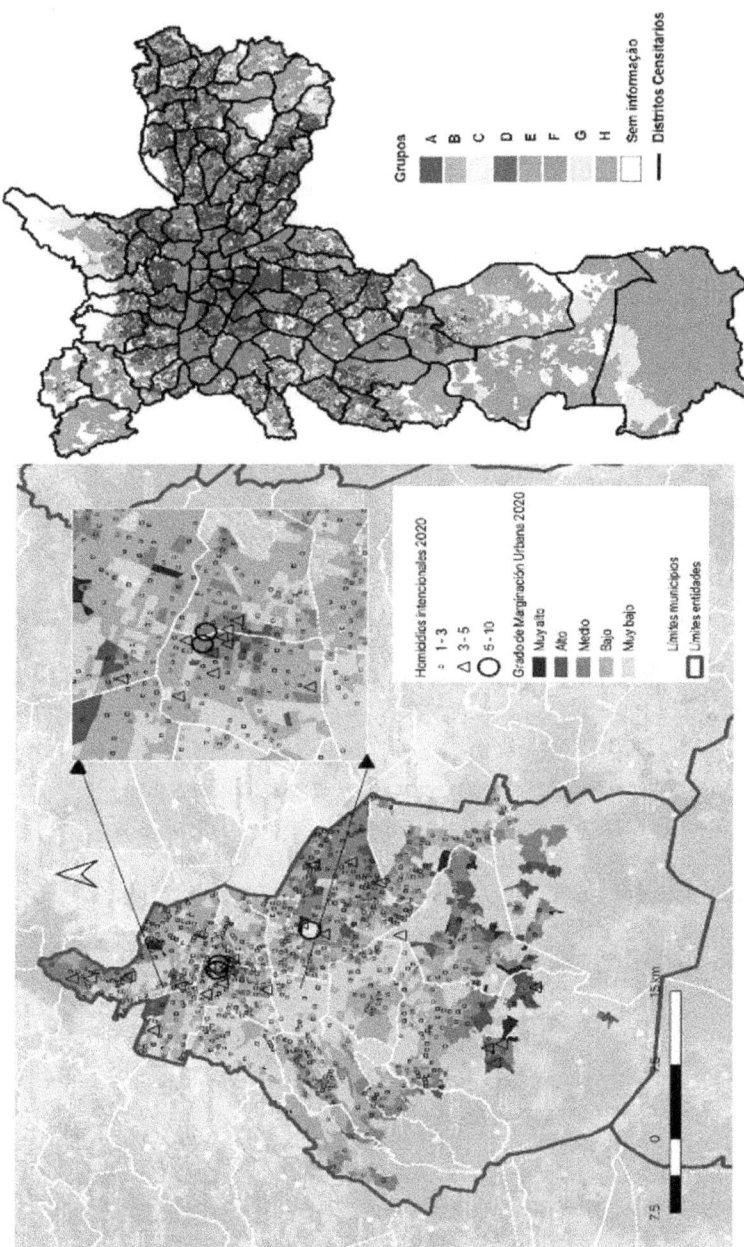

MAP 5.1 Spatial distribution of socioeconomic conditions and violence (homicide rates) in Mexico City (2020) and Sao Paulo (2019)

We use formal limits of each city or municipality. Sources: Map designed by Fernández 2023; Adorno et al. 2019. Data for Mexico city are from 2020. Data for São Paulo are estimations to 2029.

assassinations associated with social disorganization (or low social cohesion) and poor policing in certain neighborhoods.[88] In the case of São Paulo, the dominant thesis is that the consolidation of a crime regime commanded by PCC has led to a reduction of homicides, which are concentrated in the *"periferias"* of the city, with a majority of cases of young black, deprived persons living in low income, low quality of life areas.[89,90,91,92] Another difference in both cases is that police in São Paulo are a major threat to young poor populations and are responsible for a substantive proportion of their deaths.

Another worrying and salient topic is the trend in femicides, a form of extreme gender violence. Their rates have been high in both cities, but there has been a small increase in cases in recent years.

Illicit drug trafficking and drug consumption is another relevant category since there are more sites of consumption rather than production or distribution in these cities. Measure of the activity strongly varies in each city, due to different types of legal definitions and enforcement. So, to make data comparable we pose several types of trends and measures in the table. It is interesting to note that Mexico City has a much higher indication of drug consumption than São Paulo (72% vs 43%). The police department is the principal actor that prosecutes these illegalities and each city manifests a striking difference in cases of seizures, either for commerce or for consumption, in Mexico City consumption is no longer systematically persecuted.

Perception of insecurity is very high in both cases; Mexico City is the place where respondents have a stronger fear of crime. This might come as a paradox, since for the case of São Paulo several cited studies affirm that sensitivity to crime is key to explaining the behavior of the upper classes and the government. To show the strong increase in insecurity in Mexico City, we compare the situation between 2018 and 2013. They are different, since several other socio-economic trends in both cities change a lot between both years, as well as some government authorities in power. We can suggest that social reactions against crime are different and more varied in Mexico City. The most recent survey for São Paulo published by Datafolha on September 4th, 2023, shows

---

88 Mario Pavel Díaz, "Inseguridad y Narcomenudeo En La Ciudad de México: Distribución Diferenciada y Correlativos Asociados".

89 Ana Carolina Pekny and Ricardo Carolina de Mattos, "Principales retos de la violencia y la criminalidad en Brasil, 2017" (Programa de Cooperación en Seguridad Regional-Friedrich-Ebert-Stiftung (FES), diciembre de 2017), https://katalog.gfzk.de/Record/0-1659278449.

90 Feltran, "Fronteiras de tensão".

91 Gabriel Feltran (2018). *Irmãos: Uma história do PCC*.

92 Graham Denyer Willis, *The Killing Consensus: Police, Organized Crime, and the Regulation of Life and Death in Urban Brazil* (Univ of California Press, 2015).

that 22% of residents of the city feel insecure (a difference of 10 points from 2020, during the pandemic) and 18% consider that the government should do something to solve the problem of insecurity and crime.

The overall crime trends show the high prevalence of diverse types of illicit actions in the two cities. Robbery and assault, in all its modalities, represent one daunting picture of the problem. Assault in the street and while using public transportation is high in Mexico City, with a rate of 31 points.[93] Vehicle theft is high in both examples, but the statistics in São Paulo are almost ten times higher than in Mexico City, and the same trends apply for cargo-transport theft (Ostronoff, 2021: 109 & ss).[94] The theft of mobile phones is also a blatant everyday problem. The presence of firearms is evident, even by taking into consideration the number of seized guns (which might be a conservative estimation).

All other types of crimes in both cases have high rates when compared to other cities and countries. Despite the difference in policing policies implemented in both cities, Tables 5.3, 5.3b, and 5.4, show that crime and impunity are still high; they demonstrate that policies have had little impact on the reduction of these illegal activities. This produces low trust in police and in all authorities, which in turn decreases the rates of crime reporting and reinforces impunity.

When comparing the cities with international benchmarks for crime, both receive similar evaluations, of 6.5 and 7.5 scores, high-risk cities, and a high presence of criminal actors, slightly bigger in Mexico City

Table 5.2 provides information on the structures of city governments, in particular their public security apparatus. They are oversized compared with any other city or state in the country. Policing is the key figure for the provision of public services, and each city has its own organizations and spatial distribution of police corps. Each city has a central, state police (Civilian police in Mexico City, Military Police in the other) and both have a "civil" or "judiciary" police (ascribed to prosecutors' offices). Both cities are still strongly centralized, but São Paulo presents a wider distribution of police (in *delegacias*). Even though they have the largest number of police corps compared to any other city in the world, São Paulo has 130,000 policemen in the State, while Mexico has 90,000 (Only New York has a similar amount). The rate of policemen *per cápita* is very low (4.3. per one hundred thousand population in Mexico City, see Table 5.4). They also have a strong number of private police corps, resulting in better security for the ones able to afford them. Both have some military

---

93 A reliable estimation is lacking for Sao Paulo.
94 Leonardo José Ostronoff, "Não existe almoço grátis," 2021, https://aeditora.com.br/prod uto/nao-existe-almoco-gratis/.

TABLE 5.2 Government, regulatory systems and structure of public security

Dimensions/city	São Paulo	Ciudad de México	Sources
Government structure	Municipal government; Alcaldía (Mayor); Legislative Chamber; Judiciary; 24 Ministries; 2 houses (civilian and military). Multiparty system W/ Open list. City Council	Organized like State: Executive, Legislative and Judicial branches; autonomous institutions; 16 secretarías & 4 autonomous comissions & 16 Alcaldías (municipalities) W/Councils. Mixed electoral and multiparty system	1
Government (centralized-decentralized)	Decentralized since 1988 Constitution and w/ Estatuto de cidade	State-Federal Authonomy since 2017 State Constitution (weak decentralization)	
Democratic Regime Urban regulation (strong, soft)	Stable since return to democracy Strong Federal – municipal	Stable transition from Autocracy Weak	
Political composition – orientation Government coalition	Alternance; Ricardo Nunes-MDB-Center-Right (2021-2024)	Leftwing coalition since 1997 1st. election (C. Sheinbaum-Morena, 2018-2023) Morena strong majority in State Legislature; 7/16 Municipalities governed by Morena	2
Urban government (centralized-decentralized)	Semi-Centralized – municipal (32 prefecturas, 96 distritos); participatory processes	Centralized w/municipalities; participatory processes	
Rule of Law index or criminal justice index (country) 2022	0.52	0.36	3

ILLICIT URBAN ECONOMIES

(cont.)

Dimensions/city	São Paulo	Ciudad de México	Sources
Corruption (index) 2022	0.43	.26 (High perception of corruption)	4
Order and Security Score (WJP) 2020 Country)	0.64	0.53	5
Provision of Public Security	State Secretariat of Public Security & Municipal	Ministry of Public Security	
Organization of Police	Two main bodies "Polícia Militar"; "Polícia Civil", Special Operation Batallions, Polícia Científica (some neighorhood programs)	Centralized-State police (Partial municipal decentralization). Divided by Preventive (w/many corps, like SOB), Ministerial ("civil") Police. With public and private corps. Respond to Major	6
City Police	130,672 (state)	90 thousand	7
Police per cápita	10.8 Per 1000 Inhabitants	4.3 officers per 1,000 inhabitants	8
Military presence	Military Police	Military support and local operation from Guardia Nacional & Marines.	
Budget for public security	US $ 2,6 Billion	US $1,3 Billion	9
Private policing (c. 2020. Corporations) Police	1,515	1,055 (c.70 thousand employees)	
Police investigations, 2022	3,59,598	2,19,379	10
Flagrant Arrests (2021)	2,504	2,413	11

(*cont.*)

Dimensions/city	São Paulo	Ciudad de México	Sources
Arrests with warrant (2021)	88	2,930	12
Prison Population (2020)	14,819	26,148	13
Pretrial detainees (% of total)	27.20%	23.40%	14
Deaths caused by police (as % of violent deaths) (2016)	25%	n.d.	15
Number of deaths caused by police (2021)	570	n.d.	16
Perception of Police Corruption	66.9	64.6%	17
% Trust in police (2022)	n.d.	44%	18
Sources			
Note number.	Brasil	Mexico	
1	https://dialnet.unirioja.es/descarga/articulo/935612.pdf	https://www.scielo.org.mx/scielo.php?script=sci_arttext&pid=S1405-91932017000100243	
2	https://www.infobae.com/america/america-latina/2020/11/29/bruno-covas-de-centroderecha-fue-reelegido-como-alcalde-en-san-pablo/	https://elpais.com/internacional/2018/12/05/mexico/1543982951_032393.html	

(cont.)

Dimensions/city	São Paulo	Ciudad de México	Sources
3	https://worldjusticeproject.org/rule-of-law-index/country/2020/Brazil/ & Mexico	https://worldjusticeproject.mx/wp-content/uploads/2020/02/1_ReporteSpanish_MSI-2019-2020-VF2.pdf	
4	https://worldjusticeproject.org/rule-of-law-index/country/2020/Brazil/Absence%20of%20Corruption/. https://worldjusticeproject.mx/wp-content/uploads/2020/02/1_ReporteSpanish_MSI-2019-2020-VF2.pdf	https://contralacorrupcion.mx/anatomiadigital/content/corrupcion-en-mexico.php	
5	https://worldjusticeproject.org/rule-of-law-index/country/2020/Brazil/Order%20and%20Security/	https://worldjusticeproject.org/rule-of-law-index/country/2020/Mexico/Order%20and%20Security/	
6	https://www.saopaulo.sp.gov.br/spnoticias/estado-de-sao-paulo-conta-com-11-baeps	https://www.congresocdmx.gob.mx/media/documentos/851ce38484d58110 2bc726bc6795b528c815b930.pdf	
7	https://forumseguranca.org.br/wp-content/uploads/2022/06/anuario-2022.pdf?v=15		

(cont.)

Dimensions/city	São Paulo	Ciudad de México	Sources
8	https://forumseguranca.org.br/wp-content/uploads/2022/06/anuario-2022.pdf?v=15	https://secretariadoejecutivo.gob.mx//doc/Actualizacion_Diagnostico_Nacional_MOFP.pdf	
9	https://forumseguranca.org.br/wp-content/uploads/2022/06/anuario-2022.pdf?v=15	https://www.finanzas.cdmx.gob.mx/servicios-al-contribuyente/presupuesto-de-egresos-2022	
10	https://www.ssp.sp.gov.br/estatistica/pesquisa.aspx	https://www.fgjcdmx.gob.mx/procuraduria/estadisticas-delictivas	
11	http://www.ssp.sp.gov.br/Estatistica/Pesquisa.aspx	INEGI, ENPOL https://www.inegi.org.mx/programas/enpol/2021/#Tabulados	
12	http://www.ssp.sp.gov.br/Estatistica/Pesquisa.aspx	INEGI, ENPOL https://www.inegi.org.mx/programas/enpol/2021/#Tabulados	
13	Levantamento Nacional de Informações Penitenciárias. Departamento Penitenciário Nacional. Disponível em <https://www.gov.br/depen/pt-br/sisdepen>. Acesso em 12/08/1998. Brasil prison population: 835,643	https://penitenciario.cdmx.gob.mx/poblacion-penitenciaria	
14		https://www.inegi.org.mx/programas/cnsipee/2022/#Tabulados	

(cont.)

Dimensions/city	São Paulo	Ciudad de México	Sources
15	De Mattos, 2017. Instituto Sou da Paz, 2017a		
16	https://forumseguranca.org.br/wp-content/uploads/2022/07/anuario-2022-ed-especial.pdf		
17	https://sidra.ibge.gov.br/tabela/8730#resultado. (2021, nacional, si confian, policia civil)	https://www.inegi.org.mx/temas/percepciondes/	
18		https://www.inegi.org.mx/programas/envipe/2022/	

presence, in Brazil, state police are militarized. In Mexico City, the military is used as a complementary and support corporation for the civilian police, particularly to patrol very violent areas as well as prosecute federal crimes. Their budget is also quite large for any city or state measure. Even though impunity is high, the number of police inquiries appears to be significant. Mexico City has many more arrests with warrants.[95]

The relationship between prisons and poor neighborhoods has been proposed in the literature as another explanation for the high levels of crime in these urban areas. Prisons are more important in São Paulo with nearly 240,000 prisoners (nearly 40% of the country's prisoners), and more than 179 facilities in that state alone. In contrast, Mexico City has only 13 penitentiary centers with nearly 26,000 inmates, almost 10% of the former.[96] This city has a much higher prison population than São Paulo, but in contrast, its state has a huge number of prisons throughout the state. This becomes a determinant factor in public security, criminal justice, policing, governance, and social justice, with strong police profiling and punishment against poor young populations from slums and the criminalization of black youth in São Paulo. Pretrial detainees are high in both cases, at least one-quarter of total prisoners.

Both governments carry on large amounts of police personnel, but this has not led to more effective crime reduction. Policing is very selective by city zones, socio-economic residence of classes, type of delinquency, and types of offenders. Authorities are also driven by electoral incentives as citizens are sensible to how they spend money on security.

Both cities confront big problems of police violence and repressive police practices. Police violence is a strong concern in São Paulo (with 25% of total deaths caused by these actions in 2017).[97] It is expected that trust and perception of police corruption is high. São Paulo police have been involved in a vicious cyclic combat with PCC and other small gangs, leading to a dramatically large number of police killings in the city, particularly during the last decade.[98,99,100] The most recent case resulted in the deaths of 14 individuals

---

95   In São Paulo in 2016 76% of detentions were "flagrant" arrest Pekny y De Mattos, 2017 P.23. Instituto Sou da Paz, 2017: 30.
96   Subsecretaría del Sistema Penitenciario de la Ciudad de México. (2023).
97   Pekny and Ricardo, "Principales retos de la violencia y la criminalidad en Brasil, 2017".
98   Jonathan Jackson et al., "Fear and Legitimacy in São Paulo, Brazil: Police–Citizen Relations in a High Violence, High Fear City," *Law & Society Review* 56, no. 1 (March 2022): 122–45, https://doi.org/10.1111/lasr.12589.
99   Camila Dias et al., "A prática de execuções na região metropolitana de São Paulo na crise de 2012: um estudo de caso," *Revista Brasileira de Segurança Pública* 9, no. 2 (October 2, 2015): 160–79, https://doi.org/10.31060/rbsp.2015.v9.n2.507.
100 Samira Bueno (2014). *Letalidade na ação policia*. In: Lima, R., Ratton, S., José Luiz; Ghiringhelli de Azevedo, R. (eds.).

after police were searching for the person that killed one policeman, Patrick Bastos, while patrolling.[101]

The political environment is very dynamic and competitive, nested within federal systems. In the case of São Paulo, there has been a systematic alternation of municipal governments from a very competitive party system. Mexico City, by contrast, has had a dominant left-wing party in power since the transition to democracy in 1997, in permanent confrontation with national authorities from a right-wing party, which gives incentives to the government to compete and fight security policies from the Presidency. They systematically accused each other of failing policies and protecting or collaborating with criminals. But in 2018 the same coalition won the presidency and changed the dynamics of confrontation for collaboration. Their budget is also a matter of interest. For instance, the budget for public security tends to concentrate more than a quarter of the total city budget.[102] The important point is whether this type of political coalition is prepared to handle crime legally or, on the contrary, is prompt to engage in violent reactive policies or even in collusive behavior. In the case of São Paulo, evidence is that public policies have been reactive to upper-middle-class fear of crime, while in Mexico, at least formerly, authorities have been careful and promote less violent interventions. It is clear from the data and the analysis in this chapter that public policies in security have been ineffective.

5.9 The Different Forms of Criminal Organizations in the City

Tables 5.3 and 5.3b provide an overview of the different types of illicit organizations and the fields of activities they control at the city level. The literature for São Paulo evokes the hegemonic presence of the PCC. But as we show in the table, the picture needs to add several other types of illicit activities and actors in different economic sectors as well as other areas of the metropolis. In contrast, Mexico City has many organizations operating at the urban-metropolitan scale, either criminal networks, state-embedded actors, transnational cartels

---

101 Mauricio Savarese, "Sao Paulo Police Kill 14 People in Raid as They Investigate the Slaying of an Elite Officer," AP News, August 2, 2023, https://apnews.com/article/sao-paulo-police-killings-brazil-13e56cf6f1cd586f92757468d4c9601b.

102 Mendoza, *El Tamaño Del Infierno. Un Estudio Sobre La Criminalidad En La Zona Metropolitana de La Ciudad de México.*

TABLE 5.3 Typology of urban violences

Activity/city	São Paulo	Mexico city
Illicit drugs market (size, extension)	High; largest cannabis market in L.A. 1st Track w/cocaine (SP & its Port Santos-Traffick)	Generalized, retailed, bulk markets of Cocaine, Opioids, Methamphetamines, cannabis & synthetic drugs (MxCity airport as a drug-hub)
Other illicit activities (counterfeit, smuggling, piracy)	High	High
Other criminal activities	several	several, extortion,
Construction-Housing	PCC involvement; Militias in housing; collapse of squatered high rise in Downtown; new urbanizations	Traffic of land, apartments, traffic of land titles, invasions; cartel inmobiliario of A. B. Juárez
Regularization of land occupation and Autoconstruction	traffic of titles, lands, permits, housing	Legalization of irregular titles (1990's-present). Ambiguous property regimes
Water (smuggling, illegal selling, black market)		
Services, power, cable, sewage, garbage		
Public works (contracts, sub-contracts, licenses, services)	Corruption, favoritism (collusion)	Manipulation of developing plans, zoning, major public projects; corruption
Prescence of other (violent) conflicts (civil, war)	No	No

ILLICIT URBAN ECONOMIES   191

TABLE 5.3   Typology of urban violences (*cont.*)

Activity/city	São Paulo	Mexico city
National violence (criminal, civil conflicts, other conflicts, violence level)	No civil conflict; Prescence of PCC, CV, FDN. Local and regional disputes	Several small, local criminal organizations warring in different regions of the country. Some have territorial control of regions and States
Criminal organizations with territorial prescence and control	PCC Dominance (small local groups)	Several small, territorial gangs and cartels (Unión); presence of CJNG; CS and other regional and transnational groups
Other uncommon criminal actors, associations, mafias, protection rackets	Odebrecht. Cases of smuggling, counterfeit in high end stores	Informal vendors associations (and it political links); Illicit construction
Real State illicit activities (housing, developments, change of land use; environmental regulations)	Poor housing. Intrusions of PCC in housing. Occupied buildings in Centro Histórico (manipulation of real state developments)	Middle class housing: Corruption rackets (mafias?); "Cartel inmobiliario" B. Juárez. Construction of "el Dorito" in Lomas; traffic of land and property titles in Alcaldía Cuautémoc; traffic of titles and land permits in Centro Histórico. Torre Virreyes o Torre Pedregal 24 mega tower near Sta Fe
Vigilantism	Private policing, digital surveillance; private security companies; neighborhood surveillance	Iztapalapa, south-suburban; "private security" firms (Tepito) and Down Town "Centro histórico"; Surveillant system and companies.
Protection rackets	(*Police*)	Police; mafias, criminal organizations inside public security sector (Garía Luna and Garduño)

TABLE 5.3 Typology of urban violences (cont.)

Activity/city	São Paulo	Mexico city
Political elite corruption-collusion w/ criminal actors	Lava Jato, cases of corruption of Mayors; budget manipulation	Mafias in Alcaldías ("Cartel de B Juárez;" extractivism in Coyoacán (Tejera y Rodríguez, 2022)
Illicit electoral activities (illicit financing, Vote buying)	Cases of corruption	Electoral illicit actions (canvasing, vote buying, coercion to voters)
Illicit markets and markets for violence	SP-PCC-monopoly	Spaces for illicit and coercive competition
Prescence of guerrillas	No	No

(regional, foreign), militias, self-defense groups and paramilitaries, protection racket gangs, and corporations. No one can claim a hegemonic power.

Illegal activities in contention include (1) illicit drug traffic organizations (cocaine, marihuana, fentanyl, opium-based drugs, and other medicinal drugs). It is estimated that São Paulo operates the biggest drug trafficking and organized crime in any city in America (together with its nearest port Santos[103], see Table 5.4) resulting in a mixed, competitive, sometimes violent confrontation of groups to control the varied drug city markets in rich and poor areas; then (2) Car theft organizations-rings which have been consolidated, decentralized, with transnational criminal connections; (3) criminal organizations dedicated to extortion; (4) Police organizations involved in the protection rackets; (5) Networks of distributors of pirated, smuggled and stolen products, like and music, movies, clothes, garment, shoes and entertainment products. It includes leaders of merchants organizations and other gangs and mafias in large markets like Tepito in Mexico City; (6) Kidnapping groups, which include gangs and mafias (some linked to the police); (7) Human trafficking, including

---

103 Gabriel Patriarca, & S. Adorno (2023). Mergulhando aos cascos em portos brasileiros: adaptações recíprocas em torno de uma modalidade de tráfico internacional de cocaína.

ILLICIT URBAN ECONOMIES 193

TABLE 5.3B Trends in illicit activities

Illicit topics	Dimension / city	São Paulo	Mexico city	Sources
Extreme violence	Homicide rates per one hundred thousand population (per one hundred thousand. 2022)	6.44 (2,909 cases) 6.44 (2,909 cases) 6.44 (2,909 cases)	12 (1,440 cases) 12 (1,440 cases) 12 (1,440 cases)	1
	Homicide rates, 2018	6.7	16.11	2
	Femicides. State cases, 2021	136	73	3
	Femicide rate (in state) (2021)	0.60	0.79	4
	Injuries (cases, 2022)	1,22,818	1,14,932	5
	Sexual crimes rates (2018)	9.5	4.32	6
Illicit activities' trends	Crime rate (incidence) 2018-2021	58	45.33 (2021) 69.71 (2018) 45.33 (2021) 69.71 (2018) 45.33 (2021) 69.71 (2018)	7
	Overall victimization rate (Mexico, 2018; Sao Paulo 2018)	41.5	42.6	8
	Property crime rates (robbery, theft) (per one hundred thousand population)	271.07	6,582	9
	Robbery rate (with violence) 2022	1,43,936	8,622	10
	Robbery rate (without violence) 2022	2,36,145	2,064	11
	Robbery and assault rates per one hundred thousand people (includes in Public transport for Mexico City) -2021	1,079	13,654	12
	Vehicle Theft (non violent, 2022)	40,163	4,628	13

(cont.)

Illicit topics	Dimension / city	São Paulo	Mexico city	Sources
	Vehicle Theft with violence (2022)	16,020	1,628	14
	Cargo – transport theft (2021)	6,529	2,186	15
Drug traffic	Drug trafficking seizures (for distribution or trade) 2022 & 2020	41,560	6,959	16
	Drug seizures (for consumption) 2020 Drug seizures (for consumption) 2020	13,676	73,601	17
	(individual) illicit drug seizures 2020	1,990	4,837	18
	Illicit drug seizures 2021 (for distribution or commerce) (cases/product seized)	(483)	1,133.20 kg	19
	Illicit drug seizures 2021 (for distribution or commerce) (cases/product seized)			
Fire arms	Confiscation of fire arms (2021)	3,071	686	20
	Illicit gun possession (detentions, 2020)	4,441	130	21
Theft	Mobile phone thefts (year events, 2022, 2018)	2,00,000	10,24,303	22
Unreported crime	Estimated not reported crime (–2022)	n.a.	92%	23
Criminal scores	Criminality Score (GIAOC, 2020)	6.5	7.57	24
	Criminal Actors (GIAOC score)	6.5	7.13	25

(cont.)

Illicit topics	Dimension / city	São Paulo	Mexico city	Sources
Victimization	Estimated Victims of crime (per one hundred thousand population)	41.5	42.6	26
	Delinquency rate	15,382.91	69.7	27
	Individual reports o robbery or assault in streets or in Public transport (rate) (2019)	n.a.	31.0	28
	Armed assaults rates (2018–2019)	26.1	49.9	29
	Measure of perception of insecurity in population (2013–2018)	54.3% (2013)	73.0% (2013) 88.3 % (2018)	30
	Trust in Police (State)	15.8 (2013)	13.9 (2013) 9.7 (2018)	31
	Report of drug selling points	397	52	32
Sources				
Note number.	Brasil http://www.ssp.sp.gov.br/Estatistica/Pesquisa.aspx		Mexico https://www.gob.mx/sesnsp/acciones-y-programas/incidencia-delictiva-del-fuero-comun-nueva-metodologia?state=published	

(cont.)

Illicit topics	Dimension / city	São Paulo	Mexico city	Sources
2		http://www.ssp.sp.gov.br/Estatistica/Pesquisa.aspx	INEGI. Estadísticas de mortalidad https://www.inegi.org.mx/sistemas/olap/proyectos/bd/continuas/mortalidad/defuncioneshom.asp?s=est&c=28820&proy=mortgral_dh	
3		https://forumseguranca.org.br/wp-content/uploads/2022/07/anuario-2022-ed-especial.pdf	https://www.inegi.org.mx/contenidos/programas/cnpje/2022/doc/cnpje_2022_resultados.pdf	
4		https://forumseguranca.org.br/wp-content/uploads/2022/07/anuario-2022-ed-especial.pdf	https://www.inegi.org.mx/contenidos/programas/cnpje/2022/doc/cnpje_2022_resultados.pdf	
5		http://www.ssp.sp.gov.br/Estatistica/Mapas.aspx	inegi. *Encuesta Nacional de Victimización y Percepción sobre Seguridad Pública 2022 (envipe). Tabulados básicos.* https://www.inegi.org.mx/programas/envipe/2022/#Tabulados	
6		Assédio Sexual. Relatório da Pesquisa de Vitimização em São Paulo – 2018 Centro de Políticas Públicas – Insper (p. 22)	Envipehttps://www.inegi.org.mx/programas/envipe/2019/#Tabulados	
7		"Pessoas que foi victim of crime ou Agresso algumas vez na vida." Relatório da Pesquisa de Vitimização em São Paulo – 2018 Centro de Políticas Públicas – Insper (p. 4)	INEGI, ENVIPE (2021) https://www.inegi.org.mx/temas/incidencia	

(cont.)

Illicit topics	Dimension / city	São Paulo	Mexico city	Sources
8		Relatório da Pesquisa de Vitimização em São Paulo – 2018 Centro de Políticas Públicas – Insper		https://www.inegi.org.mx/programas/envipe/2019/#Tabulados
9		http://www.ssp.sp.gov.br/Estatistica/Pesquisa.aspx		https://www.inegi.org.mx/contenidos/Salvadoreans/boletines/2022/ENVIPE/ENVIPE2022.pdf
10		https://www-snsp-sp-gov-br.translate.goog/Estatistica/PainelIndicadores.aspx?_x_tr_sch=http&_x_tr_sl=pt&_x_tr_tl=es&_x_tr_hl=es&_x_tr_pto=wapp		https://www.gob.mx/sesnsp/acciones-y-programas/datos-abiertos-de-incidencia-delictiva?state=published
11		http://www.ssp.sp.gov.br/Estatistica/Mapas.aspx		https://www.gob.mx/sesnsp/acciones-y-programas/datos-abiertos-de-incidencia-delictiva?state=published
12		*Dados Estatísticos do Estado de São Paulo. Secretaria de Segurança Pública de São Paulo – Portal da Transparência. Disponível em* <http://www.ssp.sp.gov.br/Estatistica/Pesquisa.aspx>. *Acesso em 12/08/2010.Dados Estatísticos do Estado de São Paulo. Secretaria de Segurança Pública de São Paulo – Portal da Transparência. Disponível em* <http://www.ssp.sp.gov.br/Estatistica/Pesquisa.aspx>. *Acesso em 12/08/2010.* http://www.ssp.sp.gov.br/Estatistica/Mapas.aspx		https://www.inegi.org.mx/programas/envipe/2022/
13				https://www.fgjcdmx.gob.mx/procuraduria/estadisticas-delictivas

(*cont.*)

Illicit topics	Dimension / city	São Paulo	Mexico city	Sources
14		http://www.ssp.sp.gov.br/Estatistica/Mapas.aspx	https://www.fgjcdmx.gob.mx/procuraduria/estadisticas-delictivas	
15		http://www.ssp.sp.gov.br/Estatistica/Mapas.aspx	https://www.inegi.org.mx/programas/enve/2022/#Tabulados	
16		http://www.ssp.sp.gov.br/Estatistica/Pesquisa.aspx	https://www.inegi.org.mx/contenidos/programas/cnspe/2022/doc/cnspe_2022_resultados.pdf	
17		http://www.ssp.sp.gov.br/Estatistica/Pesquisa.aspx	https://www.inegi.org.mx/contenidos/programas/cnspe/2022/doc/cnspe_2022_resultados.pdf	
18		http://www.ssp.sp.gov.br/Estatistica/Pesquisa.aspx	https://www.inegi.org.mx/programas/enpol/2021/#Tabulados	
19		http://www.ssp.sp.gov.br/Estatistica/Pesquisa.aspx	https://www.inegi.org.mx/programas/cnpje/2021#Tabulados https://www.inegi.org.mx/contenidos/programas/cnpje/2022/doc/cnpje_2022_resultados.pdf	

(cont.)

Illicit topics	Dimension / city	São Paulo	Mexico city	Sources
20		https://forumseguranca.org.br/wp-content/uploads/2022/07/anuario-2022-ed-especial.pdf	https://www.inegi.org.mx/programas/cnpje/2021/#Tabulados https://www.inegi.org.mx/programas/enpol/2021/#Tabulados	
21		http://www.ssp.sp.gov.br/Estatistica/Pesquisa.aspx	https://ocindex.net/country/mexico	
22		https://g1.globo.com/fantastico/noticia/2023/03/27/sao-paulo-teve-mais-de-200-mil-registros-de-ocorrencias-de-furto-e-roubo-de-celular-em-2022-mostra-levantamento.ghtml	https://www.inegi.org.mx/programas/envipe/2022/#Tabulados	
23		n.d. hay algunos datos de crimen no reportado en Pesquisa Nacional de Vitimização 2012 Relatório completo CRISP, pero son muy pocos casos y van separados por delito	*https://www.inegi.org.mx/programas/envipe/2022/*	
24		https://ocindex.net/assets/downloads/english/ocindex_profile_brazil.pdf	https://ocindex.net/assets/downloads/english/ocindex_profile_mexico.pdf	
25		https://ocindex.net/assets/downloads/english/ocindex_profile_brazil.pdf	https://ocindex.net/assets/downloads/english/ocindex_profile_mexico.pdf	
26		Relatório da Pesquisa de Vitimização em São Paulo – 2018 Centro de Políticas Públicas – Insper	ENVIPE 2018 https://www.inegi.org.mx/programas/envipe/2018/#Tabulados	

(cont.)

Illicit topics	Dimension / city	São Paulo	Mexico city	Sources
27		http://www.ssp.sp.gov.br/Estatistica/Pesquisa.aspx https://sidra.ibge.gov.br/Tabela/6579#resultado http://www.ssp.sp.gov.br/Estatistica/Pesquisa.aspx https://sidra.ibge.gov.br/Tabela/6579#resultado	ENVIPE 2018 https://www.inegi.org.mx/programas/envipe/2018/#Tabulados	
28			ENVIPE 2019 https://www.inegi.org.mx/programas/envipe/2019/#Tabulados. ªtotal de delitos (cdmx) 4,830,779.	
29	"ameaça com arma de fogo" Relatório da Pesquisa de Vitimização em São Paulo – 2018 Centro de Políticas Públicas – Insper (p.4)		ENVIPE 2019 https://www.inegi.org.mx/programas/envipe/2019/#Tabulados. *total de delitos (cdmx) 4,830,779.	
30	Pesquisa Nacional de Vitimização (PNV) 2013, lançada agora pelo Ministério da Justiça, através da SENASP (p.229)		ENVIPE 2018: https://www.inegi.org.mx/programas/envipe/2018/#Tabulado senvipe 2013: https://www.inegi.org.mx/programas/envipe/2013/#Tabulados	
31	mucha confianza en policia estatal / Confiança na Polícia Civil (taxa de confia muito)		ENVIPE 2018 https://www.inegi.org.mx/programas/envipe/2018/#Tabulado sENVIPE 2013 https://www.inegi.org.mx/programas/envipe/2013/#Tabulados	

(cont.)

Illicit topics	Dimension / city	São Paulo	Mexico city	Sources
32		http://www.ssp.sp.gov.br/Estatistica/Trimestrais.aspx Data from SP is for drug traffic https://sidra.ibge.gov.br/Tabela/6579#resultado	ENVIPE 2019 https://www.inegi.org.mx/programas/envipe/2019/#Tabulados	

organ trafficking, migrants, sexual, children's, and other forced labor trafficking; (8) Arms trafficking; (9) Counterfeiting; (10) Forfeiting and (11) Money laundering; (12) Vigilante groups formed by residents (and in some cases with the help of police); White collar crime groups, corruption rings inside the government, particularly inside police and justice administration areas. And (13) protection rackets crafted by policemen. In certain cases, police organizations act as the principal criminal actors.[104] Judicial or civil police tend to have an extortive-collusive relationship with criminal groups.

Some criminal actors need more territorial control than others.[105] Some activities require more organization and more government protection than others. Some illegal activities in urban areas are linked to violent extortion, forced-coercive loans, fraudulent construction of housing, or illicit service provision, including trafficking of drinking water, gas, energy power, garbage collection, and paid access to government resources and public employment. Licenses to work in public transportation are sometimes acquired through corruption networks (For Mexico, see: El Universal, April 24, 2019). Some private services are offered by illicit firms, like cable, phone, internet, health, private police, and even "justice" services.

In addition, illicit electoral practices are carried out by partisan groups, sometimes by government officials, and in certain cases by criminal actors. Parties and candidates need funding and both electoral rules and competition provide incentives for candidates and parties to collect illicit money to spend during elections (*"war chests"*) usually with illegal funding (even from the government).

The citizens' reactions to the presence of criminal organizations in their neighborhood vary from different neighbors, and go from open resistance, to consent or in some cases embracing the local dominance of these actors. In Mexico City, we observed the formation of self-defense neighborhoods or vigilante organizations against crime and other gangs.[106]

---

104   Mendoza, *El Tamaño Del Infierno. Un Estudio Sobre La Criminalidad En La Zona Metropolitana de La Ciudad de México.*
105   In Arturo Alvarado, "Organizaciones criminales en América Latina: una discusión conceptual y un marco comparativo para su reinterpretación | Criminal organizations in Latin America: a comparative conceptual framework for its reinterpretation," *Revista Brasileira de Sociologia – RBS* 7, no. 17 (November 6, 2019), https://doi.org/10.20336/rbs .539, we classify the different illicit organizations by looking at the main field of activity, at the number of personnel, the labor division, the coordination and internal hierarchy, its jurisdictions and the different protection measures.
106   These associations have territorial control of public and private spaces where they operate, and power to interact with local governments. *Vigilante* associations pretend to control their territory. Each group pretends to have coercive capacity, but that is very limited.

Some criminal organizations, vigilante groups, and state-embedded criminal actors were founded in these cities. Our research shows how in Mexico City's territory, many groups have arisen, as splits of former gangs, sometimes sponsored by major transnational cartels trying to get into local markets. According to[107] Mexico City hosts at least eight illicit local groups of different sizes. Other gangs and mafias are publicly recognized by authorities, like cargo-assault and auto-theft groups; arms trading organizations; some local human trafficking rings linked to global criminal networks. Only two or three local groups have been selectively prosecuted by the government, mainly La Unión, the Tláhuac and Los Rodolfos groups (see sources in Table 5.4).[108] In addition, there are some branches of CJNG, some ex-members of Beltrán Leyva cartel or la Familia, which are also active in the city, as well as other foreign gangs not usually mentioned, from Colombia, China, or Russia (see Table 5bis). They develop corridors to distribute drugs and other merchandise and set selling points in various neighborhoods (both poor and affluent), in business districts, in the airport, and wholesale distribution centers. All of these organized criminal groups have set a foothold, a branch or a franchise to manage or outsource their business, to have a foothold in this important financial hub. They carry on covered operations without confronting or being prosecuted by government actors, as long as they don't become too visible or violent.[109]

In the majority of the cases their presence and capacity are bounded between limited territories, like informal markets (Tepito, San Felipe, Las Torres) or drug-traffic corridors, in the eastern and northern ring of the urbanized area.

107 Sérgio Adorno and Arturo Alvarado, "Crime and the Governance of Large Metropolises in Latin America: Mexico City (Mexico) and São Paulo (Brazil)," *Dilemas – Revista de Estudos de Conflito e Controle Social*, June 21, 2022, 117–51, https://doi.org/10.4322/dilemas.v15e sp4.52505.

108 A recent important article estimated the number of personnel employed by criminal organizations in Mexico at 175,000 persons. It did not provide specifics for state or local groups. The largest organizations are CJN and CS, and small gangs like the mentioned in Mexico City still employ large amounts of personnel either directly or indirectly. See: Prieto, Campedelli and Hope (2023), *Reducing cartel recruitment is the only way to lower violence in Mexico. Science*, 381, 1312–1316. September 22, 2023.

109 Evidence of the power of Criminal organizations was shown on June 26, 2020, when the Secretary of Public Security (Omar García Harfuch) was attacked but survived an assassination attempt on Reforma Blvd., one of the main arteries from an affluent residential area of the city. Three persons died at the event, among them his bodyguards. The attack was perpetrated by eight men posted in a truck blocking the street, firing several rounds of ammunition with high power Barrett firearms. Later on, eight persons were detained and the Secretary claimed that it was an attack by the Cartel Jalisco Nueva Generación (CJNG), one of the salient transnational criminal organizations. See Adorno and Alvarado, 2022. More recently there have been systematic arrests of *cells of CJNG and Sinaloa.*

In São Paulo, the PCC has extended its control from retail drug selling to arms trafficking, to bank, auto, and cargo theft, and more recently into the housing business. The group functions as an umbrella for many small gangs, lending equipment, guns, and financing operations. The city has witnessed various confrontations between PCC, the police, and the government which has paralyzed the city, dispersing fear among the population.[110] It highlights the consolidation of PCC as a political-criminal actor.

5.10   Other Criminal Activities and Actors

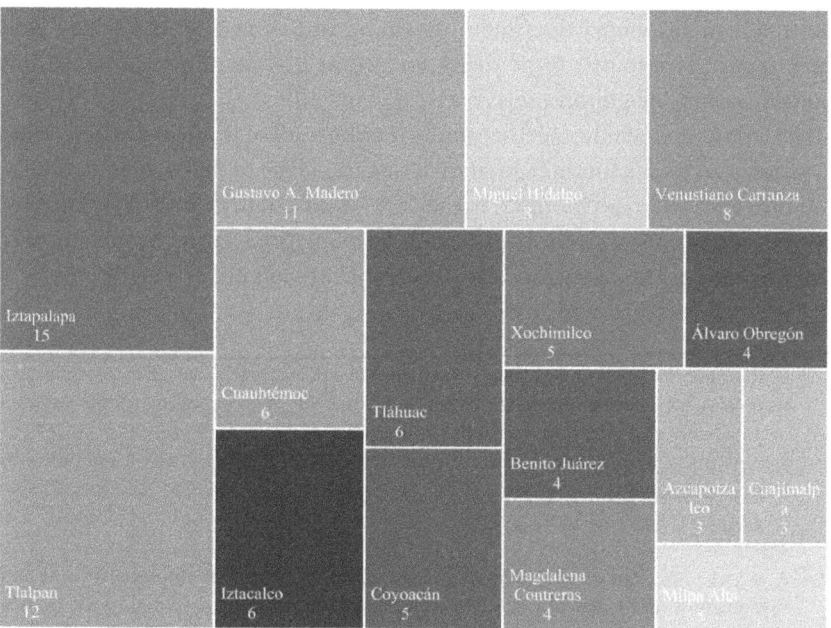

As we mentioned, criminal actors are not only those dedicated to illicit drugs and using ostensive violence. Other criminal activities are covered by political protection and present in various sectors of society, including construction,

---

110   Sao Paulo has had many confrontations orchestrated by the Primeiro Comando da Capital (PCC), in 2006, in 2012, and a parallel *Megarrebelião* de 2001 (Dias, et. Al. 2015:160–179). The organization is responsible for many murders and police assassinations. In 2006; 23 military-police killed; near 32 persons involved in the attack but also at the end of the week of May 2006 they were 439 dead. [Adorno and Salla, 2007: 7].

TABLE 5.4   Criminal actors in the Ciudad de México

Borough	Borough	no of organizations	Local/regional/ transnational coverage	Criminal organizations with activities in the borough
Iztapalapa	Iztapalapa: La Unión (Tepito); Cartel Jalisco Nueva Generación (CJNG); Cártel de Sinaloa; Cártel del Golfo; Guerreros Unidos, Los Zetas; Juan Balta; Grupo Delictivo Iztapalapa; Cártel de Tláhuac; Molina; Los Tanzanios; El Richis; Sindicato Libertad; Güero Fresa; Los OaxacosIztapalapa: La Unión (Tepito); Cartel Jalisco Nueva Generación (CJNG); Cártel de Sinaloa; Cártel del Golfo; Guerreros Unidos, Los Zetas; Juan Balta; Grupo Delictivo Iztapalapa; Cártel de Tláhuac; Molina; Los Tanzanios; El Richis; Sindicato Libertad; Güero Fresa; Los Oaxacos	15	Transnational and local	La Unión (Tepito); Cartel Jalisco Nueva Generación (CJNG); Cártel de Sinaloa; Cártel del Golfo; Guerreros Unidos, Los Zetas; Juan Balta; Grupo Delictivo Iztapalapa; Cártel de Tláhuac; Molina; Los Tanzanios; El Richis; Sindicato Libertad; Güero Fresa; Los Oaxacos

(cont.)

Borough	Borough	no of organizations	Local/regional/ transnational coverage	Criminal organizations with activities in the borough
Tlalpan	Tlalpan: La Unión (Tepito); CJNG; Cártel de Tláhuac; La Familia Michoacana; Guerreros; Maceros; Lenin; Robles; Los Papayos;Los Macedo; El H; Los ChangosTlalpan: La Unión (Tepito); CJNG; Cártel de Tláhuac; La Familia Michoacana; Guerreros; Maceros; Lenin; Robles; Los Papayos;Los Macedo; El H; Los Changos	12	Transnational and local	La Unión (Tepito); CJNG; Cártel de Tláhuac; La Familia Michoacana; Guerreros; Maceros; Lenin; Robles; Los Papayos;Los Macedo; El H; Los Changos
Gustavo A. Madero	Gustavo A. Madero: La Unión (Tepito); CJNG; Cártel del Golfo; La Familia Michoacana; Guerreros Unidos; La Ronda 88; Los Rojos; Familia Cruz; Los Chilas; Los Negros; Los Rudos	11	Transnational and local	La Unión (Tepito); CJNG; Cártel del Golfo; La Familia Michoacana; Guerreros Unidos; La Ronda 88; Los Rojos; Familia Cruz; Los Chilas; Los Negros; Los Rudos

(cont.)

Borough	Borough	no of organizations	Local/regional/ transnational coverage	Criminal organizations with activities in the borough
Miguel Hidalgo	Miguel Hidalgo: Cártel de Sinaloa; La Unión Tepito; Beltrán Leyva; Linares; Lenin; Banda el Balín; Banda el Robert; El Nopal	8	Transnational and local	Cártel de Sinaloa; La Unión Tepito; Beltrán Leyva; Linares; Lenin; Banda el Balín; Banda el Robert; El Nopal
Venustiano Carranza	Venustiano Carranza: La Unión Tepito; Cártel de Sinaloa; Juan Balta; Los Tanzanios; Paco Pacas; El Pechugas; El Patinas; Los Estúpidos	8	Transnational and local	La Unión Tepito; Cártel de Sinaloa; Juan Balta; Los Tanzanios; Paco Pacas; El Pechugas; El Patinas; Los Estúpidos
Cuauhtémoc	Cuauhtémoc: La Unión Tepito; Cártel de Sinaloa; Juan Balta; Los Tanzanios; Paco Pacas; El Pechugas; El Patinas; Los Estúpidos	6	Regional	La Unión Tepito; CJNG; Cártel de Sinaloa; Los Zetas; La Ronda 88; Fabián R88; Fuerza Anti-Unión
Iztacalco	Iztacalco: La Unión (Tepito); La Familia Michoacana; Juan Balta; Los Rodolfos; Los Tanzanios; Paco Pacas	6	National and local	La Unión (Tepito); La Familia Michoacana; Juan Balta; Los Rodolfos; Los Tanzanios; Paco Pacas

(cont.)

Borough	Borough	no of organizations	Local/regional/ transnational coverage	Criminal organizations with activities in the borough
Tláhuac	Tláhuac: CJNG, Cártel de Tláhuac; La Familia Michoacana; Molina; Los Rodolfos; Sindicato Libertad	6	Transnational and local	CJNG, Cártel de Tláhuac; La Familia Michoacana; Molina; Los Rodolfos; Sindicato Libertad
Coyoacán	Coyoacán: La Unión (Tepito); CJNG; Los Guerreros; Molina; Los Rodolfos	5	Transnational and local	La Unión (Tepito); CJNG; Los Guerreros; Molina; Los Rodolfos
Xochimilco	Xochimilco: Cártel de Tláhuac; CJNG; Los Rodolfos; Los Molina; Los Estúpidos	5	Transnational and local	Cártel de Tláhuac; CJNG; Los Rodolfos; Los Molina; Los Estúpidos
Álvaro Obregón	Álvaro Obregón: La Unión (Tepito); CJNG; Lenin; El Esparragós	4	Transnational and local	La Unión (Tepito); CJNG; Lenin; El Esparragós
Benito Juárez	Benito Juárez: La Unión (Tepito); CJNG; Fuerza Anti-Unión Tepito; Lenin	4	Transnational and local	La Unión (Tepito); CJNG; Fuerza Anti-Unión Tepito; Lenin

(cont.)

Borough	Borough	no of organizations	Local/regional/ transnational coverage	Criminal organizations with activities in the borough
Magdalena Contreras	Magdalena Contreras: La Unión (Tepito); La Familia Michoacana; Lenin; Tercera Acción Destructiva (3AD)	4	National and local	La Unión (Tepito); La Familia Michoacana; Lenin; Tercera Acción Destructiva (3AD)
Azcapotzalco	Azcapotzalco: La Unión (Tepito), Fuerza Anti-Unión Tepito; Juan Balta	3	National and local	La Unión (Tepito), Fuerza Anti-Unión Tepito; Juan Balta
Cuajimalpa	Cuajimalpa: CJNG; Beltrán Leyva; Lenin	3	Transnational and local	CJNG; Beltrán Leyva; Lenin
Milpa Alta	Milpa Alta: Cártel de Tláhuac; Molina; Loa Rodolfos	3	National and local	Cártel de Tláhuac; Molina; Loa Rodolfos
Maximal number of organizations in the city: 47				

(cont.)

Borough	no of organizations	Local/regional/ transnational coverage	Criminal organizations with activities in the borough
Number of transnational criminal organizations: 3 (+3 in extinction) Number of national-regional organizations: 2 (+1 in extinction) Number of local organizations: 39 (local gangs, mafias, charters, factions, division of other criminal actors)			

SOURCE: AUTHORS' ELABORATION WITH DATA FROM MÉXICO SOS (2017) LANTIA CONSULTING (2020); EL FINANCIERO (2021) AND SÁNCHEZ (2021)

real estate, urban development, and politics. They are not limited to specific populations or one area of the city.

In Mexico, one scandal came to public attention in the middle of a political battle in 2022, between the city government (led by the *Morena* party) and a partisan coalition from the right, the Partido Acción Nacional (PAN). It consisted of a corruption scheme, in an Alcaldía of Mexico City governed by PAN. The corruption network is operated by authorities and members of the party, today identified as the *Cartel of Benito Juárez*. The scheme consists of racketeering and trafficking construction permits and condominiums, in exchange for electoral funding and condo properties. Former mayors and authorities have been arrested (*Zócalo*, March 16th, 2023).

Another illustration happens in downtown Centro Histórico, where many properties and titles of ownership of the land of the buildings are being trafficked. These underground transactions involve extortion or agreements between informal vendor leaders, some communities working in the area, local authorities, and in some instances bureaucrats of the public registry (*Monreal, 2017*). The purpose of the illegal activity is the purchase of the land, and the acquisition of construction permits in usually cataloged historical landmark areas, hence, to illegally modify its use for commercial purposes. notably to build small informal vendor malls. In certain situations, the illegal activity involves the payment of ransom imposed by mafias like La Unión (or other lesser-known gangsters).

Another case comes from the illicit practices of architects and real estate companies. The more iconic illustration is the construction of a sky-scrapper known as *El Dorito,* in Lomas de Chapultepec, an upscale and heavily regulated area. The original project started in 2008, with an association of local construction firms and an international consortium,[111] as part of a new wave of international investments in real estate (led by a corporation launched for this specific purpose of building that tower: *Rem Koolhaas, Grupo Danhos y Pontegadea*). The project was known as the *Bicentennial Tower.* The original project was canceled by the investors because of the impossibility of getting the right permits and due to the protests of residents. The construction of the tower required circumventing laws and construction permits through complex litigation, including altering previously registered projects, aging in litigation, and even involving the Supreme Court.[112] A new tower was built in

---

111   Vicente Ugalde, "Azuela, Antonio; González, Lidia; Saavedra, Camilo (dirs.). (2020). Ciudad de México. Inercias urbanísticas y proceso constitucional. Ciudad de México: Centro de Investigación y Docencia Económicas, A.C., 288 p.," *Estudios Demográficos y Urbanos* 36, no. 3 (September 17, 2021), pp 115 & ss: 1063–69, https://doi.org/10.24201/edu.v36i3.2124.
112   Ugalde, pp115 and ss.

2014 in the same place requesting a strategy that would be legally impossible under normal-regulated permits. All these cases involve strong capital interest groups, political authorities, and constructors, showing that the city is an arena of flexible transformation of the illicit and irregular, into legal profitable real estate business. These cases demonstrate how illicit and irregular activities in the real estate sector can be transformed into legal and profitable ventures through bribery, negotiation, or litigation. When cases involve authorities, it is another form of financing illicit electoral schemes. *Alcaldías* have the right to supervise constructions and are niches of corruption networks. They are nests of different types of crime organizations capturing the rents and benefits for city making.

Additionally, there are instances where land titles and housing for the poor are subject to trafficking through political and clientelist networks. These are cases that resemble the notion of "peripheral" urbanizations,[113,114] where illicit land use and housing occupation take place. One example is the recent intrusion of PCC into peripheral areas.[115]

These examples provide a broader view where illicit actors are not the usual cliché: young destitute members (or their families) of poor origin and neighborhoods, with criminal careers and time spent in jails. Cartels, mafias, protection rackets, and corruption networks emerge in several public sectors and are typically built by the upper middle classes, by big corporations of the richest sector, and by political bosses in positions of power wishing to accumulate illegal wealth and influence. Urbanization (planned or not) creates incentives to trespass rules, together with electoral cycles, since several political coalitions in those areas finance their campaigns by negotiating, and exchanging urban projects, spaces, developments, permits, or money for votes. These include embezzlement, graft, influence peddling, tax evasion, money laundering, or extortion to constructors (see Table 5.3). The literature is scarce on these crimes. Some few benefits and a majority of people are victims of numerous illegalities in cities, due to the aggressive action of financial, political, or criminal actors (or collusion among them), insufficient regulation, and the daunting low quality of public services and high impunity.

---

113 Caldeira, "Peripheral Urbanization".
114 Rivière d'Arc, "Une radiographie de la violence dans les métropoles du Sud".
115 According to SEADE-UN Habitat (2010: 1 & 67). São Paulo's' 'precarious settlements' occupy 9 % of its territory in the surrounding periphery, characterized by irregular, unplanned favelas.

5.11 Conclusion

We have compared two metropolises to exemplify how illicit global activities affect everyday life in metropolises in Latin America. They suffer from multiple forms of criminality and the active presence of illicit organizations. Narcotraffickers, counterfeiters, corrupted architects, politicians, real estate, financial, and construction corporations play key roles as city makers. Criminals benefit from the prevalence of the economies of violence in these urban areas and grow in influence, using the corruption or coercion of public authorities and communities as critical tools. These actions are merely part of a complex web of interactions among various actors engaging in both legal and illegal transactions. While the two cities are not independent states by themselves, they are integral parts of a national state. They share sovereign powers, and resources for coercion with the state, as well as with other private groups, some of which are legal, some are legitimate, some exist in a gray area, and some are clearly illicit.

People inhabit spaces where the lines between legality and illegality are blurred, most of them residing in neighborhoods that have been victimized and stigmatized. They are subject to more than one authority and in certain cases, they must pay double taxes and obey both legal and arbitrary coercive regulations imposed by public and criminal actors. Both cities combine various normative regimes that apply to market, social, and in certain cases political behavior. Sometimes, the regulation creates obstacles to a more efficient economy and the reduction of crime, while in other cases, they incentivize transgressions. Public policies can also contribute to violence.

Both cities share several communal patterns of local and global illicit activities. The main difference between São Paulo and Mexico City lies in the dominant presence of a criminal organization, the PCC, in São Paulo, which continually challenges the government's sovereignty over the city and its population. The formation of this criminal organization is capable of controlling crime, using armed violence, and claiming territories within the city.

The narrative of illicit activities and their interconnectedness with the legal sector highlights that city-making is a complex process, which does not always align with state-making. The result is the emergence of a hybrid governance in cities. Both criminal actors and public actors, notably the police, can be a challenge to the legal governance of a city, as well as several economic actors coming from the legal, formal business sector, and the political arena. Police autonomy and privatization of policing erode the monopoly of coercion and create ample spaces without any application of the rule of law, resulting in human rights violations and hindering citizenship and democracy (Caldeira,

2000: p.13).[116] Alongside this phenomenon, segregation and the proliferation of gated communities, requiring the use of private security and vigilante groups, driven by the behavior of the upper classes, aggravate the increasing distrust in authorities and institutions, hinder public spaces, and lead to counterproductive public policies.

Urbanization is a key factor in the production of criminal activities. Whether planned or unplanned, it can create incentives for individuals and groups to bypass legislation and engage in illegal activities. Urban crimes are vibrant examples of the economies of violence, of the variety of its actors and underlying factors of success, as well as of its profound socio-political consequences. Further research is needed to explain the role of violent practices in city building and the connection between city building and the progression of the economies of violence. In some illustrated cases, the use of electoral posts and regulatory offices is key to illicit actions. The electoral cycle in the cities also plays a role, as political coalitions in these areas often finance their campaigns by exchanging permits for money and votes. Crimes associated with these activities include embezzlement, graft, influence peddling, tax evasion, money laundering, and extortion. Further research is indispensable to explain the role of these practices in city building. The examples provided highlight the complex nature of organized crime and corruption in urban environments, involving multiple sectors and actors.

These metropolises present a series of challenges to understand the development of urban life in the global south, and to the particularities of the economies of violence in these regions. Comparing these cases also raised important questions regarding the concept of city making, since cities survive, innovate, integrate, and transform despite crime and violence.

Bibliography

Adorno, Sérgio, and Arturo, Alvarado. "Crime and the Governance of Large Metropolises in Latin America: Mexico City (Mexico) and São Paulo (Brazil)." *Dilemas-Revista de Estudos de Conflito e Controle Social*, June 21, 2022, 117–51. https://doi.org/10.4322/dilemas.v15esp4.52505.

Adorno, Sérgio, Camila, Dias, and Marcelo, Nery. "A Cidade e a Dinâmica Da Violência," 381–410, 2016.

---

116 Caldeira, *Cidade de muros*.

Adorno, Sérgio, and Fernando, Salla. "Criminalidade organizada nas prisões e os ataques do PCC." *Estudos Avançados* 21 (December 2007): 7–29. https://doi.org/10.1590/S0103-40142007000300002.

Alvarado, Arturo. "Organizaciones criminales en América Latina: una discusión conceptual y un marco comparativo para su reinterpretación | Criminal organizations in Latin America: a comparative conceptual framework for its reinterpretation." *Revista Brasileira de Sociologia – RBS* 7, no. 17 (November 6, 2019). https://doi.org/10.20336/rbs.539.

Alvarado, Arturo. "Urbicide, Violence, and Destruction Against Cities by Criminal Organizations." In *Urbicide: The Death of the City*, edited by Fernando Carrión Mena and Paulina Cepeda Pico, 603–35. Cham: Springer International Publishing, 2023. https://doi.org/10.1007/978-3-031-25304-1_30.

Alvarado, Arturo, Alberto, Concha-Eastman, Hugo, Spinelli, and Maria Fernanda, Tourinho Peres. *Vidas truncadas: El exceso de homicidios en la juventud de América Latina, 1990–2010. Los casos de Argentina, Brasil, Colombia y México*. El Colegio de Mexico AC, 2015.

Arias, Enrique Desmond, ed. "Constellations of Governance: Theoretical Approaches to Micro-Level Armed Regimes." In *Criminal Enterprises and Governance in Latin America and the Caribbean*, 19–38. Cambridge: Cambridge University Press, 2017. https://doi.org/10.1017/9781316650073.002.

Bauer, Alain. "Special Issue: Economies of Violence." *International Journal on Criminology* 9, no. 2 (April 1, 2022). https://doi.org/10.18278/ijc.9.2.1.

Beckert, Jens, and Matías Dewey. *The Architecture of Illegal Markets: Towards an Economic Sociology of Illegality in the Economy*. Oxford University Press, 2017.

Beckert, Jens, and Frank Wehinger. "In the Shadow: Illegal Markets and Economic Sociology." *Socio-Economic Review* 11, no. 1 (January 1, 2013): 5–30. https://doi.org/10.1093/ser/mws020.

Benson, Todd. "Brazil's 'temple of Luxury' Becomes Symbol of Excess." *The New York Times*, July 16, 2005, sec. Business. https://www.nytimes.com/2005/07/16/business/worldbusiness/brazils-temple-of-luxury-becomes-symbol-of-excess.html.

Boucault Tranchitella, Fabio, Neil Ferreira, Novo, Ana Paula, Ribeiro, Yára, Juliano, Cintia Leci, Rodrigues, Patrícia, Colombo-Souza, Fabio, Boucault Tranchitella, et al. "Homicide Occurrence in Different Regions of the City of São Paulo and Its Risk Rate According to Male Gender between 2000 and 2014: An Analysis of 11.981 Cases." *Medicina Legal de Costa Rica* 38, no. 2 (December 2021): 105–19.

Caldeira, Teresa P. R. "Building up Walls: The New Pattern of Spatial Segregation in São Paulo." *International Social Science Journal* 48, no. 147 (1996): 55–66. https://doi.org/10.1111/j.1468-2451.1996.tb00056.x.

Caldeira, Teresa Pires do Rio. *Cidade de muros: crime, segregação e cidadania em São Paulo*. Editora 34, 2000.

Caldeira, Teresa PR. "Peripheral Urbanization: Autoconstruction, Transversal Logics, and Politics in Cities of the Global South." *Environment and Planning D: Society and Space* 35, no. 1 (February 1, 2017): 3–20. https://doi.org/10.1177/0263775816658479.

Camila Caldeira Nunes Dias. "PCC: Hegemonia Nas Prisões e Monopólio Da Violência – NEV USP," 2013. https://nev.prp.usp.br/publicacao/pcc-hegemonia-nas-prisoes-e-monopolio-da-violencia/.

Vilalta, Carlos J. José G. Castillo, and Juan A. Torres. "Delitos Violentos En Ciudades de América Latina," 2016. https://dds.cepal.org/redesoc/portal/publicaciones/ficha/?id=4409.

Davis, Diane E. "Urban Violence and the Spatial Question: The Built Environmental Correlates of (In)Security in Latin American Cities." In *The Oxford Handbook of the Sociology of Latin America*, edited by Xóchitl Bada and Liliana Rivera-Sánchez, 0. Oxford University Press, 2021. https://doi.org/10.1093/oxfordhb/9780190926557.013.41.

Dias, Camila Caldeira Nunes. "Da pulverização ao monopólio da violência: expansão e consolidação do Primeiro Comando da Capital (PCC) no sistema carcerário paulista." Text, Universidade de São Paulo, 2011. https://doi.org/10.11606/T.8.2011.tde-13062012-164151.

Dias, Camila, Maria Gorete, Marques, Ariadne, Natal, Mariana, Possas, and Caren, Ruotti. "A prática de execuções na região metropolitana de São Paulo na crise de 2012: um estudo de caso." *Revista Brasileira de Segurança Pública* 9, no. 2 (October 2, 2015): 160–79. https://doi.org/10.31060/rbsp.2015.v9.n2.507.

Díaz, Mario. "Distribución diferencial del delito en la Ciudad de México." PhD diss., Tese (Doutorado em Sociologia)–El Colegio de México, Cidade do México, 2018.

Feltran, Gabriel. *Irmãos: uma história do PCC*. Editora Companhia das Letras, 2018.

Feltran, Gabriel. "(Il)Licit Economies in Brazil: An Ethnographic Perspective: Economias (i)Lícitas No Brasil: Uma Perspectiva Etnográfica." *Journal of Illicit Economies and Development* 1, no. 2 (June 4, 2019): 145–54.

Feltran, Gabriel. "The Entangled City: Crime as Urban Fabric in São Paulo." In *The Entangled City*. Manchester University Press, 2020. https://www.manchesterhive.com/display/9781526151377/9781526151377.xml.

Feltran, Gabriel de Santis. "Fronteiras de tensão: política e violência nas periferias de São Paulo." In *Fronteiras de tensão: política e violência nas periferias de São Paulo*, 360–360, 2011. https://pesquisa.bvsalud.org/portal/resource/pt/biblio-1079927.

Fernández, J. (2021) *Controles sociales y eficacia colectiva en la localización geográfica de la violencia*. Tesis (Doctorado en Estudios Demográficos, Urbanos y Ambientales). El Colegio de México, Ciudad de México.

Fernández, José. "Violencia en la Ciudad de México: Controles sociales y eficacia colectiva en la localización geográfica de la violencia." PhD diss., Tese (Doutorado em

Estudos Demográficos, Urbanos e Ambientais)–El Colegio de México, Cidade do México, 2021 (en proceso), 2021.

Hirata, Daniel Veloso. "Sobreviver na adversidade: entre o mercado e a vida." Text, Universidade de São Paulo, 2010. https://doi.org/10.11606/T.8.2010.tde-03032 011-122251.

Instituto Nacional De Estadística Y Geografía (INEGI), *Encuesta Nacional de Victimización y Percepción sobre Seguridad Pública*, [En línea] 2018–2023. [Consultado el 14 de marzo de 2023]. Disponible en: https://www.inegi.org.mx/app/buscador/default.html?q=envipe.

Jackson, Jonathan, Krisztián, Pósch, Thiago R. Oliveira, Ben, Bradford, Sílvia M. Mendes, Ariadne Lima, Natal, and André, Zanetic. "Fear and Legitimacy in São Paulo, Brazil: Police–Citizen Relations in a High Violence, High Fear City." *Law & Society Review* 56, no. 1 (March 2022): 122–45. https://doi.org/10.1111/lasr.12589.

Leonardo, José Ostronoff. "Não existe almoço grátis," 2021. https://aeditora.com.br/produto/nao-existe-almoco-gratis/.

Lessing, Benjamin. "Criminal Governance in Latin America in Comparative Perspective: Introduction to the Special Edition." *Dilemas: Revista de Estudos de Conflito e Controle Social* 15 (September 12, 2022): 1–10. https://doi.org/10.4322/dilemas.v15esp4.52896.

Manso, Bruno Paes, and Camila, Nunes Dias. *A Guerra: a ascensão do PCC e o mundo do crime no Brasil*. Editora Todavia S.A, 2018.

Mario, Pavel Díaz. "Inseguridad y Narcomenudeo En La Ciudad de México: Distribución Diferenciada y Correlativos Asociados." Sociológica México, 2022. http://www.sociologicamexico.azc.uam.mx/index.php/Sociologica/article/view/1704.

Marques, Eduardo. "Comparative Strategies on and in Latin-American Cities." In *The Routledge Handbook of Comparative Global Urban Studies*. Routledge, 2023.

Mauricio, Savarese. "Sao Paulo Police Kill 14 People in Raid as They Investigate the Slaying of an Elite Officer." AP News, August 2, 2023. https://apnews.com/article/sao-paulo-police-killings-brazil-13e56cf6f1cd586f92757468d4c9601b.

Mendoza, Arturo Alvarado. *El Tamaño Del Infierno. Un Estudio Sobre La Criminalidad En La Zona Metropolitana de La Ciudad de México*. El Colegio de Mexico AC, 2012.

Moctezuma, Vicente (2021). *El desvanecimiento de lo popular. Gentrificación en el Centro Histórico de la Ciudad de México*. México, El Colegio de México.

Müller, F. I., & Weegels, J. (2022). *Illicit City-Making and Its Materialities*. Introduction to the Special Issue. Journal of illicit economies and development, 4(3), 230–240. https://doi.org/10.31389/jied.169.

Nery, Marcelo, Batista, Altay Alves Lino, de Souza, and Sergio, Adorno. "Os padrões urbano-demográficos da capital paulista." *Estudos Avançados* 33 (December 2, 2019): 5–36. https://doi.org/10.1590/s0103-4014.2019.3397.002.

Nery, M. B., Peres, M. F. T., Cardia, N., Vicentin, D., & Adorno, S. (2012). *Regimes espaciais: dinâmica dos homicídios dolosos na cidade de São Paulo entre 2000 e 2008*. Revista panamericana de salud pública (Impresa), 32(6), 405–412. https://doi.org/10.1590/s1020-49892012001400003.

Patriarca, Gabriel & Adorno, S. (2023). Mergulhando aos cascos em portos brasileiros: adaptações recíprocas em torno de uma modalidade de tráfico internacional de cocaína.

Pekny, Ana Carolina, and Ricardo, Carolina de Mattos. "Principales retos de la violencia y la criminalidad en Brasil, 2017." Programa de Cooperación en Seguridad Regional-Friedrich-Ebert-Stiftung (FES), diciembre de 2017. https://katalog.gfzk.de/Record/o-1659278449.

Peres, Maria Fernanda Tourinho, Juliana Feliciano, de Almeida, Diego Vicentin, Magdalena, Cerda, Nancy, Cardia, and Sérgio, Adorno. "Queda dos homicídios no município de São Paulo: uma análise exploratória de possíveis condicionantes." *Revista Brasileira de Epidemiologia* 14 (December 2011): 709–21. https://doi.org/10.1590/S1415-790X2011000400017.

Rivière d'Arc, Hélène. "Une radiographie de la violence dans les métropoles du Sud : le cas de São Paulo." *Revue internationale et stratégique* 112, no. 4 (2018): 149–57. https://doi.org/10.3917/ris.112.0149.

Robinson, Jennifer. "Introduction to a Virtual Issue on Comparative Urbanism." *International Journal of Urban and Regional Research* n/a, no. n/a. Accessed March 29, 2024. https://doi.org/10.1111/1468-2427.12171.

Rolnik, R. (2015). Guerra dos lugares. A colonização da terra e da moradia na era das finanças. São Paulo: Boi Tempo.

Rubalcava, Rosa María, Martha, Schteingart, and Jaime, Ramírez. *Ciudades Divididas: Desigualdad y Segregación Social En México*. Colegio de Mexico, 2012. https://www.jstor.org/stable/j.ctt14jxr3p.

SEADE-UN Habitat (2010) *São Paulo: A Tale of Two Cities*. United Nations Human Settlements Programme.

Silva, Carlos Freire da. "Das calçadas às galerias: mercados populares do centro de São Paulo." Text, Universidade de São Paulo, 2014. https://doi.org/10.11606/T.8.2014.tde-31032015-105012.

Steiner, Philippe, and Marie, Trespeuch, eds. *Marchés contestés : Quand le marché rencontre la morale. Marchés contestés : Quand le marché rencontre la morale*. Sociologiques. Toulouse: Presses universitaires du Midi, 2014. https://books.openedition.org/pumi/8079.

Subsecretaría del Sistema Penitenciario de la Ciudad de México. (2023). *Población penitenciaria: 25 mil 520 personas privadas de su libertad al 03 de marzo de 2023*. Available at:https://penitenciario.cdmx.gob.mx/poblacion-penitenciaria.

Telles, Vera. "A Cidade Nas Fronteiras Do Legal e Ilega," 2010. https://www.academia.edu/106442253/A_cidade_nas_fronteiras_do_legal_e_ilega.

Tilly, C. (1985). *War Making and State Making as Organized Crime*. En Cambridge University Press eBooks (pp. 169–191). https://doi.org/10.1017/cbo9780511628283.008.

Ugalde, Vicente. "Azuela, Antonio; González, Lidia; Saavedra, Camilo (dirs.). (2020). Ciudad de México. Inercias urbanísticas y proceso constitucional. Ciudad de México: Centro de Investigación y Docencia Económicas, A.C., 288 p." *Estudios Demográficos y Urbanos* 36, no. 3 (September 17, 2021): 1063–69. https://doi.org/10.24201/edu.v36i3.2124.

Willis, Graham Denyer. *The Killing Consensus: Police, Organized Crime, and the Regulation of Life and Death in Urban Brazil*. Univ of California Press, 2015.

CHAPTER 6

Warlords and Violent Entrepreneurs

Guillaume Soto-Mayor

In history,[1] throughout the world, warlords have ruled, defeated and established states.[2] A warlord can be defined as a charismatic military leader who, due to the weakness or absence of a government, ended up playing a political social role, even without political legitimacy, thanks to his capacity (real or anticipated) to use force.[3] Sometimes described as a powerful figure who provided social services in their area of influence and who possessed a private army, sometimes a "faction leader" or a "local commander," warlords, whatever their origin, the end justifies the means.

As a tool for social ascendancy favored by these war actors, violence is the basis of their power. Their legitimacy is not derived from any form of legal power. The warlords impose themselves by force, and by their ability to maintain their territorial hold in relative peace. This stability imposed by violence, or the prospect of violence is the sine qua non of the prosperity on which their authority in the eyes of their vassals and subjects depends.

What distinguishes criminal entrepreneurs/warlords from other entrepreneurs of violence is that an individual—the leader—is considered indispensable for the proper functioning, notoriety and legitimacy of the armed group. Personal strength gives the leader an almost heroic, charismatic, dimension and allows him to count on the loyalty of the communities he leads. It is interesting to note that in these holistic systems, an individual embodies the collective. The warlord is seen as the representative of what is good and right for the lot. This leader has authoritative power over all members of the organization

---

1 Ms. Alice Gagliano contributed significantly to this chapter. She is a former research assistant at SDRTI3C and French public servant with a specialization in security and political analysis in Latin America and Central America. She notably conducted a large desk research and provided high-level analysis on violent entrepreneurs operating in Latin and Central America.
2 Pierre-François Souyri, *Les guerriers dans la rizière. La grande épopée des samouraïs* (Flammarion, 2021).
3 Canada: Immigration and Refugee Board of Canada, "Afghanistan: Information Sur La Situation Des Seigneurs de Guerre En Afghanistan, y Compris Sur La Réaction de l'État Par Rapport à La Mainmise Qu'ont Les Seigneurs de Guerre Sur Les Régions (2007–2010)," January 6, 2011, https://webarchive.archive.unhcr.org/20230524234054/https://www.refworld.org/docid/4e4254682.html.

and imposes absolute loyalty on them. In return, these leaders are expected to be deeply committed to the defense of the group and its homeland.

The warlords are indeed umbilically linked to a territory, a land and sometimes to the communities that make it up, because of the filial and ethnic ties that unite these entrepreneurs of violence with the local populations. Ethnic affiliation and the defense, often instrumentalized, of this social group against an external enemy (foreign power) or internal enemy (the State) is a common rhetoric used by these warlords to justify their authoritarian power. In the Central African Republic, the Union for Peace in the Central African Republic (UPC) led by Ali Darassa, the Patriotic Movement for the Central African Republic (MPC) led by Mahamat al-Khatim, the Patriotic Rally for the Renewal of the Central African Republic (RPRC) led by Zakaria Damane, and the People's Front for the Rebirth of the Central African Republic (FPRC) led by Nourredine Adam, all have a pronounced ethnic identity.[4]

Through their coercive power, and in exchange for absolute obedience to the hierarchy and the normative order, warlords provide security and protection to their subjects. In fact, coercion, defined as "the use of overt threats and actual force to influence another decision," is central to the operation of warlords/criminal entrepreneurs.[5] The nuisance capabilities or perceived threat associated internally and externally with the strengths of criminal entrepreneurs/warlords (the human capital and technology at their disposal and the level of violence or ruthlessness associated with their leader) are a key means of enforcing agreements, ensuring the continuity of their legal order in the territories they control, and capturing targeted resources (including taxation, predation and theft).

It is also fundamentally important to note that warlords/criminal entrepreneurs encourage their members to view states and all public institutions as their enemies. They also consider the normative order and public set of values to be flawed. For example, solidarity among warlords' armed groups' ranks is often praised in contradiction to the predatory practices of public officials. Warlords determine meaning, motives, and causes. They constantly reassert their authority and visibly show their (sometimes personal) strength in order to remain the undisputed leader within their own ranks.

However, it is interesting to note that the international community pays less attention to warlords if they act in a context that does not fall into the

---

4   Thierry Vircoulon, "Écosystème des groupes armés en Centrafrique," April 2020, https://www.ifri.org/fr/publications/notes-de-lifri/ecosysteme-groupes-armes-centrafrique.
5   Warlords/criminal entrepreneurs have "enforcers" in their ranks, who maintain organizational integrity by arranging for the maiming or killing of recalcitrant members.

category of conflict under international law. According to international law,[6] two criteria must be met to qualify a situation as a non-international armed conflict: the first relates to the intensity of the violence, the second to the organization of the parties. In several cases, as we shall see later with the example of El Salvador, the intensity of the clashes between criminal groups and government forces reaches the level required to qualify as a conflict under international law. The second criterion, on the other hand, is controversial. In this case, international law only requires that "the actors of the armed violence have reached a minimal level of organization," as pointed out by the jurisprudence of the Special Court for Yugoslavia in the Limaj case.[7] In practice, an additional condition regarding the motivations of non-governmental groups is required. The absence of a claimed ideology automatically excludes criminal groups from the list of belligerents. However, as the ICRC points out, "as humanitarian law stands, there is no legal basis for this additional condition."[8] In addition, some cite the absence of limited objectives for criminal groups, unlike parties with defined political claims, as a reason why it is not possible to negotiate with this type of actor.

The purpose of this chapter is not to discuss this exclusion of criminal actors from humanitarian law and therefore from formal peace agreement negotiations. There is a great deal of debate about the reasons for and implications of this exclusion. The following reflection extends in a certain way these debates pointing out the underestimation of a warlord's effective power, especially in "peaceful" contexts, in the economic as well as in the political and social spheres. Our reflection will thus be extended to criminal actors qualified by some scholars of criminal governance as "Warlords of Crime,"[9] or even "Gangster Warlords."[10] These actors are included in our analysis because they operate in the economies of violence in a very similar way to the more traditionally "accepted warlords."

---

6   Article 3 common to the Geneva Conventions of 1949 and Article 1 of Additional Protocol II of 1977.

7   International Criminal Tribunal for the former Yugoslavia (ICTY); Trial Chamber II, "Prosecutor v. Limaj et al. (Trial Judgment)," Refworld, November 30, 2005, https://www.refworld.org/jurisprudence/caselaw/icty/2005/en/61980.

8   Sylvain Vité, "Typology of Armed Conflicts in International Humanitarian Law: Legal Concepts and Actual Situations," *International Review of the Red Cross* 91, no. 873 (March 2009): 69–94, https://doi.org/10.1017/S1816383109999021X.

9   Gerald L. Posner, *War Lords of Crime: Chinese Secret Societies: The New Mafia* (Queen Anne Press, 1989).

10 Ioan Grillo, *Gangster Warlords: Drug Dollars, Killing Fields, and the New Politics of Latin America* (Bloomsbury USA, 2017).

As we will detail next, warlords use violence for economic profit. On the other hand, the population suffers physically and mentally from this violence, but also financially. Warlords' gains come at the expense of the population, and this violence leads to multiple economic losses. Crime and violence can be measured by their welfare cost. Although imperfect and incomplete, this indicator is essential to reflect on the economic dimension of the violence exercised by criminal entrepreneurs and warlords. In the Northern Triangle of Central America, crime and violence cost 3% of the GDP in Guatemala, 6.1% in El Salvador, and 6.5% of the GDP in Honduras over the 2011–2014 period.[11] At that time of extreme violence, the homicide rates of these countries respectively reached 33.05, 40.10 and 73.09 per 100,000 population in 2013.[12] In Iraq the same year, the per capita homicide rate was 10 per 100,000.[13] This is hardly a record year, as the worst homicide rate was recorded in El Salvador in 2015 (105 per 100,000 population).[14] As the UNODC explains, organized crime kills far more people than armed conflicts do in the world: "Organized crime alone was responsible for up to 19% of all homicides in 2017. Since the start of the twenty-first century, organized crime has killed about as many people as all armed conflicts across the world combined."[15]

However, as we previously mentioned, the international community tends to pay less attention to these situations of endemic violence endemic level of violence, when they involve actors labeled as "criminals." This leads us to suggest that this lack of consideration may be due to the deep integration of these warlords into national and international economies, as we will describe later. Warlords' economic involvement, both in the legal and illegal spheres, seems to be a structuring element of their power.

6.1   Warlords and Sovereignty

The logic of sovereignty, according to the work of prominent 20th-century political theorists on the state, such as Kelsen, Carré de Malberg, and Weber,

---

11 Laura Jaitman et al., "The Costs of Crime and Violence: New Evidence and Insights in Latin America and the Caribbean," *IDB Publications*, February 3, 2017, https://doi.org/10.18235/0000615.
12 UNODC, "data UNODC," accessed March 30, 2024, https://dataunodc.un.org/.
13 UNODC.
14 UNODC.
15 UNODC, "Global Study on Homicide Executive Summary 2019," 2019, https://www.unodc.org/documents/data-and-analysis/gsh/Booklet1.pdf.

is that sovereignty is supreme and unlimited in every state. Again from a legal perspective, in modern democratic nation-states, notably through Kelsen's Grundnorm or Constitution, sovereignty is attributed to an entity endowed with the capacity to exercise public functions through an expressed collective delegation of the rights of a specific population over a delimited territory.[16] According to Weber, nation-states acquired these capacities and the legitimate authority to use force as a result of the development of military conscription and the tax system.[17] The mere assumption that warlords and criminal entrepreneurs are actors of power, let alone that they should be considered on an equal footing with nation-states, calls for a rethinking of the philosophical foundations of modern nation-state sovereignty.

In vast parts of the world, governments have ceded territorial and political sovereignty, their monopoly on taxation and violence to warlords.[18] From Afghanistan to the Democratic Republic of Congo (DRC) to El Salvador, warlords are supplanting state institutions and maintaining control through violence, favors, corruption and external support.[19]

These violent entrepreneurs have the unique ability to simultaneously offer a credible alternative form of governmental power while challenging the fundamental elements constituting the nation-state's supreme command over a defined society, as well as its absolute and independent determination of its own destiny. In fact, the *de jure* use of power by a nation-state does not mean that it is *de facto* the true political power over a specific territory. As Vircoulon argues: "The sovereignty enjoyed by the Central African state is a fictitious sovereignty that does not translate into the capacity to defend a territory or to administer it. Legitimate sovereignty is fundamentally different from the "supreme capacity to induce people to adopt a desired course of action, by exerting on them a kind of pressure, a de facto use of power."[20]

However, the quest for power by criminal entrepreneurs is inherently different from that of nation-states. Indeed, a criminal entrepreneur's view of

---

16 Ira Katznelson and Helen V. Milner, *Political Science: The State of the Discipline* (New York, Washington, D.C.: w.w. Norton ; American Political Science Assn., 2002), http://www.gbv.de/dms/sub-hamburg/347252621.pdf.
17 J. Pemberton, *Sovereignty: Interpretations* (Palgrave Macmillan UK, 2009).
18 Thierry Vircoulon, "Écosystème des groupes armés en Centrafrique".
19 Canada: Immigration and Refugee Board of Canada, "Afghanistan : Information Sur La Situation Des Seigneurs de Guerre En Afghanistan, y Compris Sur La Réaction de l'État Par Rapport à La Mainmise Qu'ont Les Seigneurs de Guerre Sur Les Régions (2007–2010)".
20 Stanley I. Benn and Richard Stanley Peters, *Social Principles and the Democratic State* (Allen & Unwin, 1959).

government power is absolutist.²¹ In fact, warlords or criminal entrepreneurs are egocentric actors whose pursuit of power is inherently a selfish quest that erases all possible obstacles, contrary even to the notion of a social contract and democratic principles. Its vitality and legitimacy come from within its own ranks.²²

The warlords' most visible challenge to the governmental power of nation-states lies in its constant ability to neutralize state responses and attempts to dismantle it or to permanently diminish its power and resources. In El Salvador, the inability of the successive repressive policy to tackle gangs' power led the governments from 2012 to change their objective toward those groups.²³ By then, the Salvadoran State had no longer sought to dismantle the gang, but rather negotiated with them to contain the level of violence. In El Salvador as in most situations, corruption is a core element to understand the ineffectiveness of state response against warlords.

However, criminal entrepreneurs and warlords not only neutralize the legitimate use of force by nation-states, they also impose their own coercive governmental authority. They have the ability to wage war and often profit directly from the duration of a conflict, as they manage the "conflict economy." In fact, criminal entrepreneurs manage a parallel system of tax collection that Weber argues is one of the oldest attributes of nation-state power.²⁴ Thus, racketeering, that is, protection against a real or imagined threat to security, is a fundamental source of wealth for all criminal entrepreneurs. The violent control of strategic economic spaces, such as mining areas, is also often seen as the raison d'être of armed groups and warlords.

In Somalia, Afghanistan, Chechnya and the Central African Republic, warlords hold fiefdoms that are not accessible to government officials. The lands, borders and customs of these territories are under their absolute or partial control. As an example, according to Vircoulon, armed groups and warlords are considered to be the "real bosses" of the Central African Republic.²⁵ They are the main employer in these lands, regulating social relations, trade and the levels of violence tolerated and perpetrated. They can negotiate contracts and

---

21 David Held, *Political Theory and the Modern State: Essays on State, Power, and Democracy*, Reprinted (Cambridge: Polity Press, 2000).
22 Jean-François Gayraud, "Le Monde des mafias Géopolitique du crime organisé," www.odi lejacob.fr, 2005, https://www.odilejacob.fr/catalogue/histoire-et-geopolitique/geopoliti que-et-strategie/monde-des-mafias_9782738121325.php.
23 Juan José Martínez, "El Niño de Hollywood," July 2023, https://www.revistadelauniversi dad.mx/articles/68938586-850d-4382-9614-21ee87d2af07/el-nino-de-hollywood.
24 Held, *Political Theory and the Modern State*.
25 Thierry Vircoulon, "Écosystème des groupes armés en Centrafrique".

maintain diplomatic relations with other national and international actors, both public and private. Warlords are therefore often a signal and embodiment of state failure and the inability of a government to rule over a given territory.

Moreover, like nation-states and as noted earlier, warlords are deeply embedded in the social and historical realities of the territory from which they originate. It can be argued that territory is part of the biotope of criminal entrepreneurs.[26] The territory of the warlords is first and foremost their historical cradle and their strength depends heavily on this living space. The presence of strongholds does not limit the constant attempt of criminal entrepreneurs to expand their territory.[27] Sometimes powerful entrepreneurs of violence have the ability to create a Potemkin village, giving an illusion of control to nation-states over their own territory.

These entrepreneurs of violence keep their communities under their dominance through the use of armed forces of various sizes, often a few hundred permanent soldiers and additional recruits as needed from time to time.[28] These non-state armed forces vary in size, participate in legal and illegal economic activities, and the smallest of them engage in mercenaryism by offering security or protection services to the highest bidder. The most powerful warlords maintain prolonged control over a territory, from which they profit to set up a system of parallel taxation and to manage the exploitation and illicit resale of natural resources.

In areas where warlords operate, a new form of governance, and in particular a new form of justice, is emerging: arbitrary arrests of civilians by the armed forces under his control, and the warlord imposes his rules in both civil and criminal cases, as well as in the judgment and imposition of fines. Fearful justice, sometimes appreciated, the warlords set themselves up as the only legitimate rulers, the only ones to bring a semblance of justice. They impose their own courts, their standard set of rules, their sentences, and their prisons.[29]

Relationships between warlords are often fluid and opportunistic. These entrepreneurs of violence regularly change sides in conflicts, joining rebel

---

26 Petra Reski, "The Honored Society: A Portrait of Italy's Most Powerful Mafia," 2008, https://www.goodreads.com/book/show/15814205-the-honored-society.

27 James Cockayne, *Hidden Power: The Strategic Logic of Organized Crime* (Oxford University Press, 2016).

28 Kasper Agger, "Warlord Business: CAR's Violent Armed Groups and Their Criminal Operations for Profit and Power," *The Enough Project* (blog), June 17, 2015, https://enoughproject.org/reports/warlord-business-cars-violent-armed-groups-and-their-criminal-operations-profit-and-power.

29 Interviews with members of non-state armed groups conducted in Mali, Cote d'Ivoire and DRC, from 2014 to 2023.

states or alliances depending on the expected economic and power benefits or losses. Violence and warlord alliances can be the result of competition or partnership for leadership positions, control of profitable routes, trade centers and natural resource production.[30]

6.2 A Prime Example of Actors in the Economies of Violence

It is through violence that warlords gain power and maintain their hold on territories, communities, and economic resources. Warlords and violent entrepreneurs often rule through terror and have structural advantages because they do not fear competition; they can use coercion to eliminate it, and thus, they can influence labor and partners through bribery and/or violent threats. Unlike other actors, warlords/criminal entrepreneurs are not constrained by moral considerations, and they opportunistically take advantage of any enrichment prospects, any favorable developments, that liberal markets offer them.

In the territories controlled by the warlords, the lives of the populations are constantly marked by violence in many forms, physical, sexual and psychological. For example, Congolese warlord Bosco Ntaganda, known as "The Terminator," is currently on trial before the International Court of Justice for committing 18 counts of war crimes in the Democratic Republic of Congo (Congo), including murder, rape, pillaging, and enlisting child soldiers. In the Central African Republic, the Front Populaire pour la Renaissance de Centrafrique (FPRC), formed in July 2014, and the Unité pour la Paix en Centrafrique (UPC) led by Ali Darrassa and Mahamat Alkhatim, are responsible for killings of civilians, attacks on public authorities and widespread looting.[31] Warlords Michel Djotodia and Nourredine Adam, who led the FPRC, are under international sanctions.[32]

The violence committed and perpetuated by warlords is primarily physical and sexual. In territories controlled by armed groups and warlords in the DRC, Congolese girls are forced into forced prostitution in makeshift brothels and camps, as well as around mines and markets.[33] In territories controlled

---

30 Agger, "Warlord Business".
31 Agger.
32 Agger.
33 "Convention C182—Convention (N° 182) Sur Les Pires Formes de Travail Des Enfants, 1999—Discussion: 2017, Cas Individuel-Republique Democratique Du Congo," 2017, https://www.ilo.org/dyn/normlex/fr/f?p=NORMLEXPUB:12100:0::NO::P12100_INSTRUMENT_ID:312327.

by warlords, communities, including children, often work in conditions akin to slavery. In the Central African Republic, the UPC and FPRC use terrible violence, recruit child soldiers, and commit sexual abuse. They terrorize populations throughout CAR to control profitable mining areas, imposing illegal taxes that fund the group.[34] In the Democratic Republic of Congo, at least 50,000 children are believed to be working in mines, and armed groups regularly organize abductions and trafficking of vulnerable people, particularly children who are subjected to mutilation and sexual violence.[35] Miners work up to 12 hours a day, for one or two dollars, in scorching temperatures, without any protection and in contact with high concentrations of minerals.[36]

Many warlords are also accused of directing ethnically motivated killings and fuelling inter-ethnic violence.[37] Inter-ethnic rivalries and correlated acts of violence, such as the ones opposing the Hemas and Lindusi's ethnies in Kivu (DRC), are occasionally manipulated by warlords in order to reinforce their violence grasp on a territory.[38] Warlords encourage and commit multiple acts of violence (including murder, summary executions and torture) against another ethnic group, stoking conflict to justify their authoritarian rule and protection of one community.[39]

The violence at the heart of warlords' and criminal entrepreneurs' power is self-replicating and impunity is encouraged, creating a powerful and enduring culture of violence in a territory. During the war in Liberia, warlords recruited orphans and street children as security guards. They joined the ranks of the militia at clan checkpoints to rape, pillage and kill people.[40] Often drugged, they lived in a constant state of violence. In Central America, family disintegration was and remains a primary factor in the recruitment of children by gangs.[41]

---

34 Agger, "Warlord Business".
35 "Convention C182—Convention (N° 182) Sur Les Pires Formes de Travail Des Enfants, 1999-Discussion: 2017, Cas Individuel—Republique Democratique Du Congo".
36 "Convention C182—Convention (N° 182) Sur Les Pires Formes de Travail Des Enfants, 1999-Discussion: 2017, Cas Individuel—Republique Democratique Du Congo".
37 "Congolese Warlord Stands Trial on 18 Counts of War Crimes, But Many More Crimes Have Gone Unreported," HuffPost, September 1, 2015, https://www.huffpost.com/entry/congolese-warlord-stands-_b_8069584.
38 Philippe Le Billon, *Fuelling War: Natural Resources and Armed Conflicts* (London: Routledge, 2013), https://doi.org/10.4324/9781315019529.
39 Agger, "Warlord Business".
40 Billon, *Fuelling War*.
41 Juan José Martínez, "El Niño de Hollywood".

Operating in Guatemala, Honduras and El Salvador,[42] the Mara Salvatrucha 13 and the Barrio 18[43] are two gangs born in the United States, more specifically in the suburbs of Los Angeles where many Central Americans had emigrated during the civil wars.[44] From the 90s, the US federal government, in response to growing security issues linked to the development of gangs, deported a large number of Salvadorans, Hondurans and Guatemalans, who had been convicted in the United States, to their country of origin where they established the first "cliques." Then, the socio-economic situation of these countries destroyed by civil wars helped to fill the ranks of these gangs imported from the United States. In disadvantaged neighborhoods, many children have to grow up without their parents who emigrated, at first because of the civil wars, and then to escape gangs' violence or economic predation. Joining a gang, beyond a livelihood, means being part of a group that replaces an absent family. The need to belong is vital for these children and youth, even if this affiliation is based on extreme daily violence.[45] Violence is the essence of the Maras culture, as shown by the different norms and rites of these gangs documented by anthropologists. One of the first rites of passage consists of being violently beaten for 13 seconds by different members of the gang without being able to fight back. This is why the Mara Salvatrucha carries the number 13.[46]

---

42 It should be mentioned here that the establishment on March 28, 2022 of a state of exception still in force in February 2023, led to the arrest of over 60,000 individuals in 10 months. President Bukele's war against gangs is out of all proportion to the repressive policies implemented by previous governments, which proved ineffective. Among these 60,000 arrests, NGOs have identified a large number of arbitrary detentions, including people with no relations to the gangs. However, there is clear evidence that gangs' activities are currently at a standstill and that security forces took back control of almost all territory. This unprecedented move has been done at the cost of serious human rights violations and an erosion of state of law documented by NGOs and International Organization. Experts cannot say with certainty what the criminal panorama will look like in the middle term and what will happen to these gangs (there is evidence that some members have fled to neighboring countries). We therefore voluntarily not address this recent evolution and when mentioning gangs' power in this chapter we refer to a time that ends (or stops momentarily) in 2022.

43 In 2005 in El Salvador, a division occurred within the Barrio 18 between its incarcerated members and those outside the prisons, which gave birth to two distinct and rival entities: the Revolutionaries and Sureños.

44 Juan José Martínez, "El Niño de Hollywood".

45 Roberto Valencia, *Carta desde Zacatraz*, Primera edición, El Faro (Madrid: Libros del K.O., 2018), http://bookdata.stanford.edu/casalini/suauth/60/81/60818226.pdf.

46 Martínez, Óscar and Juan José Martínez D'Aubuisson. El Niño de Hollywood: cómo Estados Unidos y El Salvador moldearon a un sicario de la Mara Salvatrucha 13. Primera edición. Ciudad de México: Debate, 2018.

It is interesting to note that all forms of violence in the warlord territories are linked. Since the beginning of oil exploitation, from the Biafran war of succession in the 1960s to the Ogoni uprising in the early 1990s, the Niger Delta region has been the scene of interconnected inter-ethnic conflicts and criminal and political violence.[47] Among others, two warlords have shaped the conflict since the 1990s in the Niger Delta: the Niger Delta People Voluntary Forces (NDPVF) of Alhaji Asari Dokubo and the Niger Delta Vigilante of Ateke Tom.[48] Smaller armed groups, known as sects, have been affiliated with these two large armed forces. Many of these "cult" groups, with names such as the Icelanders, Greenlanders, KKK, Germans, Dey Gbam, Mafia Lords, and Vultures, were formed in the early 1990s as university fraternities, but later largely transformed into criminal gangs.[49] In late 2003, in an effort to increase their access to weapons and other resources, many of the "cult" groups formed alliances with either the Asari or Tom's armed group, with the two leaders vying for control of oil bunkering routes.[50] Although the smaller groups retained their names and leadership structures, the Asari and Tom assumed command and control responsibilities over the militant actions of these smaller groups. The two rival armed groups and their affiliates fought, and hundreds died, for control of territory that allowed them to access and control lucrative oil bunkering sites and oil transportation routes.[51]

The economic dimension of the violence committed by the warlords is central. This dimension is highlighted in the context of the exploitation of profitable raw materials in territories plagued by violence. In countries plagued by civil war, illegal and legal activities have long been intertwined and have created so-called "war economies."[52] Liberian warlord Charles Taylor used his control of the port of Buchanan to sell tropical hardwood and iron ore

---

47   Human Rights Watch, "Testing Democracy: Political Violence in Nigeria," *Human Rights Watch*, April 10, 2003, https://www.hrw.org/report/2003/04/10/testing-democracy/political-violence-nigeria.
48   Energy Intelligence, "Nigeria: Gangsta Power," Energy Intelligence, September 22, 2004, https://www.energyintel.com/0000017b-a7a5-de4c-a17b-e7e7768f0000.
49   Energy Intelligence.
50   Human Rights Watch, "Testing Democracy: Political Violence in Nigeria".
51   Oil bunkering is the illegal tapping directly into oil pipelines, often at manifolds or wellheads, and the extraction of crude oil which is piped into river barges that are hidden in small tributaries. The crude is then transported to ships offshore for sale, often to other countries in West Africa but also to other farther destinations.
52   Transformation des conflits et construction de la paix Cadre d'orientation de la Diaconie œcuménique Rédaction: Barbara Müller, Martin Petry, Dr. Klaus Seitz, juillet 2010.

to international buyers seeking cheap natural resources.[53] Liberian warlord Charles Taylor's Revolutionary United Front has used sheer brutality, physical and sexual violence, to take total control of territory for the sole purpose of exploiting its natural resources. Within the areas they control, members of the ex-Séléka groups kill, threaten, and use other forms of violence to claim taxes from civilians, businesses, and public institutions.[54]

Finally, the centrality of violence in warlords' and criminal entrepreneurs' daily operations is directly highlighted by their implication in arms trafficking. The illicit flow of arms embodies the link between illicit economies and conflict, with the proliferation of arms being a major factor in the escalation of conflict.[55] Arms trafficking in Africa is thriving and armed militias are strongly linked to it. In 2017, 28% of violent deaths were caused by bullets; 40 million small arms are held by "non-state groups," representing 80% of pistols and rifles in circulation.[56] These weapons ensure that warlords have the technical capacity to maintain a violent government system over their territory.

Mercenaries and criminal intermediaries are often the main suppliers of weapons to warlords. For example, Frenchman Pierre Dadak is suspected of having delivered 200,000 Kalashnikov assault rifles, rocket launchers and tanks to South Sudan.[57] Pierre Dadak is said to have traveled with a diplomatic passport from Guinea-Bissau on the plane of the president of the Gambia to conclude this deal, while having benefited from the support of the Polish intelligence service and the Corsican-Marseille criminal organization.[58] These connections are particularly useful for the transit of arms to countries under embargo. This was the case, for example, in Côte d'Ivoire, where arms trafficking was organized during and after the civil war (2001–2011) via companies registered in Israel and under the supervision of the Ivorian National Security Council, an institution placed under the direct supervision of President

---

53 Stephen Ellis, *The Mask of Anarchy: The Destruction of Liberia and the Religious Dimension of an African Civil War* (NYU Press, 2001), pp. 90–91.
54 Agger, "Warlord Business".
55 Lucia Bird, "Criminalité Organisée et Dynamiques D'instabilité: Cartographie Des Plaques Tournantes Illicites En Afrique de l'Ouest," September 2022, https://wea.globalinitiat ive.net/illicit-hub-mapping/assets/pdfs/illicit_hubs_methodology_fr.pdf.
56 Nicolas Florquin, Sigrid Lipott, and Francis Wairagu, *L'atlas Des Armes: Une Cartographie Des Flux Illicites d'armes Légères En Afrique*, 2019.
57 "La Chute d'un Seigneur de La Guerre," November 20, 2016, https://www.lejdd.fr/Intern ational/La-chute-d-un-seigneur-de-la-guerre-825928.
58 Karam Henni, "Un Célèbre Trafiquant d'armes et Seigneur de Guerre Français Arrêté En Espagne," November 23, 2021, https://www.rap2france.com/news/un-celebre-trafiqu ant-d-armes-et-seigneur-de-guerre-francais-arrete-en-espagne-14922.

Alassane Ouattara. These arms deliveries were allegedly made to the army and to warlords close to the government.[59] This case illustrates the common benefits that arms-selling states, criminals and intermediaries derive from this market of violence linked to warlords.

6.3 Economies of Violence—Typology of Illegal Activities

Warlords and their armies are involved in a range of illicit and often violent activities that generate income and resources to finance their operations, purchase weapons, recruit soldiers and supporters, and generate profits for individual commanders.[60] Thus, economic resources derived from violence often fuel the cycle of violence. Depending on the geography of the territories they control and their capacity to exercise violence, rebel groups may derive financial resources from the control of lucrative economic sectors and natural resources, remittances from diasporas, financial support from third parties, voluntary (membership fees) or involuntary transfers (looting, forced taxes), detour of aid, or their economic activities as service providers. Warlords can both control these economic rents during conflict and/or in peacetime.

In times of conflict, warlords use all means and methods of violence at their disposal to seize resources that allow them to get rich in a short time and/or to strengthen their power and thus increase their chances of survival in the medium term. Warlords can enrich themselves by paying for their protection, by participating in the trade of arms, food and other necessities, by exploiting often enslaved labor, by seizing land, by stealing foreign aid or by allowing their fighters to pillage, extort, plunder and rob villages or travelers.[61] In the Central African Republic, armed groups such as the FPRC and UPC engage in a wide range of illicit fiscal activities, as well as looting of personal property, attacks and extortion.[62] These warlords and their men also loot money and other resources belonging to foreign or national communities affiliated with

---

59 Conseil de Sécurité des Nations Unies, "Rapport de La Mission Du Conseil de Sécurité En Côte d'Ivoire et En Guinée-Bissau," April 10, 2019, https://documents.un.org/doc/undoc/gen/n19/106/15/pdf/n1910615.pdf?token=i97uEFTVqmCdIzX3vz&fe=true.
60 Conseil de Sécurité des Nations Unies.
61 Philippe Hugon, L' économie de l'Afrique / Philippe Hugon, Repères (la Découverte, 2009), https://documentation.insp.gouv.fr/insp/doc/SYRACUSE/136353/l-economie-de-l-afrique-philippe-hugon.
62 Agger, "Warlord Business".

the "enemy," such as the cattle or coffee trade, but always for the benefit of the commander.[63]

Whether in peacetime or wartime, the core of the fortune of the violent entrepreneurs lies in the absolute control of a certain number of territories. The warlords can profit from the coinage of passage grants, prebends on smuggling or on the various baksheesh along the routes they control. Warlords and their armed groups often demonstrate their territorial control by building up roadblocks and imposing highly profitable taxes. Kasper Agger estimates that "ex-Séléka members make a total annual profit of between $1.5 and $2 million from all road taxes in the areas they control."[64] Territorial control at the borders also allows warlords to sell secure customs passage from one border to another. In Kivu, the Rassemblement Congolais pour la Démocratie/Mouvement de Libération (RCD-ML) of Antipas Mbusa Nyamwisi and the Forces Armées Populaires du Congo of Commander Jérôme Kakwavu Bukande, under international sanctions (resolution 1596, 2005),[65] controlled most of the border to Kenya and Uganda.[66] A key economic issue for the warlords will therefore be the location of the territories they control, particularly the importance of road and cross-border trade and the presence of trading centers.

The predation of economic resources is guaranteed by a more or less organized form of violent governance by the warlords. At the same time, it is a demonstration of strength, of territorial control, and the basis of their economic model: the "economy of barriers" consists of the imposition by force (or the threat of potential violence) of taxes of all kinds, particularly customs taxes.[67] The armed groups focus on the main trade routes, especially those through which gold, diamonds and cattle move. Revenues from these taxations are estimated to exceed 10 million euros annually.[68] According to IPIS, more than two-thirds of the trade routes essential to the Central African economy

---

63   Agger.
64   Agger.
65   Conseil de sécurité des Nations Unies, "Jerome Kakwavu Bukande," October 29, 2014, https://www.un.org/securitycouncil/fr/sanctions/1533/materials/summaries/individual/jerome-kakwavu-bukande.
66   Tim Raeymaekers, "Network War. An Introduction to Congo's Privatised War Economy," IPIS (blog), June 16, 2002, https://ipisresearch.be/publication/network-war-an-introduction-to-congos-privatised-war-economy/.
67   Alexandre Jaillon, Peer Schouten, and Soleil Kalessopo, "The Politics of Pillage: The Political Economy of Roadblocks in the Central African Republic (2017)," IPIS (blog), December 7, 2017, https://ipisresearch.be/publication/politics-pillage-political-economy-roadblocks-central-african-republic-2/.
68   Alexandre Jaillon, Peer Schouten, and Soleil Kalessopo.

were under the control of armed groups, including the movement of livestock and the trade routes linking the country to Chad and Sudan.[69]

Territorial control also allows warlords to establish and impose parallel administrative and fiscal structures to tax all economic resources.[70] In addition to systematically looting civilians, public administrators, associations, or businesses in their territories, warlords often establish regular and pseudo-regulated taxation.

According to a Global Financial Integrity study, extortion in the northern triangle (Guatemala, Honduras, and El Salvador) is estimated to generate $1.1 billion a year.[71] As Sean Doherty explains: "Extortion is so common that some victims view it as an inevitable expense and differentiate between what they call *renta* (rent), which are regular payments to criminal groups, and extortion, which is an additional payment on top of these."[72] This taxation system is so well established that when gangs are temporarily unable to collect the rent, individuals, and businesses set aside the necessary amount in anticipation of a later catch-up, as during the Covid-19 pandemic or periods of high conflict between gangs or with the governments.[73] Of these three countries, El Salvador is the most affected by this predatory system, with extortion against individuals alone reaching $190 to $245 million per year, compared to $40 to $57 million in Guatemala and $30 to $50 million in Honduras.[74]

The Salvadoran gangs do not have the opportunity to exploit coveted natural resources, nor do they enjoy a monopoly on drug transportation, which mainly remains under the control of the Texis Cartel and the Peronnes.[75] As

---

69 Alexandre Jaillon, Peer Schouten, and Soleil Kalessopo.
70 Conseil de sécurité des Nations Unies, "Rapport de Mi-Mandat Du Groupe d'experts En En Application de l'alinéa c du Paragraphe 32 de La Résolution 2399 (2018)," juillet 2018, https://documents.un.org/doc/undoc/gen/n18/218/64/pdf/n1821864.pdf?token=AVG QSlSvbXMkSwvklO&fe=true.
71 Julia Yansura, "Extortion in the Northern Triangle of Central America: Following the Money," *Global Financial Integrity* (blog), September 7, 2022, https://gfintegrity.org/report/extortion-in-the-northern-triangle-of-central-america-following-the-money/.
72 Sean Doherty, "Extortion in Northern Triangle Worth Over $1 Billion Annually: Report," InSightCrime, October 3, 2022, http://insightcrime.org/news/extortion-northern-triangle/.
73 Interview with an investigative journalist, San Salvador, October 2022.
74 Julia Yansura, "Extortion in the Northern Triangle of Central America".
75 There is one exception to this rule: In the region of La Union, in the south of the country on the border with Nicaragua, an MS13 clique called Hempstead Locos Salvatruchos (HLS) has taken control of drug transportation following a deadly succession among the Peronnes. This event has given rise to small replications at other strategic points, and specialists have been paying close attention to a possible evolution in the control of drug transportation in El Salvador, although a transfer of power has not yet taken place.

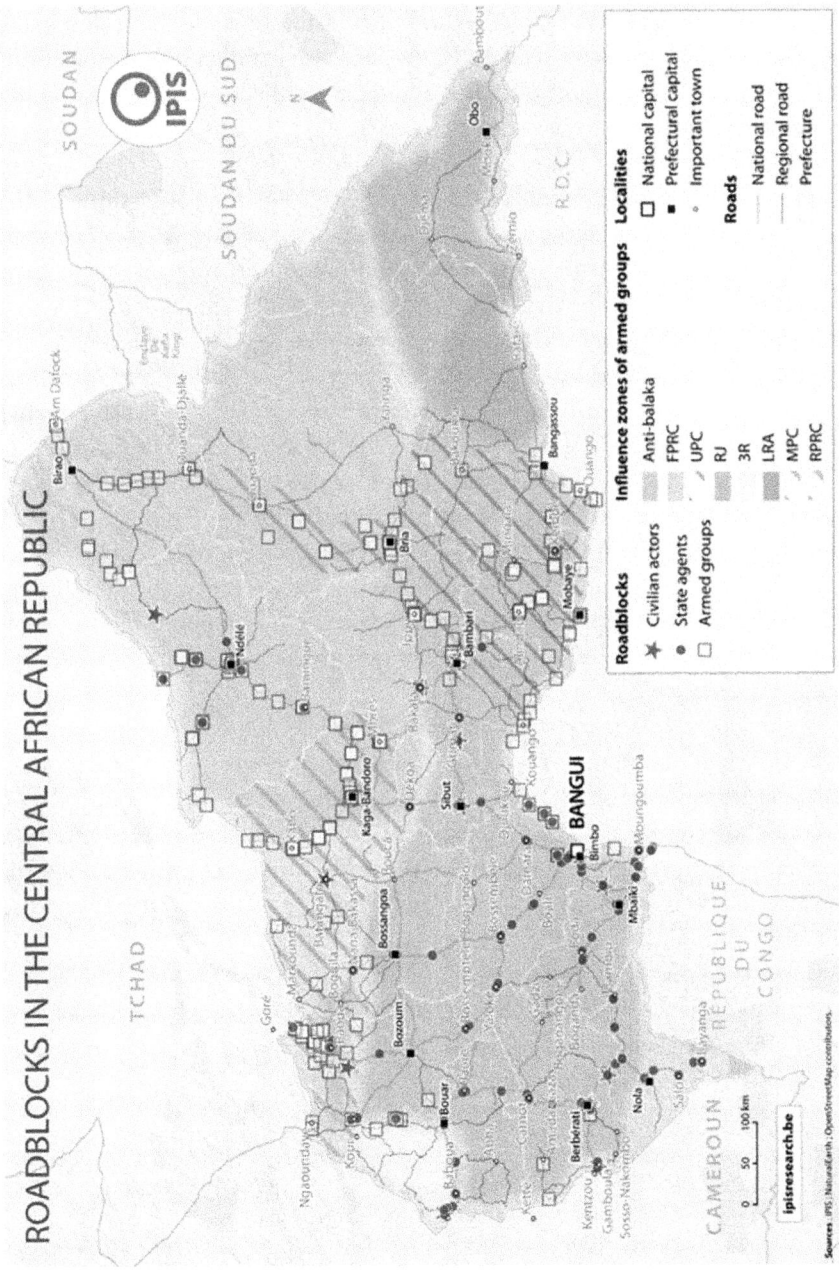

MAP 6.1 Roadblocks in the Central African Republic
SOURCE: NATURAL EARTH OPENSTREETMAP CONTRIBUTORS, IPIS, SEPTEMBER 2017

mentioned in an *Insight Crime*'s investigation, "The MS13 has never been particularly good at international drug trafficking. Internal rivalries, inexperience, sloppiness, a penchant for violence and high visibility made them unreliable partners for more experienced and practiced drug trafficking organizations (DTOs)."[76] Therefore, extortion is Salvadoran criminal entrepreneurs' primary source of income.

Gangs, composed of many small, locally-based cliques, have been able to establish extensive territorial control. Fiscal control is the cornerstone of the Salvadoran gangs' economic scheme ensuring their survival. All businesses in an area under the control of a gang must pay a monthly rent, as well as merchandise trucks and collective transports transiting through the area. This rent can range from $10 a month for a street vendor to $5,000 for the largest distribution companies like the Coca-Cola Company.[77] In addition to extortion, the two factions of Barrio 18 and MS13 have also managed to infiltrate parts of the legal economy. In gang-controlled neighborhoods, the cliques exercise a monopoly on the sale of essential consumer goods from gasoline to bread. Transportation is an emblematic example of the fiscal monopoly of gangs in certain areas. When traveling, residents of a gang-controlled area cannot escape the control of the established cliques. Cabs are owned by pandilleros, public transport must pay rent to operate, and the few people who own their own vehicles are not exempt from the gangs who control gas stations, garages, and parking spots.[78]

In the Central African Republic, armed groups such as the FPRC and the UPC, and their commanders, benefit greatly from the taxation of the production and transportation of natural resources and agricultural products such as coffee. By capturing land, warlords can also sell it, allocate it to relatives, distribute favors, and strengthen their power through this process. Warlords can also sell their arbitration skills, particularly in regulating access to and use of land.

Depending on the circumstances and its control over the land, the armed group will either negotiate access to an external operator who will take over production itself, or sell the result of its exploitation to a national or foreign

---

76 Hector Silva, Victoria Dittmar, and Alicia Florez, "How an MS13 Clique in El Salvador Took a Cocaine Corridor," InSight Crime, March 23, 2021, http://insightcrime.org/investigations/how-an-ms13-clique-in-el-salvador-took-a-cocaine-corridor/.
77 Juan José Martínez, "El Niño de Hollywood".
78 Juan José Martínez D'Aubuisson, "The Omnipresent Business of the MS13 in El Salvador," InSight Crime, January 25, 2022, http://insightcrime.org/investigations/the-omnipresent-businesses-of-the-ms13/.

buyer.[79] In the case of production delegated by armed groups to an external operator, payment can be made in cash but is more generally made through a percentage of the minerals or wood exploited that the group will itself resell. In exchange, the armed groups provide security to the operators by preventing the incursion of an opposing armed force, such as the warlord "Chance" in the northeast of the Democratic Republic of Congo.[80]

Warlords and their militias can benefit directly from the trade in natural resources (minerals, timber, oil, drug fields, etc.) that they exploit through the people they employ (and often enslave) and/or the businesses they own. Louise Shelley reminds us that: "as competition for scarce resources intensifies, they become the currency of criminal groups who take advantage of this scarcity for their own benefit. As a result, environmental and natural resource crimes are among the fastest growing forms of illicit trade. UNEP and Interpol have estimated their value at up to 250 billion euros in 2016."[81] In fact, environmental crimes have become one of the largest sources of funding for non-state armed groups and militias, which use them to support their involvement in conflicts.[82] Warlords are indeed involved in wildlife crime, including the trafficking and trade in elephant tusks, tiger and panther parts, and pangolins.[83]

During wartime, diamonds were the main resource of the Angolan rebellion called Uniao Nacional para a Independencia Total de Angola (UNITA). In the mid-1990s, UNITA was exporting more than $1 million worth of diamonds a day to pay for weapons of war.[84] In South Sudan, warlords are paid largely through oil, timber and coal trafficking.[85] In Côte d'Ivoire, in 2014, during peacetime, former warlord Issiaka Ouattara, alias Wattao, controlled artisanal gold mining in the town of Doropo. He reportedly sold the "exploitation rights" for 25 million CFA francs ($50,000), with monthly revenues of 60 million CFA francs

---

[79] Parfait Kaningu Bushenyula et al., "Conflits armés et autorité publique en RDC : vers la gestion de l'environnement par les groupes armés," October 5, 2021, https://www.eca-creac.eu/sites/default/files/pictures/conflits_armes_et_autorite_publique_rdc_vers_la_gestion_de_lenvironnement.pdf.
[80] Interview with the head of a local NGO, Dakar, 18 janvier 2023.
[81] Louise I. Shelley, "Dark Commerce: How a New Illicit Economy Is Threatening Our Future," *Princeton University Press—E-Book*, 2018, 1–376.
[82] *World Atlas of Illicit Flows*, 2018, https://www.youtube.com/watch?v=_gygyRvujQ4.
[83] *World Atlas of Illicit Flows*.
[84] Ian Smillie, *Blood on the Stone: Greed, Corruption and War in the Global Diamond Trade* (Anthem Press, 2010).
[85] "Criminality in South Sudan—The Organized Crime Index," 2023, https://ocindex.net/assets/downloads/2023/english/ocindex_profile_south_sudan_2023.pdf.

($120,000).[86] Wattao and his men also reportedly take a handsome tithe from the trade in rough diamonds in Séguéla, facilitating their illegal export for a fee. The gems are smuggled out of the country via Mali, Guinea or Liberia, before being sold in the United Arab Emirates, particularly in the Dubai market.

Another telling example is that the lion's share of the profits from the gold trade go to armed groups, fueling the cycle of violence in the Congo and Central African Republic.[87] In the DRC, a warlord named "Bosco" got rich from the gold mines he owned and from illegally taxing mineral trade routes. He oversaw a lucrative smuggling operation illegally exporting minerals to Rwanda through the territory he controlled and his own private residence strategically located on the border with Rwanda.[88] In the Central African Republic, FPRC leader and warlords Zakaria Damane and Oumar Younouss, also known as Oumar Sodiam, after the Central African diamond company Sodiam, are said to be profiting from the diamond trade in two ways, either by employing diggers—sometimes under duress—to find diamonds directly, which they then sell to diamond collectors, or indirectly by taxing diamond miners, traders and company employees.[89]

In Nigeria, highly organized criminal syndicates of oil bunkers, reportedly composed of expatriate and local businessmen, senior politicians and military personnel, and even employees of the oil companies themselves, have recruited young warlords to help provide security for their criminal activities, granting or securing access to the oil fields.[90] By 2009, the main warlords in the Niger Delta—including the Movement for the Emancipation of the Niger Delta (MEND)—were already important players in the local economy of the conflict.[91] Although revenues from oil bunkering fluctuate widely, they account for about 10% of Nigeria's daily production and bring in between $1.5 billion

---

86 "Les juteux trafics des seigneurs de guerre devenus militaires—L'Humanité," https://www.humanite.fr (blog), April 29, 2014, https://www.humanite.fr/monde/cote-divoire/les-juteux-trafics-des-seigneurs-de-guerre-devenus-militaires.

87 Sasha Lezhnev, "From Mine to Mobile Phone: The Conflict Minerals Supply Chain," *The Enough Project* (blog), November 10, 2009, https://enoughproject.org/reports/mine-mobile-phone.

88 "Congolese Warlord Stands Trial on 18 Counts of War Crimes, But Many More Crimes Have Gone Unreported".

89 Agger, "Warlord Business".

90 Christina Katsouris and Aaron Sayne, *Nigeria's Criminal Crude: International Options to Combat the Export of Stolen Oil* (Chatham House, 2015).

91 Aaron Sayne, "What's Next for Security in the Niger Delta?," United States Institute of Peace, April 26, 2013, https://www.usip.org/publications/2013/04/whats-next-security-niger-delta.

and $4 billion annually for the actors involved.[92] These large revenues are used to pay off local warlords against their security services. It is their capacity for violence and territorial control that compels criminal conglomerates to hire them for contracts to monitor pipelines and clean up oil spills, as well as to rent their barges and other equipment.[93] These legitimate revenues flow back to the armed groups and warlords, fueling the violence as they gain additional income and weapons to expand their militant actions.

In Myanmar, warlords have been involved in the plundering of natural resources, including jade and timber, worth billions of dollars for decades. Due to growing demand from China, Myanmar has recently seen a rapid and massive expansion of illegal mining of heavy rare earth minerals in the north of its territory, an area that has long been controlled by various warlords.[94] In fact, over the past decade, China has outsourced much of its heavy rare earth mining industry across the border to Kachin State, which is now one of the world's largest sources of these minerals, which are vital to the production of new technologies.[95] Nevertheless, Global Witness found that this illegal trade has benefited local warlords linked to the military regime and senior army officers, particularly warlord Zakhung Ting Ying, whose militia controls much of the mining territory through a climate of terror.[96]

Finally, warlords can enrich themselves through their direct or indirect participation in transnational criminal operations, linked to organized crime. A first example is the participation of Somali warlords in the trafficking of toxic waste in the 1990s, in connection with Italian criminal organizations and politicians. In Côte d'Ivoire, at the end of the conflict, trafficking in drugs and counterfeit medicines multiplied in the territories controlled by the former warlords.[97] Another famous example is the warlords who operated during

---

92   Working Paper for SPDC, "Peace and Security in the Niger Delta: Conflict Expert Group Baseline Report," yumpu.com, December 2003, https://www.yumpu.com/en/document/view/8937981/peace-and-security-in-the-niger-delta-npr, pp 46.
93   Working Paper for SPDC.
94   Global Witness, Press release, "New Evidence Shows Massive and Rapid Expansion of Illicit Rare Earths Industry in Myanmar, Fuelling Human Rights Abuses, Environmental Destruction and Funding Military-Linked Militias," National Wind Watch, August 9, 2022, https://www.wind-watch.org/news/2022/08/10/new-evidence-shows-massive-and-rapid-expansion-of-illicit-rare-earths-industry-in-myanmar-fuelling-human-rights-abuses-environmental-destruction-and-funding-military-linked-militias/.
95   Global Witness, "Myanmar's Poisoned Mountains," Global Witness, August 9, 2022, https:///en/campaigns/natural-resource-governance/myanmars-poisoned-mountains/.
96   Global Witness.
97   http://www.douanes.ci/?page=Infos.Actualite.News&id=334&rub=actualite&typrub=srub.

the Balkan wars in the 90s. An alliance of interdependent criminal and rebel groups thrived by selling drugs, weapons, oil, clothes, food, migrants, and information, sometimes also participating directly in combat, notably during the siege of Sarajevo.[98] The Kosovo Liberation Army (KLA) was notoriously financed through various trafficking controlled by Albanian clans, notably organs smuggling through the Yellow Houses network.[99]

The Burmese, Laotian, and Thai armed groups, financed underhand or tolerated by Southeast Asian governments for decades, are textbook cases in terms of the economies of violence and the enrichment of warlords through international trafficking. Indeed, the power of these warlords was and still is correlated to their control of remote territories, giving them the possibility to produce and sell various hard drugs (heroin and methamphetamine in particular), but also to exploit and sell several minerals (jade and emeralds for example).[100]

For example, in the middle of the Cold War, two Chinese from Burma, the Lo Hsing-Han and Lo Hsing-Minh brothers, founded the Shan State Revolutionary Army (SSRA), a seemingly secessionist movement that served as a front for a gigantic Asian heroin trade that made the Lo brothers very rich. The military junta finally let them do it, and SSRA became a useful tool in the fight against the communist maquis. SSRA received financial support from the CIA in exchange for sending agents to "Red" China. In dissidence against the Burmese central power, the warlord Chan Shee-Fu, nicknamed Khun Sa, became a major player in the production and trade of poppies at the head of the Shan United Army. From 1978, in order to buy peace with the secessionist Hmong populations, the Laotian state authorized the purchase, refining and transport of opium cultivated in the mountains by the warlords. The production, of 50 tons in 1984, increased to 250 tons in 1987, the poppy became the first agricultural resource of Laos.[101]

The reshipment of these goods to the Western world was the work of another type of actor: the Asian mafias. Relying on the Chinese diaspora, the new international Asian heroin network was in fact dominated from the 1970s

---

98 Jean-François Gayraud, "Nouveau Capitalisme criminel," www.odilejacob.fr, 2014, https://www.odilejacob.fr/catalogue/sciences-humaines/droit-justice/nouveau-capitalisme-criminel_9782738130723.php.
99 "The Bloody Yellow House," The Bloody Yellow House, October 15, 2009, https://thebloodyellowhouse.wordpress.com/.
100 Alexandre Marchant, "Histoire et géopolitique du trafic des opiacés en Asie du Sud-Est," vih.org, September 25, 2017, https://vih.org/drogues-et-rdr/20170925/histoire-et-geopolitique-du-trafic-des-opiaces-en-asie-du-sud-est/.
101 Alexandre Marchant.

onwards by the Chinese Triads: 14 K, the most powerful, based in Hong Kong; Ka Ki Nang, based in Thailand; Gi Kin San, operating out of Singapore; and Sap Baat Chai, or the 18 Immortals group, based in Malaysia.[102] The alliances between armed groups and mafias underline the existence, since the 1990s, of new forms of economic relations outside the spectrum of states and the international community between key actors in the economies of violence. Despite some positive developments and their retreat in the 1990s under international pressure, guerrillas and mafias remain active in the Golden Triangle and new drug lords, such as the Chinese-Burmese Wei Shao Kang, head of the United Wa State Army, a new guerrilla group federating the Wa ethnic group, have set up synthetic drug laboratories in the 1990s.[103] Ecstasy and especially methamphetamine, after having saturated the Thai market, are now spreading throughout Asia.

6.4 Social Power and Political Connections

Warlords/criminal entrepreneurs are always part of a particular ecosystem. In social spaces characterized by extreme poverty and communal antagonisms, the business conflict model of armed groups led by warlords is quite attractive.[104] It is a guarantee of insurance, survival, protection, and income for the population, as well as for politicians. Armed groups and warlords have economic claims rooted in the defense of their communities, which aim at the political legitimization of their control over certain territories. The Kosovo Liberation Army used the war as a self-validation of all their criminal activities and personal enrichment while using violent means.[105] In Nigeria, the warlords in the Niger Delta, while unappreciated, often symbolize a vanguard rebellion against an allegedly exploitative federal government in Abuja and the patronage-based and "clientelistic" distribution of power it has installed in the region.[106] In fact, the socio-economic inequalities are staggering in these impoverished and underdeveloped regions, as the benefits of oil production are not visible to the vast majority of the population, who suffer enormously

---

102 Roger Faligot, *La mafia chinoise en Europe: Paris, Marseille, Amsterdam, Anvers, Bruxelles* … (Calmann-Lévy, 2001).
103 Alexandre Marchant, "Histoire et géopolitique du trafic des opiacés en Asie du Sud-Est".
104 Thierry Vircoulon, "Écosystème des groupes armés en Centrafrique".
105 Jean-François Gayraud, "Le Monde des mafias Géopolitique du crime organisé".
106 "Armed Gangs Dominate Nigeria's Oil-Rich Region," Voice of America, November 2, 2009, https://www.voanews.com/a/a-13-2009-04-19-voa18-68684917/355754.html.

from the lack of public services as well as the environmental damage caused by legal and illegal extraction and transportation.

The exercise of power by armed groups is evident in their appropriation of all state responsibilities. The warlords play the role of protector and thus intervene in the resolution of community problems in these villages. It can be argued that warlords derive their legitimacy, in some territories, from trading goods outside of the predatory taxation levied by the state (sometimes compounded by additional personal taxes of state officials)—thereby protecting local populations from these predatory practices and allegedly redistributing wealth belonging to local communities more efficiently.

As mentioned, violent entrepreneurs collect taxes and regulate entry and exit into the controlled territory. When armed groups are from the same territory and ethnic grouping, loyalty to the warlords is strengthened and makes it more difficult to dislodge them from the area. For exploitation activities by armed groups, the workforce is mainly recruited from within the community. Warlords buy popular support by distributing land and jobs, especially among their own ranks. Warlords regulate the entire economy of a territory. The control of food resources also provides warlords with several advantages: it allows them to meet the needs of the population in terms of food but also the prospect of possible rapid enrichment and thus reduces the potential risks of discontent; it plays a role of legitimization of these parties, as it proves that they are capable of managing the lives of the populations under their control; it serves as a tool of submission and blackmail in their relationship both with the populations under their control and with the various other parties they are fighting against.[107] In El Salvador, gangs use the population to collect rent from businesses. Victims of extortion themselves are forced to participate in this system and are thus considered to be agents of the justice system.[108] Citizens can neither oppose the gangs against this illegal taxation, exposing themselves to a gradually increasing violence up to and including death,[109] nor can they assert their rights as victims before the State and its institutions. Gang's taxing power is thus uncontested.

---

107 Jeroen Cuvelier and Stefaan Marysse, "Les enjeux économiques du conflit en Ituri," in *L'Afrique des grands-lacs: annuaire 2003–2004* (L'Harmattan, 2004), 171–203, http://hdl.handle.net/1854/LU-1863604.
108 D'Aubuisson, "The Omnipresent Business of the MS13 in El Salvador".
109 Luis Enrique Amaya and Juan José Martínez d'Aubuisson, "Renta O Extorsión Victimarios y Víctimas de Las Maras En El Salvador" (Global Initiative Against Transnational Organized Crime, October 2021), https://globalinitiative.net/wp-content/uploads/2021/11/GITOC-Renta-o-extorsion-Victimarios-y-victimas-de-las-maras-en-El-Salvador.pdf.

It is visible that in many territories where warlords operate, they build both commercial and political relationships of interest with local elites, both in economic circles and in government (local or national). Relationships of interdependence, cooperation, and competition are established between warlords and the political and economic elites. The latter will sometimes use a warlord, and support him and his violent action, for personal enrichment. The elites benefit from insecurity as long as they can control the intensity of the violence. Through the dependence and vulnerability of the population due to continued insecurity, members of the elites secure the support of several easily manipulated bands of fighters ready to be engaged in an armed struggle for control over economic resources. Conflict legitimizes actions that would be considered crimes in times of peace. It provides a direct incentive for the warlords, and all their official business partners, to perpetuate the war.[110]

As early as 1998, links between the Museveni family, the Ugandan army and its expeditionary force in the DRC, and Indian and Israeli mineral magnates were demonstrated around gold trafficking.[111] Some businessmen in Ituri allegedly collaborated with the Ugandan military to transport out of the country raw materials excavated under the control of armed groups under the control of warlords.[112] In Rwanda, Uganda and Burundi, companies illegally importing minerals from Congolese mines under the control of warlords are working closely with officers of the security services—the country's military and police—to ensure that their investments are "protected."[113] These are striking examples of the willful perpetuation of violence for personal and corporate gain.

Ceding control of a territory and its natural resources to a warlord to ensure stability can be a voluntary compromise by governments and sometimes the international community. Having a single interlocutor, a strongman, with whom to interact is seen as facilitating commercial transactions and supposedly guaranteeing a mutually beneficial form of capitalist peace, as both actors, warlords, and political elites, become dependent on the same economic rent. Alliances are formed between politicians, national or foreign companies, private security firms, and/or armed groups to create new rents based on the

---

110 Kathryn Nwajiaku-Dahou, "The Political Economy of Oil and 'rebellion' in Nigeria's Niger Delta," *Review of African Political Economy* 39, no. 132 (2012): 295–313.
111 Cuvelier and Marysse, "Les enjeux économiques du conflit en Ituri".
112 Lezhnev, "From Mine to Mobile Phone".
113 Lezhnev.

exploitation of a resource present in the territory of a warlord.[114] These deals are often validated or even negotiated by the international community.

The agreements (e.g., "internationally sanctioned" illicit trades between political elites and warlords) are often accompanied by the rehabilitation of the most violent warlords and are accompanied by an exchange that systematically includes willful blindness and complacency about their legal and illegal economic revenues, as well as "forgetting" about their past and current abuses. In the DRC, the transition from rebel to army general in an indirect peace agreement in 2009 gave warlord Bosco Ntaganda control over lucrative mining areas, allowing him to effectively run his own state within a state.[115]

These arrangements are best exemplified by the Karzai government in Afghanistan (2001–2014). The Afghan warlords played a prominent role in the government of Hamid Karzai.[116] The Karzai clan made Faustian pacts with warlords to ensure his two successive elections as head of the country.[117] This exchange of favors allowed the warlords to obtain key positions in the government. Mohammad Qasim Fahim became vice-president of the country, while General Abdul Rashid Dostum became chief of staff of the Afghan army. In addition to impunity for their multiple crimes,[118] access to high positions in the Afghan administration has allowed the warlords to make an excellent financial operation by obtaining total immunity for their illegal activities (drug and mineral trafficking in particular) and access to lucrative public contracts.[119]

Indispensable post-conflict partners for the new political elites, Albanian criminal clans acquired unparalleled political and mediatic power in the

---

114   William Reno, "African Weak States and Commercial Alliances," *African Affairs* 96, no. 383 (1997): 165–85.
115   "Congolese Warlord Stands Trial on 18 Counts of War Crimes, But Many More Crimes Have Gone Unreported".
116   Kenneth Katzman, "Afghanistan: Post-Taliban Governance, Security, and U.S. Policy," Refworld, December 22, 2015, https://www.refworld.org/reference/countryrep/uscrs/2015/en/108828.
117   Jonathan S. Landay and Tom Lasseter, "Notorious Warlord Returns Just before Afghan Election," The Seattle Times, August 17, 2009, https://www.seattletimes.com/seattle-news/politics/notorious-warlord-returns-just-before-afghan-election/.
118   In 2007 the Afghan parliament passed a law granting amnesty to warlords and others who committed human rights abuses during the previous wars in Afghanistan. Underscoring the power of warlords in the Afghan administration, this U.S.-backed law illustrates the disbelief in justice and the foolish belief in the malleability of violence as a catalyst for peace.
119   Candace Rondeaux, "Dealing with brutal Afghan warlords is a mistake," Afghanistan Analysts Network—English, January 17, 2010, https://www.afghanistan-analysts.org/en/reports/war-and-peace/dealing-with-brutal-afghan-warlords-is-a-mistake/.

post-communism institutional void. It is therefore no surprise that the Albanese Mafia developed a new stronghold in Kosovo following the footsteps of NATO.[120] At the end of the war, former Kosovar paramilitaries engaged full-time in the transit of cigarettes, heroin, migrants, and women to Western Europe, developing a new platform for the Albanian Mafia between Turkey and Italy. In July 2001, an Italian prosecutor formally accused then-prime minister of Montenegro Milo Dujkanovic, Minister of Foreign Affairs Branko Petrovic, and local police chiefs, of being active associates of Camorra and Sacra Corona Unita bosses in the running of the largest Mediterranean cigarette trafficking network, smuggling over 1000 tons of cigarettes per month.[121] Cigarettes were mainly sold to Tobacco multinational companies based in Switzerland including R.J Reynolds and Philip Morris. Experts affirm that during Dujkanovic' reign half of Montenegro's GDP originated in criminal activities.[122]

Once integrated into the state apparatus, warlords derive a considerable part of their power and wealth from bribes received in exchange for access to public contracts, the misappropriation of public resources, and contracts related to the security employing their armed forces. In Afghanistan, warlord militias were employed by NATO through numerous contracts, organizing and extorting money from the US military's supply chain.[123,124] Conflict after conflict, the state and its allies in the international community believe that social peace can be obtained in exchange for the purchase and remuneration of the violence of its main contractors. This calculation has been, is, and will continue to be a serious mistake.[125] Delegating security, community protection, and the economy to violent actors never leads to lasting peace because it is against their interests.

Since 2012 in El Salvador, governments in power have negotiated with the gangs, leading to an overall reduction in homicides.[126] The breakdown of the

---

120 "The Bloody Yellow House".
121 Ian Traynor, "Montenegrin PM Accused of Link with Tobacco Racket," *The Guardian*, July 11, 2003, sec. World news, https://www.theguardian.com/world/2003/jul/11/smoking.internationalcrime.
122 Jean-François Gayraud, "Nouveau Capitalisme criminel".
123 Tom A. Peter, "A Changing of the Guard for Afghanistan's Warlords," *Christian Science Monitor*, accessed March 30, 2024, https://www.csmonitor.com/World/Asia-South-Central/2010/1027/A-changing-of-the-guard-for-Afghanistan-s-warlords.
124 John F. Tierney, *Warlord, Inc.: Extortion and Corruption along the U.S. Supply Chain in Afghanistan* (Washington, DC: U.S. House of Representatives, 2010), http://media.washingtonpost.com/wp-srv/world/documents/warlords.pdf.
125 "Selling Justice Short," *Human Rights Watch*, July 7, 2009, https://www.hrw.org/report/2009/07/07/selling-justice-short/why-accountability-matters-peace.
126 Óscar Martínez y Daniel Reyes, "Cronología Del Pacto Entre El Gobierno de Bukele y Las Pandillas," Cronología del pacto entre el Gobierno de Bukele y las pandillas, January 18,

first truce between the Barrio 18 and MS13 cliques negotiated by the government in 2012, led to an outbreak of violence in 2014 and 2015. That year, El Salvador registered the highest per capita homicide rate in the world (115 per 100,000 inhabitants).[127] Since then, successive governments have maintained a constant dialogue with the gangs to avoid any outbreak of violence that would cost them a lot in the polls. Thus, since 2015 the annual homicide rate has been decreasing. However, these "truces" and negotiations do not reduce the power of the Maras. On the contrary, in exchange for a reduction in clashes and deaths, the gangs obtain favors. These favors mainly concern the incarcerated leaders, privileged intermediaries of the governments. Successive arrangements have made Salvadoran prisons a command center for the gangs and have shaped Maras' organization.[128]

At first, the numerous small cliques of the Barrio 18 and the Mara Salvatrucha were horizontally organized. The leaders of these cliques would meet during "meering"[129] (a term specific to pandilleros, derived from the English "meeting"), but there were no designated leaders above all at that time. It was in the mid-2000s that a vertical structure and leaders representing the entire maras emerged. This organizational change is the result of successive Salvadoran governments' carceral policies during these years.[130] In order to be able to negotiate with all of the disparate cliques of these three gangs, the governments need interlocutors capable of imposing an agreement on all of these small structures. Those in power need a small number of uncontested leaders, and therefore a strong verticality. Political power has thus become dependent on these gangs, which control the level of violence in the country, a central element of Salvadoran politics. The periodic outbreaks of violence illustrate this power play between gangs and the government.

These negotiations create de facto links between gang leaders and the country's top leaders. The escape of one of the MS13's top leaders, Crook, at the end of 2021 is one example of this high-level complicity. Elmer Canales Rivera, alias Crook, was at that time facing an extradition request from the United States. An investigation by the newspaper El Faro[131] revealed that his escape was

---

2023, https://elfaro.net/es/202301/el_salvador/26676/Cronolog%C3%ADa-del-pacto-entre-el-Gobierno-de-Bukele-y-las-pandillas.htm.

127 United Nations Office on Drugs and Crime. Data UNODC available at: https://dataunodc.un.org.
128 Juan José Martínez, "El Niño de Hollywood".
129 Valencia, *Carta desde Zacatraz*.
130 Juan José Martínez, "El Niño de Hollywood".
131 Carlos García, "Transnational Escape of MS-13 Leader 'Crook' Caught on Social Media," Transnational Escape of MS-13 Leader "Crook" Caught on Social Media, July 11, 2022,

orchestrated by Carlos Maroquin, head of the "social tissue," one of the most important officials of the Ministry of Security, who personally drove him to the Guatemalan border. He was not the only member of the government involved in this case.[132] Rodolfo Antonio Delgado Montes, the current Attorney General of El Salvador, worked as a lawyer for a close collaborator of MS13: Jorge Manuel Vega Knight.[133] Yet no one questioned his ties to the gang during his confirmation hearings in 2021. One of his first acts in office was to dismantle the Special Investigation Commission, which was investigating Vega Knight and about a hundred other gang members. 5 months after being appointed prosecutor, he succeeded in having the seizure of his former client's assets lifted: two motels that had been proven to be used as money laundering sites for MS13.[134]

In the Central African Republic, too, peace (or rather a semblance of stability) is decided around the distribution of control over revenues from the illegal exploitation and resale of natural resources (minerals, timber, livestock, wildlife) between political and economic elites and warlords. Central African warlords sell diamonds to buyers in the two Central African buying offices—the Central African Diamond Buying Office (Badica) and the Central African Diamond Company (Sodiam)—both of which are linked to political elites in the capital.[135] Warlords sometimes sell their products across the border in South Darfur and Chad, again to local political and commercial elites. Here too, the integration of these warlords into the state apparatus is only of interest if they gain access to positions of power and impunity for war crimes. This is the case of the Central African rebel Ali Darassa, the leader of the Union for Peace in the Central African Republic (UPC), a group that has repeatedly massacred civilians, who in March 2019 became a deputy minister and advisor to the Prime Minister's Office with the blessing of the United Nations.[136] In the Bambari locality he controlled, Ali Darassa had set up a parallel administration

---

       https://elfaro.net/en/202207/el_salvador/26264/Transnational-Escape-of-MS-13-Leader-%E2%80%9CCrook%E2%80%9D-Caught-on-Social-Media.htm.

132 Carlos García.

133 Juan Martínez d'Aubuissson and Efren Lemus, "El Salvador's Attorney General Worked for Top MS13 Ally," InSight Crime, October 31, 2022, http://insightcrime.org/investigations/el-salvador-attorney-general-worked-top-ms13-ally/.

134 Efren Lemus y Juan José Martínez d'Aubuisson "El fiscal general trabajó 29 meses para uno de los principales colaboradores de la MS-13" El Faro, 31 oct 2022.
       https://elfaro.net/es/202210/el_salvador/26427/El-fiscal-general-trabajó-29-meses-para-uno-de-los-principales-colaboradores-de--la-MS-13.htm.

135 Agger, "Warlord Business".

136 Célian Macé, "En Centrafrique, Les Seigneurs de Guerre Tirent Profit de La Paix," April 18, 2019, https://www.liberation.fr/planete/2019/04/18/en-centrafrique-les-seigneurs-de-guerre-tirent-profit-de-la-paix_1722223/.

that was responsible, among other things, for running a system of systematic racketeering, natural resource, and arms trafficking networks.[137]

6.4.1 Case Study: The Links between Secret Cults, Organized Crime, and Warlords in Nigeria

Secret cults have always existed in some parts of Nigeria, and the origins of some of the country's crime syndicates can be traced back to brotherhoods.[138][139] In Nigeria, a brotherhood is a nominally academic group, although "street and stream" brotherhoods emerged in the 1990s.[140] In 1968, the formation of the notorious Eiye brotherhood at the University of Ibadan marked an evolution of these traditional socio-political institutions. In the 1990s, an array of new cults emerged, and by the end of the 1990s, many of the brotherhoods and cults were operating largely as criminal gangs.[141] One of the most feared cults on Nigerian campuses is the Black Axe. Investigations and several arrests of NBM members by the Italian police have brought to light various crimes committed by members of NBM and other cults, who have been convicted of drug trafficking, extortion, 419 fraud, prostitution, passport forgery, and credit card cloning.[142]

The transition to democracy in 1999 exacerbated youth militancy, as unscrupulous politicians used hired thugs to commit violence to ensure their electoral victory. Brotherhoods were simultaneously co-opted by military governments anxious to consolidate their control over university students who might challenge their authority, as fierce student unionism was seen by military

---

137 Célian Macé.
138 Adewale Rotimi, "Violence in the Citadel: The Menace of Secret Cults in the Nigerian Universities," *Nordic Journal of African Studies* 14 (January 1, 2005), https://doi.org/10.53228/njas.v14i1.282.
139 "Nigerian Crime Syndicates And Their Routes To Europe And The West," accessed March 30, 2024, http://hellasfrappe.blogspot.com/2012/12/nigerian-crime-syndicates-and-their.html.
140 "Nigerian Crime Syndicates And Their Routes To Europe And The West".
141 It includes the Second Son of Satan, Night Cadet, Sonmen, Mgba Brothers, Temple of Eden, Trojan Horse, Jurists, White Bishops, Gentlemen Clubs, Fame, Executioners, Dreaded Friend of Friends, Eagle Club, Black Scorpion, Red Sea Horse and Fraternity of Friends. A list of 41 cults active in 2003 is provided by Christopher Oyemwinmina and Stanley Aibieyi in Christopher Oyemwinmina and Stanley Aibieyi, "Cultism: A Destructive Concept in the Educational Development of Tertiary Institutions in Nigeria," *African Research Review* 9 (October 27, 2015): 221, https://doi.org/10.4314/afrrev.v9i4.17.
142 Adesanya, Adeleke. *Unraveling Nigerian Organised Crime and Activities*, Newswatch Times. Accessed March 3, 2016 at http://www.mynewswatchtimesng.com/unravelling-nigerian-organised-crime-activities/.

authorities as a threat to the consolidation of their power.[143] Secret cults were used to counterbalance student unions and their anti-government activities, which challenged or defied the military dictatorship and school administrations, and were sometimes used to exact political revenge. In exchange for their help, the cults received support and patronage from the government and school authorities.[144] Involved in violent intimidation campaigns, assassinations of political opponents, and impunity for lucrative criminal activities, the cults have become both essential elements of Nigerian political systems and key bases for the expansion of Nigerian crime syndicates around the world.[145] By 2005, the majority of the Brotherhoods were engaged in a variety of criminal activities ranging from drug trafficking to armed robbery to kidnapping.[146] In the Niger River Delta, the brotherhoods were deeply involved in the oil-rich delta conflict, and most of the university cults were accused of kidnapping foreign oil workers for ransom. Militant groups, such as the Movement for the Emancipation of the Niger Delta (MEND), employ members of the brotherhoods as fighters.[147]

After a long conflict in southeastern Nigeria that left thousands dead over the years, an amnesty between the Niger Delta armed groups representing 26,000 militants and the Nigerian government was signed in June 2009.[148] In several regions, their de facto sovereignty over the territory was recognized, with militant leaders being integrated into state institutions, given police protection and given official mandates, including securing oil production and transportation. One of its main effects has been the "legalization" of illicit activities, as young warlords retain their military forces and use them to strengthen their economic power through the signing of lucrative official contracts that recognize the dependence of external actors on them, redistributing their capacity for violence while diminishing the economic damage it might cause. The small armies of warlords are often hired within the private security companies they create and control, which are themselves hired by the official and criminal oil production/transportation conglomerates.

---

143 "Nigeria's 2003 Elections," *Human Rights Watch*, June 1, 2004, https://www.hrw.org/report/2004/06/01/nigerias-2003-elections/unacknowledged-violence.
144 Rotimi, "Violence in the Citadel," pp. 93.
145 Okafor Ofiebor, "Portrait of Ateke Tom," The News, September 13, 2004.
146 Interview with Jack Jackson (PhD), December 2022.
147 "Nigerian Crime Syndicates And Their Routes To Europe And The West".
148 Jan Pospisil, Alina Rocha Menocal, and Markus Schultze-Kraft, "Understanding Organised Violence and Crime in Political Settlements: Oil Wars, Petro-Criminality and Amnesty in the Niger Delta," *Journal of International Development* 29, no. 5 (2017): 613–27.

Putting former militants in charge of protecting the oil infrastructure is, in a way, like appointing a bank robber as head of bank security. This suggests that federal elites have identified the militants' ability to limit oil production through violent means as the main problem, without being as concerned about oil bunkering.[149]

Interestingly, young activists and cult members presented themselves as modern-day Robin Hoods, reclaiming oil revenues that supposedly belong to local communities. By the late 2000s, the activists who had set out to challenge the abuses of the leaders had become big men themselves.[150] As a result, the number of small armed groups and "small" warlords increased dramatically, and the criminal alliances between local warlords, businessmen, security forces, criminal gangs, and members of the local/federal political elites did not cease after the signing of the amnesty. So, the large-scale oil bribing continued, and the warlords got richer and richer, winning on all fronts since they were now politicians and therefore politically protected. In 2021, crime and separatist actions were the main cause of violence in the delta regions: they increased by 87% and 573%, respectively, in 2021 compared to 2020.[151] A burgeoning financial capacity has also strengthened their socio-political hold, as they have become the official providers of education, health, and agricultural services. Growing social power translates into greater political power. In recent presidential and legislative elections, warlords and small criminal groups have thus become prime targets for the main political parties, trading the support and votes of the communities they control for more money and protection.

6.4.2   Case Study: Post-conflict Socio-economic Power of Warlords in Côte D'ivoire

Following the rebellion in Côte d'Ivoire (2001–2011), the northern part of the country was entirely ruled by the rebel commanders of the Forces Nouvelles (FN) who came to power in 2011. The capital of the northern region and the stronghold of the rebellion has long been Bouaké. The region was divided into ten sectors or zones, each of which was headed by a zone commander, commonly known as a "Comezone," a true warlord. For a long period, the leader of the rebellion was Guillaume Soro, who later became president of the

---

149   Pospisil, Menocal, and Schultze-Kraft.
150   Aaron Sayne, "What's Next for Security in the Niger Delta?"
151   Foundation for Partnership Initiatives in the Niger Delta (PIND), "Niger Delta Annual Conflict Report: January-December 2021," 2021, https://pindfoundation.org/wp-content/uploads/2022/02/Niger-Delta-Annual-Conflict-Report-2021-Draft.pdf.

National Assembly. Important Comezones included Mourou Ouattara, Cherif Ousmane, "Wattao," Ousmane Coulibaly alias "Ben Laden" and Losséni Fofana alias "Fofie."[152]

The financial and economic systems that supported the rebellion varied over time. In addition to revenues from allies and foreign businessmen, the warlords sought revenues from the administration of trade in the territories they controlled. Cocoa and cotton, for example, were sent south, with the warlords giving lower prices to producers and then making large profits from resale. Large volumes of these products were then exported via Guinea, then Burkina Faso, Ghana and even Togo. The revenues generated by these activities were more than enough for the Comezones to finance the control of their respective regions.[153]

The ten regions were also required to send a portion of their revenues to the capital, Bouaké, in a unified financial mechanism called "la centrale".[154] In theory, this central financial institution was to redistribute a portion of the revenues to pay soldiers and other expenses. In reality, however, the finances of the rebellion were highly decentralized. The Comezones became financially independent of the revenues collected in each of their regions. In fact, these regional commanders became the rulers of their sectors and ran these territories as their personal fiefdoms with their own sources of income, in charge of their own private armies, and often administered justice and governed many aspects of society.

After the 2011 post-election crisis, Alassane Ouattara became president, most of the former FAFN leaders moved to Abidjan and joined the Ouattara government and the military in one capacity or another. It is difficult to know the exact number of troops that the former Comezones had under their command. However, it is safe to say that they maintained affiliated troops in the areas where they were deployed. For example, Ousmane Cherif was deployed with his troops to Yopougon and then became the deputy head of the Security Group of the Presidency of the Republic. His famous battalion, Guepard, remains entirely under his command in the GSPR. Ousmane Cherif is currently in charge of the security of the First Lady, Dominique Ouattara, and is considered the protégé of Me Ouattara.[155] Ousmane Coulibaly has deployed all

---

152 Interviews conducted with former rebels and law enforcement officers in Abidjan and Yopougon, Ivory Coast, 2015 and 2016.
153 Interviews conducted with former rebels and law enforcement officers in Abidjan and Yopougon, Ivory Coast, 2015 and 2016.
154 Interviews conducted with former rebels and law enforcement officers in Abidjan and Yopougon, Ivory Coast, 2015 and 2016.
155 http://cujema.unblog.fr/2012/02/04/cherif-ousmane-est-le-protege-de-ouattara/.

his troops in the northern part of Yopougon and along the western coastline, almost to San Pedro. He has been appointed prefect of the country's second-largest city, San Pedro, a key maritime center. Losséni Fofana remains in the Man area with his troops and becomes commander of the Western Security Battalion. Tuo Fozie, one of the main leaders of the rebellion, became the prefect of Buna, where he controlled most of the border with Burkina Faso.

The thousands of infantrymen who participated in the standard DDR process received a certain amount of money from the national DDR commission. Once this money is spent, they no longer have a reliable source of income, suggesting that their loyalty is at the disposal of whoever pays them. Warlords have used the DDR process to maintain and even strengthen their forces. As one UNOCI official confirmed, their influence on the DDR process has allowed each of the former Comezones to place their associated soldiers in the gendarmerie, prison administration, customs, and in the water and forestry departments as forest guards.[156] Thus, their integration into the Rule of Law did not reduce their human and financial power.

In 2011, the warlords were recycled into key positions in the civil and military administration within the new regime. Appointed to positions of authority in the territories they already controlled, these "Com Zone" (zone commanders) still oversee the illegal exploitation and export of natural resources (raw diamonds, gold, cocoa, cashew nuts, timber, etc.) for arms purchases or personal enrichment.[157] This territorial control provides them with revenues derived from any criminal activity and the flow of illicit goods through their areas. One of the main trafficking hubs in Côte d'Ivoire, the port of Abidjan, is under the jurisdiction of the Ministry of Transport, which happens to be headed by a former rebel, hence the network's control of the port. Since warlords control most of the law enforcement officers, conditions are conducive to impunity.[158] The complicity of law enforcement in Ivorian ports and airports is so widespread that criminals have claimed to be able to receive and ship drugs directly to runways or port terminals.[159] Trust between business partners involved in these networks is largely based on informal ties, whether ethnic, familial or personal, and on their shared experience as warlords.

---

156   Interviews conducted with former rebels and law enforcement officers in Abidjan and Yopougon in 2015 and 2016.
157   Interviews conducted with former rebels.
158   Interviews conducted with former rebels and law enforcement officers in Abidjan and Yopougon in 2015 and 2016.
159   *Interviews conducted with former rebels.*

The integration of warlords into legal positions has further opacified and provided a legal front for the illegal exploitation of natural resources for their benefit. Access to the state apparatus has also made it easier for them to launder their dirty money, notably by gaining access to public contracts and being able to create legal businesses, particularly in the flourishing construction sector.[160]

6.5 Warlords and the International Economy

Warlords are not confined to the black market; they and their violence are closely linked to the global economy.

Whether mutual benefit or accepted lesser evil, the potential violence of warlords and their correlating ability to impose their laws by force, such as threats of kidnapping and racketeering, means that economic actors often comply with the taxation systems imposed on these territories. Large national and foreign companies, telephone companies, mining exploration companies, and even NGOs calculate the cost/benefit of their (non)presence in territories controlled by warlords and regularly agree to pay high taxes in order to be able to operate safely in the area. Warlords also try to present these forced taxation systems as "attractive" by making them more competitive than those imposed by public officials. In the Central African Republic, predation by ex-Seleka fighters in the commercial heart of Bangui is accepted by traders as a lesser evil than predation by the state.[161] In Honduras, the Mara Salvatrucha 13, whose business model is based primarily on the systematic extortion of businesses and residents in controlled areas, has made a strategic change in recent years. The gang has decided to reduce the pressure on small businesses and citizens. Benefiting from an increase in income from drug trafficking, MS13 has bet on a reduction in tax pressure to gain legitimacy among the population.[162]

Partners, members of government, and businessmen find their financial interests in commercial deals with the warlords, whom they sometimes protect in return. Indeed, as they are often the only potential outlets and buyers of products or commodities illegally sold by the warlords, they acquire them at a lower cost. For example, Central African warlords do business with Sudanese businessmen who are close to the military authorities and who support them

---

160 "Les juteux trafics des seigneurs de guerre devenus militaires—L'Humanité".
161 Thierry Vircoulon, "Écosystème des groupes armés en Centrafrique".
162 *MS13's Toxic Weed That's "More Addictive Than Cocaine"* | *High Society*, 2022, https://www.youtube.com/watch?v=-ZhxFtmAoXg.

in return because they can sell the coffee produced/taxed under the control of armed groups at a higher price.[163]

It is interesting to note that the warlords mimic the criminal and money-laundering practices in the real economy of the political leaders of the regions in which they operate. For example, most of the Central African warlords of the ex-Seleka, such as the so-called "Bahar," have become livestock owners.[164] Livestock farming is indeed one of the main opportunities for enrichment, as well as being one of the main methods of money laundering for Sahelian leaders, such as Chadian dignitaries.[165] The securing of transhumance and the acquisition of herds are therefore ways for warlords to gain respectability and earn an "honorable" living through money laundering tolerated by all.

Concerning the exploitation, production, export, and protection of the production and export of natural resources or drugs (mainly), several situations can be observed. At the heart of the war economy, all these scenarios lead to the same result for the past decades until today: the enrichment of the warlords, the entrenchment of violent practices, and the integration of the products into the legal economy. As a matter of fact, the FBI and Congolese intelligence services are currently investigating a large network of American buyers fuelling violence in South Kivu as they discretely acquire minerals produced by local militias.[166]

In the first case, warlords strive to control mining, forestry, or hydrocarbon production sites, to become recognized vendors, and/or to tax production for security purposes. A perfect example is diamonds, which, by selling them through back channels on the international market and buying back arms, the rebel forces of warlord Fodeh Sankoh in Sierra Leone were able to hold out and even overthrow the existing government of Tejan Kabbah. The same is true

---

163 « *La face cachée du conflit centrafricain,* » International Crisis Group, Briefing Afrique, n°105, décembre 2014.

164 Thierry Vircoulon, "Ecosystème des groupes armés en Centrafrique," *Notes de l'Ifri,* Ifri, avril 2020.

165 "La Face Cachée Du Conflit Centrafricain" (International Crisis Group, Briefing Afrique, n°105, décembre 2014), https://www.files.ethz.ch/isn/186507/b105-la-face-cachee-du-conflit-centrafricain.pdf.

166 Olivier Liffran and Antoine Rolland, "DRC : From Texas to South Kivu's Highlands, Mahoro Peace Association's Complex Channels Finance Militia," Africa Intelligence, January 16, 2023, https://www.africaintelligence.com/central-africa/2023/01/16/from-texas-to-south-kivu-s-highlands-mahoro-peace-association-s-complex-channels-finance-militia,109902191-geo.

of the situation in Liberia or even Angola, where Jonas Savimbi's UNITA sold diamonds worth over $3.7 billion between 1992 and 1998.¹⁶⁷

The second situation is that foreign companies pay access to groups to prospect for or exploit natural resources. In the Central African Republic, a Chinese oil company and mining companies, as well as the Russian company Lobaye Invest, linked to Wagner, are allying themselves with armed groups by sharing the revenues from these illicit exploitations.¹⁶⁸ In the DRC and Angola, the British-Canadian company Heritage Oil, led oil exploration and exploitation throughout the years of civil war.¹⁶⁹

Third, private national or foreign militias impose control of natural resources by force and use local warlords to bypass local governments. This privatization of disorder also opens the way to the informalization of war. This mercantilism allows private military companies, often mercenaries, to exploit a market in unstable states. This is done in the context of what is described as security and equity exchanges. Military companies protect a country or territory in exchange for mining concessions often held by rebels. This is currently the case with the Wagner militia in the Central African Republic and Mali.¹⁷⁰

As observed earlier, the maintenance of a security and political status quo can be negotiated between warlords and members of the government in exchange for a share of the revenues linked to illicit exploitation and trafficking. In both Côte d'Ivoire and Afghanistan, criminal strongmen often join the government to mark this alliance.¹⁷¹ In the Central African Republic, warlords have thus gained access in 2020 to several strategic ministries for the exploitation of natural resources, such as the Ministry of Water and Forests and the Ministry of State, the Ministry of Mines, Oil and the Ministry of Energy.¹⁷²

In the final scenario, warlords establish control over resources with the complicity of international companies such as oil companies, mining companies, security companies and airlines. Reno calls this "private management of disorder," the willingness and ability of large corporations to maintain a presence in

---

167   Global Witness, *A Rough Trade: The Role of Companies and Governments in the Angolan Conflict* (Global Witnesss, 1998).
168   Thierry Vircoulon, "Ecosystème des groupes armés en Centrafrique," *Notes de l'Ifri,* Ifri, avril 2020.
169   Tim Raeymaekers, "Network War. An Introduction to Congo's Privatised War Economy".
170   Benjamin Roger, "Mali: comment Wagner compte faire main basse sur des mines d'or," JeuneAfrique.com, September 7, 2022, https://www.jeuneafrique.com/1374898/politi que/russie-comment-wagner-compte-faire-main-basse-sur-des-mines-dor-au-mali/.
171   Thierry Vircoulon, "Écosystème des groupes armés en Centrafrique".
172   Thierry Vircoulon.

a territory at all costs in order to secure their access to a key resource.¹⁷³ This resolution often results in the company establishing simultaneous business ties with a rebel warlord and the government. This model is exemplified by the support provided by the Elf oil company to President Dos Santos and the rebel forces of the National Union for the Total Independence of Angola (UNITA) led by warlord Jonas Savimbi during the 1975–2002 bloody war in Angola.¹⁷⁴ The MPLA, led by Agostinho Neto, and opposed to UNITA, an armed movement supported by the United States and also in collusion with the Portuguese secret police and apartheid South Africa, exploited and sold oil illegally throughout the civil war.¹⁷⁵ The rebel movements supplied the United States with cheap oil through multinationals such as the Gulf, which accounted for 65% of Angola's export revenues during the Reagan Administration.¹⁷⁶

Interestingly, in all of these scenarios, corruption and the complicity of government forces are key to the integration of natural resources produced and/or exported under the control of warlords into international circuits. As Louise Shelley states, "Corruption is the grease that allows all forms of illicit trade to operate smoothly, for illicit trade run by warlords and criminal entrepreneurs managing territories not controlled by the state, it is often state officials who facilitate the trade at any given time, both domestically and globally, by creating a system that allows illicitly acquired products to be laundered into the global flows of licit trade."¹⁷⁷ Corruption affects both private companies (export-import, transport companies but also banking institutions) and state officials (politicians, police, border and customs officials, licensing authorities, etc.).¹⁷⁸

The proximity and intertwining of government leaders, both national and foreign, with warlords can be such that they become a conduit for foreign buyers to gain access to armed groups and purchase the natural resources under their control. For example, a significant portion of the mineral resources produced under the control of Ivorian zone commanders during the civil war

---

173   W. Reno, "Internal Wars, Private Enterprise, and the Shift in Strong State—Weak State Relations," *International Politics* 37, no. 1 (2000): 57–74, https://doi.org/10.1023/A:1009869405384.
174   Hugon, *L' économie de l'Afrique / Philippe Hugon*.
175   Sharife Khadija, "La bataille pour le pétrole angolais," ritimo, September 1, 2010, https://www.ritimo.org/La-bataille-pour-le-petrole-angolais.
176   Sharife Khadija.
177   Shelley, "Dark Commerce".
178   Marina Caparini, "Organized Environmental Crime: Why It Matters for Peace Operations," May 12, 2022, https://www.sipri.org/commentary/topical-backgrounder/2022/organized-environmental-crime-why-it-matters-peace-operations.

were exported via Burkina Faso, where these warlords had complicities in the state apparatus.[179] Second, in the late 1990s, the allocation of mining concessions on Congolese soil was negotiated in Kampala with the leaders of Yoweri Museveni's Uganda People's Defense Forces (UPDF).[180]

Since the 1990s, Rwanda and Uganda have provided arms and training to their respective rebel allies and have established extensive links to facilitate the exploitation of mineral resources in their own territories.[181] Together with their warlord allies, high-ranking members of the Rwandan and Ugandan military (including those close to Kagame and Museveni) have established significant control over the illegal exploitation of minerals. They supply arms to their allies and transport mineral resources from the DRC to Rwanda and Uganda using private companies owned or controlled by friends and relatives of Presidents Kagame and Museveni. In the late 1990s, when Rwanda had its troops in the DRC, Rwanda's diamond exports rose from about 166 carats in 1998 to some 30,500 carats in 2000, even though the country has virtually no mineral reserves of its own.[182] This example illustrates the scale of the financial benefit to both countries and their elites.

6.6 Globalization and Neoliberal Economics: Warlords' Best Allies

Warlords thrive in a globalized neoliberal economy. Their socio-economic power is directly linked to the increase in economic and political competition, the growing mobility of goods, money, and people, more efficient means of transportation as well as social media and new internet technologies (darknet, encrypted communication, etc.).[183] The development of cyber illicit trade has for instance facilitated the expansion of warlords/criminal entrepreneurs' operations.[184] Silk Road 2.0 processed billions in transactions every year.[185] The cover of their business is improving, putting more distance between real buyers and their violent exploitation of natural resources.

---

179   Conseil De Sécurité Des Nations Unies, "Rapport de La Mission Du Conseil de Sécurité En Côte d'Ivoire et En Guinée-Bissau".
180   Tim Raeymaekers, "Network War. An Introduction to Congo's Privatised War Economy".
181   "Loupe Holes: Illicit Diamonds in the Kimberley Process," Global Witness, October 28, 2008, https:///en/archive/loupe-holes-illicit-diamonds-kimberley-process/.
182   Tim Raeymaekers, "Network War. An Introduction to Congo's Privatised War Economy".
183   Shelley, "Dark Commerce".
184   Shelley.
185   Shelley.

Essential elements of the neo-liberal market economy, free ports are tax-free warehouses originally created to store raw materials and then manufactured goods for a short time before they are transported, transited, and reshipped. They are exempt from taxes and customs duties. If the goods are sold within the free port, the owner also does not pay tax on the transaction.[186] In March 2010, the Financial Action Task Force (FATF) issued a special report highlighting the potential misuse of free trade zones by money launderers and other financial criminals, including warlords.[187] Indeed, free ports such as Dubai are particularly useful for selling and laundering illegally produced and transported natural resources, and then integrating them into international sales channels.

In the 1970s, when offshore tax havens became an accepted and natural financial tool, they were used to maximize the wealth of warlords and illicit entrepreneurs and for their operations. Tax havens have been used to launder money for warlords more easily and to expand their operations. The illicit arms trade of intermediary Pierre Dadak was facilitated by the creation and use of multiple companies around the world with nominees—Politica Holding in Delaware, a tax haven, or in Cyprus (Vinams Enterprises Ltd.).[188]

In the DRC, companies and subsidiaries domiciled in tax havens such as Bermuda, the British Virgin Islands or Panama have signed agreements with warlords, on the one hand, or with the government, on the other, in order to conceal their purchases of natural resources and related financial transactions.[189] This is the case, for example, of Emaxon, a company owned by the multi-convicted Israeli diamond magnate Dan Gertler, which has several subsidiaries in tax havens.[190] The diamond consortium ORYX Natural Resources, based in the tax haven of the Cayman Islands and linked to the Russian company Petra Diamonds and the Kabila clan when they were warlords, was used in the early 2000s to illegally export Congolese diamonds via Zimbabwean companies and the Zimbabwean military (through Operation Sovereign Legitimacy, the economic arm of the Zimbabwean military).[191]

---

186   "Free Ports and Risks of Illicit Trafficking of Cultural Property," 2016, https://unesdoc.unesco.org/ark:/48223/pf0000372793.
187   "Money Laundering Vulnerabilities of Free Trade Zones" (The Financial Action Task Force (FATF), March 2010), https://www.fatf-gafi.org/content/dam/fatf-gafi/reports/ML%20vulnerabilities%20of%20Free%20Trade%20Zones.pdf.
188   "La Chute d'un Seigneur de La Guerre".
189   Alain Deneault, "Dossier Special RDC: Les mines du Congo-Kinshasa vues des paradis fiscaux," Survie, September 2006, https://survie.org/billets-d-afrique/2006/150-septembre-2006/article/dossier-special-rdc-les-mines-du.
190   Hugon, L'économie de l'Afrique / Philippe Hugon.
191   Hugon.

Western companies and financial institutions have encouraged the exploitation of natural resources while being wilfully blind as to where these products come from and who benefits from them. For example, in 1999, the financial arm of RCD-Goma—known as SONEX—received $5 million in loans from Citibank New York.[192] Most of the mineral production at the time was destined for the United States, whose government also helped broker deals between US companies and local armed groups.

There is ample evidence of the growing links between criminal entrepreneurs and legal economic channels. In fact, over the past few decades, criminal entrepreneurs have been able to increase and diversify their presence in the legal economy, either by establishing their own businesses or by taking over existing companies.[193] Although difficult to quantify, the increasing reliance on "criminal" money following successive economic shocks in Russia, Japan, the United States, and Europe may have further opened businesses to the liquidity of criminal organizations and extended their pernicious influence in our economies.[194] This reality is even more problematic in weak states where warlords/criminal entrepreneurs operate.

There are also many cases of warlords who have been converted to the legal economy, using their networks and capacity for violence to gain comparative advantage and enrich themselves. For example, in 1992, Lo Hsing-Han, whose heroin empire we have already mentioned under the guise of a rebellion manipulated for this purpose, officially became a businessman at the head of the Asia World Group, between Rangoon and Singapore, while continuing his trafficking activities under the radar.[195]

6.7 Minerals and Warlords: A Gray Area in the Global Economy

Conflicts involve an interweaving of intermediaries within the chains with regional and international ramifications, a gray zone that is skilfully constructed and maintained. The economy of plunder, particularly regarding natural resources, is ensured by conglomerates or joint ventures between

---

192 Dena Montague and Frida Berrigan, "The Business of War in the Democratic Republic of Congo," Dollars and Sense magazine, August 2001, https://thirdworldtraveler.com/Africa/Business_War_Congo.html.
193 Cláudia Costa Storti and Paul de Grauwe, eds., *Illicit Trade and the Global Economy* (MIT Press, 2012), pp.5.
194 Michael D. Lyman and Gary W. Potter, *Organized Crime* (Pearson/Prentice Hall, 2007), pp 9.
195 Alexandre Marchant, "Histoire et géopolitique du trafic des opiacés en Asie du Sud-Est".

businessmen, mercenaries, politicians, and armed groups.[196] The extent of the connections between international economic operators and warlords is matched only by the associated profits in an economy increasingly dependent on these minerals. Over the past decades, examples of such collusion have been legion.

The constant thread is that these criminal alliances always fuel violence and serve the interests of a few. As early as 1994, the Human Rights Watch report on Angola accused De Beer, the leading diamond trading company, and several states such as Belgium, of collaborating with UNITA and buying gems mined in rebel-held territory, in violation of Angolan and international sanctions.[197] Several years later, in 1998, the Human Rights Watch report "A Rough Trade" provided further evidence of the blood diamond trade.[198]

In the DRC, the mineral and arms trade is closely linked to rebel movements, local and neighboring governments, and foreign business networks, mainly Israeli, Chinese, Lebanese but also American and Australian. In May 1997, American Mineral Fields (AMF)—whose chairman is Mike McMurrough, a personal friend of President Clinton—signed a billion-dollar mining deal with Kabila while he was still a warlord.[199]

A key player in Ituri gold mining since the 1990s, Russell Resources Group is owned by Israeli Gad Raveh and Australian David Russel and headed by David Agmon, a retired Israeli general and Chief of Staff to former Prime Minister Benjamin Netanyahu.[200] Since then, the mine has been the focus of desire and fighting between several armed groups and former warlords, such as Jean-Pierre Bemba and Thomas Lubanga, all of whom are more or less affiliated with Congolese, Rwandan and Ugandan officials, and foreign mining companies.[201]

While in the early 1990s Burundi was the most important transit zone for gold exports from the Congo, this function was taken over by Uganda after 1997.

---

196 Paul Collier and Anke Hoeffler, "On the Incidence of Civil War in Africa," *The Journal of Conflict Resolution* 46, no. 1 (2002): 13–28.
197 "Angola: Arms Trade and Violations of the Laws of War since the 1992 Elections," *Human Rights Watch*, November 1, 1994, https://www.hrw.org/report/1994/11/01/arms-trade-and-violations-laws-war-1992-elections.
198 Global Witness, *A Rough Trade*.
199 Dena Montague and Frida Berrigan, "The Business of War in the Democratic Republic of Congo".
200 Kennes, E., "Le secteur minier au Congo: déconnexion et descente aux enfers," L'Afrique des Grands Lacs. Annuaire 1999–2000, Paris, L'Harmattan, 2000, pp.322–323.
201 "DRC: UPC Rebels Grab Mongbwalu's Gold," Africa Intelligence, January 15, 2003, https://www.africaintelligence.com/central-africa/2003/01/15/upc-rebels-grab-mongbwalu-s-gold,5962134-art.

According to US Geological Survey figures, Uganda's gold exports amounted to 6,819 kg in 1997 compared to 225 kg in 1994.[202] Uganda's gold exports more than doubled after the UPDF entered Congolese territory and deployed around Kilo Moto, one of Congo's most productive gold mines.

Under the Mobutu regime, in August 1996, the Canadian-American company Barrick Gold Corporation was able to sign a mining contract for the exploration and exploitation of a gold site twice the size of Belgium.[203] In exchange for a contract, cash and infrastructure were promised, including an airport (Bunia) used for diamond trafficking by a general close to Mobutu and to facilitate arms transfers to Ugandan rebel movements. At the time of Barrick's entry into Zaire, the members of its International Advisory Board were all "strongmen": former Canadian Prime Minister Brian Mulroney, Vernon Jordan (a close associate of Bill Clinton), and former US President George Bush Sr. Other Barrick advisors included former US Senator Howard Baker Jr.—the White House Chief of Staff during Ronald Reagan's presidency—and Karl Otto Pöhl, the former President of the German Central Bank.[204]

6.8 Desired and Maintained by the Main Public and Private Decision-Makers of the Global Economy

The blood minerals, which enrich the warlords, are extracted by men and children who dig the ground with rudimentary tools, risking their lives underground for a handful of dollars. The permanent violence they endure is this extreme poverty, the constant danger to their lives, and the multiple abuses perpetrated by the armed groups and state forces that oversee these operations.[205] These minerals are exported, often clandestinely to avoid laws and taxes. They are processed by smelters and bought, with their eyes closed, in Europe, Asia, and the United States by the electronics industry. A trade fueled by unbridled demand, corruption, and relentless pressure to cut costs. The companies that buy these ores are in fact perfectly aware that children work in the ore supply chains. It is "thanks to child labor" that the minerals they

---

202 US Geological Survey 1997, The Mineral Industry of Uganda.
203 Kennes, E., "Le secteur minier au Congo: déconnexion et descente aux enfers," L'Afrique des Grands Lacs. Annuaire 1999–2000, Paris, L'Harmattan, 2000, pp.322–323.
204 Wayne Madsen, *Genocide and Covert Operations in Africa, 1993–1999*, African Studies (Lewiston, N.Y.) (Lewiston, N.Y.: Edwin Mellen Press, 1999), pp.73–74.
205 Vincent Georis, "Sur La Piste Des Minerais Du Sang Du Congo," L'Echo, 2011, https://multimedia.lecho.be/congo/.

buy are so cheap that their production costs are minimized and their margins increased.

The DRC, particularly the Kivu and Ituri regions in eastern DRC, contains millions of tons of diamonds, copper, cobalt, zinc, manganese, uranium, niobium and 80% of the world's reserves of tantalum, also known as coltan, a resource that is particularly valuable because it is used to make cell phones, night vision goggles, fiber optics and capacitors (the component that holds the electrical charge in computer chips).[206] In neo-capitalist global economies, control of these minerals is vital to maintaining military dominance and economic prosperity.[207]

On paper, mechanisms have been put in place by states, with the support of the United Nations, to make the production and trade of these minerals more virtuous and to ensure that this trade does not finance conflict and the maintenance of an endless cycle of violence.[208] However, the stakes and financial interests of states, political and economic elites, and multinationals around the world are too high for these mechanisms to be truly effective. According to specialists in the sector interviewed, the control mechanisms put in place over the last twenty years following the numerous scandals involving "blood minerals" have been at best useless and at worst have voluntarily or involuntarily served as a perfect cover for perpetuating these criminal practices.[209]

The Kimberley Process, established in 2003, is a perfect example of the shortcomings of this control system.[210] Without adequate resources, financial or technical, the Kimberley Process is inoperative. Its mechanism for alerting and monitoring, and then imposing decisions, relies almost exclusively on the goodwill of governments and private companies, and is, therefore, de facto inoperative.[211] In reality, the Kimberley Certification consists only of a piece of paper issued by a state stipulating that diamonds do not come from a conflict zone. Or, as a 2008 Global Witness report put it. "A written guarantee simply

---

206 Dena Montague and Frida Berrigan, "The Business of War in the Democratic Republic of Congo".
207 "La laverie ITSCI," Global Witness, May 30, 2022, https:///fr/itsci-laundromat-fr/.
208 Marx Eric, "The Kimberley Process: Conflict diamonds cut out," the Guardian, 31 August 2010.
209 David Rhode, "The Kimberley Process Is a 'perfect Cover Story' for Blood Diamonds," *The Guardian*, March 24, 2014, sec. Guardian Sustainable Business, https://www.theguardian.com/sustainable-business/diamonds-blood-kimberley-process-mines-ethical.
210 See the Kimberley Process website: https://www.kimberleyprocess.com/.
211 Dina Siegel, Toine Spapens, and Daan P. Van Uhm, "Regulators and Villains: The Dual Role of Private Actors in Diamonds and Caviar," *Crime, Law and Social Change* 74 (December 1, 2020): 509–23, https://doi.org/10.1007/s10611-020-09902-5.

stating that diamonds do not come from conflict areas is meaningless if it is not backed up by actions and policies to verify that this statement is true."[212] The process has also willfully ignored the fact that these new regulations could create new opportunities for criminal entrepreneurs to obtain an official, internationally recognized certificate guaranteeing their bona fides while mixing conflict and non-conflict diamonds in large export projects.[213]

Another example is the Tin Supply Chain Initiative (ITSCI), created in 2009, which also aims to provide a reliable chain of custody for minerals, ensuring that their extraction does not contribute to child labor or enrich armed groups and the military.[214] In the case of the DRC, this means that the minerals must come from mines validated by the authorities as free of these crimes. In Rwanda, this chain of custody ensures that the minerals have not been smuggled in from the DRC. In both countries, officials responsible for implementing ITSCI seal and label bags of legitimate minerals, before they are transported for processing or export. In 2012 and 2018, the OECD reviewed ITSCI's standards and found them to be fully consistent with its own guidance for due diligence in mineral supply chains.[215]

However, research by International Peace Information Service (IPIS) and Global Witness shows that ITSCI facilitates the laundering of minerals from militia-controlled mines, or produced through child labor.[216] This mechanism is used by many international companies to guarantee the "responsibility" of their mineral supply. Large volumes of labeled minerals are falsely attributed to validated but inactive mines in the locality when in fact they originate in militia-controlled areas and are then sent to Uganda, Burundi, Rwanda, or Tanzania.[217] In these numerous mines, warlords and their militias often force artisanal miners to work without pay and levy a tax on traders.[218] Poorly paid and easily corrupted government officials, not effectively monitored by the ITSCI, validate the origin of the minerals and compromise their entire supply chain.

The initial reliability of the ITSCI as a control mechanism, and the very intention of its creators, can be questioned when one considers that the main

---

212 "Loupe Holes".
213 Siegel, Spapens, and Uhm, "Regulators and Villains".
214 "La laverie ITSCI".
215 Kay Nimmo and Richard Burt, "iTSCi: Contributing to Minerals Traceability and Due Diligence in Central Africa," May 2012, https://www.oecd.org/investment/investmentfordevelopment/50473045.pdf.
216 "La laverie ITSCI".
217 Vincent Georis, "Sur La Piste Des Minerais Du Sang Du Congo".
218 "La laverie ITSCI".

international buyers of minerals are also the heads of its control body, or that the control mechanism is financed according to the volume of minerals validated and exported.[219] Moreover, several sources interviewed confirm the findings of Global Witness' investigations, which highlighted Rwanda's interest in setting up this control mechanism, which several people close to the Rwandan government helped to design to satisfy the pseudo-requirements of Western importers. The smuggling and export of illicitly mined minerals from the DRC has been a major source of enrichment for political and economic elites in Rwanda for the past three decades, for example for Minerals Supply Africa (MSA), one of Rwanda's main mineral exporters. ITSCI has enabled Rwandan exporters to label fraudulent minerals for legitimate export.[220]

Today, the journey of a conflict mineral from the mines to cell phones, car batteries, or airplanes can be broken down into several stages, all of which illustrate the lack of willingness of the international community, both public and private, to properly regulate and stop this illicit trade.[221] In mines controlled or supervised by armed groups, local miners all work in terrible conditions. The violence used to enslave them ensures that production costs of finished products will be minimized and profit margins will increase. The transport and sale of minerals in large quantities to buy houses requires the bribery of officials and private company workers who conceal the origin of the minerals and begin the laundering process.[222]

Once acquired from illicit producers, the traders sell the minerals to foreign buyers and international traders from China, Malaysia, Belgium, Israel, Australia, the United States, and other foreign countries. There has not been a single case where an exporter has refused a shipment of minerals because he thought it would enrich a warlord and/or the minerals were from a conflict mine.[223] One famous example of traders operating in the coltan trade in eastern Congo for the past twenty years is Valentina Piskounova.[224] Her company, La Conmet, is based in Butembo and owned by the Ugandan company Kullinan Finance Investment. Under the protection of Salim Saleh, a brother of Ugandan President Museveni, and sourcing minerals through its connections

---

219 Interviews conducted with confidential informants working for the mining industry in DRC and Rwanda, December 2022.
220 "La laverie ITSCI".
221 Lezhnev, "From Mine to Mobile Phone".
222 "La laverie ITSCI".
223 Lezhnev, "From Mine to Mobile Phone".
224 Tim Raeymaekers, "Network War. An Introduction to Congo's Privatised War Economy".

with armed groups in Ituri, including the RCD-ML, Conmet has agreements with clients in South Africa, Kazakhstan, and Germany.²²⁵

The exported ore still passes through a "buffer" stage in the international circuits: smelters and intermediaries based in Hong Kong, Dubai, Thailand, Kazakhstan, Austria, Malaysia, and China. It is in these transit countries that the true origin of the ores is hidden. In forges and refineries, conflict and non-conflict minerals from various sources are used to create metals for electronic products and are often mixed and matched in ways that prevent them from being traced. Finally, these actors sell these reworked ores to manufacturers of components used in electronic device customers of global brands such as Apple, Intel, Samsung, Nokia, Motorola, and Tesla. For example, illegally mined rare earth minerals from Myanmar, notably controlled by warlord Zakhung Ting Ying, are processed in China by state-owned enterprises, which sell them to permanent magnet manufacturers supplying some of the world's best-known brands of electric vehicles, wind turbines, and electronic devices, including General Motors, Mitsubishi Electric, Siemens, Tesla, and Volkswagen.²²⁶

Depending on the competitiveness of their business models on the low purchase cost of the mineral, guaranteed by its illegal exploitation and export, these multinationals do not seek (nor do they wish) to detect smuggling, fraud, contribution to conflicts, and child labor in their supply chain. Fully aware of the flaws in this system, they place their trust in ITSCI and the Responsible Minerals Initiative (RMI), which itself builds on the ITSCI program.²²⁷

The dependence of the international economy on resources under their control protects the warlords. This protection is illustrated primarily by the fact that these unregulated industries are significantly under-policed and under-punished criminally: "the global community is pseudo regulating the sale of flora, fauna, fishing, timber logging and mining. Criminals have always profited by getting involved in time-sensitive sectors."²²⁸ This lack of international political will is particularly visible in the major Western countries that benefit the most. For example, when a bill to improve transparency and rigorous controls on the tantalum and tungsten trade was introduced in the US Congress a few years ago, the electronics industry spent more than $2 million a month lobbying Senate offices to relax the legislation.²²⁹

---

225 "Covered in Blood: Ethnically Targeted Violence in Northern DRC," *Human Rights Watch*, July 7, 2003, https://www.hrw.org/report/2003/07/07/covered-blood/ethnically-targe ted-violence-northern-drc.
226 Global Witness, "Myanmar's Poisoned Mountains".
227 "La laverie ITSCI".
228 Shelley, "Dark Commerce".
229 Lezhnev, "From Mine to Mobile Phone".

The actions of entire states can be aligned with the interests of their private sector: "During the 1990s, Belgian customs recorded the import of billions of dollars of rough diamonds from Liberia, a country with negligible diamond resources (...) Anything a Belgian importer wrote on an invoice was dutifully recorded as fact by the Belgian authorities. Although no one who knew anything about diamonds would have believed the statistics, they were never questioned."[230] This deliberate omission is a perfect example of how a Western industry, with the support of its government, brings illegally purchased natural resources into the legitimate trade. It also demonstrates how the greed of the leaders of the capitalist system perpetuates wars and is at the heart of the power of warlords around the world.

6.9 Conclusion: Deeply Anti-democratic Violence

Increasing the wealth and power of individuals without regard for the well-being of societies/communities is not only antithetical to democracy, sustainable economic growth, and innovation, but it threatens the future of our world as violent entrepreneurs continue to expand their power. In fact, warlords and illicit entrepreneurs are often promoted economically and socially through violence because the resources they own and sell are vital to the international economy.[231] With the complicity of a predatory political class and multinationals eager for quick profits to plunder natural resources, the multiple acts of violence committed by warlords against the population are ignored.[232] In the DRC, the story of the warlord Bosco Ntaganda is a striking example of the impunity enjoyed by warlords and members of the Congolese national army as they profit from the mineral trade at the expense of local communities.[233]

At the same time, as warlords increase their power, government revenues are reduced and businesses are lost. The state can no longer collect enough taxes to meet its obligations, as most economic activities take place outside the formal rules of trade. This context of informalization of the economy linked to corruption violence only accelerates the collapse of many countries. This situation leads to a lasting criminalization of politics, which in turn only feeds

---

230   Ian Smillie, "Blood Diamonds and Non-State Actors," *Vanderbilt Journal of Transnational Law* 46, no. 4 (January 1, 2013): 1003.
231   Thierry Vircoulon, "Écosystème des groupes armés en Centrafrique".
232   Shelley, "Dark Commerce".
233   "Congolese Warlord Stands Trial on 18 Counts of War Crimes, But Many More Crimes Have Gone Unreported".

instability. The resources and wealth of elites have become intrinsically linked to bad governance practices, corrupt schemes, international trafficking, and alliances with entrepreneurs of violence. These same entrepreneurs of violence sometimes become one with the state.

However, the international community has often been short-sighted and continues to be so, as powerful states view warlords as agents of peace or state-building, or assume that their interests coincide with those of the government or populations they control. Warlords are conflict entrepreneurs whose positions depend on violence, and they usually resort to violence, with varying degrees of success, to get what they want. As a result, internationally negotiated peace treaties or ceasefires give violent actors a new political status and cover to engage in crime. In Afghanistan and Somalia, for example, these warlords, criminals, businessmen, and pseudo-statesmen have been the US's preferred allies in fighting Islamic militants.[234] In both cases, these pacts have been absolute failures and have led to absolute chaos.

Bibliography

Aaron, Sayne. "What's Next for Security in the Niger Delta?" United States Institute of Peace, April 26, 2013. https://www.usip.org/publications/2013/04/whats-next-security-niger-delta.

Africa Intelligence. "DRC: UPC Rebels Grab Mongbwalu's Gold," January 15, 2003. https://www.africaintelligence.com/central-africa/2003/01/15/upc-rebels-grab-mongbwalu-s-gold,5962134-art.

Agger, Kasper. "Warlord Business: CAR's Violent Armed Groups and Their Criminal Operations for Profit and Power." *The Enough Project* (blog), June 17, 2015. https://enoughproject.org/reports/warlord-business-cars-violent-armed-groups-and-their-criminal-operations-profit-and-power.

Alexandre, Marchant. "Histoire et géopolitique du trafic des opiacés en Asie du Sud-Est." vih.org, September 25, 2017. https://vih.org/drogues-et-rdr/20170925/histoire-et-geopolitique-du-trafic-des-opiaces-en-asie-du-sud-est/.

"Angola: Arms Trade and Violations of the Laws of War since the 1992 Elections." *Human Rights Watch*, November 1, 1994. https://www.hrw.org/report/1994/11/01/arms-trade-and-violations-laws-war-1992-elections.

---

234   Olivier Rogez, "Somalie—Bashir Ragé, Seigneur de Guerre," RFI, June 21, 2006, http://www1.rfi.fr/actufr/articles/078/article_44565.asp.

Benjamin, Roger. "Mali : comment Wagner compte faire main basse sur des mines d'or." JeuneAfrique.com, September 7, 2022. https://www.jeuneafrique.com/1374898/politique/russie-comment-wagner-compte-faire-main-basse-sur-des-mines-dor-au-mali/.

Benn, Stanley I., and Richard Stanley Peters. *Social Principles and the Democratic State*. Allen & Unwin, 1959.

Billon, Philippe Le. *Fuelling War: Natural Resources and Armed Conflicts*. London: Routledge, 2013. https://doi.org/10.4324/9781315019529.

Bushenyula, Parfait Kaningu, Elisée Cirhuza, Balolage, Emery, Mudinga, and Aymar Nyenyezi, Bisoka. "Conflits armés et autorité publique en RDC : vers la gestion de l'environnement par les groupes armés," October 5, 2021. https://www.eca-creac.eu/sites/default/files/pictures/conflits_armes_et_autorite_publique_rdc_vers_la_gestion_de_lenvironnement.pdf.

Canada: Immigration and Refugee Board of Canada. "Afghanistan : Information Sur La Situation Des Seigneurs de Guerre En Afghanistan, y Compris Sur La Réaction de l'État Par Rapport à La Mainmise Qu'ont Les Seigneurs de Guerre Sur Les Régions (2007–2010)," January 6, 2011. https://webarchive.archive.unhcr.org/20230524234054/https://www.refworld.org/docid/4e4254682.html.

Carlos, García. "Transnational Escape of MS-13 Leader 'Crook' Caught on Social Media." Transnational Escape of MS-13 Leader "Crook" Caught on Social Media, July 11, 2022. https://elfaro.net/en/202207/el_salvador/26264/Transnational-Escape-of-MS-13-Leader-%E2%80%9CCrook%E2%80%9D-Caught-on-Social-Media.htm.

Célian, Macé. "En Centrafrique, Les Seigneurs de Guerre Tirent Profit de La Paix," April 18, 2019. https://www.liberation.fr/planete/2019/04/18/en-centrafrique-les-seigneurs-de-guerre-tirent-profit-de-la-paix_1722223/.

Cockayne, James. *Hidden Power: The Strategic Logic of Organized Crime*. Oxford University Press, 2016.

Collier, Paul, and Anke, Hoeffler. "On the Incidence of Civil War in Africa." *The Journal of Conflict Resolution* 46, no. 1 (2002): 13–28.

Conseil de sécurité des Nations Unies. "Jerome Kakwavu Bukande," October 29, 2014. https://www.un.org/securitycouncil/fr/sanctions/1533/materials/summaries/individual/jerome-kakwavu-bukande.

Conseil De Sécurité Des Nations Unies. "Rapport de La Mission Du Conseil de Sécurité En Côte d'Ivoire et En Guinée-Bissau," April 10, 2019. https://documents.un.org/doc/undoc/gen/n19/106/15/pdf/n1910615.pdf?token=i97uEFTVqmCdIzX3vz&fe=true.

Conseil De Sécurité Des Nations Unies. "Rapport de Mi-Mandat Du Groupe d'experts En En Application de l'alinéa c du Paragraphe 32 de La Résolution 2399 (2018)," juillet 2018. https://documents.un.org/doc/undoc/gen/n18/218/64/pdf/n1821864.pdf?token=AVGQSlSvbXMkSwvklO&fe=true.

"Convention C182—Convention (N° 182) Sur Les Pires Formes de Travail Des Enfants, 1999—Discussion: 2017, Cas Individuel-Republique Democratique Du Congo," 2017. https://www.ilo.org/dyn/normlex/fr/f?p=NORMLEXPUB:12100:0::NO::P12100_IN STRUMENT_ID:312327.

"Covered in Blood: Ethnically Targeted Violence in Northern DRC." *Human Rights Watch*, July 7, 2003. https://www.hrw.org/report/2003/07/07/covered-blood/ethnically-targeted-violence-northern-drc.

"Criminality in South Sudan—The Organized Crime Index," 2023. https://ocindex.net/assets/downloads/2023/english/ocindex_profile_south_sudan_2023.pdf.

Cuvelier, Jeroen, and Stefaan, Marysse. "Les enjeux économiques du conflit en Ituri." In *L'Afrique des grands-lacs : annuaire 2003–2004*, 171–203. L'Harmattan, 2004. http://hdl.handle.net/1854/LU-1863604.

D'Aubuisson, Juan José Martínez. "The Omnipresent Business of the MS13 in El Salvador." InSight Crime, January 25, 2022. http://insightcrime.org/investigations/the-omnipresent-businesses-of-the-ms13/.

David, Rhode. "The Kimberley Process Is a 'perfect Cover Story' for Blood Diamonds." *The Guardian*, March 24, 2014, sec. Guardian Sustainable Business. https://www.theguardian.com/sustainable-business/diamonds-blood-kimberley-process-mines-ethical.

Deneault, Alain. "Dossier Special RDC : Les mines du Congo-Kinshasa vues des paradis fiscaux." Survie, September 2006. https://survie.org/billets-d-afrique/2006/150-septembre-2006/article/dossier-special-rdc-les-mines-du.

Doherty, Sean. "Extortion in Northern Triangle Worth Over $1 Billion Annually: Report." InSight Crime, October 3, 2022. http://insightcrime.org/news/extortion-northern-triangle/.

Ellis, Stephen. *The Mask of Anarchy: The Destruction of Liberia and the Religious Dimension of an African Civil War*. NYU Press, 2001.

Energy Intelligence. "Nigeria: Gangsta Power." Energy Intelligence, September 22, 2004. https://www.energyintel.com/0000017b-a7a5-de4c-a17b-e7e7768f0000.

Faligot, Roger. *La mafia chinoise en Europe: Paris, Marseille, Amsterdam, Anvers, Bruxelles ...* Calmann-Lévy, 2001.

Florquin, Nicolas, Sigrid, Lipott, and Francis, Wairagu. *L'atlas Des Armes: Une Cartographie Des Flux Illicites d'armes Légères En Afrique*, 2019.

Foundation for Partnership Initiatives in the Niger Delta (PIND). "Niger Delta Annual Conflict Report: January-December 2021," 2021. https://pindfoundation.org/wp-content/uploads/2022/02/Niger-Delta-Annual-Conflict-Report-2021-Draft.pdf.

"Free Ports and Risks of Illicit Trafficking of Cultural Property," 2016. https://unesdoc.unesco.org/ark:/48223/pf0000372793.

Global Witness, Press release. "New Evidence Shows Massive and Rapid Expansion of Illicit Rare Earths Industry in Myanmar, Fuelling Human Rights Abuses,

Environmental Destruction and Funding Military-Linked Militias." National Wind Watch, August 9, 2022. https://www.wind-watch.org/news/2022/08/10/new-evidence-shows-massive-and-rapid-expansion-of-illicit-rare-earths-industry-in-myanmar-fuelling-human-rights-abuses-environmental-destruction-and-funding-military-linked-militias/.

Global Witness. "La laverie ITSCI," May 30, 2022. https:///fr/itsci-laundromat-fr/.

Global Witness. "Loupe Holes: Illicit Diamonds in the Kimberley Process," October 28, 2008. https:///en/archive/loupe-holes-illicit-diamonds-kimberley-process/.

Global Witness. "Myanmar's Poisoned Mountains." Global Witness, August 9, 2022. https:///en/campaigns/natural-resource-governance/myanmars-poisoned-mountains/.

Global Witness. *A Rough Trade: The Role of Companies and Governments in the Angolan Conflict*. Global Witnesss, 1998.

Grillo, Ioan. *Gangster Warlords: Drug Dollars, Killing Fields, and the New Politics of Latin America*. Bloomsbury USA, 2017.

Held, David. *Political Theory and the Modern State: Essays on State, Power, and Democracy*. Reprinted. Cambridge: Polity Press, 2000.

https://www.humanite.fr. "Les juteux trafics des seigneurs de guerre devenus militaires- L'Humanité," April 29, 2014. https://www.humanite.fr/monde/cote-divoire/les-juteux-trafics-des-seigneurs-de-guerre-devenus-militaires.

HuffPost. "Congolese Warlord Stands Trial on 18 Counts of War Crimes, But Many More Crimes Have Gone Unreported," September 1, 2015. https://www.huffpost.com/entry/congolese-warlord-stands-_b_8069584.

Hugon, Philippe. *L' économie de l'Afrique / Philippe Hugon*. Repères. la Découverte, 2009. https://documentation.insp.gouv.fr/insp/doc/SYRACUSE/136353/l-economie-de-l-afrique-philippe-hugon.

Human Rights Watch. "Testing Democracy: Political Violence in Nigeria." *Human Rights Watch*, April 10, 2003. https://www.hrw.org/report/2003/04/10/testing-democracy/political-violence-nigeria.

International Criminal Tribunal for the former Yugoslavia (ICTY); Trial Chamber II. "Prosecutor v. Limaj et al. (Trial Judgment)." Refworld, November 30, 2005. https://www.refworld.org/jurisprudence/caselaw/icty/2005/en/61980.

Jaillon, Alexandre, Peer Schouten, and Soleil Kalessopo. "The Politics of Pillage: The Political Economy of Roadblocks in the Central African Republic (2017)." *IPIS* (blog), December 7, 2017. https://ipisresearch.be/publication/politics-pillage-political-economy-roadblocks-central-african-republic-2/.

Jaitman, Laura, Dino, Caprirolo, Rogelio Granguillhome, Ochoa, Philip, Keefer, Ted, Leggett, James Andrew, Lewis, José Antonio, Mejía-Guerra, Marcela, Mello, Heather, Sutton, and Iván, Torre. "The Costs of Crime and Violence: New Evidence and

Insights in Latin America and the Caribbean." *IDB Publications*, February 3, 2017. https://doi.org/10.18235/0000615.

Jean-François, Gayraud. "Nouveau Capitalisme criminel." www.odilejacob.fr, 2014. https://www.odilejacob.fr/catalogue/sciences-humaines/droit-justice/nouveau-capitalisme-criminel_9782738130723.php.

Jean-François, Gayraud. "Le Monde des mafias Géopolitique du crime organisé." www.odilejacob.fr, 2005. https://www.odilejacob.fr/catalogue/histoire-et-geopolitique/geopolitique-et-strategie/monde-des-mafias_9782738121325.php.

Juan José, Martínez. "El Niño de Hollywood," July 2023. https://www.revistadelauniversidad.mx/articles/68938586-850d-4382-9614-21ee87d2af07/el-nino-de-hollywood.

Juan Martínez, d'Aubuisson and Efren, Lemus. "El Salvador's Attorney General Worked for Top MS13 Ally." InSight Crime, October 31, 2022. http://insightcrime.org/investigations/el-salvador-attorney-general-worked-top-ms13-ally/.

Julia, Yansura. "Extortion in the Northern Triangle of Central America: Following the Money." *Global Financial Integrity* (blog), September 7, 2022. https://gfintegrity.org/report/extortion-in-the-northern-triangle-of-central-america-following-the-money/.

Karam, Henni. "Un Célèbre Trafiquant d'armes et Seigneur de Guerre Français Arrêté En Espagne," November 23, 2021. https://www.rap2france.com/news/un-celebre-trafiquant-d-armes-et-seigneur-de-guerre-francais-arrete-en-espagne-14922.

Katsouris, Christina, and Aaron, Sayne. *Nigeria's Criminal Crude: International Options to Combat the Export of Stolen Oil*. Chatham House, 2015.

Katzman, Kenneth. "Afghanistan: Post-Taliban Governance, Security, and U.S. Policy." Refworld, December 22, 2015. https://www.refworld.org/reference/countryrep/uscrs/2015/en/108828.

Katznelson, Ira, and Helen V. Milner. *Political Science: The State of the Discipline*. New York, Washington, D.C.: w.w. Norton ; American Political Science Assn., 2002. http://www.gbv.de/dms/sub-hamburg/347252621.pdf.

Kennes, Erik. "Le secteur minier au Congo:"déconnexion" et descente aux enfers." *L'Afrique des Grands Lacs. Annuaire 1999–2000* (1999): pp.322–323.

Landay, Jonathan S. and Tom, Lasseter. "Notorious Warlord Returns Just before Afghan Election." The Seattle Times, August 17, 2009. https://www.seattletimes.com/seattle-news/politics/notorious-warlord-returns-just-before-afghan-election/.

Lezhnev, Sasha. "From Mine to Mobile Phone: The Conflict Minerals Supply Chain." *The Enough Project* (blog), November 10, 2009. https://enoughproject.org/reports/mine-mobile-phone.

"La Chute d'un Seigneur de La Guerre," November 20, 2016. https://www.lejdd.fr/International/La-chute-d-un-seigneur-de-la-guerre-825928.

"La Face Cachée Du Conflit Centrafricain." International Crisis Group, Briefing Afrique, n°105, décembre 2014. https://www.files.ethz.ch/isn/186507/b105-la-face-cachee-du-conflit-centrafricain.pdf.

Lucia, Bird. "Criminalité Organisée et Dynamiques D'instabilité: Cartographie Des Plaques Tournantes Illicites En Afrique de l'Ouest," September 2022. https://wea.globalinitiative.net/illicit-hub-mapping/assets/pdfs/illicit_hubs_methodology_fr.pdf.

Luis Enrique, Amaya and Juan José, Martínez d'Aubuisson. "Renta O Extorsión Victimarios y Víctimas de Las Maras En El Salvador." Global Initiative Against Transnational Organized Crime, October 2021. https://globalinitiative.net/wp-content/uploads/2021/11/GITOC-Renta-o-extorsion-Victimarios-y-victimas-de-las-maras-en-El-Salvador.pdf.

Lyman, Michael D., and Gary W. Potter. *Organized Crime*. Pearson/Prentice Hall, 2007.

Madsen, Wayne. *Genocide and Covert Operations in Africa, 1993–1999*. African Studies (Lewiston, N.Y.). Lewiston, N.Y.: Edwin Mellen Press, 1999.

Marina, Caparini. "Organized Environmental Crime: Why It Matters for Peace Operations," May 12, 2022. https://www.sipri.org/commentary/topical-backgrounder/2022/organized-environmental-crime-why-it-matters-peace-operations.

Montague, Dena and Frida, Berrigan. "The Business of War in the Democratic Republic of Congo." Dollars and Sense magazine, August 2001. https://thirdworldtraveler.com/Africa/Business_War_Congo.html.

"Money Laundering Vulnerabilities of Free Trade Zones." The Financial Action Task Force (FATF), March 2010. https://www.fatf-gafi.org/content/dam/fatf-gafi/reports/ML%20vulnerabilities%20of%20Free%20Trade%20Zones.pdf.

MS13's Toxic Weed That's "More Addictive Than Cocaine" | High Society, 2022. https://www.youtube.com/watch?v=-ZhxFtmAoXg.

Nimmo, Kay, and Richard, Burt. "iTSCi: Contributing to Minerals Traceability and Due Diligence in Central Africa," May 2012. https://www.oecd.org/investment/investmentfordevelopment/50473045.pdf.

"Nigeria's 2003 Elections." *Human Rights Watch*, June 1, 2004. https://www.hrw.org/report/2004/06/01/nigerias-2003-elections/unacknowledged-violence.

"Nigerian Crime Syndicates And Their Routes To Europe And The West." Accessed March 30, 2024. http://hellasfrappe.blogspot.com/2012/12/nigerian-crime-syndicates-and-their.html.

Nwajiaku-Dahou, Kathryn. "The Political Economy of Oil and 'rebellion' in Nigeria's Niger Delta." *Review of African Political Economy* 39, no. 132 (2012): 295–313.

Ofiebor, Okafor. "Portrait of Ateke Tom." *The News* (2004).

Olivier, Liffran and Antoine, Rolland. "DRC : From Texas to South Kivu's Highlands, Mahoro Peace Association's Complex Channels Finance Militia." Africa Intelligence,

January 16, 2023. https://www.africaintelligence.com/central-africa/2023/01/16/from-texas-to-south-kivu-s-highlands-mahoro-peace-association-s-complex-channels-finance-militia,109902191-geo.

Olivier, Rogez. "Somalie—Bashir Ragé, Seigneur de Guerre." RFI, June 21, 2006. http://www1.rfi.fr/actufr/articles/078/article_44565.asp.

Óscar, Martínez y Daniel, Reyes. "Cronología Del Pacto Entre El Gobierno de Bukele y Las Pandillas." Cronología del pacto entre el Gobierno de Bukele y las pandillas, January 18, 2023. https://elfaro.net/es/202301/el_salvador/26676/Cronolog%C3%ADa-del-pacto-entre-el-Gobierno-de-Bukele-y-las-pandillas.htm.

Oyemwinmina, Christopher, and Stanley, Aibieyi. "Cultism: A Destructive Concept in the Educational Development of Tertiary Institutions in Nigeria." *African Research Review* 9 (October 27, 2015): 221. https://doi.org/10.4314/afrrev.v9i4.17.

Pemberton, J. *Sovereignty: Interpretations*. Palgrave Macmillan UK, 2009.

Peter, Tom A. "A Changing of the Guard for Afghanistan's Warlords." *Christian Science Monitor*. Accessed March 30, 2024. https://www.csmonitor.com/World/Asia-South-Central/2010/1027/A-changing-of-the-guard-for-Afghanistan-s-warlords.

Petra, Reski. "The Honored Society: A Portrait of Italy's Most Powerful Mafia," 2008. https://www.goodreads.com/book/show/15814205-the-honored-society.

Posner, Gerald L. *War Lords of Crime: Chinese Secret Societies: The New Mafia*. Queen Anne Press, 1989.

Pospisil, Jan, Alina Rocha, Menocal, and Markus, Schultze-Kraft. "Understanding Organised Violence and Crime in Political Settlements: Oil Wars, Petro-Criminality and Amnesty in the Niger Delta." *Journal of International Development* 29, no. 5 (2017): 613–27.

Reno, W. "Internal Wars, Private Enterprise, and the Shift in Strong State—Weak State Relations." *International Politics* 37, no. 1 (2000): 57–74. https://doi.org/10.1023/A:1009869405384.

Reno, William. "African Weak States and Commercial Alliances." *African Affairs* 96, no. 383 (1997): 165–85.

Rondeaux, Candace. "Dealing with brutal Afghan warlords is a mistake." Afghanistan Analysts Network—English, January 17, 2010. https://www.afghanistan-analysts.org/en/reports/war-and-peace/dealing-with-brutal-afghan-warlords-is-a-mistake/.

Rotimi, Adewale. "Violence in the Citadel: The Menace of Secret Cults in the Nigerian Universities." *Nordic Journal of African Studies* 14 (January 1, 2005). https://doi.org/10.53228/njas.v14i1.282.

"Selling Justice Short." *Human Rights Watch*, July 7, 2009. https://www.hrw.org/report/2009/07/07/selling-justice-short/why-accountability-matters-peace.

Sharife, Khadija. "La bataille pour le pétrole angolais." ritimo, September 1, 2010. https://www.ritimo.org/La-bataille-pour-le-petrole-angolais.

Shelley, Louise I. "Dark Commerce: How a New Illicit Economy Is Threatening Our Future." *Princeton University Press—E-Book*, 2018, 1–376.

Siegel, Dina, Toine, Spapens, and Daan P. Van Uhm. "Regulators and Villains: The Dual Role of Private Actors in Diamonds and Caviar." *Crime, Law and Social Change* 74 (December 1, 2020): 509–23. https://doi.org/10.1007/s10611-020-09902-5.

Silva, Hector, Victoria, Dittmar, and Alicia, Florez. "How an MS13 Clique in El Salvador Took a Cocaine Corridor." InSight Crime, March 23, 2021. http://insightcrime.org/investigations/how-an-ms13-clique-in-el-salvador-took-a-cocaine-corridor/.

Smillie, Ian. "Blood Diamonds and Non-State Actors." *Vanderbilt Journal of Transnational Law* 46, no. 4 (January 1, 2013): 1003.

Smillie, Ian. *Blood on the Stone: Greed, Corruption and War in the Global Diamond Trade*. Anthem Press, 2010.

Souyri, Pierre-François. *Les guerriers dans la rizière. La grande épopée des samouraïs*. Flammarion, 2021.

Storti, Cláudia Costa, and Paul de Grauwe, eds. *Illicit Trade and the Global Economy*. MIT Press, 2012.

The Bloody Yellow House. "The Bloody Yellow House," October 15, 2009. https://thebloodyellowhouse.wordpress.com/.

Thierry, Vircoulon. "Écosystème des groupes armés en Centrafrique," April 2020. https://www.ifri.org/fr/publications/notes-de-lifri/ecosysteme-groupes-armes-centrafrique.

Tierney, John F. *Warlord, Inc.: Extortion and Corruption along the U.S. Supply Chain in Afghanistan*. Washington, DC: U.S. House of Representatives, 2010. http://media.washingtonpost.com/wp-srv/world/documents/warlords.pdf.

Tim, Raeymaekers. "Network War. An Introduction to Congo's Privatised War Economy." IPIS (blog), June 16, 2002. https://ipisresearch.be/publication/network-war-an-introduction-to-congos-privatised-war-economy/.

Traynor, Ian. "Montenegrin PM Accused of Link with Tobacco Racket." *The Guardian*, July 11, 2003, sec. World news. https://www.theguardian.com/world/2003/jul/11/smoking.internationalcrime.

UNODC. "dataUNODC." Accessed March 30, 2024. https://dataunodc.un.org/.

UNODC. "Global Study on Homicide Executive Summary 2019," 2019. https://www.unodc.org/documents/data-and-analysis/gsh/Booklet1.pdf.

Valencia, Roberto. *Carta desde Zacatraz*. Primera edición. El Faro. Madrid: Libros del K.O., 2018. http://bookdata.stanford.edu/casalini/suauth/60/81/60818226.pdf.

Vincent, Georis. "Sur La Piste Des Minerais Du Sang Du Congo." L'Echo, 2011. https://multimedia.lecho.be/congo/.

Vité, Sylvain. "Typology of Armed Conflicts in International Humanitarian Law: Legal Concepts and Actual Situations." *International Review of the Red Cross* 91, no. 873 (March 2009): 69–94. https://doi.org/10.1017/S181638310999021X.

Voice of America. "Armed Gangs Dominate Nigeria's Oil-Rich Region," November 2, 2009. https://www.voanews.com/a/a-13-2009-04-19-voa18-68684917/355754.html.

Working Paper for SPDC. "Peace and Security in the Niger Delta: Conflict Expert Group Baseline Report." yumpu.com, December 2003. https://www.yumpu.com/en/document/view/8937981/peace-and-security-in-the-niger-delta-npr.

World Atlas of Illicit Flows, 2018. https://www.youtube.com/watch?v=_gygyRvujQ4.

CHAPTER 7

The Digital Realm: An Amplifier of the Economy of Violence

Julien Dechanet

Economic violence can be defined as any form of physical, psychological, or financial aggression aimed at controlling, exploiting, or dominating an individual or group in an economic context.

Digital technology is a powerful tool that has revolutionized the global economy by enabling the development of new production methods. Unfortunately, it is becoming increasingly clear that the digital realm can be utilized to support and even amplify existing forms of economic violence.

7.1 How Does Digitalization Amplify Physical Violence?

Physical violence is the first form of economic violence that can be amplified by digitalization. Social networks are the main vectors of violence amplification, be it urban violence during riots, surveillance of a population, or particularly the exacerbation of the scourge of digital harassment, or cyberbullying, spreading from Hollywood to playgrounds and worldwide.

Since 2005, The use of social networks during riots has disrupted public space, allowing all parties to profit from it. This was the case during the Capitol riots in the United States in January 2021[1] and in France in 2023. Rioters use it to organize and coordinate, law enforcement to keep an eye on the rioters and are also watched by the population, the general public gets information and journalists look for testimonies. The "online" and "offline" worlds are deeply intertwined, and it is challenging to separate one from the other. Extremist groups can also use social networks to recruit new members and spread their ideology.

Another role of social networks in the context of urban uprisings is to enable the public to show itself. Observing the extent of the movement on platforms

---

1 "The Jan. 6 Capitol Attack: Inquiries and Fallout—The New York Times," accessed March 30, 2024, https://www.nytimes.com/news-event/jan-6-committee.

like Snapchat or TikTok has enabled young people to realize their power, and potentially amplified the riots. However, blaming social networks for causing violence is also a way of depoliticizing and delegitimizing the revolt, denying the rioters the right to revolt against police violence, as if the objective itself were not legitimate, despite long-standing criticisms of France on this matter. Many protests have already resulted in documented damages shared on social networks, without questioning their legitimacy.

Facial recognition technologies can be used for population surveillance and control, constituting a form of indirect physical violence. For instance, in China, facial recognition is used to monitor and control the Uighur population in the Xinjiang region.[2] The city of Urumqi, situated in the Chinese territories adjacent to Central Asia, is arguably one of the most tightly controlled regions on the planet. Security checkpoints equipped with identification scanners guard access to the railway station and the city. Facial recognition scanners track movements in hotels, shopping malls, and banks. The police use portable devices to search smartphones for encrypted online chat applications, politically charged videos, or other suspicious content. To refuel, motorists must first swipe their identity card in a terminal and face a camera. China's efforts to eliminate a violent separatist movement led by some members of the Uighur Muslim ethnic group, the majority in the Xinjiang Uighur Autonomous Region (XUAR), have transformed it and its capital, Urumqi, into a high-tech laboratory for social control—a model that the government aims to expand nationwide, according to advocates for individual freedoms.

Cyberbullying is an insidious form of online behavior that can have serious consequences on the mental, physical, and emotional health of its victims. Recent statistics and examples underscore the magnitude of this issue and its impact on individuals.

According to a 2020 survey by the Pew Research Center, approximately 41% of American adults reported being victims of online harassment. This encompasses a range of behaviors, from insults and disdain to threats and sexual harassment.[3] Among the victims, 25% reported severe experiences, including threats of physical violence or public humiliation.

The case of Caroline Flack is a recent example of cyberbullying. She was a British television personality who faced intense online harassment before

---

2 "China's Algorithms of Repression," *Human Rights Watch*, May 1, 2019, https://www.hrw.org/report/2019/05/01/chinas-algorithms-repression/reverse-engineering-xinjiang-police-mass.
3 Emily A Vogels, "The State of Online Harassment," *Pew Research Center*, January 2021, https://www.pewresearch.org/internet/wp-content/uploads/sites/9/2021/01/PI_2021.01.13_Online-Harassment_FINAL-1.pdf.

her death in 2020.[4] Hateful comments and constant attacks on social media had a detrimental impact on her mental health, highlighting the tragic consequences of cyberbullying.

Another illustration is the case of actress Kelly Marie Tran, who fell victim to online harassment and cyberbullying after portraying the character Rose Tico in the Star Wars saga.[5] The hateful and racist attacks directed at her led to her decision to withdraw from social media to protect her mental health.

Cyberbullying among young adolescents in schools is a concerning issue that can have profound consequences on the mental and emotional well-being of the victims. Recent statistics and examples shed light on the extent of this problem within educational environments.

According to a 2019 survey conducted by UNESCO, approximately one in three adolescents worldwide has been a victim of online harassment.[6] Studies have revealed that online bullying is particularly prevalent in schools, where adolescents may be subjected to offensive messages, insults, malicious rumors, and the sharing of humiliating content.

A striking example of cyberbullying-associated violence consequences in a school setting is the case of the 16-year-old English teenager, Sian Waterhouse, who took her own life after a dispute with friends on Snapchat and Facebook.[7]

Another instance involves online messaging groups where students can become targets of their peers. Derogatory comments, manipulated images, and threatening messages can quickly spread, creating a toxic and harmful environment for victims, sometimes pushing them to take their own lives.[8]

7.1.1 *Cyberbullying Comes in Various Forms*

First, there's "doxing," which involves exposing an individual on the internet. Unfortunately, photos and videos, often offensive and demeaning to the person

---

4 "Caroline Flack Inquest: 'No Doubt' Presenter Intended to Take Own Life," August 6, 2020, https://www.bbc.com/news/uk-england-london-53676793.
5 Rebecca Rubin, "Kelly Marie Tran Speaks Out About Online Harassment: 'I Won't Be Marginalized,'" *Variety* (blog), August 21, 2018, https://variety.com/2018/film/news/kelly-marie-tran-speaks-out-online-harassment-star-wars-1202911512/.
6 "From Ideas to Action: Addressing Barriers to Comprehensive Sexuality Education in the Classroom," UNESCO Digital Library, 2019, https://unesdoc.unesco.org/ark:/48223/pf0000371091.
7 Amie Gordon, "'Bubbly and Fun-Loving' Schoolgirl, 16, Hanged Herself after She Was Bullied on Social Media," Daily Mail Online, July 11, 2018, https://www.dailymail.co.uk/news/article-5941297/Bubbly-fun-loving-schoolgirl-16-hanged-bullied-social-media.html.
8 David D. Luxton, Jennifer D. June, and Jonathan M. Fairall, "Social Media and Suicide: A Public Health Perspective," *American Journal of Public Health* 102, no. Suppl 2 (May 2012): S195–200, https://doi.org/10.2105/AJPH.2011.300608.

involved, spread rapidly. Even if the aggressor deletes the images, they have likely already reached the hands of strangers, creating a particularly violent multiplier effect against the victim. Imagine sharing an embarrassing story on Instagram or a provocative photo on Snapchat. "It's not a big deal; it disappears automatically after some time," most teenagers think. Until someone takes screenshots and shares them with the entire class. Then, classmates share them again with their friends. Before even realizing it, the images go viral, but for all the wrong reasons.

The second form is exclusion. It often takes more subtle forms than the typical cliques on the playground. For example, the class creates a WhatsApp group for everyone except one child. Subsequently, all sorts of messages, photos, and videos are shared within this group. As these children do not see them, they become less and less able to participate in discussions, even offline. They increasingly isolate themselves from their classmates.

The third form is "fraping," a term derived from a combination of Facebook and raping—cyberbullies use a victim's online profile to destroy their reputation. After quickly glancing at your social media on the school/work computer, the person following you discovers that your profile is still open and sees a unique opportunity. The cyberbully begins posting unpleasant messages in your name, posting racist comments, and sharing embarrassing photos. In the worst cases, they may even change your password so that you can no longer access your account.

Another form is "slut-shaming," which often targets young girls and women. "Slut-shaming" involves publicly shaming a person because of their sexuality. Whether it's wearing a too-short skirt, entering a first sexual relationship, or sharing a nude photo with a boyfriend, cyberbullies seize upon these situations to insult the young girl publicly, or worse, post photos and videos on online forums. Often, victims are forced to pay a ransom to cyberbullies to remove the media or prevent it from being published online. This was the case in Australia when a young man, Craig,[9] was filmed in a private moment without his knowledge. He was compelled to pay $2,000 to a cyberbully to prevent the videos and photos from being published to all his friends on social media.

It is often necessary to pay a ransom to cyber harassers to remove the media or to prevent it from being published online. This was the case in Australia when Craig was unknowingly filmed in his privacy and later faced a demand

---

9 South Australia Police, "Scams, Cybercrime and Cyberbullying" (South Australia Police, 2021), https://www.police.sa.gov.au/your-safety/scams-and-cybercrime.

to pay $2,000 to a cyber harasser to prevent the videos and photos from being shared with all his friends on social media.

Finally, there's "masquerading." In this scenario, perpetrators hide behind an anonymous identity. For instance, they create a new profile on social media using a fake name and false photos. They then use this fake account to inundate their victim with unpleasant (and often personal) messages. Since the victim has no idea of the identity behind this account, the psychological damage is often significant.

7.2 How Does Digitalization Exacerbate Exploitation, Discrimination, and Exclusion in the Workplace?

Digital technologies can be harnessed to facilitate exclusionary practices in the workplace by enabling heightened surveillance of workers, automating recruitment processes, and providing profiling tools that can be used for discriminatory purposes.

Digital technologies, such as electronic monitoring tools, can be used to remotely monitor workers, record their communications and internet usage, and track their productivity. This can contribute to a surveillance culture that may be exploited to the detriment of workers.

Remote work has surged following the global crisis linked to Covid-19, bringing forth numerous advantages that warrant examination.

7.2.1 *Enhanced Productivity Monitoring*

Electronic surveillance has assisted employers in more effectively tracking the tasks and projects of remote workers, contributing to improved time management and enhanced productivity. A study conducted by Prodoscore, a productivity analytics software company, revealed a 47% increase in productivity for remote workers under surveillance during the Covid-19 pandemic.[10]

7.2.2 *Enhanced Performance Management*

It enables employers to obtain objective data on the performance of remote workers, facilitating assessments and feedback. According to a survey conducted by Gallup, employees who have regular check-ins with their managers

---

10 "Surprising Working From Home Productivity Statistics," Apollo Technical LLC, February 7, 2024, https://www.apollotechnical.com/working-from-home-productivity-statistics/.

are 3.5 times more likely to be engaged in their work.[11] Electronic surveillance can assist managers in having informed and data-driven conversations with their remote employees.

7.2.3   Enhanced Data Security
Surveillance can help prevent leaks of sensitive data by monitoring communications and preventing unauthorized access to confidential information. According to the IBM Cost of a Data Breach report, the average cost of a data breach in 2023 was approximately $4.45 million.[12]

7.2.4   Reduced Fraud
Surveillance can contribute to detecting internal fraud by monitoring financial activities and transactions.

Unfortunately, the downsides of remote work are undeniable. A technological revolution always brings its share of disadvantages.

7.2.5   Privacy Invasion?
Electronic surveillance can encroach upon the privacy of employees, creating an atmosphere of distrust and a sense of constant scrutiny. A survey conducted by NordVPN Teams revealed that 63% of employees feel monitored by their employer while working remotely, leading to feelings of privacy violation and distrust.[13]

7.2.6   A Source of Stress and Dissatisfaction
Employees may experience increased stress knowing they are constantly under surveillance, which can harm their mental and emotional well-being. According to a survey by FlexJobs and Mental Health America, 75% of workers reported higher stress levels due to the Covid-19 pandemic and the demands of remote work.[14]

---

11   Gallup, "Employees Want a Lot More From Their Managers," Gallup.com, April 8, 2015, https://www.gallup.com/workplace/236570/employees-lot-managers.aspx.
12   "Cost of a Data Breach Report 2023," IBM, 2023, https://www.ibm.com/reports/data-breach.
13   Paulius Ilevičius, "Why Is Employee Surveillance on the Rise?," NordVPN, August 23, 2021, https://nordvpn.com/blog/employee-surveillance-2021/.
14   Brie Weiler Reynolds, "FlexJobs, Mental Health America Survey: Mental Health in the Workplace," FlexJobs Job Search Tips and Blog, August 21, 2020, https://www.flexjobs.com/blog/post/flexjobs-mha-mental-health-workplace-pandemic/.

7.2.7 A Decrease in Creativity and Autonomy
Excessive surveillance can stifle employees' creativity and initiative as they feel constrained to always adhere strictly to guidelines.

7.2.8 A Breakdown in Trust
The implementation of electronic surveillance can lead to a loss of mutual trust between employers and employees, impacting long-term commitment and loyalty. According to a survey conducted by Gartner, 30% of companies actively monitor remote employees, contributing to a loss of trust employees may have in their employers.[15]

7.2.9 Misinterpretation of Data
Electronic surveillance may not accurately reflect an employee's actual performance, as some crucial activities may go uncaptured. Social interactions, informal discussions, the exchange of tacit knowledge, and other non-directly measurable activities can play a crucial role in the productivity and creativity of workers.[16] Creative tasks, such as solving complex problems or team collaboration, may not be effectively captured by electronic monitoring systems. An employee might spend more time on a task actively seeking innovative solutions, but this wouldn't be clearly visible in raw data.

7.2.10 An Increase in Complexity and Costs
Implementing electronic surveillance systems can be complex and costly, especially in terms of technical and financial resources. It may require integration with other company IT systems, which can be complex depending on the existing architecture and the varied requirements and roles of each department. Introducing a new surveillance system also necessitates training employees and managers for effective use, adding a layer of complexity and requiring significant financial and time resources. Ensuring legal and regulatory compliance may demand investments in time and money to ensure that the systems adhere to prevailing standards.

In a professional working scenario, digitization exacerbates discrimination in the recruitment of new employees, contributing to the economy of violence.

---

15 "The Future Of Employee Monitoring," Gartner, May 3, 2019, https://www.gartner.com/smarterwithgartner/the-future-of-employee-monitoring.

16 Sven Horak et al., "Informal Networks: Dark Sides, Bright Sides, and Unexplored Dimensions," *Management and Organization Review* 16, no. 3 (July 2020): 511–42, https://doi.org/10.1017/mor.2020.28.

Digital technologies can be employed to automate recruitment processes, including candidate selection. Recruitment automation tools typically rely on modern technologies such as artificial intelligence, machine learning, predictive analytics, and natural language processing to perform simple but repetitive and time-consuming recruitment tasks consistently and reliably. However, these tools can be biased and perpetuate discriminatory practices by relying on selection criteria that exclude certain groups of candidates.[17]

Indeed, Applicant Tracking Systems (ATS) use algorithms to sort resumes based on keywords or specific criteria. This can exclude qualified candidates whose resumes don't perfectly match the predefined criteria, creating a bias in favor of candidates who know how to format their resumes optimally for the ATS.

Furthermore, job advertisements posted on digital platforms can be targeted in a way that only reaches a specific demographic group, inadvertently excluding candidates based on their age, gender, or other protected characteristics.[18]

Additionally, some recruiters utilize online tests to assess candidates' skills. These tests may exhibit bias toward certain populations if the questions are culturally specific or favor particular groups.[19]

Asynchronous video interviews, where candidates record their responses to pre-recorded questions, can introduce biases by not accounting for cultural differences in communication styles or inadvertently evaluating candidates based on race, gender, or appearance.[20]

Finally, recruiters may review candidates' social media profiles to learn more about them.[21] This can lead to biases based on candidates' privacy and the subjectivity of interpreting online posts.[22]

---

17 Miranda Bogen, "All the Ways Hiring Algorithms Can Introduce Bias," *Harvard Business Review*, May 6, 2019, https://hbr.org/2019/05/all-the-ways-hiring-algorithms-can-introduce-bias.
18 Kirsten Martin, *Ethics of Data and Analytics: Concepts and Cases* (New York: Auerbach Publications, 2022), pp 4, https://doi.org/10.1201/9781003278290.
19 Amit Datta, Michael Carl Tschantz, and Anupam Datta, "Automated Experiments on Ad Privacy Settings: A Tale of Opacity, Choice, and Discrimination" (arXiv, March 16, 2015), https://doi.org/10.48550/arXiv.1408.6491.
20 Nicolas Roulin et al., "Bias in the Background? The Role of Background Information in Asynchronous Video Interviews," *Journal of Organizational Behavior* 44 (November 4, 2022), https://doi.org/10.1002/job.2680.
21 Marysol Villeda et al., "Use of Social Networking Sites for Recruiting and Selecting in the Hiring Process," *International Business Research* 12 (February 11, 2019): 66, https://doi.org/10.5539/ibr.v12n3p66.
22 Alessandro Acquisti and Christina Fong, "An Experiment in Hiring Discrimination via Online Social Networks," *Management Science* 66, no. 3 (March 2020): 1005–24, https://doi.org/10.1287/mnsc.2018.3269.

Digital technologies[23] can be harnessed to profile consumers through the use of advertising[24] targeting algorithms. These tools may be employed to discriminate based on criteria such as age, race, or gender. Advertisers on LinkedIn and Facebook purchase ads to achieve various marketing objectives. Both LinkedIn and Facebook have three types of objectives: awareness, consideration, and conversion, each with multiple additional options. The chosen objective determines the ad format, bidding strategy, and payment options available to the advertiser. If the advertiser discloses that it is a job-related ad, the platforms disable or limit age and gender targeting. LinkedIn, being a professional network, also allows targeting based on job title, education, and professional experience.

ProPublica journalists were among the first to reveal that Facebook's targeting options enabled job and housing advertisers[25] to practice discrimination based on age,[26] race,[27] and gender. In response to these findings and as part of a settlement agreement, Facebook made changes to restrict the targeting capabilities offered to advertisers for ads in the employment and housing sectors.

Other advertising platforms, like Google, have announced similar restrictions. The question of whether these restrictions are sufficient to prevent discrimination by a malicious advertiser remains open, as studies have shown that advanced features of advertising platforms, such as custom audiences and "lookalike" audiences, can be used by advertisers to manipulate user behavior.[28] This may include creating specific ads to exploit individuals' psychological vulnerabilities, encourage harmful behaviors, or push them to make economic decisions against their interests.[29] It can also lead to the extraction

---

23 Shoshana Zuboff, *The Age of Surveillance Capitalism: The Fight for a Human Future at the New Frontier of Power* (PublicAffairs, 2019).

24 Mike Smith, *Targeted: How Technology Is Revolutionizing Advertising and the Way Companies Reach Consumers* (AMACOM, 2014).

25 Julia Angwin, Ariana Tobin, and Madeleine Varner, "Facebook (Still) Letting Housing Advertisers Exclude Users by Race," ProPublica, November 21, 2017, https://www.propublica.org/article/facebook-advertising-discrimination-housing-race-sex-national-origin.

26 Julia Angwin, Noam Scheiber, and Ariana Tobin, "Facebook Job Ads Raise Concerns About Age Discrimination," *The New York Times*, December 20, 2017, sec. Business, https://www.nytimes.com/2017/12/20/business/facebook-job-ads.html.

27 Julia Angwin, Ariana Tobin, and Madeleine Varner, "Facebook (Still) Letting Housing Advertisers Exclude Users by Race".

28 Allen Finn, "Big Changes to Facebook Custom Audiences: What You Need to Know," *WordStream* (blog), November 1, 2022, https://www.wordstream.com/blog/ws/2018/04/23/facebook-custom-audience-changes.

29 Daniel Susser, Beate Roessler, and Helen Nissenbaum, "Online Manipulation: Hidden Influences in a Digital World," SSRN Scholarly Paper (Rochester, NY, December 23, 2018), https://doi.org/10.2139/ssrn.3306006.

and exploitation of personal data on a large scale, often without users' informed consent, raising privacy concerns and potentially resulting in violent economic exploitation through the misuse of collected information.[30]

In January 2023, Facebook introduced a technology in the United States aimed at reducing discriminatory biases in ads displayed on its platforms. Named the Variance Reduction System (VRS), it was developed under the guidance of the US Department of Justice after reaching an agreement. The platform was accused of discriminatory practices by offering the ability to precisely target certain ads, particularly for housing. To promote fairer ad distribution, the tool relies on a machine learning technique to acquire new insights. In essence, the ad is initially shown to a test group of users. The profiles that viewed the ad are then analyzed and compared to the demographic distribution of the target audience selected by the advertiser. If disparities are identified by the program, the ad targeting algorithm works to reduce the difference between the audiences. According to Facebook, the VRS relies on publicly available statistics from the US Census to estimate ethnic origin.

Another example of economic violence facilitated by digital means is the exploitation of workers. Indeed, workers in smartphone production factories in China are often paid low wages and work in hazardous conditions.[31] They are also subjected to extremely long working hours and intense pressure to increase production. Workers are frequently subjected to precarious labor practices, such as the use of temporary workers or outsourcing, which limit their rights and social protection. According to a report by China Labor Watch in 2018, workers at the Jabil Circuit factory (a subcontractor for Apple) in China were compelled to work excessive overtime, reaching up to 100 hours per month, well beyond the legal limit of 36 hours.[32]

Another example concerns call centers, an essential tool in the commercial apparatus of many companies worldwide. They are often located in developing countries where wages are low. Workers are predominantly underpaid, work unpaid overtime, and endure stressful working conditions. Moreover, most call center workers do not have long-term contracts and are often terminated

---

30 Dipayan Ghosh and Ben Scott, "Digital Deceit: The Technologies behind Precision Propaganda on the Internet," Report (New America, January 23, 2018), https://apo.org.au/node/130646.
31 *Inside Apple's iPhone Factory In China,* 2021, https://www.youtube.com/watch?v=9XkX6EGk_CA.
32 *Inside Apple's iPhone Factory In China.*

without notice.³³ In India, one of the major countries for outsourced call centers, the average salary for a call center employee can be around 15,000 to 25,000 rupees per month (approximately $200–340), which is well below the average salary in India (around 500 euros).³⁴

A new report conducted by the Communications Workers of America and worker organizations in India shows that call center reps in India are often working 48 to 54 hours a week.³⁵ This is also the case for freelance writers working through online platforms, struggling to find well-paying and stable jobs, sometimes accepting contracts at low rates to make a living. Similarly, independent workers offering their services on micro-work platforms like Amazon Mechanical Turk may earn only a few cents for certain tasks, making it difficult to achieve a decent income.³⁶

Drivers working for online transportation platforms like Uber or Lyft are often considered independent contractors, meaning they do not benefit from the social protections and benefits offered to employed workers.³⁷ They are also often paid at low rates that do not allow them to earn a decent wage. According to an analysis by Ridester, a driver information platform, the median hourly income for Uber drivers in the United States was around $9.73 in 2020, after accounting for expenses related to vehicle maintenance and operation. In comparison, companies like Amazon, Target, or Chipotle surpassed the $15 per hour mark in 2022. However, $15 per hour amounts to $30,000 per year, well below the $50,000 to $60,000 for the median salary in the United States.³⁸

Finally, digital technologies can also be used to exploit workers, especially in industries that depend on remote work. Digital platforms often enable worker exploitation by offering them precarious contracts, low wages, and inadequate

---

33 Snigdha Poonam, "The Scammers Gaming India's Overcrowded Job Market," *The Guardian*, January 2, 2018, sec. News, https://www.theguardian.com/news/2018/jan/02/the-scammers-gaming-indias-overcrowded-job-market.

34 "Call Center Agent Salary in India in 2024," PayScale, accessed March 30, 2024, https://www.payscale.com/research/IN/Job=Call_Center_Agent/Salary.

35 "Report Cites Poor Working Conditions in India's Call Centers," Workforce.com, October 17, 2006, https://workforce.com/news/report-cites-poor-working-conditions-in-indias-call-centers.

36 David Martin et al., "Turking in a Global Labour Market," *Computer Supported Cooperative Work (CSCW)* 25 (February 1, 2016), https://doi.org/10.1007/s10606-015-9241-6.

37 Andrew J. Hawkins, "Uber and Lyft Face an Existential Threat in California—and They're Losing," The Verge, September 2, 2019, https://www.theverge.com/2019/9/2/20841070/uber-lyft-ab5-california-bill-drivers-labor.

38 Jeff Cox, "Raising Minimum Wage to $15 Would Cost 1.4 Million Jobs, CBO Says," CNBC, February 8, 2021, https://www.cnbc.com/2021/02/08/raising-minimum-wage-to-15-would-cost-1point4-million-jobs-cbo-says.html.

social protection. In 2020, a study by the International Labour Organization (ILO) estimated that 22.9% of the global workforce, approximately 1.1 billion people, consisted of independent workers, many of whom operate through digital platforms.[39] About 40% of independent workers in the United States do not have access to employer-provided health insurance, according to the Bureau of Labor Statistics.[40] Recognizing this alarming situation, the European Union adopted a directive in 2021 requiring platform workers to have the right to basic social protection and fair working conditions.[41]

7.3 How Does Digital Technology Amplify Financial Violence?

The third form of economic violence that can be amplified by digital technology is financial violence, which is characterized by fraudulent and corrupt practices impacting the economy. Digital tools can be utilized to manipulate financial markets, create speculative bubbles, and access sensitive financial information. Online financial fraud is also on the rise, with increasingly sophisticated online scams that often employ psychological manipulation techniques to deceive users.

Banks have faced allegations of manipulating the LIBOR[42] interest rate, a benchmark rate used in many loans and financial transactions, using high-frequency trading algorithms to manipulate prices.[43] In 2010, such manipulation led to a flash crash in the US financial markets, causing a 9% drop in the Dow Jones in just a few minutes.

The shift to automated exchanges, the rise of Big Data, and machine learning have led to the emergence of High-Frequency Trading (HFT) during the

---

39 "World Employment and Social Outlook—Trends 2020" (International Labour Organization, 2020), https://www.ilo.org/wcmsp5/groups/public/---dgreports/---dcomm/---publ/documents/publication/wcms_734455.pdf.
40 "Health Plan Provisions for Private Industry Workers in the United States, 2020: U.S. Bureau of Labor Statistics," accessed March 31, 2024, https://www.bls.gov/ebs/publications/health-care-plan-provisions-for-private-industry-2020.htm.
41 "Commission Welcomes Political Agreement on Improving Working Conditions in Platform Work," Text, European Commission, December 13, 2023, https://ec.europa.eu/commission/presscorner/detail/en/ip_23_6586.
42 Established in 1970, Libor is a benchmark interest rate set in London by the British Bankers' Association (BBA). Every day, this rate is used by major banks around the world to lend trillions of dollars to finance their activities.
43 Dan Davies, "How to Get Away with Financial Fraud," *The Guardian*, June 28, 2018, sec. News, https://www.theguardian.com/news/2018/jun/28/how-to-get-away-with-financial-fraud.

2000s. This practice significantly expanded between 2005 and 2009. According to TABB Group and Deutsche Bank, in 2014, HFT represented 35% of stock market trades in Europe and 50% in the United States.[44] This manipulation had consequences for the global economy, affecting interest rates for mortgages. High-frequency traders are daily traders who use advanced algorithms to execute trades in milliseconds or even microseconds. They place and cancel millions of orders in a day, liquidating their positions quickly before the end of the trading session. If HFTs have a strategy based on transaction volume, speed is a key element. Being the first to receive and process information from databases allows them to spot market signals and anticipate price movements before other traders. Therefore, an HFT will not hesitate to invest considerable sums to gain even a few nanoseconds. After optimizing their algorithms, HFTs have three options to increase speed:

Become clients of market-making firms using the colocation system—For this, HFTs will rent a box where they can directly connect their computers via fiber optics to the platform's servers.

Invest in advanced telecommunication networks—This comes with a significant cost: Spread Network LLC connected the stock exchanges of New York and Chicago with fiber optics in 2010. The estimated cost of this 1,200 km network, where information circulates in 0.0065 seconds, is $300 million.

Become clients of companies specializing in advanced telecommunication networks—For example, the cost of using Spread Network LLC's network ranges from $3 to $5 million per year.

The technological arms race has been such that today this network is "obsolete" as transmissions by wave and then by laser are faster than those performed by fiber optics. The best HFTs conduct their trades at the limit of physical laws. As evidence, an order sent from Frankfurt to London takes 2.21 milliseconds, while light takes 2.12 milliseconds.[45]

Digital technologies enable tax evaders to conceal their financial transactions by using offshore accounts or shell companies to hide their money.[46] This

---

44 Badr Berrada, "The Dark Side of High Frequency Trading," June 18, 2017, https://www.bbntimes.com/financial/the-dark-side-of-high-frequency-trading.

45 "Les Effets, Enjeux et Réglementations Du Trading Haute Fréquence," accessed March 31, 2024, https://www.alumneye.fr/les-effets-enjeux-et-reglementations-du-trading-haute-frequence/.

46 Juliette Garside, Holly Watt, and David Pegg, "The Panama Papers: How the World's Rich and Famous Hide Their Money Offshore," *The Guardian*, April 3, 2016, sec. News, https://www.theguardian.com/news/2016/apr/03/the-panama-papers-how-the-worlds-rich-and-famous-hide-their-money-offshore.

practice is common in tax havens, often employed by corporations to avoid paying taxes.

Offshore accounts are bank accounts located in foreign jurisdictions, often in tax havens, where laws are designed to protect financial privacy. Tax evaders use these accounts to hide income, capital gains, and other financial transactions. The 2016 Panama Papers scandal, where millions of sensitive documents were leaked, exposed how political figures, celebrities, and companies utilized offshore companies to evade taxes.[47]

Digital technologies facilitate the creation of shell companies, fictitious entities often registered in jurisdictions with lax regulatory oversight. These companies are used to mask the true owners of assets and conceal financial transactions. A notable example is the use of shell companies in real estate transactions to hide the identity of the actual owners and avoid tax reporting.[48]

Tax havens, often territories with favorable tax regulations, are used by corporations to minimize their tax obligations. These jurisdictions often offer strict laws on financial privacy and low tax rates. Multinational corporations can shift their profits to these locations, thereby reducing their tax liability in the countries where they conduct their operations.[49]

Data theft is also a common form of cybercrime. Hackers can steal financial information, health records, and personal information such as email addresses, credit card numbers, and social security numbers. This stolen data can be sold on the black market and used for fraud, identity theft, and other crimes.

An example of data theft is the one that affected the consumer credit reporting company Equifax in 2017.[50] This breach compromised the personal information of over 147 million individuals, including their names, social security numbers, birthdates, addresses, and other sensitive details. This incident led to a congressional investigation and a $575 million fine for the company.

Another instance of data theft occurred in 2013 when the retail chain Target was targeted, resulting in the theft of credit and debit card information from over 40 million customers.[51] The attack was attributed to a group of

---

47   Garside, Watt, and Pegg.
48   "'Shell Companies' In Real Estate Transactions," Nisar Law Gro-up, P.C., March 17, 2015, https://www.nisarlaw.com/blog/2015/march/understanding-the-use-of-shell-companies-in-real/.
49   "Tax Havens: Super-Rich 'hiding' at Least $21tn," BBC News, July 22, 2012, sec. Business, https://www.bbc.com/news/business-18944097.
50   "The Equifax Breach Was Entirely Preventable," WIRED, September 14, 2017, https://www.wired.com/story/equifax-breach-no-excuse/.
51   "Target 2015 Annual Report" (Target, 2015), https://corporate.target.com/getmedia/e503afc7-58e1-468c-8ff2-8442b3a4a699/Target-2015-Annual-Report.pdf.

Ukrainian and Russian hackers, costing Target over $18.5 million in legal fees and reparations.

In 2018, the online marketing company Exactis experienced a massive data leak, exposing the personal information of 340 million individuals and businesses.[52] This data breach was described as one of the largest in history.

Cyberattacks on major corporations and governments can also have significant financial consequences, particularly by disrupting financial markets. In May 2017, a massive cyberattack known as WannaCry struck thousands of organizations worldwide, crippling computer systems and encrypting data.[53] This attack was executed using malicious software that exploited a vulnerability in the Microsoft Windows operating system. Several major companies were affected, including FedEx, a transportation and logistics company, and Renault, a French automobile manufacturer. The computers of these companies were infected with the malware, leading to a halt in their business operations. Employees were unable to access their data, and production systems were temporarily shut down. This disruption impacted these companies' ability to deliver products and services, resulting in a decline in their stock values. In addition to these major corporations, numerous other organizations, including hospitals and governments, fell victim to WannaCry. According to the National Center for Cyber Security (CNSSI), WannaCry affected more than 150 countries and over 200,000 computers worldwide. This attack underscored the vulnerability of businesses and organizations to cyber threats and emphasized the importance of implementing cybersecurity measures to protect data and information systems.

Another form of cybercrime, online financial fraud, is steadily increasing, with increasingly sophisticated online scams that often use psychological manipulation techniques to deceive users. A study by the French *Observatoire de la sécurité des cartes de paiement* (observatory of the security of bank credit cards) revealed that online payment fraud increased by 16% in 2020 in France.[54] Among the techniques used, "phishing" stands out, involving the

---

52 "The Exactis Data Breach: What Consumers Need to Know," *McAfee Blog* (blog), June 28, 2018, https://www.mcafee.com/blogs/privacy-identity-protection/exactis-d-ata-breach/.
53 "The WannaCry Attack Reveals the Risks of a Computerised World," *The Economist*, May 20, 2017, https://www.economist.com/leaders/2017/05/20/the-wannacry-attack-reveals-the-risks-of-a-computerised-world.
54 "Rapport annuel de l'Observatoire de la sécurité des moyens de paiement 2018," Banque de France, July 9, 2019, https://publications.banque-france.fr/rapport-annuel-de-lobservatoire-de-la-securite-des-moyens-de-paiement-2018.

sending of fraudulent emails to induce people to disclose their personal and banking information, as well as online investment scams.

Another example of online fraud is related to online purchases. Fraudsters can create fake online retail websites to entice users to buy products that are never delivered or are of lower quality than promised. Fraudsters may also use online payment services to persuade users to send money for products or services that are never delivered.

In 2018, the European Commission published a report on online fraud, estimating that annual losses caused by online fraud in Europe were approximately 1.3 billion euros.[55] The report also identified phishing scams as the most common form of online fraud.

In 2020, the cybersecurity company Proofpoint published a report on online fraud trends,[56] revealing an increase in fraud related to the Covid-19 pandemic. Fraudsters employed tactics such as selling fake Covid-19 vaccines, fraudulent charity donations, and impersonating healthcare service providers to deceive online users.

7.4   How Does Digital Technology Amplify the Structural and Democratic Violence of a State?

The fourth form of economic violence that can be amplified by digital technology is structural violence. This form of violence, theorized by Johan Galtung, is often invisible and manifests itself in economic policies and practices that limit people's access to resources, opportunities, and economic rights.[57] Digital technology can reinforce this form of violence by creating barriers to accessing digital resources, establishing digital monopolies, and enabling the exploitation of users' personal data.

---

55 "Rapport de l'olaf 2018" (Commission européenne, 2018), https://anti-fraud.ec.europa.eu/system/files/2021-09/olaf_report_2018_fr_0.pdf.
56 "Proofpoint's Annual Human Factor Report Reveals How 2020 Transformed Today's Threat Landscape," Proofpoint, August 3, 2021, https://www.proofpoint.com/us/newsroom/press-releases/proofpoints-annual-human-factor-report-reveals-how-2020-transformed-todays.
57 Johan Galtung, "Violence, Peace, and Peace Research," *Journal of Peace Research* 6, no. 3 (September 1, 1969): 167–91, https://doi.org/10.1177/002234336900600301.

Digital technology has facilitated the emergence of new forms of precarious work, such as independent work, online gig platforms, and the gig economy.[58] These forms of work are often characterized by low wages, a lack of social protection, and uncertainty about future employment. A study by the International Labour Organization revealed that 56% of the global workforce was engaged in the gig economy in 2016, highlighting the extent of labor precarity.

The digital realm has also contributed to the exacerbation of economic inequalities. On one hand, technology companies often play key roles in the global economy, yet they tend to concentrate a disproportionate share of the profits. On the other hand, economic inequalities can be heightened by the new forms of precarious work mentioned earlier. In 2020, Oxfam revealed that global billionaires had increased their wealth by $3.9 billion during the pandemic, while the most precarious workers were the hardest hit.[59]

Technology companies also wield considerable economic power, which can enable them to influence public policies and circumvent competition regulations. For instance, in 2017, the European Commission imposed a record fine of 2.42 billion euros on Google for abusing its dominant position in the online search engine market.[60]

While access to the Internet and online resources can potentially reduce educational inequalities, disadvantaged populations may have limited access to these resources due to a lack of infrastructure and digital skills.[61]

Digital technology can also be a source of democratic violence. Social networks and online platforms have given rise to new forms of violence that can harm democracy. Hate speech, manipulation of public opinion, and violations of privacy are examples of the amplification of this democratic violence facilitated by the widespread use of digital technology in our societies.

---

58   Tom Montgomery and Simone Baglioni, "Defining the Gig Economy: Platform Capitalism and the Reinvention of Precarious Work," *International Journal of Sociology and Social Policy* 41, no. 9/10 (January 1, 2020): 1012–25, https://doi.org/10.1108/IJSSP-08-2020-0400.

59   "Power, Profits and the Pandemic: From Corporate Extraction for the Few to an Economy That Works for All," Oxfam, 2020, https://policy-practice.oxfam.org/resources/power-profits-and-the-pandemic-from-corporate-extraction-for-the-few-to-an-econ-621044/.

60   "Commission fines Google €2.42 billion for abusing dominance as search engine by giving illegal advantage to own comparison shopping service—Factsheet," Text, European Commission—European Commission, 2017, https://ec.europa.eu/commission/presscorner/detail/es/MEMO_17_1785.

61   "Global Education Monitoring Report Summary, 2020: Inclusion and Education: All Means All," UNESCO Digital Library, 2020, https://unesdoc.unesco.org/ark:/48223/pf0000373721.

Online hate speech has become common on social networks. Users can make insults, threats, and discriminatory speeches without being held accountable for their actions. According to a study by the European Union Agency for Fundamental Rights in 2020, nearly one-third of the respondents stated that they had been victims of online hate speech.[62]

Manipulation of public opinion has also become common on social networks. Interest groups can create fake news, manipulated videos, or bots to spread false ideas and influence public opinion. These manipulations can have serious consequences, such as the polarization of society. In 2016, the US presidential election was marked by accusations of manipulation of public opinion by foreign actors. In September 2017, Facebook announced that it had identified 3,000 ads displayed on its site in 2016, seen by 10 million American internet users. These ads were notable for addressing highly controversial topics in the United States, such as the reception of refugees, the Black Lives Matter movement, gun control, Islam, and LGBT rights (lesbian, gay, bisexual, transgender). Some ads also directly targeted Hillary Clinton, Donald Trump's opponent in the 2016 US presidential election. These campaigns were purchased for a total of $100,000, according to Facebook figures, a relatively small amount, especially when compared to the $70 million and $30 million spent by Donald Trump and Hillary Clinton, respectively, on online advertising during the campaign. In addition to ads, Facebook also identified 470 accounts linked to the Russian entity called the Internet Research Agency (IRA), which posts non-paid content, traditional posts. Between 2015 and 2017, the Internet Research Agency posted 80,000 times on Facebook, and 29 million users received these posts in their news feeds, bringing this number to 126 million when considering shares, comments, and likes these posts received.

The proliferation of online hate has profound economic implications for both major digital platforms and political and economic actors, illustrating a complex interconnection between the digital sphere and financial and power-related issues. For major digital platforms, the spread of hateful content can have significant repercussions on their reputation, leading to a loss of user trust and potentially a decline in the company's valuation. Moreover, they face legal challenges, with potential lawsuits and costs associated with managing abusive content. On the side of political and economic actors, online hate becomes a strategic tool to accentuate social divides. Notable examples such as the Cambridge Analytica scandal underscore how data manipulation and

---

62 "Fundamental Rights Report 2021," European Union Agency for Fundamental Rights, June 1, 2021, http://fra.europa.eu/en/publication/2021/fundamental-rights-report-2021.

targeted diffusion of hate speech can be used to influence public opinion and maintain or seize power. In South Africa, the Gupta family has been accused of employing similar tactics, exacerbating divisions to evade corruption charges and illicitly seize public resources. This instrumentalization of online hate reveals a deliberate strategy aimed at consolidating dominant positions, avoiding legal consequences, and illegitimately exploiting resources, highlighting the close links between the digital, political, and economic spheres. Addressing these issues requires stringent legislative measures, effective regulations, and increased awareness to prevent the exploitation of digital media for harmful economic and political purposes.

Finally, privacy violations represent another form of democratic violence associated with the digital realm. Technology companies collect massive amounts of data on users, which can be used for malicious purposes. Governments can also leverage this data to monitor citizens and limit their freedom of expression.[63] In 2013, Edward Snowden's revelations exposed massive internet surveillance programs implemented by the US and UK governments. This included the Prism program and XKeyscore, the latter providing broader net surveillance without hierarchical or judicial oversight.[64]

7.5 The Weight of the Underground Digital Economy and Cybercrime

The underground digital economy, also known as the Darknet, has grown significantly over the years, evolving into a thriving marketplace for a diverse range of online criminal activities. The darknet hosts approximately 300,000 active sites, and its ecosystem is estimated to be worth several billion dollars annually.[65] Studies have shown that nearly 60% of the content available on the darknet is related to illegal activities, spanning from the sale of counterfeit products and illicit substances to sophisticated hacking services.[66]

---

63 Owen Bowcott and Spencer Ackerman, "Mass Internet Surveillance Threatens International Law, UN Report Claims," *The Guardian*, October 15, 2014, sec. World news, https://www.theguardian.com/world/2014/oct/15/internet-surveillance-report-edward-snowden-leaks.

64 "Après Prism, la NSA espionne un peu plus avec XKeyscore," Le Monde Informatique, August 1, 2013, https://www.lemondeinformatique.fr/actualites/lire-apres-prism-la-nsa-espionne-un-peu-plus-avec-xkeyscore-54589.html.

65 "Internet Organised Crime Threat Assessment (IOCTA) 2019" (Europol, 2019), https://www.europol.europa.eu/sites/default/files/documents/iocta_2019.pdf.

66 Roberta Liggett et al., "The Dark Web as a Platform for Crime: An Exploration of Illicit Drug, Firearm, CSAM, and Cybercrime Markets," in *The Palgrave Handbook of International*

Regarding cybercrime in general, the statistics are equally alarming. According to McAfee's Cybercrime Report, global losses due to cybercrime reached around $1 trillion in 2020.[67] Ransomware attacks saw a dramatic increase, rising by 62% during the year 2022, with average ransom demands nearly doubling. The healthcare and finance sectors were particularly targeted, with attacks exploiting the Covid-19 pandemic and the transition to online financial operations.

The underground digital economy has thrived in recent years, fueled by the growing demand for illicit products and services.[68] Sales on the darknet reached staggering levels, illustrating the scale of this clandestine economy. According to a Chainalysis study, darknet markets generated over $1.7 billion in cryptocurrency revenue in 2020.[69] This substantial sum is the result of a diversification of offered products and services, ranging from narcotics to weapons, stolen data, and hacking services.

7.5.1 The Sale of Stolen Data, Ransomware, and Malware Attacks in the Underground Digital Economy

The sale of stolen data is a cornerstone of the underground digital economy. In 2021, the cybersecurity company Cyble revealed that a database containing over 3.2 billion pairs of credentials and passwords had been uploaded to a darknet forum.[70] These details, originating from breaches in various companies, were available for purchase, allowing cybercriminals to exploit this information for phishing attacks and other forms of online fraud.

The rise of ransomware has also contributed to the expansion of the underground digital economy. According to Coveware's Ransomware Report, the average ransom demand significantly increased from $115,123 in 2020 to

---

  Cybercrime and Cyberdeviance, ed. Thomas J. Holt and Adam M. Bossler (Cham: Springer International Publishing, 2020), 91–116, https://doi.org/10.1007/978-3-319-78440-3_17.

67 "McAfee Labs 2020 Threats Predictions Report," *McAfee Blog* (blog), December 5, 2019, https://www.mcafee.com/blogs/other-blogs/mcafee-labs/mcafee-labs-2020-threats-predictions-report/.

68 Mike McGuire, "The Web of Profit: A Look at the Cybercrime Economy," *VentureBeat* (blog), April 21, 2018, https://venturebeat.com/security/the-web-of-profit-a-look-at-the-cybercrime-economy/.

69 "Geographic Distinctions in Crypto Darknet Market Activity," *Chainalysis* (blog), February 1, 2021, https://www.chainalysis.com/blog/crypto-darknet-markets-2021-geographic-breakdown/.

70 "COMB: Largest Breach of All Time Leaked Online with 3.2 Billion Records," Cybernews, February 12, 2021, https://cybernews.com/news/largest-compilation-of-emails-and-passwords-leaked-free/.

$220,298 in 2021.[71] This trend reflects the growing financial efficiency of ransomware, phishing attacks, and the increasing value of stolen data.

An illustrative example is the "DarkMarket" operation, one of the largest darknet markets dedicated to illegal trade. In January 2021, European authorities shut down this market and arrested its administrator, a 34-year-old Australian.[72] DarkMarket had 20 servers located in Moldova and Ukraine, over 500,000 users, and 2,400 vendors, facilitating more than 320,000 transactions.

Finally, the spread of malware is another form of economic violence that can cause substantial harm to businesses and individuals. Malware such as computer viruses, Trojans, and ransomware can result in data loss, service interruptions, and hardware damage.

Malware can be shared through various means, including phishing emails, pirated software downloads, or infected websites. Once a user has downloaded or installed malware, it can begin collecting sensitive information or causing damage to the computer system.

A well-known example of malware diffusion is the NotPetya attack in 2017.[73] Starting with a phishing campaign, users were tricked into opening an infected Microsoft Word document. The malware then rapidly spread across the networks of businesses and organizations worldwide, causing significant financial losses. One notable victim was the shipping company Maersk, which fell prey to the NotPetya ransomware, paralyzing its operations for several days and costing the company millions of dollars in lost revenue and data restoration expenses. Overall, the NotPetya attack incurred approximately $10 billion in costs for the affected businesses.

7.5.2   *Cybercriminal Groups and Notable Attacks*

Another example is the Emotet malware attack, which began in 2014 and has continued to evolve since.[74] Emotet is a Trojan-type malware used to steal sensitive information such as usernames and passwords. In 2020, German

---

71   "Ransomware Attack Vectors Shift as New Software Vulnerability Exploits Abound," Coveware, April 26, 2021, https://www.coveware.com/blog/ransomware-attack-vect ors-shift-as-new-software-vulnerability-exploits-abound.

72   "Les autorités européennes démantèlent DarkMarket, un important site de vente en ligne du marché noir," *Le Monde.fr*, January 12, 2021, https://www.lemonde.fr/pixels/arti cle/2021/01/12/les-autorites-europeennes-demantelent-darkmarket-un-important-site -de-vente-en-ligne-du-marche-noir_6065989_4408996.html.

73   "NotPetya Technical Analysis," LogRhythm, June 30, 2017, https://logrhythm.com/blog /notpetya-technical-analysis/.

74   "Emotet Malware," CISA, January 23, 2020, https://www.cisa.gov/news-events/alerts/2018 /07/20/emotet-malware.

authorities, under the coordination of Europol, alongside authorities from the Netherlands, the United States, the United Kingdom, France, Lithuania, Canada, and Ukraine, conducted an operation as part of the European Multidisciplinary Platform Against Criminal Threats (EMPACT) to shut down Emotet's command and control server, which had infected over 1.6 million computers worldwide.[75]

Due to the clandestine and rapidly changing nature of cybercrime, it is important to note that the activities[76] of cybercriminal groups evolve swiftly, and providing precise and up-to-date information on each group can be challenging. Here are a few examples of global cybercriminal groups:

- *Wizard Spider (REvil/Sodinokibi)*—This group is responsible for the REvil ransomware, also known as Sodinokibi. In 2020 and 2021, the group targeted large companies and organizations worldwide with sophisticated ransomware attacks. They were involved in ransomware operations against companies such as Acer, JBS (a major meat company), and Kaseya, where their attack had a global impact.
- *Lazarus Group*—Backed by the North Korean state, the Lazarus Group is known for data theft, espionage, and financial attacks. They have been involved in notorious attacks, including the hacking of Sony Pictures in 2014 and stealing funds from online banks.
- *FIN7 (Carbanak)*—This criminal group is associated with attacks against financial institutions and businesses globally. They are involved in stealing financial data and credit cards. FIN7 is known for its technical sophistication and ability to target the financial and retail sectors.
- *APT29 (Cozy Bear)*—A cyberespionage group attributed to Russia, APT29 is known for hacking governments and strategic organizations. They have been involved in espionage and political interference campaigns, including election-related attacks.
- *DarkTequila*—This cybercriminal group primarily targets users in Latin America, stealing financial and identification information. In 2020, they were linked to phishing campaigns and system infections via malicious USB drives.

---

75   "World's Most Dangerous Malware EMOTET Disrupted through Global Action," Europol, January 27, 2021, https://www.europol.europa.eu/media-press/newsroom/news/world%e2%80%99s-most-dangerous-malware-emotet-disrupted-through-global-action.

76   Marshall Heilman, "Mandiant and CrowdStrike Join Forces in the Fight Against Evil," Mandiant, April 6, 2023, https://www.mandiant.com/resources/blog/mandiant-crowdstrike-join-forces.

- *Maze Group*—Maze is a notorious ransomware group known for the practice of disclosing stolen data if victims refuse to pay the ransom. In November 2020, the group announced the end of its operations, but other similar ransomware groups have emerged to fill the void.
- *TA505*—This group is involved in massive phishing and malware distribution campaigns, including the Dridex banking Trojan and the Locky ransomware. They have targeted businesses and financial institutions worldwide.

7.5.3 Consequences of the Underground Digital Economy and Cybercrime

The consequences of the underground digital economy and cybercrime are profound, impacting not only businesses and governments but also individuals worldwide. However, significant efforts are being made to combat these growing threats and mitigate their impacts.

According to cybersecurity reports from Accenture in 2021 and IBM,[77] in 2023, the direct and indirect costs of cyberattacks have increased significantly. In 2023, the average direct costs of a data breach were approximately $4.45 million, while indirect costs, such as revenue losses, averaged $1.76 million. Furthermore, the report states that 68% of organizations reported an increase in costs related to data breaches over the past five years.

7.6 International Efforts to Combat the Underground Digital Economy and Cybercrime

Governments and international organizations are actively collaborating to combat the underground digital economy and cybercrime. The United Nations (UN) has established the United Nations Office on Drugs and Crime (UNODC) to coordinate global efforts to combat cybercrime.[78] In 2021, Europol coordinated "Operation EMMA 95," leading to the dismantling of one of the largest networks selling stolen data on the darknet, involving more than 40 countries.[79]

---

77 "Cost of a Data Breach Report 2023".
78 "Comprehensive Study on Cybercrime," UNODC, accessed March 31, 2024, //www.unodc .org/unodc/en/organized-crime/comprehensive-study-on-cybercrime.html.
79 "IOCTA 2021: Internet Organised Crime Threat Assessment 2021" (LU: EUROPOL, 2021), https://www.europol.europa.eu/cms/sites/default/files/documents/internet_organised _crime_threat_assessment_iocta_2021.pdf.

7.6.1 The Role of Businesses and Public Awareness in Combating Cybercrime

Businesses also play a crucial role in the fight against cybercrime. According to a Deloitte[80] study, 75% of businesses are increasing their cybersecurity spending to address growing threats. Investments in advanced security technologies, employee training for security awareness, and the implementation of incident response protocols are measures taken to mitigate risks.

Public awareness is another essential element in the fight against cybercrime. According to a Pew Research Center[81] survey, 64% of US adults reported experiencing some form of online identity theft. Public awareness and education campaigns, promoting good cybersecurity practices such as using strong passwords, verifying online sources, and regularly updating software, contribute to strengthening resilience against online attacks.

The underground digital economy and cybercrime have significant consequences globally. Financial costs, data losses, and impacts on online trust are challenges faced by individuals and organizations. However, concerted efforts from governments, businesses, and the general public to combat these threats show signs of effectiveness. International cooperation, investments in cybersecurity, and ongoing awareness are key elements in mitigating these risks and protecting the digital world.

7.7 Digital as an Amplifying Factor in the Economy of War

7.7.1 Digital Transformation and Military Competitiveness

The integration of digital technology into military operations can provide advantages in terms of speed, precision, and coordination. Real-time collection and analysis of data through advanced sensors and surveillance systems, for instance, can help anticipate enemy movements and make more informed decisions. The use of digital technologies in the armed forces can increase operational efficiency in certain areas.[82] For example, the utilization of

---

80 "2021 Future of Cyber Survey," Deloitte, 2021, https://www.deloitte.com/global/en/servi ces/risk-advisory/analysis/future-of-cyber.html.
81 Richard Wike et al., "Social Media Seen as Mostly Good for Democracy Across Many Nations, But U.S. Is a Major Outlier," *Pew Research Center's Global Attitudes Project* (blog), December 6, 2022, https://www.pewresearch.org/global/2022/12/06/social-media-seen -as-mostly-good-for-democracy-across-many-nations-but-u-s-is-a-major-outlier/.
82 P Binuraj, "Digitalisation of Armed Forces," DEFSTRAT, 2020, https://www.defstrat.com /magazine_articles/digitalisation-of-armed-forces/.

surveillance drones equipped with advanced cameras enables the military to gather real-time intelligence in challenging-to-reach areas,[83] facilitating more targeted and responsive operations. This, in turn, reduces risks for personnel and improves the accuracy of data.

Moreover, the implementation of advanced satellite communication systems ensures reliable connectivity in remote environments, facilitating the coordination of operations and the sharing of crucial information.[84]

In terms of logistics, the use of the Internet of Things (IoT) allows armies to monitor troop and equipment movements in real time, optimizing resource management and reducing costs.[85]

Finally, AI-based combat simulation provides realistic and cost-effective training for soldiers, enhancing their skills and readiness for real-life situations.[86]

7.7.2 Technological Innovation and Military Complexity

The digital realm has profoundly influenced technological innovation in the military domain, triggering a series of sophisticated developments that have significantly enhanced the capabilities of armed forces to anticipate and address increasingly complex threats. Among these major technological advances, artificial intelligence (AI) holds a central position. AI systems are now used to analyze vast amounts of intelligence data, allowing for a better understanding of emerging trends and threats while improving the accuracy of strategic forecasts. Additionally, advanced cyber defense has become essential in an increasingly interconnected world. Digital technologies have enabled the creation of sophisticated intrusion detection systems and advanced security protocols to protect military networks against cyber-attacks. Furthermore, the evolution of digital technologies has also given rise to autonomous weapons, sparking ethical and legal debates. However, these systems offer

---

83   Tarek Rakha and Alice Gorodetsky, "Review of Unmanned Aerial System (UAS) Applications in the Built Environment: Towards Automated Building Inspection Procedures Using Drones," *Automation in Construction* 93 (September 1, 2018): 252–64, https://doi.org/10.1016/j.autcon.2018.05.002.

84   Gerard Maral, Michel Bousquet, and Zhili Sun, *Satellite Communications Systems: Systems, Techniques and Technology* (John Wiley & Sons, 2020).

85   Vlada Sokolovic and Goran Markovic, "Internet of Things in Military Applications," *Vojnotehnicki Glasnik* 71 (January 1, 2023): 1148–71, https://doi.org/10.5937/vojtehg71-46785.

86   L. Campbell et al., "The Use of Artificial Intelligence in Military Simulations," in *Computational Cybernetics and Simulation 1997 IEEE International Conference on Systems, Man, and Cybernetics*, vol. 3, 1997, 2607–12 vol.3, https://doi.org/10.1109/ICSMC.1997.635328.

the opportunity to react quickly and effectively to real-time threats without exposing military personnel to imminent danger. According to the Stockholm International Peace Research Institute (SIPRI),[87] in 2022, global defense spending amounted to over $2 trillion (with $800 billion for the United States). Among these expenditures, those related to research and development have seen a significant increase, largely due to digital technologies, reflecting the major impact of these advancements on military strategy and global security. For the United States, R&D increased by 24% over the 2012–2021 period.

The current conflict between Russia and Ukraine is a perfect example of the use of digital technology by civilians and the military to gain an advantage on the battlefield.

In 2022, Ukrainians turned to SpaceX CEO Elon Musk to receive terminals from the Starlink satellite internet service, thwarting the Russian strategy to disable Ukrainian communications.[88] Other business leaders and donors distributed funds to Ukraine to purchase Starlink terminals, and the number now reaches 20,000 in the country.[89]

Among the initiatives taken by the young Ukrainian parliament at the beginning of the Russian offensive on February 24, 2022, was the repeal of a law preventing the government from storing its data in a dematerialized database. They decided to move all their data from government servers to the cloud to ensure the resilience of their information without fearing the destruction of data centers on their territory.

The Diia application, meaning "action" in French, serves as a one-stop-shop for Ukrainians. The mobile application, initially launched to combat the pandemic, later served the military during the invasion in February 2021. Today, no less than 17 million Ukrainians are registered on this application, where data is collected and used for various purposes.

Ukrainian Deputy Prime Minister Mykhailo Fedorov explains, "You can report where the enemy is using the Diia application," adding that "a chatbot, based on geolocation, has been created to help citizens know the location of enemy troops." Coupled with satellite images and reports from the population,

---

87 "SIPRI Yearbook 2022 | SIPRI," accessed March 31, 2024, https://www.sipri.org/yearbook/2022.

88 "Ukraine Seeking Action to Stop Russian Use of Starlink, Minister Says | Reuters," Reuters, February 20, 2024, https://www.reuters.com/world/europe/ukraine-seeking-action-stop-russian-use-starlink-minister-says-2024-02-19/.

89 "Mykhaïlo Fedorov, ministre ukrainien de la Tech : 'C'est la guerre du passé contre le futur,'" L'Express, August 21, 2022, https://www.lexpress.fr/economie/high-tech/mykhailo-fedorov-ministre-ukrainien-de-la-tech-c-est-la-guerre-du-passe-contre-le-futur_2178430.html.

it notifies the Ukrainian military of the presence of the Russian army, as well as the bodies of soldiers. The leader specifies that artificial intelligence is also used to identify these bodies and find their presence on social networks. Thus, they can report it to the families.

Moreover, Diia offers people in combat zones access to the online payment system to receive aid from the state without the need to travel on the territory. A refund and virtual credit card service has been set up to receive this assistance. Ukrainian citizens can declare the destruction of their homes by taking multiple photos and sending them to the application's service to receive specific aid.

Thanks to the eEnemy (eVorog) feature launched within two days on the Diia application, civilians send thousands of photos of enemy troops and positions to analysts responsible for transmitting them to military intelligence. In response, the Russians began to shoot down 3G and 4G antennas. The result is catastrophic.

This will also affect the Russians because their supposedly inviolable encrypted ERA phones are unable to function. Russian soldiers begin to steal Ukrainian SIM cards, revealing their positions, and movements, and allowing jamming and interception of their communications. This leads to regrettable consequences: the assassination of generals, and the destruction of ammunition depots, and barracks (Wagner in Luhansk).

But the real reason for the Ukrainian success is the formidable efficiency of artillery. Faced with the 50,000 Russian shells raining down on their country every day, the Ukrainians have modern cannons, Howitzers M-177, Himars, Caesar cannons ... which would be of limited effect if they were not integrated into the Kill Chain of a future warfare laboratory.

Networked warfare functions like a feedback loop; it all starts with the 300 satellites directed at Ukraine, synthetic aperture radars that pierce through clouds, commercial remote sensing (CRS) satellites, and others; the images, of unprecedented resolution, are sent in real-time to supercomputers which, through differential analysis, compare them to the most recent shots to identify troop or equipment movements and shots, artillery, cruise missiles ... (with thermal imaging software). The hypotheses, verified by humans, are superimposed on the digital model of the battlefield, and transmitted to military intelligence with target recommendations; these are immediately entered into artillery piece selection software such as GIS Arta, and in record time, the shot is fired. The outcome is immediately observed by the satellite and then relayed for machine-learning data processing by the same supercomputers that learn through experience. The fusion of satellite intelligence, big data, and artificial intelligence is the true secret behind this warfare.

7.7.3 Economic Impact and Controversies

The Integration of digital technology into the war economy can have complex economic consequences. On the one hand, it can stimulate the technological sector and create jobs in the defense and cybersecurity industries. However, it can also lead to massive spending on research and development, potentially reducing resources available for other economic sectors and having environmental consequences.

In the defense sector, the evolution of global threats such as the conflict in Ukraine has increased pressure to accelerate defense acquisitions.[90] In 2015, the United States Department of Defense (DoD) established a division called the Defense Innovation Unit (DIU), utilizing advances in commercial technology to help the military deploy cutting-edge defense systems more rapidly, without the constraints of traditional procurement systems.[91]

For example, in 2022, the DIU transformed 17 commercial prototypes into fully operational military capabilities, marking an increase of over 50% from the previous year.[92] One of the prototypes' awaiting launch is GigEagle, a platform that uses machine learning to identify experts within the US National Guard and Army Reserve for specific missions. The algorithm searches for hidden skills that may not necessarily be part of someone's military specialty but are highly relevant to evolving military needs. This could include an infantryman who is also a freelance developer for a major tech company or a doctor who is a champion-level esports player, capable of quickly learning to operate drones.

To compete in this new world, defense sector companies are looking to shift their spending and accelerate investments in research and development. In fact, 59% of engineering executives in the sector expect budgets to increase over the next three years as they ramp up production. In January 2023, Boeing, for example, announced the hiring of an additional 10,000 workers, and Airbus stated plans to add over 13,000 workers in 2023 to increase production.[93]

---

90 Pieter D Wezeman, Justine Gadon, and Siemon T Wezeman, "Trends in International Arms Transfers, 2022," March 2023, https://www.sipri.org/sites/default/files/2023-03/2303_at_fact_sheet_2022_v2.pdf.
91 "DIU Making Transformative Impact Five Years In," U.S. Department of Defense, accessed March 31, 2024, https://www.defense.gov/News/News-Stories/Article/Article/2327021/diu-making-transformative-impact-five-years-in/.
92 "Annual Report FY 2022" (Defense Innovation Unit (DIU), 2022), https://downloads.ctfassets.net/3nanhbfkropc/5guJIhcMGwIgoop4z9r5QM/a724a6935a7e5a8d516cc58328e47796/DIU_Annual_Report_FY22_FINAL.pdf.
93 Bruno Trévidic, "Airbus prévoit encore plus de 13.000 recrutements en 2023," Les Echos, January 26, 2023, https://www.lesechos.fr/industrie-services/air-defense/airbus-prevoit-encore-plus-de-13000-recrutements-en-2023-1900947.

Leading companies like these are investing in digital initiatives, modularity, and sustainability across the entire value chain.

In the case of the Russo-Ukrainian conflict, the example of cryptocurrency is interesting on several levels: the economy, technology, and diplomacy. While Western governments and NATO categorically opposed military intervention against Russia, they swiftly applied draconian sanctions against the Kremlin, as well as against President Putin and his inner circle, including Russian banks and oligarchs. Similarly, individuals and businesses rallied to support Ukraine. Major industry players, including international law firms, withdrew from the Russian market, while people worldwide mobilized to donate millions of euros directly to the Ukrainian army, government, and displaced Ukrainians. Cryptocurrencies unexpectedly played a central role in the war in Ukraine, with Ukraine receiving millions in cryptocurrency donations.

Ukraine is no stranger to cryptocurrency, ranking first in the world in terms of cryptocurrency adoption, with over 12.7% of its population owning it.[94] On March 16, 2022, President Volodymyr Zelensky approved a bill officially legalizing cryptocurrencies in Ukraine.[95] From the outset of the war, Ukraine quickly leveraged the speed and decentralized nature of crypto by using it to raise funds. These efforts took two main forms: the sale of NFTs[96] and direct donations in cryptocurrencies. According to Alex Bornyakov, Ukraine's Deputy Minister of Digital Transformation, Ukraine's cryptocurrency wallets received nearly $100 million in donations after one month of conflict.[97] The Economist reports that by early March, Ukraine had already spent more than half of its crypto donations on purchasing military equipment and medical aid, with about one-fifth of the funds collected spent in crypto directly.[98]

---

[94] Aija Lejniece, "La crypto est au centre de la guerre de la Russie contre l'Ukraine," https://geopolitique.eu/, 2023, https://geopolitique.eu/articles/la-crypto-est-au-centre-de-la-guerre-de-la-russie-contre-lukraine/.

[95] David Walsh, "Ukraine Officially Legalises Crypto after Zelenskyy Signs New Law," euronews, March 17, 2022, https://www.euronews.com/next/2022/03/17/ukraine-war-zelenskyy-signs-a-new-law-officially-legalising-bitcoin-and-other-cryptos.

[96] An NFT is a unique digital identifier that cannot be copied, substituted, or subdivided, recorded on a blockchain and used to certify the authenticity and ownership (such as of a specific digital asset and the specific rights associated with it).

[97] Amitoj Singh, "Ukraine Has Received Close to $100M in Crypto Donations," March 10, 2022, https://www.coindesk.com/business/2022/03/09/ukraine-has-received-close-to-100-million-in-crypto-donations/.

[98] "How Is Ukraine Using Crypto to Fund the War?," *The Economist*, accessed March 31, 2024, https://www.economist.com/the-economist-explains/2022/04/05/how-is-ukraine-using-crypto-to-fund-the-war.

The EU has explicitly confirmed that sanctions against Russia include cryptocurrencies.[99] However, in an attempt to circumvent international sanctions, Russia launched the trial phase of a digital ruble on August 15, 2023, leveraging blockchain technology, hoping to limit the long-term impact of international sanctions following the outbreak of the war in Ukraine.[100]

The true utility of cryptocurrencies in the fight against sanctions can be found among ordinary Russian citizens who have been deprived of certain services. Take a mundane example: Instagram is no longer accessible to Russian IP addresses; this issue can be circumvented by using a VPN to shift the user's actual IP address outside of Russia. Even if Russian credit cards or other payment methods no longer work for paying foreign services, a VPN subscription can be purchased with cryptocurrency. Therefore, payments to and from non-sanctioned Russian citizens and entities, which would have been impossible due to current banking restrictions and commercial service withdrawals, can still be possible via cryptocurrency.

Despite undeniable advantages in terms of economic development, the digital realm unfortunately has an impact on the environment, particularly the planet's natural resources. According to figures established by a GreenIT study published in October 2019[101] billion smartphones, computers, game consoles, and TVs worldwide play a central role in environmental impact. According to the same study, it takes 80 times more energy to produce a gram of a smartphone than a gram of a car.

However, it is not their usage that has the most consequences for the environment; 90% of the energy consumed by a smartphone is generated during its manufacturing. The construction of information technology tools impacts the quantity of available natural resources, and these primary resources do not replenish as fast as we consume them. Every year, the Global Footprint Network, in partnership with WWF, calculates the "overshoot day," the date from which we have consumed all the resources that the Earth can produce

---

99 "Council Regulation (EU) 2022/394 of 9 March 2022 Amending Regulation (EU) No 833/2014 Concerning Restrictive Measures in View of Russia's Actions Destabilising the Situation in Ukraine," 081 OJ L § (2022), http://data.europa.eu/eli/reg/2022/394/oj/eng.

100 "La Russie lance un rouble numérique, espérant contourner les sanctions internationales," Le Monde.fr, August 15, 2023, https://www.lemonde.fr/international/article/2023/08/15/la-russie-lance-un-rouble-numerique-esperant-contourner-les-sanctions-internationales_6185479_3210.html.

101 "Empreinte Environnementale Du Numérique Mondial," GreenIT, 2019, https://www.greenit.fr/etude-empreinte-environnementale-du-numerique-mondial/.

in a year.¹⁰² Their study shows that it would take 1.7 Earths to meet humanity's needs.

The digital sector demands a significant amount of energy to operate, being a major consumer of non-renewable natural resources. If the Internet were a country, it would be the world's third-largest electricity consumer after China and the United States. Between 7% and 10% of the world's electricity would be consumed by the Internet alone. Moreover, 35% of digital greenhouse gas emissions will be due to the manufacturing of user terminals in 2025. The energy intensity of the digital industry increases by an average of 4% per year.¹⁰³

If we take the example of data centers, they consume an average of 5.15 MWh/m2/year in France. In summary, a 10,000 m2 data center consumes on average as much as a city of 50,000 inhabitants, and 40% of this electrical consumption is used solely for cooling.¹⁰⁴

However, our society is increasingly centered around data (90% of data was produced between 2015 and 2017), and its accumulation is continually increasing. It's worth noting that humanity has never generated as much data: every two days, the world's population produces as much information as it generated from the dawn of its existence until 2003.¹⁰⁵

7.8   Conclusion

While digital technology amplifies the economy of violence and warfare, its development is inevitable for future economic growth. It provides increased operational efficiency for businesses through automation and process optimization. Furthermore, it opens new horizons by enabling global market access through the Internet and stimulates innovation by fostering technological research and development. The creation of jobs in the digital sector and the growing need for digital skills also reinforce its significance. At the

---

102   "About Earth Overshoot Day," *Earth Overshoot Day* (blog), accessed March 31, 2024, https://overshoot.footprintnetwork.org/about-earth-overshoot-day/.
103   www.ETEnergyworld.com, "Energy Intensity of Global ICT Sector Expanding at 4 per Cent Annually," ETEnergyworld.com, accessed March 31, 2024, https://energy.economicti mes.indiatimes.com/news/power/energy-intensity-of-global-ict-sector-expanding-at-4 -per-cent-annually-study/68284500.
104   "L'efficacite Energetique Dans Les Data Centers" (ATEE, November 2016), https://www .actu-environnement.com/media/pdf/news-27968-data-center-atee.pdf.
105   "L'incroyable impact de la pollution numérique et les bonnes pratiques à adopter très vite !," June 24, 2022, https://www.grizzlead.com/lincroyable-impact-de-la-pollut ion-numerique-et-les-bonnes-pratiques-a-adopter-tres-vite/.

national and even international levels, digital technology serves as an engine for innovation and economic growth, especially in advanced sectors. Digital public services simplify government-citizen interactions, and investments in digital infrastructure promote connectivity. In summary, digital technology is an indispensable component of the modern economy, propelling competitiveness, sustainability, and prosperity on a national and international scale. Its intelligent integration is essential for shaping a flourishing economic future.

Bibliography

Acquisti, Alessandro, and Christina, Fong. "An Experiment in Hiring Discrimination via Online Social Networks." *Management Science* 66, no. 3 (March 2020): 1005–24. https://doi.org/10.1287/mnsc.2018.3269.

Aija, Lejniece. "La crypto est au centre de la guerre de la Russie contre l'Ukraine." https://geopolitique.eu/, 2023. https://geopolitique.eu/articles/la-crypto-est-au-centre-de-la-guerre-de-la-russie-contre-lukraine/.

Amie, Gordon. "'Bubbly and Fun-Loving' Schoolgirl, 16, Hanged Herself after She Was Bullied on Social Media." Daily Mail Online, July 11, 2018. https://www.dailymail.co.uk/news/article-5941297/Bubbly-fun-loving-schoolgirl-16-hanged-bullied-social-media.html.

Amitoj, Singh. "Ukraine Has Received Close to $100M in Crypto Donations," March 10, 2022. https://www.coindesk.com/business/2022/03/09/ukraine-has-received-close-to-100-million-in-crypto-donations/.

Angwin, Julia, Ariana, Tobin, and Madeleine, Varner. "Facebook (Still) Letting Housing Advertisers Exclude Users by Race." ProPublica, November 21, 2017. https://www.propublica.org/article/facebook-advertising-discrimination-housing-race-sex-national-origin.

Angwin, Julia, Noam, Scheiber, and Ariana, Tobin. "Facebook Job Ads Raise Concerns About Age Discrimination." *The New York Times*, December 20, 2017, sec. Business. https://www.nytimes.com/2017/12/20/business/facebook-job-ads.html.

"Annual Report FY 2022." Defense Innovation Unit (DIU), 2022. https://downloads.ctfassets.net/3nanhbfkr0pc/5guJIhcMGwIg0op4z9r5QM/a724a6935a7e5a8d516cc58328e47796/DIU_Annual_Report_FY22_FINAL.pdf.

Apollo Technical LLC. "Surprising Working From Home Productivity Statistics," February 7, 2024. https://www.apollotechnical.com/working-from-home-productivity-statistics/.

Banque, de France. "Rapport annuel de l'Observatoire de la sécurité des moyens de paiement 2018," July 9, 2019. https://publications.banque-france.fr/rapport-annuel-de-lobservatoire-de-la-securite-des-moyens-de-paiement-2018.

BBC News. "Tax Havens: Super-Rich 'hiding' at Least $21tn." July 22, 2012, sec. Business. https://www.bbc.com/news/business-18944097.

Berrada, Badr. "The Dark Side of High Frequency Trading," June 18, 2017. https://www.bbntimes.com/financial/the-dark-side-of-high-frequency-trading.

Binuraj, P. "Digitalisation of Armed Forces." DEFSTRAT, 2020. https://www.defstrat.com/magazine_articles/digitalisation-of-armed-forces/.

Bogen, Miranda. "All the Ways Hiring Algorithms Can Introduce Bias." *Harvard Business Review*, May 6, 2019. https://hbr.org/2019/05/all-the-ways-hiring-algorithms-can-introduce-bias.

Bowcott, Owen, and Spencer, Ackerman. "Mass Internet Surveillance Threatens International Law, UN Report Claims." *The Guardian*, October 15, 2014, sec. World news. https://www.theguardian.com/world/2014/oct/15/internet-surveillance-report-edward-snowden-leaks.

Brie, Weiler Reynolds. "FlexJobs, Mental Health America Survey: Mental Health in the Workplace." FlexJobs Job Search Tips and Blog, August 21, 2020. https://www.flexjobs.com/blog/post/flexjobs-mha-mental-health-workplace-pandemic/.

Bruno, Trévidic. "Airbus prévoit encore plus de 13.000 recrutements en 2023." Les Echos, January 26, 2023. https://www.lesechos.fr/industrie-services/air-defense/airbus-prevoit-encore-plus-de-13000-recrutements-en-2023-1900947.

Campbell, L., A. Lotmin, M.M.G. DeRico, and C. Ray. "The Use of Artificial Intelligence in Military Simulations." In *Computational Cybernetics and Simulation 1997 IEEE International Conference on Systems, Man, and Cybernetics*, 3:2607–12 vol.3, 1997. https://doi.org/10.1109/ICSMC.1997.635328.

"Caroline Flack Inquest: 'No Doubt' Presenter Intended to Take Own Life." August 6, 2020. https://www.bbc.com/news/uk-england-london-53676793.

Chainalysis. "Geographic Distinctions in Crypto Darknet Market Activity," February 1, 2021. https://www.chainalysis.com/blog/crypto-darknet-markets-2021-geographic-breakdown/.

"China's Algorithms of Repression." *Human Rights Watch*, May 1, 2019. https://www.hrw.org/report/2019/05/01/chinas-algorithms-repression/reverse-engineering-xinjiang-police-mass.

CISA. "Emotet Malware," January 23, 2020. https://www.cisa.gov/news-events/alerts/2018/07/20/emotet-malware.

Council Regulation (EU) 2022/394 of 9 March 2022 amending Regulation (EU) No 833/2014 concerning restrictive measures in view of Russia's actions destabilising the situation in Ukraine, 081 OJ L § (2022). http://data.europa.eu/eli/reg/2022/394/oj/eng.

Coveware. "Ransomware Attack Vectors Shift as New Software Vulnerability Exploits Abound," April 26, 2021. https://www.coveware.com/blog/ransomware–attack–vectors–shift–as–new–software–vulnerability–exploits–abound.

Cox, Jeff. "Raising Minimum Wage to $15 Would Cost 1.4 Million Jobs, CBO Says." CNBC, February 8, 2021. https://www.cnbc.com/2021/02/08/raising-minimum-wage-to-15-would-cost-1point4-million-jobs-cbo-says.html.

Cybernews. "COMB: Largest Breach of All Time Leaked Online with 3.2 Billion Records," February 12, 2021. https://cybernews.com/news/largest-compilation-of-emails-and-passwords-leaked-free/.

Datta, Amit, Michael Carl, Tschantz, and Anupam, Datta. "Automated Experiments on Ad Privacy Settings: A Tale of Opacity, Choice, and Discrimination." arXiv, March 16, 2015. https://doi.org/10.48550/arXiv.1408.6491.

David, Walsh. "Ukraine Officially Legalises Crypto after Zelenskyy Signs New Law." euronews, March 17, 2022. https://www.euronews.com/next/2022/03/17/ukraine-war-zelenskyy-signs-a-new-law-officially-legalising-bitcoin-and-other-cryptos.

Davies, Dan. "How to Get Away with Financial Fraud." *The Guardian*, June 28, 2018, sec. News. https://www.theguardian.com/news/2018/jun/28/how-to-get-away-with-financial-fraud.

Deloitte. "2021 Future of Cyber Survey," 2021. https://www.deloitte.com/global/en/services/risk-advisory/analysis/future-of-cyber.html.

Earth Overshoot Day. "About Earth Overshoot Day." Accessed March 31, 2024. https://overshoot.footprintnetwork.org/about-earth-overshoot-day/.

European Commission. "Commission Welcomes Political Agreement on Improving Working Conditions in Platform Work." Text, December 13, 2023. https://ec.europa.eu/commission/presscorner/detail/en/ip_23_6586.

European Commission—European Commission. "Commission fines Google €2.42 billion for abusing dominance as search engine by giving illegal advantage to own comparison shopping service—Factsheet." Text, 2017. https://ec.europa.eu/commission/presscorner/detail/es/MEMO_17_1785.

European Union Agency for Fundamental Rights. "Fundamental Rights Report 2021," June 1, 2021. http://fra.europa.eu/en/publication/2021/fundamental-rights-report-2021.

Europol. "World's Most Dangerous Malware EMOTET Disrupted through Global Action," January 27, 2021. https://www.europol.europa.eu/media-press/newsroom/news/world%e2%80%99s-most-dangerous-malware-emotet-disrupted-through-global-action.

Finn, Allen. "Big Changes to Facebook Custom Audiences: What You Need to Know." *WordStream* (blog), November 1, 2022. https://www.wordstream.com/blog/ws/2018/04/23/facebook-custom-audience-changes.

Gallup. "Employees Want a Lot More From Their Managers." Gallup.com, April 8, 2015. https://www.gallup.com/workplace/236570/employees-lot-managers.aspx.

Galtung, Johan. "Violence, Peace, and Peace Research." *Journal of Peace Research* 6, no. 3 (September 1, 1969): 167–91. https://doi.org/10.1177/002234336900600301.

Garside, Juliette, Holly, Watt, and David, Pegg. "The Panama Papers: How the World's Rich and Famous Hide Their Money Offshore." *The Guardian*, April 3, 2016, sec. News. https://www.theguardian.com/news/2016/apr/03/the-panama-papers-how-the-worlds-rich-and-famous-hide-their-money-offshore.

Gartner. "The Future Of Employee Monitoring," May 3, 2019. https://www.gartner.com/smarterwithgartner/the-future-of-employee-monitoring.

Ghosh, Dipayan, and Ben, Scott. "Digital Deceit: The Technologies behind Precision Propaganda on the Internet." Report. New America, January 23, 2018. https://apo.org.au/node/130646.

GreenIT. "Empreinte Environnementale Du Numérique Mondial," 2019. https://www.greenit.fr/etude-empreinte-environnementale-du-numerique-mondial/.

Hawkins, Andrew J. "Uber and Lyft Face an Existential Threat in California—and They're Losing." The Verge, September 2, 2019. https://www.theverge.com/2019/9/2/20841070/uber-lyft-ab5-california-bill-drivers-labor.

"Health Plan Provisions for Private Industry Workers in the United States, 2020 : U.S. Bureau of Labor Statistics." Accessed March 31, 2024. https://www.bls.gov/ebs/publications/health-care-plan-provisions-for-private-industry-2020.htm.

Horak, Sven, Fida Afiouni, Yanjie Bian, Alena Ledeneva, Maral Muratbekova-Touron, and Carl F. Fey. "Informal Networks: Dark Sides, Bright Sides, and Unexplored Dimensions." *Management and Organization Review* 16, no. 3 (July 2020): 511–42. https://doi.org/10.1017/mor.2020.28.

IBM. "Cost of a Data Breach Report 2023," 2023. https://www.ibm.com/reports/data-breach.

Inside Apple's iPhone Factory In China, 2021. https://www.youtube.com/watch?v=9XkX6EGk_CA.

"Internet Organised Crime Threat Assessment (IOCTA) 2019." Europol, 2019. https://www.europol.europa.eu/sites/default/files/documents/iocta_2019.pdf.

"IOCTA 2021: Internet Organised Crime Threat Assessment 2021." LU: EUROPOL, 2021. https://www.europol.europa.eu/cms/sites/default/files/documents/internet_organised_crime_threat_assessment_iocta_2021.pdf.

Le Monde Informatique. "Après Prism, la NSA espionne un peu plus avec XKeyscore," August 1, 2013. https://www.lemondeinformatique.fr/actualites/lire-apres-prism-la-nsa-espionne-un-peu-plus-avec-xkeyscore-54589.html.

Le Monde.fr. "La Russie lance un rouble numérique, espérant contourner les sanctions internationales." August 15, 2023. https://www.lemonde.fr/international/article/2023/08/15/la-russie-lance-un-rouble-numerique-esperant-contourner-les-sanctions-internationales_6185479_3210.html.

Le Monde.fr. "Les autorités européennes démantèlent DarkMarket, un important site de vente en ligne du marché noir." January 12, 2021. https://www.lemonde.fr/pixels/article/2021/01/12/les-autorites-europeennes-demantelent-darkmarket-un-important-site-de-vente-en-ligne-du-marche-noir_6065989_4408996.html.

"l'efficacite energetique dans les data centers." ATEE, November 2016. https://www.actu-environnement.com/media/pdf/news-27968-data-center-atee.pdf.

"Les Effets, Enjeux et Réglementations Du Trading Haute Fréquence." Accessed March 31, 2024. https://www.alumneye.fr/les-effets-enjeux-et-reglementations-du-trading-haute-frequence/.

L'Express. "Mykhaïlo Fedorov, ministre ukrainien de la Tech : 'C'est la guerre du passé contre le futur,'" August 21, 2022. https://www.lexpress.fr/economie/high-tech/mykhailo-fedorov-ministre-ukrainien-de-la-tech-c-est-la-guerre-du-passe-contre-le-futur_2178430.html.

Liggett, Roberta, Jin R. Lee, Ariel L. Roddy, and Mikaela A. Wallin. "The Dark Web as a Platform for Crime: An Exploration of Illicit Drug, Firearm, CSAM, and Cybercrime Markets." In *The Palgrave Handbook of International Cybercrime and Cyberdeviance*, edited by Thomas J. Holt and Adam M. Bossler, 91–116. Cham: Springer International Publishing, 2020. https://doi.org/10.1007/978-3-319-78440-3_17.

"L'incroyable impact de la pollution numérique et les bonnes pratiques à adopter très vite !," June 24, 2022. https://www.grizzlead.com/lincroyable-impact-de-la-pollution-numerique-et-les-bonnes-pratiques-a-adopter-tres-vite/.

LogRhythm. "NotPetya Technical Analysis," June 30, 2017. https://logrhythm.com/blog/notpetya-technical-analysis/.

Luxton, David D., Jennifer D. June, and Jonathan M. Fairall. "Social Media and Suicide: A Public Health Perspective." *American Journal of Public Health* 102, no. Suppl 2 (May 2012): S195–200. https://doi.org/10.2105/AJPH.2011.300608.

Maral, Gerard, Michel, Bousquet, and Zhili Sun. *Satellite Communications Systems: Systems, Techniques and Technology*. John Wiley & Sons, 2020.

Marshall, Heilman. "Mandiant and CrowdStrike Join Forces in the Fight Against Evil." Mandiant, April 6, 2023. https://www.mandiant.com/resources/blog/mandiant-crowdstrike-join-forces.

Martin, David, Jacki, O'neill, Neha, Gupta, and Benjamin, Hanrahan. "Turking in a Global Labour Market." *Computer Supported Cooperative Work (CSCW)* 25 (February 1, 2016). https://doi.org/10.1007/s10606-015-9241-6.

Martin, Kirsten. *Ethics of Data and Analytics: Concepts and Cases*. New York: Auerbach Publications, 2022. https://doi.org/10.1201/9781003278290.

McAfee Blog. "McAfee Labs 2020 Threats Predictions Report," December 5, 2019. https://www.mcafee.com/blogs/other-blogs/mcafee-labs/mcafee-labs-2020-threats-predictions-report/.

McAfee Blog. "The Exactis Data Breach: What Consumers Need to Know," June 28, 2018. https://www.mcafee.com/blogs/privacy-identity-protection/exactis-data-breach/.

Mike McGuire. "The Web of Profit: A Look at the Cybercrime Economy." *VentureBeat* (blog), April 21, 2018. https://venturebeat.com/security/the-web-of-profit-a-look-at-the-cybercrime-economy/.

Montgomery, Tom, and Simone, Baglioni. "Defining the Gig Economy: Platform Capitalism and the Reinvention of Precarious Work." *International Journal of Sociology and Social Policy* 41, no. 9/10 (January 1, 2020): 1012–25. https://doi.org/10.1108/IJSSP-08-2020-0400.

Nisar Law Group, P.C. "'Shell Companies' In Real Estate Transactions," March 17, 2015. https://www.nisarlaw.com/blog/2015/march/understanding-the-use-of-shell-companies-in-real/.

Oxfam. "Power, Profits and the Pandemic: From Corporate Extraction for the Few to an Economy That Works for All," 2020. https://policy-practice.oxfam.org/resources/power-profits-and-the-pandemic-from-corporate-extraction-for-the-few-to-an-econ-621044/.

Paulius, Ilevičius. "Why Is Employee Surveillance on the Rise?" NordVPN, August 23, 2021. https://nordvpn.com/blog/employee-surveillance-2021/.

PayScale. "Call Center Agent Salary in India in 2024." Accessed March 30, 2024. https://www.payscale.com/research/IN/Job=Call_Center_Agent/Salary.

Poonam, Snigdha. "The Scammers Gaming India's Overcrowded Job Market." *The Guardian*, January 2, 2018, sec. News. https://www.theguardian.com/news/2018/jan/02/the-scammers-gaming-indias-overcrowded-job-market.

Proofpoint. "Proofpoint's Annual Human Factor Report Reveals How 2020 Transformed Today's Threat Landscape," August 3, 2021. https://www.proofpoint.com/us/newsroom/press-releases/proofpoints-annual-human-factor-report-reveals-how-2020-transformed-todays.

Rakha, Tarek, and Alice, Gorodetsky. "Review of Unmanned Aerial System (UAS) Applications in the Built Environment: Towards Automated Building Inspection Procedures Using Drones." *Automation in Construction* 93 (September 1, 2018): 252–64. https://doi.org/10.1016/j.autcon.2018.05.002.

"Rapport de l'OLAF 2018." Commission européenne, 2018. https://anti-fraud.ec.europa.eu/system/files/2021-09/olaf_report_2018_fr_0.pdf.

Reuters. "Ukraine Seeking Action to Stop Russian Use of Starlink, Minister Says | Reuters," February 20, 2024. https://www.reuters.com/world/europe/ukraine-seeking-action-stop-russian-use-starlink-minister-says-2024-02-19/.

Roulin, Nicolas, Eden–Raye Lukacik, Joshua Bourdage, Lindsey Clow, Hayam Bakour, and Pedro Diaz. "Bias in the Background? The Role of Background Information in Asynchronous Video Interviews." *Journal of Organizational Behavior* 44 (November 4, 2022). https://doi.org/10.1002/job.2680.

Rubin, Rebecca. "Kelly Marie Tran Speaks Out About Online Harassment: 'I Won't Be Marginalized.'" *Variety* (blog), August 21, 2018. https://variety.com/2018/film/news/kelly-marie-tran-speaks-out-online-harassment-star-wars-1202911512/.

"SIPRI Yearbook 2022 | SIPRI." Accessed March 31, 2024. https://www.sipri.org/yearbook/2022.

Smith, Mike. *Targeted: How Technology Is Revolutionizing Advertising and the Way Companies Reach Consumers*. AMACOM, 2014.
Sokolovic, Vlada, and Goran Markovic. "Internet of Things in Military Applications." *Vojnotehnicki Glasnik* 71 (January 1, 2023): 1148–71. https://doi.org/10.5937/vojteh g71-46785.
South Australia Police. "Scams, Cybercrime and Cyberbullying." South Australia Police, 2021. https://www.police.sa.gov.au/your-safety/scams-and-cybercrime.
Susser, Daniel, Beate Roessler, and Helen Nissenbaum. "Online Manipulation: Hidden Influences in a Digital World." SSRN Scholarly Paper. Rochester, NY, December 23, 2018. https://doi.org/10.2139/ssrn.3306006.
"Target 2015 Annual Report." Target, 2015. https://corporate.target.com/getme dia/e503afc7-58e1-468c-8ff2-8442b3a4a699/Target-2015-Annual-Report.pdf.
The Economist. "How Is Ukraine Using Crypto to Fund the War?" Accessed March 31, 2024. https://www.economist.com/the-economist-explains/2022/04/05/how-is -ukraine-using-crypto-to-fund-the-war.
The Economist. "The WannaCry Attack Reveals the Risks of a Computerised World." May 20, 2017. https://www.economist.com/leaders/2017/05/20/the-wannacry-att ack-reveals-the-risks-of-a-computerised-world.
"The Jan. 6 Capitol Attack: Inquiries and Fallout—The New York Times." Accessed March 30, 2024. https://www.nytimes.com/news-event/jan-6-committee.
UNESCO Digital Library. "From Ideas to Action: Addressing Barriers to Comprehensive Sexuality Education in the Classroom," 2019. https://unesdoc.unesco.org/ark:/48223 /pf0000371091.
UNESCO Digital Library. "Global Education Monitoring Report Summary, 2020: Inclusion and Education: All Means All," 2020. https://unesdoc.unesco.org /ark:/48223/pf0000373721.
UNODC. "Comprehensive Study on Cybercrime." Accessed March 31, 2024. //www .unodc.org/unodc/en/organized-crime/comprehensive-study-on-cybercrime.html.
U.S. Department of Defense. "DIU Making Transformative Impact Five Years In." Accessed March 31, 2024. https://www.defense.gov/News/News-Stories/Article/Arti cle/2327021/diu-making-transformative-impact-five-years-in/.
Villeda, Marysol, Randy McCamey, Eyo Essien, Christian Amadi, and Rajunor Anani. "Use of Social Networking Sites for Recruiting and Selecting in the Hiring Process." *International Business Research* 12 (February 11, 2019): 66. https://doi.org/10.5539/ibr .v12n3p66.
Vogels, Emily A. "The State of Online Harassment." *Pew Research Center*, January 2021. https://www.pewresearch.org/internet/wp-content/uploads/sites/9/2021/01/PI_2 021.01.13_Online-Harassment_FINAL-1.pdf.

Wezeman, Pieter D, Justine Gadon, and Siemon T Wezeman. "Trends in International Arms Transfers, 2022," March 2023. https://www.sipri.org/sites/default/files/2023-03/2303_at_fact_sheet_2022_v2.pdf.

WIRED. "The Equifax Breach Was Entirely Preventable," September 14, 2017. https://www.wired.com/story/equifax-breach-no-excuse/.

Wike, Richard, Laura, Silver, Janell, Fetterolf, Christine, Huang, Sarah, Austin, Sneha, Gubbala, and Laura, Clancy. "Social Media Seen as Mostly Good for Democracy Across Many Nations, But U.S. Is a Major Outlier." *Pew Research Center's Global Attitudes Project* (blog), December 6, 2022. https://www.pewresearch.org/global/2022/12/06/social-media-seen-as-mostly-good-for-democracy-across-many-nations-but-u-s-is-a-major-outlier/.

Workforce.com. "Report Cites Poor Working Conditions in India's Call Centers," October 17, 2006. https://workforce.com/news/report-cites-poor-working-conditions-in-indias-call-centers.

"World Employment and Social Outlook—Trends 2020." International Labour Organization, 2020. https://www.ilo.org/wcmsp5/groups/public/---dgreports/---dcomm/---publ/documents/publication/wcms_734455.pdf.

www.ETEnergyworld.com. "Energy Intensity of Global ICT Sector Expanding at 4 per Cent Annually." ETEnergyworld.com. Accessed March 31, 2024. https://energy.economictimes.indiatimes.com/news/power/energy-intensity-of-global-ict-sector-expanding-at-4-per-cent-annually-study/68284500.

Zuboff, Shoshana. *The Age of Surveillance Capitalism: The Fight for a Human Future at the New Frontier of Power*. PublicAffairs, 2019.

Conclusion

Clotilde Champeyrache and Guillaume Soto-Mayor

In the contemporary fabric of our societies lies the prevailing illusion that asserts our capacity to forge ahead without heed to the pervasive presence and pernicious impacts of violence within the very foundations of our economies. Alain Bauer's work, *Tu ne tueras point*[1] resonates with a clarion call, reverberating the stark reality that violence is omnipresent, woven intricately, and currently thriving into the tapestry of our socio-economic structures. This book has shown that the illusions in the 90s showing how violence and war were on the decline were seductive veils, obscuring the centrality of violence in the fabric of our economies and its far-reaching ramifications in our societies. Alain Bauer's thesis underscores the futility of such a delusion, heralding the demise of any semblance of hypocrisy.

With that in mind, this book unveils a sobering truth: without reckoning the economies of violence and the powerful actors that perpetuate them, we stand at an impasse. The illusion of peace, thriving economic development, the sanctity of human rights and the rule of law, the battle against climate change—each aspiration remains elusive within a system entrenched in violence. The foundations of our modern economic systems, upon closer examination, reveal a disconcerting truth: they necessitate a tacit acceptance of violence, coercing humanity to traverse perilous lengths. This imperative begs the question: who truly benefits from these economies of violence? The answer, often obscured by rhetoric and obfuscation, is clear: it is those who wield power within these structures who reap the spoils at the expense of human suffering. Indeed, violence has become so insidiously integrated into our daily lives that its normalization has become all but inevitable. Our common narrative, spanning across the chapters of this collective work, paints a vivid tableau of this normalization—from the microcosms of interpersonal relationships to the macrocosm of global geopolitics. The call to action embedded within our research is unequivocal: to dismantle the illusion, to confront the economies of violence head-on, and to forge a new paradigm wherein peace, prosperity, and justice are not mere aspirations, but tangible realities for all.

This scholarly work has strived to enrich ongoing academic discourse concerning the intricate interplay between violence and economic frameworks. It

---

1 Alain Bauer, *Tu ne tueras point* (Fayard, 2024), https://cnam.hal.science/hal-04414363.

presents a discerning critique, shedding light on the nuanced manners through which violence eludes detection and comprehension within the contemporary capitalist milieu. Moreover, it accentuates the diverse manifestations and pivotal roles of agents of violence across global landscapes, spanning varied political regimes and cultural contexts. Employing a rigorous analytical approach grounded in theoretical underpinnings, empirical substantiation, and ethical deliberations, the text endeavors to cultivate heightened consciousness, foster dialogic engagement, and galvanize concerted endeavors aimed at dismantling entrenched structures of violence within both economic and, by extension, political spheres.

Drawing upon an interdisciplinary tapestry woven from criminological, sociological, economic, and political perspectives, alongside insights gleaned from experiential wisdom, the work probes into the mechanisms by which violence becomes ingrained within economic frameworks and unpacks the ramifications of such normalization. Illuminating multifaceted dimensions of invisibility encompassing structural, symbolic, and systemic violence, this exposition underscores the enduring grip and surreptitious operations of violence within economic paradigms. Introducing innovative conceptual frameworks tailored to scrutinize violence within economic realms and buttressed by incisive analyses of diverse case studies delineating actors within economies of violence, their methodologies, and evolutionary trajectories, the volume elucidates key dynamics perpetuating the cloak of invisibility shrouding violence, while delineating its far-reaching implications for social equity and communal well-being.

Understanding violence within economic systems unveils the foundational structural complexities inherent in contemporary economic operations. Economic architectures not only dictate the allocation of material resources but also configure intricate webs of social interactions and identities. The pervasive influence of global capitalism, characterized by interwoven markets, capital flows, and transnational corporate entities, profoundly shapes social, economic, and environmental landscapes worldwide, thereby molding patterns of systemic violence across heterogeneous contexts. Through mechanisms such as inequitable resource distribution, labor exploitation, and exclusionary policies, economic frameworks can perpetuate manifestations of structural violence that disproportionately impact marginalized communities. The often-overlooked role of violence as a determinant of profitability within modern economic frameworks underscores its significance. Similarly, the remarkable adeptness of agents of violence in leveraging the intricacies of the economic system for their gain merits scrutiny. By scrutinizing these structural dynamics, scholars can unravel the mechanisms by which economic processes contribute to the perpetuation of social injustices and fortify systems of dominance and subjugation. Thus, Clotilde Champeyrache cogently demonstrates violence's centrality within the underpinnings of our economic systems.

The intricate nexus between actors of violence and neoliberalism evinces a multifaceted interplay, notably reflecting the manner in which neoliberal economic doctrines engender circumstances conducive to the proliferation and perpetuation of criminal enterprises. Neoliberalism, functioning both as an ideological framework and a suite of economic policies, prioritizes market deregulation, privatization, and individualistic ethos, often at the expense of communal welfare, public goods, and democratic governance. As underscored by Arturo Alvarado, David Izadifar, and Nazia Hussain, the observation of how actors of violence, encompassing criminal organizations among others, thrive within contemporary economic paradigms is indeed striking.

Moreover, neoliberal globalization engenders avenues for actors of violence by streamlining the movement of commodities, capital, and individuals across borders and jurisdictions. The liberalization of trade and investment, a hallmark of neoliberal regimes, may precipitate the proliferation of illicit markets, including but not limited to drug trafficking, human trafficking, and arms smuggling, exploiting lacunae in regulatory frameworks, and deficiencies in law enforcement collaboration.

Mafias and other actors of violence have indeed significantly leveraged the emergence of new trade routes and transportation networks. Their strategic positioning in key trade hubs and control over vital resources, such as those in Hong Kong or New York, have facilitated the expansion of both historical and novel licit and illicit trafficking networks. It is noteworthy that multinational corporations also have their share of responsibilities in these developments. For instance, Albanian criminal syndicates have flourished due to their geographical proximity to Turkey and Europe. Collaborating with Turkish and Italian mafias, the largest Albanian criminal factions have asserted control over a substantial portion of the heroin and human trafficking operations originating from Southeast Asia and North Africa bound for Europe. Similarly, the Camorra's expansion into Romania's waste management sector, including the transportation and disposal of hazardous materials, exemplifies the transnational reach of criminal enterprises. Additionally, Nigerian syndicates have gained notoriety for orchestrating human trafficking networks, particularly in the realm of prostitution, from West Africa to Europe and the Middle

East, exploiting the cost advantages of their workforce compared to Eastern European counterparts, thus capitalizing on market principles.[2]

Moreover, criminal organizations such as the Nigerian Crime Syndicates have amalgamated the exploitation of newfound trade avenues with innovative strategies, notably by establishing a decisive competitive edge in the realm of transnational drug smuggling through the use of human couriers.[3] By enticing financially desperate individuals with lucrative prospects, training "mules" in specialized facilities, employing logistical experts to optimize flight connections, and leveraging diasporic networks, the Nigerian Crime Syndicates (NCS) have refined and deployed these smuggling techniques extensively in recent years. Notably, they pioneered the "shot-gun" method, whereby multiple couriers are dispatched on the same flight while one is deliberately flagged by an accomplice passenger under NCS directives, thereby allowing the others to bypass security checks unnoticed. Through astute exploitation of globalization dynamics, the NCS has ascended the criminal hierarchy incrementally, emerging as prominent figures within the global underworld.

From an economic and financial standpoint, neoliberal policies such as deregulation, privatization, and austerity measures provide fertile ground for the flourishing of organized crime by enfeebling state institutions, undermining public services, and exacerbating societal disparities Furthermore, neoliberal economic policies that accord primacy to free trade accords and deregulation may compromise endeavors to combat organized crime by prioritizing market access and economic interests over considerations of security and the risks to enhance the power of actors of violence. Violent market economies are violent actors' best ally and source of inspiration.

Increasingly loose fiscal legislation is a good example as it encompassed one of the criminal actor's key strategic objectives; i.e. "the creation of venues for the private accumulation of capital, without the loss of any of that capital to public governmental purposes through redistributive taxation, social welfare or the provision of public goods."[4] Moreover, as Holton highlights, the global multiplication of stock markets, the complexification of financial operations, and the rapidity of information sharing match criminal organizations' desire to stay invisible while conducting their illegal activities.[5] Criminal organizations

---

2 "Serious and Organised Crime Threat Assessment (SOCTA)," Europol, December 14, 2021, https://www.europol.europa.eu/publications-events/main-reports/socta-report.
3 Stephen Ellis, *This Present Darkness: A History of Nigerian Organized Crime* (Oxford University Press, 2016).
4 James Cockayne, *Hidden Power: The Strategic Logic of Organized Crime* (Oxford University Press, 2016).
5 Robert Holton, "Global FInance," in *Global Finance* (Routledge, 2012), pp 23.

have notably considerably extended their activities thanks to the development of modern capitalism, offshore shell companies, tax evasion schemes, and tax havens.

The conspicuous infiltration of mafia entities into the financial sector has been increasingly exposed in the wake of successive financial crises. Numerous instances disclosed by whistleblowers underscore the burgeoning influence of mafia syndicates within the banking systems, notably in countries such as the United States and the United Kingdom, characterized by Saviano as "criminal capitalism capitals." For instance, in 2016, HSBC agreed to a $1.9 billion settlement with the US government for irregularities in handling funds linked to Mexican cartels.[6] Similarly, in 2010, Wachovia Bank faced a meager $160 million fine from US authorities for inadequate oversight in transactions involving a staggering $378.4 billion from Mexican currency exchange houses.[7] Utilizing local exchange bureaus, the Sinaloa Cartel channeled millions in cash and established numerous bank accounts through the Miami branch of Wachovia.[8]

As underscored in Walter Howie's "Red Capitalism," the infiltration of criminal capital and conduct within the state-owned banking system of China mirrors concerns in the US and the UK.[9] Furthermore, jurisdictions known for their lenient financial regulations such as the Bahamas, Luxembourg, and Switzerland have attracted significant attention from mafia entities, as evidenced by a 2008 investigation revealing €44 billions of 'Ndrangheta assets in Zurich banks.[10] Additionally, mafias exert influence over banks and even entire banking systems in countries like Nigeria, Cyprus, or the Bahamas. Thus, criminal actors have entrenched themselves as significant stakeholders in the global banking and financial infrastructure across both developed and developing regions, wielding a potentially formidable political instrument, and reinforcing their capacity of nuisance as actors of violence. A catastrophic vicious circle.

Politically and culturally, neoliberalism cultivates an environment conducive to corruption, cronyism, and impunity, potentially facilitating collusion

---

6   Jean-François Gayraud, "Nouveau Capitalisme criminel," www.odilejacob.fr, 2014, https://www.odilejacob.fr/catalogue/sciences-humaines/droit-justice/nouveau-capitalisme-criminel_9782738130723.php.
7   "Banking Standards: Written Evidence from Martin Woods," UK Parliament, 2013, https://publications.parliament.uk/pa/jt201314/jtselect/jtpcbs/27/27v_we107.htm.
8   Roberto Saviano, *Extra pure. Voyage dans l'économie de la cocaïne* (Editions Gallimard, 2016).
9   Carl Walter and Fraser Howie, *Red Capitalism: The Fragile Financial Foundation of China's Extraordinary Rise* (John Wiley & Sons, 2012).
10 Petra Reski, "The Honored Society: A Portrait of Italy's Most Powerful Mafia," 2008, https://www.goodreads.com/book/show/15814205-the-honored-society.

between organized crime syndicates and corrupted political elites. Neoliberal policies that prioritize market mechanisms and profit maximization at the expense of public welfare and democratic governance can erode institutional integrity, undermine the rule of law, and engender opportunities for rent-seeking behavior and illicit enrichment. Additionally, the privatization of public assets and services may engender regulatory capture, as private interests wield undue influence over governmental policies and decision-making processes, thereby affording organized crime entities the latitude to operate with impunity and evade accountability.

In local and global liberal markets, violent actors benefit from similar structural advantages as they don't fear competition, use coercion to eliminate it, and inflect workforce and clients using violent threats of corruption. Unlike other violent actors, they aren't limited by any moralistic considerations and they opportunistically take advantage of any enrichment prospect, any favorable evolution, that liberal markets offer them. In the 70s, all types of actors (multinational companies, corrupted politicians, mafias, etc.) started to exploit legislative weaknesses to launder criminal assets in off-shore fiscal paradises, often relying on the same banks, and financial and law firms as advisers.[11] Drawing inspiration from the cartels of multinational corporations, criminal actors, and more expansively, agents of violence have devised oligopolistic tactics. The symbiotic relationship between warlords and multinational corporations, rogue states, and prominent criminal entities, as elucidated in the book, serves as a poignant example of such alliances.

Actors of the economies of violence, and especially criminal actors, are porous biological creatures living in symbiosis with their environment from which they constantly learn. They seem to be at the forefront, and/or to master all innovations in economic and political systems. Actors of violence constantly develop new sources of illicit revenues thanks to their global connections and deep understanding of our consumerist societies. One example is the involvement of actors of violence in the counterfeiting industry, one of the most profitable illicit activities on earth. Another example is the criminal innovative use of digital tools not only to better secure their communication and operations but also as a new source of revenue. In fact, Russian, Chinese, Japanese, and, famously, Nigerian criminals started cyber-crime, but also large-scale online welfare, insurance, or student loan fraud already in the 1980s. Nowadays, as

---

11 *Mafia and Banks (3/3)—Crime without Limits*, accessed March 31, 2024, https://www.arte.tv/en/videos/102289-003-A/mafia-and-banks-3-3/.

Julien Dechanet highlighted, the various forms of cybercrime generate billions in revenue annually across the globe.

The phenomenon of globalization has engendered multifaceted and contradictory impacts on the dynamics of violence, fostering avenues for collaboration and advancement while simultaneously exacerbating disparities and tensions. The proliferation of global markets, the liberalization of trade, and the relaxation of financial regulations have empowered transnational corporations and criminal entities to accrue unparalleled wealth and influence, often at the expense of local communities, labor forces, and ecological integrity. This consolidation of economic authority serves to perpetuate structural violence primarily through the augmentation of resources and socio-political clout wielded by agents of violence, alongside the perpetuation of cycles of impoverishment, joblessness, and social marginalization. This phenomenon is notably pronounced, though not exclusively so, in regions of the Global South, where vulnerable demographics bear a disproportionate burden of the adverse repercussions stemming from the processes of globalization.

Some contend that a notable manifestation of systemic violence within global capitalism lies in the exploitation of labor to maximize profits. Transnational corporations frequently endeavor to minimize production expenditures by outsourcing labor to jurisdictions with minimal wage standards and deficient regulatory oversight. As articulated by Louise Shelley, this exploitation of inexpensive labor fuels the persistence of destitution, precarious labor conditions, and human rights transgressions across numerous regions globally, including but not limited to the agricultural, mining, fishing, and garment sectors. Furthermore, the commodification of labor under capitalist frameworks relegates workers to mere cogs in the production apparatus, stripping them of autonomy, dignity, and substantive involvement in economic decision-making processes.

Another facet of systemic violence inherent to global capitalism manifests in the environmental degradation and ecological devastation stemming from unsustainable production and consumption paradigms, culminating in human suffering. Industries characterized by extraction, industrialized agriculture, and consumerist behaviors spurred by capitalist consumption imperatives collectively exacerbate deforestation, pollution, climate alteration, and biodiversity depletion. Capitalist exploitation of labor is systematically led by actors of violence (warlords, criminal actors, multinational companies, corrupted politicians etc.) and often occurs in official or artisanal industries that extract and exploit natural resources, leading to the degradation of both human and environmental well-being. For example, extractive industries such as mining, logging, and agribusiness often rely on cheap labor and environmental destruction to maximize profits, leading to the displacement of indigenous communities, land grabbing, and environmental pollution. These ecological detriments disproportionately impact marginalized communities, notably those residing in the Global South, who endure the lion's share of ecological catastrophes and environmental injustices. Confronted with both direct and indirect manifestations of violence, marginalized and vulnerable populations, comprising women, children, indigenous groups, and rural communities, encounter significant obstacles in accessing resources, wielding political influence, and availing themselves of legal recourse to safeguard their well-being.

Sand mining stands out as a salient example of an economically lucrative yet ecologically detrimental activity, which to some extent, benefits actors of violence. Given its integral role as a primary ingredient in concrete, the global construction sector, which has experienced sustained growth over decades, drives the unprecedented scale of sand extraction—the largest industry of its kind worldwide. According to a report by the United Nations Environment Program, approximately 50 billion metric tons of sand are consumed annually.[12] Specialists estimate that the illicit global sand trade yields profits ranging from $200 billion to $350 billion annually, exceeding the combined profits from illegal logging, gold mining, and fishing.[13] A 2022 study conducted by researchers at the University of Amsterdam warns that the rate at which river sand is being dredged far surpasses nature's capacity for replenishment, raising concerns that the world may confront a shortage of construction-grade sand by 2050.[14] The environmental repercussions are profound, with river dredging leading to the destruction of estuaries and habitats, exacerbation of flooding, and coastal ecosystem disruption that disrupts marine life, exacerbating social tensions in regions where sand trafficking occurs. Thus, addressing the economies of violence remains indispensable for effectively combating climate change.

Illegal mining operations often evade scrutiny from law enforcement agencies, masquerading as legitimate enterprises with no property owners lodging complaints, and complicit officials possibly profiting from such activities. This

---

12   David A. Taylor, "Inside the Crime Rings Trafficking Sand," Scientific American, February 1, 2024, https://www.scientificamerican.com/article/sand-mafias-are-plundering-the-earth/.

13   "Sand and Sustainability: 10 Strategic Recommendations to Avert a Crisis," UNEP, April 25, 2022, http://www.unep.org/resources/report/sand-and-sustainability-10-strategic-recommendations-avert-crisis.

14   E. S. Rentier and L. H. Cammeraat, "The Environmental Impacts of River Sand Mining," Science of The Total Environment 838 (September 10, 2022): 155877, https://doi.org/10.1016/j.scitotenv.2022.155877.

phenomenon extends to various natural resources, including those crucial for the global economy's purported transition to sustainability, such as the so-called "green industries," which heavily rely on illegally extracted resources. Consequently, for crime syndicates, multinational corporations, warlords, and corrupt politicians—key stakeholders in economies of violence—illicit mining represents a lucrative and low-risk venture. Across the globe, protesters and victims of such illegal operations, including local villagers, farmers, and fishermen, are systematically subjected to intimidation or violence. However, given sand's critical importance in pivotal sectors of the global neoliberal economy, buyers seldom scrutinize its provenance or the beneficiaries of its commerce.

Through empirical observation of the functioning economic system, an analysis emerges delineating a recurrent trend wherein certain individuals and institutions consistently reap benefits from prevailing rules and political maneuvers. Notably, it is glaring to note the apparent oversight of economies of violence and the phenomenon of violence itself within major political paradigms, exemplified by initiatives such as the war on drugs, terrorism, and immigration. Despite the staggering investments made by the international community, particularly the Western powers, the proliferation of illicit drugs persists, terrorist organizations maintain operational capacities across numerous continents, and human smuggling activities escalate to unprecedented scales. These political undertakings engender economies of violence, thereby directly empowering their most prominent actors. An example is the current war on immigration, and its massive backfiring on practical levels, its direct fueling of the illicit migration business, human exploitation, and the benefits of actors of violence. Technological tools, notably drones and satellite surveillance, originally deployed in the context of the "war on terror" have been repurposed for surveillance at the borders of the European Union (EU) and at the Southern border of the United States. New surveillance tools and intrusive technologies are a burgeoning market that might soon exceed $65 billion in value.[15] In parallel, Western States have considerably increased the budget of their border agencies and simultaneously condoned increasing violence against asylum seekers.[16] In parallel, the closing of legal migration channels has been exploited at large scales by criminal organizations operating in Central America and the southeastern borders of the European Union.

---

15   Mark Akkerman, "Financing Border Wars: The Border Industry, Its Financiers and Human Rights," April 9, 2021, https://www.tni.org/en/publication/financing-border-wars.
16   "The Cost of Immigration Enforcement and Border Security," American Immigration Council, January 20, 2021, https://www.americanimmigrationcouncil.org/research/the-cost-of-immigration-enforcement-and-border-security.

In the context of Libya, local warlords, adept at both combating and facilitating migration, capitalize handsomely while wielding the specter of further "invasions" to Europe and concurrently profiting from orchestrated human smuggling operations. In a noteworthy instance, a militia leader in the northwestern Libyan city of Zawiya, identified as Al Bija, was discovered by journalists to preside over the smuggling market, exacting substantial commissions from departing vessels. Notably, he would "rescue" those who failed to pay, towing them back to shore only to incarcerate them within brutal detention facilities operated by his own tribal faction. This duplicity in migration control—extracting financial gains and securing impunity through intimidation while offering to redress the same threats—evolved into a high-stakes pursuit of profit and dominance amid Libya's tumultuous conflict.

As demonstrated throughout this book, the primary facilitators of the flourishing economies of violence often remain conspicuously absent from the agendas of the international community. Consequently, we contend that these issues ought to assume a more prominent position in international policy formulation to effectively address both political and economic violence. Corruption stands out as a pivotal catalyst for the proliferation of economies of violence, yet it frequently eludes substantive attention in development assistance programs and conflict resolution endeavors. Historically, as exemplified by the cases of the Central African Republic and Afghanistan discussed herein, corruption has been regarded as a pragmatic necessity by peacebuilding actors seeking to engage all stakeholders in peacebuilding initiatives. However, as corruption takes root and becomes entrenched within state institutions, it transcends mere technical challenges to evolve into a breeding ground for renewed socio-political instability and the attendant economies of violence. Therefore, efforts to combat corruption must be significantly bolstered not only to counter the economies of violence but also to safeguard the effective functioning, and possibly even democratic integrity, of the state, thereby ensuring the sustainability of social harmony.

As a matter of fact, within the framework of global capitalism, actors of violence flourish by capitalizing on a multitude of interconnected mechanisms, encompassing the exploitation of labor, corruption, environmental degradation, and the implementation of neoliberal policies, all of which serve to bolster their interests at the detriment of broader societal cohorts. The direct consequences of international policies in the fostering of economies of violence and its actors must be critically assessed. Economies of violence, and violence in general, have to be taken into account more seriously in modern time policy making. The comprehension and mitigation of these systemic manifestations of violence necessitate a rigorous examination of the structural inequities, power dynamics, and ideological constructs that undergird the fabric of global capitalist economies. Through the conscientious contestation and reshaping of these foundational structures, prospects emerge for envisioning alternative economic frameworks that prioritize human flourishing, equitable distribution of resources, and the sustainable stewardship of ecological systems over the imperatives of profit maximization and unchecked accumulation.

The scrutiny of violence within economic frameworks elucidates the intricate junctures where economic exploitation intersects with a spectrum of other violent manifestations, spanning physical, psychological, and symbolic dimensions. Economic disparities frequently intersect with axes of identity such as race, gender, class, and nationality, amplifying the ordeals of violence and subjugation endured by marginalized cohorts. For instance, marginalized communities may encounter disproportionate levels of impoverishment, unemployment, and housing instability owing to systemic prejudices and structural impediments entrenched within economic systems. In territories governed by the economies of violence, it is also likely that populations in general are losing revenues and quality of life. A meticulous examination of these interstices yields invaluable insights into the labyrinthine interplay between economic dynamics and overarching systems of oppression, thereby engendering more nuanced strategies for grappling with issues of violence and inequity. Subsequent inquiries should delve into the variegated disparities and asymmetric adversities inflicted by economies of violence upon diverse communities contingent upon their racial, gender, and national affiliations.

Nonetheless, amid the challenges, promising solutions do exist, often originating from grassroots initiatives. Notably, in the realm of regulating the exploitation and trade of natural resources, local governing bodies have emerged, exemplified by the establishment of the local sand authority in Kenya, which has garnered notable success. This entity has effectively prosecuted egregious offenders and enforced stringent penalties on illicit mining activities, underscoring the feasibility of regulating mineral production and showcasing its broader societal and economic benefits for the community at large. Another illustrative case can be found in Italy, a country profoundly impacted by the economic influence of violent actors.

Italian and French mafia experts have reported to us a reduction in mafia crime in Sicily in recent years. This is due to a combination of factors. First, the adoption of a law in 1982, the only one of its kind in the world, which condemns mafia associations and systematically confiscates the assets of mafia members and their accomplices. Mafiosi kill for money and possessions. Civil society has not been forgotten by these laws: confiscated property cannot be resold and can be made available to public services and local authorities. Associations that help citizens cope with the damage caused by the mafia are housed in former mafia-owned premises. For example, on the land confiscated from Giovanni Brusca, the probable mastermind of Judge Falcone's assassination, agricultural cooperatives have sprung up, such as Placido Rizzoto—Libera Terra,[17] which produces wine and bears the name of a trade unionist killed by the mafia. This cooperative makes profits, employs more people, and pays them better than the mafia did. Thanks to these cooperatives, or businesses seized from companies and reassigned to new owners, the whole criminal economy is being transformed into a legal one, with profits more widely shared. Some grassroot initiatives, such as the Erasmus program (a "European network for the promotion of economic and social alternatives to serious crime,")[18] promote the aforementioned initiatives beyond Italy's borders, particularly in France. They deserve to be better known and replicated more widely throughout the world. It shows that only a transverse effort implicating simultaneously the State (providing an adapted legislative framework), law enforcement's efficient efforts, local populations, and civil society directly contributes to the building of a viable economic future for the former victims of the economies of violence. If an honest critical look is given to the functioning of our economic and political systems, that leaders and populations work hand in hand, there is indeed hope for a better, more peaceful, and just society, to exist in the future.

As we have done in this book, examining the different forms that violence can take (from conspicuous physical violence to more discreet forms of economic conditioning) gives us a fresh look at the inner workings of our economies. It should encourage us to think in less Manichean terms. Only in theory can we represent a legal world driven by peaceful methods and an illegal world characterized by violence. It's only by breaking out of this framework, and the illusion of knowledge that goes with it, that we can fully appreciate the paradoxical yet structuring dynamics at work here. For example, decrypting the Encrochat and Sky ECC messaging systems reveals a considerable capacity for cooperation between criminal organizations. Conversely, questioning the true nature of wage relations in the context of Uberization raises questions about economic violence in the legal economy. The admittedly relative pacification of the illegal world, while the legal world increasingly resorts to coercion by agents in asymmetrical situations of power, opens up new research perspectives. The issue of the economies of violence therefore aspires to take a major

---

17 "Placido Rizzotto- Official Website," accessed March 31, 2024, https://www.confiscatibene.it/riuso/placido-rizzotto-libera-terra.
18 "Crim'HALT-Official Website," March 16, 2021, https://crimhalt.org/.

place on the agenda of both research and the development of appropriate public policies.

Bibliography

Akkerman, Mark. "Financing Border Wars: The Border Industry, Its Financiers and Human Rights," April 9, 2021. https://www.tni.org/en/publication/financing-border-wars.

American Immigration Council. "The Cost of Immigration Enforcement and Border Security," January 20, 2021. https://www.americanimmigrationcouncil.org/research/the-cost-of-immigration-enforcement-and-border-security.

Bauer, Alain. *Tu ne tueras point*. Fayard, 2024. https://cnam.hal.science/hal-04414363.

Cockayne, James. *Hidden Power: The Strategic Logic of Organized Crime*. Oxford University Press, 2016.

"Crim'HALT-Official Website," March 16, 2021. https://crimhalt.org/.

Ellis, Stephen. *This Present Darkness: A History of Nigerian Organized Crime*. Oxford University Press, 2016.

Europol. "Serious and Organised Crime Threat Assessment (SOCTA)," December 14, 2021. https://www.europol.europa.eu/publications-events/main-reports/socta-report.

Gayraud, Jean-François. "Nouveau Capitalisme criminel." www.odilejacob.fr, 2014. https://www.odilejacob.fr/catalogue/sciences-humaines/droit-justice/nouveau-capitalisme-criminel_9782738130723.php.

Holton, Robert. "Global FInance." In *Global Finance*. Routledge, 2012.

Mafia and Banks (3/3)—Crime without Limits. Accessed March 31, 2024. https://www.arte.tv/en/videos/102289-003-A/mafia-and-banks-3-3/.

Petra, Reski. "The Honored Society: A Portrait of Italy's Most Powerful Mafia," 2008. https://www.goodreads.com/book/show/15814205-the-honored-society.

"Placido Rizzotto- Official Website." Accessed March 31, 2024. https://www.confiscatibene.it/riuso/placido-rizzotto-libera-terra.

Rentier, E. S., and L. H. Cammeraat. "The Environmental Impacts of River Sand Mining." *Science of The Total Environment* 838 (September 10, 2022): 155877. https://doi.org/10.1016/j.scitotenv.2022.155877.

Saviano, Roberto. *Extra pure. Voyage dans l'économie de la cocaïne*. Editions Gallimard, 2016.

Taylor, David A. "Inside the Crime Rings Trafficking Sand." Scientific American, February 1, 2024. https://www.scientificamerican.com/article/sand-mafias-are-plundering-the-earth/.

UK Parliament. "Banking Standards: Written Evidence from Martin Woods," 2013. https://publications.parliament.uk/pa/jt201314/jtselect/jtpcbs/27/27v_we107.htm.

UNEP. "Sand and Sustainability: 10 Strategic Recommendations to Avert a Crisis," April 25, 2022. http://www.unep.org/resources/report/sand-and-sustainability-10-strategic-recommendations-avert-crisis.

Walter, Carl, and Fraser Howie. *Red Capitalism: The Fragile Financial Foundation of China's Extraordinary Rise*. John Wiley & Sons, 2012.

Index

A Rough Trade   255, 260, 270
Abdullah, Dr. Abdullah   66, 71
Abizaid, John   73
Absolutist   225
Accepted Warlords   222
Ad distribution   285
Ad hoc approach   96
Adam, Nourredine   221, 227
Advertising platforms   284
  Google   145, 151, 284, 292, 309
Aemilia investigation   37
Afghan Border Police (*See* ABP)   77
Afghan National Civil Order Police (*See*
  ANCOP)   77
Afghan National Defense and Security Forces
  (*See* ANDSF)   77, 78
Afghan National Police (*See* ANP)   77, 78
Afghan New Beginning Programme (*See*
  ANBP)   87
Afghan Uniformed Police (*See* AUP)   77
Afghanistan National Auxiliary Police (*See*
  ANAP)   77
Afghanistan Security Forces Fund (*See*
  ASFF)   86
Africa Corp   4
Agger, Kasper   267
Akhund, Mullah Dadullah   100
Akhundzada, Mullah Muhammad   102
Akhundzada, Sher Mohammad   75
Al-Baraka group   109
Al-Faisal, Muhammad   109
Al-Haramain Foundation   107
Al-Khatim, Mahamat   221
Al-Qaeda (*See* AQ)   61, 62, 79, 98, 112
Alan   123, 124, 126, 141–143
Albanese Mafia   245
Alizai, Abdul Habib   104
Alizai, Haji Azizullah   104
Alvarado, Arturo   215
Amarkhil, Zia ul-Haq   70
Amaya, Rances Ulices   47
American firepower   63
American institutionalism   20, 28, 30
American Mineral Fields (*See* AMF)   260
Amphetamine-type stimulants   12

Antagonistic   12
Anti-American Shiite group   114
Anti-terrorism effort   61
Anti-trust legislation   25
Applicant Tracking System (*See* ATS)   283
Armed Forces   10, 86, 226, 230, 245, 299,
  300, 308
Armor for individuals   29
Arms trafficking   171, 174, 202, 204, 231, 248
Artificial Intelligence   55, 283, 300, 302, 308
Artificial scarcity   37, 38, 39, 143
Assassination   64, 68, 80, 83, 85, 113, 180, 203,
  204, 249, 302, 326
Atlanta spas   49
Attorney General Sabit   94
Azimi's influence   97

Badica   247
Baker Jr., Howard   261
Balkh   76
Balkan   44, 240
Ballentine   4, 7, 15
Baltimore   45, 49, 56, 59
Bargaining power   31, 33, 34
Barrick Gold Corporation   261
Barrio   18, 229, 236, 246
Bastos, Patrick   189
Battalions   85
Bauer, Alain   215, 327
Bayat, Ehsanullah   69
Beckert   156, 157, 159, 160, 163, 165, 215
Bemba, Jean-Pierre   260
Bermuda   258
Bicentennial Tower   211
Biden administration   54
Black Axe   248
Black markets   5
Blackmail   19, 20, 23, 32, 40, 242
Blood minerals   261, 262
Bolster   2, 104, 324
Bonn Conference   64–66, 68, 73, 84
Brahui, Haji Karim   63
Brazil's wealth   156
Breakdown in trust   282
Brotherhood   248, 249

Burkina Faso 251, 252, 257
Bush, George W. 65

Caloocan 2 (resettlement site) 133
Cartel de Jalisco Nueva Generacion (*See* CJNG) 170
Cartels 23, 167, 189, 191, 203, 212, 319, 320
Cathy 59, 123, 124, 126, 140, 148
Champeyrache, Clotilde 39, 150
Cherif, Ousmane 251
Child soldiers 42, 227, 228
Chinese Elite 7
Chinese territories 277
Civil Code 39
Client-perpetrated violence 49, 56
Clientelism 157, 163, 171
Clientelistic 241
Clinton, Hillary 293
Cliques 46, 229, 236, 246, 279
Coalition forces 86, 87, 96, 112, 115
Coase's world 27, 29
Coasian logic 26
Cochabamba 146, 147
Coercive measures 2
Cogitations of two influential figures 64
    Brahimi, Lakhtar 64, 65
    Khalilzad, Zalmay 65, 69
Cold Blooded Cartel 45
Collier, Paul 15, 268
Colonial powers 9
Colonias 171
Coltan 10, 262, 264
Comezone 250–252
Commons, John R. 40
Communal antagonisms 241
Community-based organizations 52, 131
Concessionaires 124–126, 130, 132, 136–140, 147–149
Condominiums 211
Confidential information 281
Confiscation 29–30, 64, 74, 173, 194
Conflict economy 33, 225
Conflict theory 19, 27, 29, 30, 40
Conflict-ridden region 10
Congolese government 11
Congolese mines 243
Conservatoire National des Arts et Metiers (*See* CNAM) IX, XII, XIII

Coping strategies XI, 132, 134, 135
Corruption XIV, 1, 12, 13, 23, 28, 64, 66, 67, 69, 70, 72, 73, 76, 78, 79, 83, 88, 91, 92, 95–98, 116, 119, 122, 127, 159, 163, 164, 166, 171, 174, 183, 188, 190–192, 202, 211–214, 224, 225, 237, 245, 256, 261, 266, 274, 294, 319, 320, 324
Corsican-Marseille criminal organization 231
Council of Ulemas 102
Counter Narcotic Police of Afghanistan (*See* CNPA) 77
Counternarcotics strategy 79
Countries, XIII 1, 7, 11, 42, 43, 62, 65, 99, 104, 107, 108, 109, 125–127, 146, 152, 167, 170, 174, 176, 178, 181, 233, 229–231, 234, 257, 263–266, 285, 286, 289, 290, 298, 319
    Libya 7, 16, 324
    North American 7
    North Korean 7, 12, 18, 297
    United Aram Emirates 7, 107, 238
COVID-19 Pandemic 234, 280, 281, 291, 295
Craig 57, 69, 122, 279
Criminal activities 5, 11, 72, 74, 82, 98, 104, 190, 204, 214, 238, 241, 245, 249, 294
    Cigarette trafficking 5, 245
    Counterfeiting 5, 54, 171, 174, 202, 320
    Cybercrime 5, 7, 12, 279, 289, 290, 294, 295, 297–299, 311, 313, 321
    Drug trafficking 5, 12, 69, 81, 85, 99, 101, 102, 112, 114, 162, 172, 180, 192, 194, 236, 248, 249, 253, 317
    Human trafficking VII, XIV, 2, 5, 7, 12, 14, 17, 42–47, 49–60, 171, 174, 192, 203, 317
    Medicine trafficking 5
    Natural resources trafficking 5
    Thefts and robberies 5
Criminal actors in the Ciudad de Mexico XI, 205–210
Criminal behavior 2
Criminal capitalism capitals 319
Criminal entrepreneurs 220, 221, 223, 224–228, 231, 236, 241, 256, 257, 259, 263
Criminal governance 163–165, 169, 217, 222
Criminal Procedure Code 95
Criminal rivalries 43
Crook, Alias 246
Crop destruction 79

INDEX 331

Cryptocurrency 295, 304, 305
Cunning 100, 101
Cyber illicit trade 257
Cybercriminals 7, 295
Cyprus Group 65

Dadak, Pierre 231, 258
Dallago, Bruno 40
Dallah Albaraka Group 109
Damane, Zakaria 221, 238
Darassa, Ali 221, 247
DarkMarket 296, 310
Data theft 289, 297
David, Agmon 260
Dechanet, Julien VII, XIII, 15, 276, 321
Defense Innovation Unit (*See* DIU) 303, 307
Delgado Montes, Rodolfo Antonio 247
Delinquency XIII, 13, 15, 169, 175, 188, 195
Democratic Republic of Congo (*See* DRC) 10, 15, 224, 227, 228, 237, 259, 260, 262, 272
Demsetz, Harold 40
Department of Defense (*See* DOD) 86, 303, 313
Derogatory comments 278
Des-industrialization 171
Deutsche Bank 54, 288
Dewey 137, 152, 156, 157, 159, 160, 163, 165, 215
Dey Gbam 230
Diplomacy 1, 16, 112, 304
Disarmament of Illegal Armed Groups (*See* DIAG) 86, 87
Disarmament, Demobilization, and Reintegration (DDR) program 86
Disastrous civil war in 1861, 9
Disband Illegally Armed Groups (*See* DIAG) 77
Discrimination 157, 280, 282–284, 307, 309
Djotodia, Michel 227
Dobbins, James 117
Doherty, Sean 269
Dokubo, Alhaji Asari 230
Dostum, Mohammad Qasim 63, 244
Double blindness 19
Double game 112
Dow Jones 287
Downtown areas 176
Dujkanovic, Milo 245

Durrani tribes 82
 Alokozai 82, 83
 Barakzai 82
 Popalzai 80, 82

East of the Democratic Republic of the Congo (*See* DRC) 10
Economic power to withhold 31, 33, 38, 39, 143, 150
Economic science 22, 40
Economies of violence I, III, IX, X, XV, 1–3, 5–10, 12–15, 39, 50, 67, 126, 144, 149, 155, 163, 213–215, 222, 227, 232, 240, 241, 315, 316, 320, 322–326
Economy of barriers 233
Economy of Violence in Afghanistan VII, 14, 61, 63, 65, 67, 69, 71, 73, 75, 77, 79, 81, 83, 85, 87, 89, 91, 93, 95, 97, 99, 101, 103, 105, 107, 109, 111, 113, 115, 117, 119, 121
Edna 124, 126
eEnemy (eVorog) 302
Egocentric actors 225
EI Faro 229
EI Salvador 222–225, 229, 234, 236, 242, 245–247, 268, 269, 271–274
El Dorito 191, 211
Electronic surveillance systems 282
Eluded justice 98
Emilia-Romagna 37
Emotet malware attack 296
Environmental legislation 26
Ethnic affiliation 221
Ethnocentrism 71
Ethnographic approaches 165
European Commission 287, 291, 292, 309
European imperialism 9
European Multidisciplinary Platform Afains Criminal Threats (*See* EMPACT) 297
Ex-Seleka group 231
Exploitation rights 237
External enemy (*See* foreign power) 221
Extremist groups 276

Faction leader 220
Fahim, Marshal 86, 88, 89
Fahim, Qasim 66, 88, 244
Fall of the Taliban 61, 92, 110
Fasenfest, David I, X

Fauzi, General Hamayoun 89
Favelas 171, 176, 212
Fayeq, Abdul Karim 83
Fearon, James 4
FedEx 290
Fedorov, Mykhailo 301, 311
Felbab-Brown, Vanda 5
Fiber optics 262, 288
Fiefdoms 225, 251
Financial Action Task Force (*See* FATF) 258, 272
Financial sectors 2, 319
Fiscal monopoly 236
Flack, Caroline 277, 278, 308
FlexJobs 281, 308
Fofie 251
Forces Nouvelles (*See* FN) 250
Forms of violence 2, 7, 44, 171, 230, 231, 292
    Assault 7, 35, 43, 47, 48, 157, 174, 181, 194, 195, 203, 231
    Forced prostitution 7, 227
    Immolation 7
    Rape 7, 43, 227, 228
Fozie, Tuo 252
Free from violence 3
Freedom 21, 23, 25, 30–33, 62, 98, 101, 277, 294
    In action 31, 165
    In vacuo 30
Front for the Rebirth of Central African Republic (*See* FPRC) 221

Gagliano, Alice 10
Galtung, Johan 309
Gambia 231
Gang assessment 46
Geyer, Michael 16
Ghani, Ashraf 67, 70, 71, 76, 78, 89, 118
Ghost soldiers 78
Gini index 158, 176
Giovanni Brusca 326
Global cybercriminal group 297
    APT29 (Cozy Bear) 297
    DarkTequila 297
    FIN7 (Carbanak) 297
    Lazarus Group 297
    Maze Group 298
    TA505 298

    Wizard spider 297
Global Footprint Network 305
Global illicit activities 155, 156, 171, 173, 213
    Arms trafficking 171, 174, 202, 204, 231, 248
    Money laundering XIV, 104, 171, 174, 202, 212, 214, 247, 254, 258, 272
    Narcotraffic 169, 171, 174, 213
Global North 1, 14, 146
Global South 1, 14, 16, 127, 129, 146, 150, 165, 214, 216, 321, 322
Global witness 106, 239, 255, 257, 260, 262–265, 269, 270
Golden era 113
Golden Triangle 241
Good governance 146
Governance structures 157, 160
Government-sponsored organizations 14
Graveyard of empires 92
Gray zone 174, 259
Green industries 323
GreenIT study 305
Growth sectors 36
    Transportation 36, 42, 103, 158, 173, 178, 181, 202, 230, 234, 236, 242, 249, 257, 286, 290, 317
Guatemala 46, 223, 229, 234, 247
Guatemalan border 247
Guilty-victim 26
Guinea-Bissau 231
Gul, Mawlawi Ajab 102
Gullible people 7

Habibi, Abdul Samad 89
Hackers 289, 290
Harold, Demsetz 26, 40
Harrison, Mark 4
Hazara, Khodaidad 69
Hegemonic control 172
Heinous acts 7
Hekmatyar, Gulbuddin 98
Hekmatyar's Hezb-e Islami (*See* HIG) 75
Helmand Province 68
Herat Province 114
Heritage Oil 255
Hidden Forces VII, 14, 19
High-Frequency Trading (*See* HFT) 287
Hirshleifer, Jack 40

INDEX   333

Hmong populations   240
Hoeffler, Anke   3, 260
Homestead Strike   36
Homicide rate   XI, 171, 178, 179, 193, 223, 246
Honorable   254
Hoods, Robin   81, 250
Hotlines   52
Hsing-Han, Lo   240, 259
Hsing-Minh, Lo   240
Human trafficking networks   2, 317
Hussain, Nazia   130

Ignorant savages   45
Illicit drug traffic organizations   192
    Cocaine   174, 190, 192, 236, 253, 272, 274, 319, 327
    Fentanyl   192
    Marihuana   175, 192
    Medicinal drugs   192
    Opium-based drugs   192
Illicit economies   10, 156, 160, 168, 216, 217, 231
Illicit Urban Economies   VII, 14, 155, 157, 159, 161, 163, 165, 167, 169, 171, 173, 175, 177, 179, 181, 183, 185, 187, 189, 191, 193, 195, 197, 199, 201, 203, 205, 207, 209, 211, 213, 215, 217, 219
Illusion of the dichotomy   19
Imperils liberties   157
Impoverished class   145
Impunity   79, 97, 98, 124, 172, 181, 188, 212, 228, 244, 247, 249, 252, 266, 319, 320, 324
Independent Electoral Commission (See IEC)   93
Indigenous people   3
Industrial Revolution   28
Influential leaders   73
Infringement of laws   157
    Aggressions   157
    Assaults   43, 157, 195
    Homicides   20, 30, 157, 162, 164, 171, 174, 176, 177, 178, 180, 223, 245
    Pirating   157
    Robberies   5, 157, 162
Initial endowments   23
    Budgetary   23, 72
    Material   11, 23, 29, 30, 37, 52, 60, 176, 230, 233, 243, 258, 268, 316, 317

Social   11–326
Insight Crime's investigation   236
Insurgent groups   72, 98, 100, 106
Insurgent operations   81
Intangible violence   20
Inter-communal dimension   10
Inter-Service Intelligence (See ISI)   111
Internal enemy (See the State)   221
International Labour Organization (See ILO)   287, 292, 314
International Peace Information Service (See IPIS)   263
International Security Assistance Force (See ISAF)   62, 79
Internationally sanctioned   244
Internet of Things (See IOT)   300, 313
Internet Research Agency (See IRA)   293
Intimidation   10, 20, 35, 45, 249, 323, 324
Invisible hand   20, 24, 28
Involuntary transfers   232
    Forced taxes   232
    Looting   227, 232, 234
Irenic   27, 30, 31
Irenique vision   22
Irenism   20, 21, 26, 27
Islamabad   111, 112
Islamic Development Bank   108
Islamic jurisprudence   101
    Al-hayal   101
Islamic law   101, 102, 122
    Quran   101, 102
    Sunnah   101
Islamic Republic of Iran (See IRI)   62, 113, 115
Istislah   102
Ituri   242, 243, 260, 262, 265, 269
IUU fishing   51
Ivorian National Security Council   231
Ivorian ports   252
Izadifar, David   VII, XIV, 14, 61, 317

Jabil Circuit factory   285
Jalali, Ali Ahmad   68, 70
Jan, Lahore   104
Japanese territories   1
Jawhari, Baz Mohammad   89
Jeffrey Epstein case   54
Jihad   62, 68, 83, 90, 93, 97, 102
JP Morgan   54

Judiciary 92–94, 96–98, 119, 181, 182
  Courts of Appeal 92, 96
  Primary Courts 92, 96
  Supreme Court 92, 93, 96, 97, 211
Jurisprudence 39, 101, 222, 270
Juvenile prostitution 47
Juxtaposed 27, 29

Kabul bank scandal 98
Kabul government 90, 111
Kalashnikov 74, 118, 231
Kaldor, Mary 16
Kamel, Saleh Abdullah 109
Kapisa Province 84
Karzai, Ahmad Wali 69, 74, 75, 82, 83
Karzai, Hamid 63, 66–70, 74, 80, 85, 94, 106, 116, 244
Kashmir issue 111
Khalid, Assadullah 85
Khalili, Karim 63
Khalilzad, Zalmay 65, 69
Khan, Haji Juma 81
Khan, Jan Muhammad 68
Khan, Matiullah 80
Khudam, Abdul Karim 76
Kidnapping for Ransom 99
Knotty problems 146
Koistinen, Paul A.C. 4
Kullinan Finance Investment 264

Labor exploitation 42, 316
Labour-value; three classes 23
  The capitalists 23
  The landowners 23
  The working class 23
Laden, Osama bin 61, 62, 104
Laghman Province 94
Laitin, David 4
Land grabbing 3, 7, 74, 120, 322
Lapis-lazuli 106, 115, 117
Law Enforcement 37, 44, 49, 50, 52, 53, 76, 102, 118, 251, 252, 276, 317, 322, 326
Law of the strongest 22
Lead nation 94
Legal economy VII, 14, 37, 38, 123, 144, 149, 236, 254, 259, 326
Legislative elections 250
Legitimacy stems 139

Legitimate expression 2
Libera Terra 326
Liberal economists 22
Liberal peace 3, 17
Liberal thought 24
Limaj case 222
Local commander 62, 91, 95, 220
Locke's thought 32
Loya Jirga 66
Lubanga, Thomas 260
Lucrative revenue 104

Machiavellian world 28
Mafia Lords 230
Mafias XIII, 2, 7, 20, 129, 143, 152, 154, 154, 170, 191, 192, 203, 210–212, 225, 240, 241, 271, 317, 319, 320, 322, 327
Malabon (informal settlement) 133
Malicious rumors 278
Malware attack 295, 296
Malware distribution campaign 298
  Dridex banking Trojan 298
  Locky ransomware 298
Manichean way 26
Mara Salvatrucha 13, 229, 253
Marcos era 145
Marginalized communities 316, 322, 325
Maroquin, Carlos 247
Marshall's Principles of Economics 24
Marxist currents 23
Maslaha 101, 102, 120
Masquerading 280, 324
Massoud, Ahmad Shah 64
Maynilad 124, 130, 132, 148
Mazar-e Sharif 113
Maze Group 298
McMurrough, Mike 260
Medicinal drugs 192
Meering 246
Mercenaryism 226
Meritocratic State 67
Meshrano Jirga 75
Methamphetamine 82, 190, 240, 241
Methamphetamine production 82
Metro Manila VII, 14, 123–125, 130–133, 136, 144, 145, 147, 148, 150, 153
Metropolitan Waterworks and Sewerage System (See MWSS) 124, 130

INDEX 335

Mexico City XI, 14, 155, 156, 162, 166, 168–181, 188–203, 211, 213, 214
Micro-work platforms 286
   Amazon Mechanical Turk 286
Microsoft Windows 290
Military cooperation 113
Miller, Ruth Antuanet 45
Mineral Supply Africa (*See* MSA) 264
Mining areas 225, 228, 244
Minister of Defense 69, 85, 87–90, 104
Minister of the Interior 68, 83
Ministry of Transport 252
Ministry of Water and Forest 255
Misinterpretation of data 282
Mitsubishi Electric 265
Mohaqiq, Mohammad 63
Mohib, Hamdullah 71
Mohseni, Muhammad Asef 63
Monetary impact 103
Monopoly of violence 19, 23, 36, 38
Moral ramifications 8
Morris, Philip 245
Movement for the Central African Republic (*See* MPC) 221
Movement for the Emancipation of the Niger Delta (*See* MEND) 238, 249
MS-13 gang member 47
MS13 234, 236, 242, 246, 247, 253, 269, 271, 272, 274
McAfee's Cybercrime report 295
Mujaheddin 64
Mujahid, Mullah Yaqoob 104
Multimillion-dollar contract 80
Multinational corporations 6, 11, 289, 317, 320, 323
Municipal government 182, 189
Municipal infrastructures 127
Muqbil, Zarar Ahmad 70
Murder 35, 204, 227, 228
Museveni family 243
Mushahid, Ahmad 69
Musk, Elon 301
Muttaqi, Amir Khan 105
Myanmar government 11

Naderi, Nader 95
Naim, Moises 7, 17
Naissance 14, 227

National Center for Cyber Security (*See* CNSSI) 290
National Directorate of Security (*See* NDS) 85
National Union for the Total Independence of Angola (*See* UNITA) 256
National Water Crisis Act 123, 149
Nations XIV, 1, 6, 9–12, 24, 29, 42, 59, 61, 62, 64, 65, 81, 98, 99, 103, 106, 107, 108, 110, 111, 122, 174, 218, 225, 226, 232–234, 246, 247, 257, 262, 268, 298, 299, 314, 322
   Iran 11, 61, 62, 65, 102, 109, 110, 113–118, 122
   Syria 11, 12
   Venezuela 11, 16
Natural order 20, 21, 24, 25, 31, 34
Natural resources 2–6, 10, 14, 15, 36, 106, 226, 228, 231, 232, 234, 236, 237, 239, 243, 247, 252–259, 266, 268, 305, 306, 321, 323, 325
   Coltan 10, 262, 264
   Diamonds 10, 233, 237, 238, 247, 252, 254, 255, 257, 258, 262, 263, 266, 269, 270, 274
   Gold 5, 10, 11, 16, 17, 106, 233, 237, 238, 241, 243, 252, 260, 261, 267, 322
Natural rights 25
Ndrangheta 37, 319, 329, 330
Neoclassical core 18
Neoliberal Economies 257, 317, 318
Nepotism 97
Netanyahu, Benjamin 260
Neto, Agostinho 256
New wars 6
NGOS 52, 60, 80, 101, 137, 138, 140, 143, 206, 229, 233, 253, 274
Niang, Mame Yacine x
Niger Delta People Voluntary Forces (*See* NDPVF) 230
Niger Delta Vigilante 230
Nigerian Crime Syndicate (*See* NCS) 248, 249, 272, 318
Nimruz Province 63
Nitzschke 4, 15
Non-conflictual way 22
Non-denominational 52
Non-drinking purposes 132
   Bathing 132, 134
   Washing 51

Non-governmental organizations (*See* NGOS) 52, 57, 137
Non-Mafiosi 38
Non-patrimoniality of the human body 25
Non-profit organizations (*See* NPOS) 107
Non-state groups 231
Noorzai, Haji Bashir 104, 105, 117
Normative regimes 161, 167, 213
North American 7
North Atlantic Treaty Organization (*See* NATO) 61
North Korean 7, 12, 18, 297
Northern Alliance 61–63, 65–69, 73, 90
    Harakat-e Islami 63
    Hezb-e Wahdat-Islami 63
    Jamiat-e Islami 63, 83, 88
    Junbish-e Islami 63
    Partisan of the National Liberation, Movement of Afghanistan 63
    The Eastern Shura 63
Northern Virginia 45, 48, 57
NotPetya attack 296
Notions of victim (the polluted) 25
Ntaganda, Bosco 227, 244, 266
Nur, Atta Mohammad 76

Offshore bank accounts 12
Old American institutionalism 20
Oligopolistic tactics 320
Omar, Mullah 99, 104
Online gig platforms 292
Online transportation platforms 286
    Lyft 286, 310
    Uber 286, 310
Operation EMMA 95, 298
Operation Enduring Freedom (*See* OEF) 62
Opiate trade 79
Opium cultivation 63, 81, 102
Opium taxation 105
Original institutionalist economics (*See* OIE) 30
Ouattara, Alassane 232, 251
Ouattara, Issiaka 237
Overshoot day 305, 306, 309
Overy, Richard 4
Oxfam 292, 312

Packer, George 71

Pakistani cities 112
    Miranshah 112
    Peshawar 65, 112
    Quetta 112
Panama Papers controversy 12
Panama Papers scandal 289
Panjshir Valley 68, 88
Partido Accion Nacional (*See* PAN) 211
Pasay (mixed-use development) 133
Pashtun tribes 64
Pasig River 137
Paul II, Pope John 61
Payenda, Khalid 70, 76, 78, 91, 117
Penal Code 95
Penitentiary centers 188
Periferias 163, 180, 216
Perilous terrain 101
Peronnes 234
Perpetrator (the polluter) 25
Persian Gulf 105, 107, 114
Pervasive phenomenon 1
Petrovic, Branko 245
Pew Research Center 277, 299, 313, 314
Philippines 130, 131, 143, 145, 146, 148–151, 153
Philosophers of the Enlightenment 24
    Montesquieu 24
    Voltaire 24
Physical violence 2, 36, 37, 48, 124, 276, 277, 326
    Economic coercion 2
    Media manipulation 2
    Psychological repression 2
Pillaging 227
Pimp sticks 48
Pistol-whipped 48
Placido Rizzoto 326
Plundering of natural resources 239
    Jade 239, 240
    Timber 237, 239, 247, 252, 265
Pohl, Karl Otto 261
Policies of structural changes 171
    Decentralization 171, 182, 183
    Des-industrialization 171
    Liberalization 171, 317, 321
    Prevarication of labor 171
Political maneuvering 1, 113, 114
Political patronage 67, 157
Political repercussions 110

INDEX 337

Political-criminal actor 204
Popal, Ghulam Jelani 69
Post-communism 245
Post-Soviet 44
Postcolonial scholarship 143
Potemkin village 226
Pre-pandemic years 53
Predatory Sate 67
Premeditation 2
President Corazon Aquino 145
President Marcos 143, 144
Price makers 23
Price takers 23
Primeiro Comando da Capital (*See* PCC) 161, 165, 169, 172, 204, 216
Principles of scarcity 33
Privacy invasion 281
Private management of disorder 255
Problem of power (*See* power asymmetry) 23
Prodi, Romano 100
Producing power 33
Proletarian revolution 23
Property rights 22, 24–26, 32, 33, 39, 40, 160, 171, 174
  Alienability 24
  Exclusivity 24
  Rights of use 24
ProPublica journalists 284
Provincial Reconstruction Team (*See* PRT) 68, 69
Pseudo-statesmen 267
Public-private partnerships 128
Puerto Santos 173
Pullman Strike 36
Pure and perfect 21, 23, 25, 28, 33

Qadeer, Abdul Zahir 93
Qadir, Abdul 63, 71, 121
Qanuni, Yunus 66, 68
Qiyas 101
Quasi-monopoly 172
Quezon City 131–134

Rabbani government 113
Rabbani, Burhanuddin 63
Ramos, Fidel 145
Ransomware attack 295–297, 308

Ransomware operations against companies 297
  Acer 297
  JBS 297
  Kaseya 297
Rape 7, 43, 227, 228
Real bosses 225
Rebel groups 11, 232, 240
  Rwanda 10, 11, 15, 238, 243, 257, 260, 263, 264
  Uganda 11, 233, 243, 257, 260, 261, 263, 264
Reconciliation 115
Recruitment automation tools 283
  Machine learning 283, 285, 287, 303
  Natural language processing 283
  Predictive analytics 283
Red Capitalism 319, 328
Red china 240
Red flags 55
Remote work 280, 281, 286
Repercussions of violence 8
Resolute Support Mission (*See* RSM) 89, 120
Responsible Minerals Initiative (*See* RMI) 265
Reuter, Peter 5
Revil ransomware 297
Reynolds, R.J. 245
Riba Duties 107
Richar, Dawson 34, 40
Rioters 276, 277
Risk of confiscation 29
Rivalrous relations 30
Rivera, Elmer Canales 246
Robber barons 36, 40
Robbins, Lionel 40
Robin Hoods 81, 250
Rogers, John 20, 34, 40
Rule of Law 1, 13, 92–94, 96, 119, 121, 160, 163, 173, 182, 213, 252, 315, 320
Rumsfeld, Donald 65
Russel, David 260
Rwanda 10, 11, 15, 238, 243, 257, 260, 263, 264

Saleh, Salim 264
Salvation of Afghanistan 63
San Jose del Monte (resettlement site) 133
San Pedro 252

Sanctioned norms 159, 163
Sanctuaries 111, 112
Sand mining 322, 327
Sankoh, Fodeh 254
Santos, Dos 256
Sao Paulo metropolitan Regions 14
Sayyaf, Abdul Rasul 97, 108
Scarcity 20–22, 32, 33, 37–39, 76, 143, 237
Second World War 4, 16, 87
Secret cults 248, 249, 273
Security and Defense Research Team (See SDRT13C) IX, XII, XIV
Security Sector Reform (See SSR) 76, 77, 82, 120
Self-employment 156
Self-help 136, 147
Self-interest 5, 14
Sell violence 5
Sex trafficking 44–50, 53–59, 44
Sexual abuse 228
Sexual exploitation 14
Sexual violence 228, 231
Shah, Mohammed Zaher 65
Shan State Revolutionary Army (See SSRA) 240
Shantytowns 171
Shelley, Louise 17, 58, 274
Shelley, Pr. Louise 5
Sherzai, Gul Agha 76
Shinwari, Fazl Hadi 97
Shot-gun 318
Shuray-e Nizar 68, 88
Sian Waterhouse 278
Sicily's Palermo Province 37
Siemens 265
Sinaloa Cartel 170, 319
Sirat, Abdul Sattar 66
Skepticism 69
Slut-shaming 279
Smith, Adam 20, 24, 27, 40
Snowden, Edward 294
Social networks 149, 276, 277, 283, 292, 293, 302, 307
   Facebook 278, 279, 284, 285, 293, 307, 309
   LinkedIn 284
   Snapchat 277–279
   TikTok 277

WhatsApp 279
Social tissue 247
Socio-territorial governance 162
Socioeconomic system 9
Sodiam 238, 247
Sodinokibi 297
Sodiam, Oumar 238
Soto, Gaston V
Soto-Mayor, Guillaume III, IV, VII, XIV, 1, 15, 220, 315
South Carolina 48
Soviet troops 102
SpaceX 301
Spanta, Dr. Rangin Dadfar 69
Sparrow Unit 143
Spread Network LLC 288
State Authority 94, 136, 157
State deconstruction 97
State-society relations 129, 145, 148
State-sponsored actors 5
Stockholm International Peace Research Institute (See SIPRI) 301
Street and stream 248
Strongmen 73, 82, 137, 149, 255, 261
Structural violence 291, 316, 321
Sub-Saharan 44, 129, 152
Sudanese businessmen 253
Suicide attacks 99
Sweet trade 24
Syndicates 100, 103, 107, 123, 124, 130, 136, 139, 143, 144, 149, 238, 248, 249, 272, 317, 318–320, 323
Systemic violence 316, 321

T-visa 52, 53
TABB Group 288
Takhar 69, 76
Takhar Province 69
Taliban 61–271
Tax evasion 174, 212, 214, 319
Tax-free 258
Taylor, Charles 230, 231
Tejan Kabbah 254
Tesla 265
Texis Cartel 234
The Black Lives Matter movement 293
The Calabrian mafia 37, 329
The Commonsian approach 35

INDEX

The Digital Realm   VII, 15, 276, 277, 279, 281, 283, 285, 287, 289, 291–295, 297, 299–301, 303, 305, 307, 309, 311, 313
   Cyberbullying   276–279, 313
   Digital harassment   276
The entrepreneur   141
The Haqqani network   105
The Kimberley process   257, 262, 269, 270
The Kosovo Liberation Army (See KLA)   240, 241
The social cost problem   25
The Terminator   227
The UN Protocol   42, 59
Three-man republic   71
Thwarted   8
Tico, Rose   278
Tin Supply Chain Initiative (See ITSCI)   263
Tom Ateke   230, 249, 272
Tooze, Adam   4
Trafficking Victims Protection Act   44, 52
Tran, Kelly Marie   278, 312
Transgressive activities   155, 156
Transgressive actors   166
   Architects   10, 166, 211, 213
   Counterfeits   166
   Firms   2, 159, 160, 162, 166, 170, 174, 191, 202, 211, 243, 288, 304, 320
   Narcotic traffickers   166
   Pirates   166
Transitional Government   64
Transparency in Supply Chain Act   54
Trends in illicit activities   XI, 193–201
Tribal elders   73
Trump, Donald   293

Ubiquitous characteristics   14
Uganda   11, 233, 243, 257, 260, 261, 263, 264
Uganda People's Defense Forces (See UPDF)   257
Uighur population   277
Ul- Haq, Lt. Gen. Ehsan   65
Ulumi, Nur-ul-Haq   72
UN Charter   61, 62
Unaccounted Tales   VI, 14, 19
Uncontested Natural Order   20
Unethical executives   5
   Bribery   5, 72, 95, 97, 212, 227, 264
   Environmental abuse   5

Fraud   5, 7, 42, 51, 58, 66, 70, 71, 90, 98, 116, 248, 264, 281, 287, 289, 290, 291, 295, 309, 312, 320
Uniao Nacional para a Independencia Total de Angola (See UNITA)   237
Union for Peace in the Central African Republic (See UPC)   221, 247
United Kingdom   78, 297, 319
United Nationals Secretary-General Special Representatives   64, 65
United Nations Assistance Mission in Afghanistan (See UNAMA)   65
United Nations Conventions   42, 59
United Nations Office on Drugs and Crime (See UNODC)   103, 122, 246, 298
United Nations Security Council (See UNSC)   61, 62, 98, 99, 106, 107, 108, 122
United State Geological Survey (See USGS)   105
Upon to evolve   31
Urban centers   79, 156, 170
   Sao Paulo   XI, 218
   Mexico City   XI, 14, 155, 156, 162, 166, 168–181, 188–203, 211, 213, 214
Urban Water Supply   126, 128
Uruzgan Province   68, 81
USB drives   297
Uyghur Forced Labor Protection Act   54
Uzzle, Cordario Marcell   47

Variance Reduction System (See VRS)   285
Vega Knight, Jorge Manuel   247
Victim-blame view   25
Vigilante groups   167, 202, 203, 214
Vigilantism   171, 172, 191
Violence   1, 326
Violent behavior   35
Violent Entrepreneurs   VII, 15, 35, 36, 41, 220, 221, 223–225, 227, 229, 231, 233, 235, 237, 239, 241–243, 245, 247, 249, 251, 253, 255, 257, 259, 261, 263, 265, 266, 267, 269, 271, 273, 275
Violent repression   11
Vircoulon   221, 224, 225, 241, 253–255, 266, 274
Visible violence   23, 35, 36
Visionary technocrat   71

Volkov, Vadim   41
Volkswagen   265
Vote of exchange   37
VPN subscription   305
Vultures   230

Wagner Group   4
WannaCry   290, 313
War economies   4, 230
War economy   3, 64, 120, 233, 254, 255, 257, 264, 274, 303
War on terror   96, 323
Wardak, Ghulam Faruq   70
Wardak, Rahim   69, 89
Warlord(s)   VII, 324
Warlords of Crime   222
Warlords' Best Allies   257
Wasiri community   105
Watan Group   80
Water Code of 1975   148
Water tariffs   146
Wattao, Alias   237
Will-in-action   32, 33, 38
Women selling sex   49

Xinjiang region   277
Xinjiang Uighur Autonomous Region (*See* XUAR)   277

Yaqoob, Mullah   99, 104
Yellow Houses network   240
Ying, Zakhung Ting   239, 265
Yopougon   251, 252
Younouss, Oumar   238

Zakat   107–109
Zelensky, Volodymyr   304
Zimbabwean companies   258
Zulmai Mujadid   106
Zurich banks   319, 330

www.ingramcontent.com/pod-product-compliance
Lightning Source LLC
Chambersburg PA
CBHW070609030426
42337CB00020B/3729